Geoffrey Hill

W

edited by

Peter Robinson

Open University Press
Milton Keynes . Philadelphia

Open University Press
12 Cofferidge Close, Stony Stratford, Milton Keynes MK11 1BY, England
and
242 Cherry Street, Philadelphia, PA 19106, U.S.A.

First published 1985

British Library Cataloguing in Publication Data

Geoffrey Hill: essays on his work.
  1. Hill, Geoffrey——Criticism and
interpretation
I. Robinson, Peter, 1953 Feb. 18
821'.914   PR6015.14735Z/

ISBN 0-335-10588-2
ISBN 0-335-10587-4 Pbk

Text design by Clarke Williams

Typeset by Butler & Tanner Ltd,
Frome and London

Printed in Great Britain by M. & A. Thomson Litho Limited, East Kilbride,
Scotland

Contents

Notes on contributors

Peter Robinson has published *Overdrawn Account* (1980), a collection of poems, and edited *With All the Views: Collected Poems of Adrian Stokes* (1981). With Marcus Perryman, he translates modern Italian poetry. His poems, translations, and criticism have appeared in such magazines as *Essays in Criticism*, *English*, *The Grosseteste Review*, and *PN Review*.

Henry Hart is an American. He has undertaken graduate studies at New College, Oxford, and completed his doctoral thesis on Geoffrey Hill's poetry in April 1983. He intends to return to teach in the USA.

Jeremy Hooker was born at Warsash in 1941, and educated at Southampton University. Formerly Senior Lecturer in English at the University College of Wales, Aberystwyth, and creative-writing fellow at Winchester School of Art, 1981–3, he is now a freelance writer and teacher. He has published seven collections of poetry, and critical studies of David Jones and John Cowper Powys. His selected poems, *A View from the Source*, and a selection of critical essays, *Poetry of Place*, were published in 1982.

Gabriel Pearson is a Professor of Literature at the University of Essex. He has taught at the Universities of Keele, Michigan and Delaware. He edited *Dickens and the Twentieth Century* with John Gross, was founder-editor of *New Left Review* and has contributed essays to a number of books on Thomas Mann, Dickens, T.S. Eliot, Matthew Arnold, Henry James, Robert Lowell, John Berryman, Yvor Winters, Saul Bellow and Bernard Malamud.

Martin Dodsworth is a Senior Lecturer in English Literature at the Royal Holloway College, University of London. He edited *The Survival of Poetry* (1970) and is editor of *English*, the journal of the English Association.

Christopher Ricks is a Professor of English at the University of Cambridge. He is the author of *Milton's Grand Style*, *Tennyson*, and *Keats and Embarrassment*, and he edited *The Poems of Tennyson*. In 1978 he published 'Geoffrey Hill and "The Tongue's Atrocities"'.

Adrian Poole is a Fellow of Trinity College, Cambridge. He is the author of *Gissing in Context* (1975), and has also written on Euripides, George Eliot, Hardy and James.

Jeffrey Wainwright was born in Stoke-on-Trent, Staffordshire, in 1944. He studied at Leeds University and has taught at Aberystwyth and Long Island University in Brooklyn; he currently teaches at Manchester Polytechnic. His collections of poetry are *The Important Man* (1971), and *Heart's Desire* (1978).

Jon Silkin was born in London in 1930. Awarded a Gregory Fellowship in Poetry at the University of Leeds in 1958, he stayed on to take a degree in English there in 1962. Since 1965 he has lived in Newcastle-upon-Tyne, where he edits *Stand*. In recent years he has held a number of visiting lectureships and fellowships in the USA, Australia, Israel, and the UK. His principal publications are *The Peaceable Kingdom* (1954), *Nature with Man* (1965), *Out of Battle: Poets of the First World War* (1972), *The Penguin Book of First World War Poetry* (1979), *The Psalms with their Spoils* (1980) and *Selected Poems* (1980).

Hugh Haughton was born in Cork, studied at Cambridge, and after a period as a Research Fellow in Merton College Oxford, lectures in the Department of English and Related Literature at the University of York. He has reviewed for the TLS.

Henry Gifford was born in 1913. He taught in the English Department at Bristol (1946–76), and is now Emeritus Professor of English and Comparative Literature there. His publications include *The Novel in Russia* (1964), *Comparative Literature* (1969), *Pasternak: A Critical Study* (1977) and *Tolstoy* (Past Masters, 1982).

Michael Edwards was educated at Christ's College, Cambridge, and is Reader in Literature at the University of Essex. He has published several volumes of poetry and a radio play, as well as many translations from French, Italian and Spanish. His critical books include *La Tragédie racinienne* and *Towards a Christian Poetics*.

Eric Griffiths is a Fellow of Trinity College, Cambridge.

John Bayley is a Professor at St. Catherine's College, Oxford. Among his books are *Pushkin* (1971), *The Uses of Division* (1976), *An Essay on Hardy* (1978), and *Shakespeare and Tragedy* (1981).

Philip Horne is a Research Fellow of Christ's College, Cambridge. He has written on Henry James, and on contemporary fiction in the *London Review of Books*.

Jenny Polak, who painted the portrait of Geoffrey Hill reproduced on the cover, has exhibited in Cambridge at the Gonville and Caius, and Clare College Galleries, and in London at the National Portrait Gallery and the King's Street Gallery, St James's. She lives in London, and teaches art.

Acknowledgements

Grateful acknowledgement is made for the use of quotations from the works of Geoffrey Hill published by Andre Deutsch Ltd (and listed in full detail in the Bibliography); and for quotations from T.S. Eliot's *Four Quartets* published by Faber and Faber Publishers.

Editor's introduction

Geoffrey Hill was born in Bromsgrove, Worcestershire, in 1932. He is an only child. His father and paternal grandfather were both policemen, the latter becoming Deputy Chief Constable of Worcestershire. Geoffrey Hill's mother, whose family was Baptist, joined the Church of England when he was three; he sang in the church choir from about the age of seven until going up to Oxford in 1950. Hill gained a First in English Language and Literature in 1953. The previous autumn the Fantasy Press had issued a pamphlet of his poems.[1] During the academic year 1954–5, he accepted a post at the University of Leeds. There he became Professor of English in 1977, and remained at Leeds until the end of 1980. In January 1981, he took up a fellowship at Emmanuel College, Cambridge.

By the autumn of 1953, Geoffrey Hill was sufficiently distinguished a figure in Oxford literary circles to merit a personality profile in *Isis*.[2] Yet it was not until 1959 that his first collection of poems, *For the Unfallen*,[3] was published by André Deutsch. Hill is not an easy or very prolific composer of poetry, and his readers were obliged to wait until 1968 for *King Log*[4] (though a pamphlet, *Preghiere*, in 1964, and part of *Penguin Modern Poets 8* in 1966 had shown his continuing development)[5]. *King Log* was a Poetry Book Society Choice, as was the relatively quickly written *Mercian Hymns* of 1971,[6] and *Tenebrae* which appeared in 1978.[7] Though Hill has produced relatively few collections, each has significantly confirmed his poetry's distinction. A measure of the importance attached to a new Geoffrey Hill work may be indicated by the broadcast of 'The Mystery of the Charity of Charles Péguy' on BBC Radio 3 in February 1983 and its almost simultaneous appearance in the *Times Literary Supplement*, followed two months later by its publication in book form.[8] Within a year of its release the poem had received more than fifteen respectful reviews, and had stimulated an epistolary controversy in one of the literary magazines. Geoffrey Hill is also a writer of closely argued, scrupulously presented literary essays; a collection of them, *The Lords of Limit*, was published in 1984.[9]

Geoffrey Hill: Essays on his Work is the first volume of critical writing devoted to his poetry, literary criticism, and version for the stage of Ibsen's *Brand* (1978).[10] The contributions have been arranged in two parts. The first section offers a series of discussions in chronological order of individual volumes by Geoffrey Hill. There is one exception: the opening essay, Henry Hart's commentary on the early poems, considers work published between 1951 and 1954 while Hill was a student at Oxford. Only a small proportion of these poems were collected in *For the Unfallen;* the sources for all of them may be found in Philip Horne's bibliography at the end of this book.

The second section consists of essays on subjects prompted by Hill's work as a whole. Here too there is one exception. Eric Griffiths had written on Geoffrey Hill's critical essays before a number of them were collected to make *The Lords of Limit*; it was thought better to retain it among the contributions focused on subjects rather than on published volumes, for it had been conceived as such. The ordering of the first four essays in the second section has been planned to echo the development of Hill's work: the matters discussed in each have particular bearing on concerns manifested in the continuities between his first four volumes of poetry and *Brand*. The final two essays attempt to describe the position and significance of Geoffrey Hill's work in relation to his contemporaries, and to the reader.

The cohesion of this volume is itself a tribute to the coherence of Geoffrey Hill's work. His paternal grandmother as a child and young woman was a maker of hand-made nails. She is commemorated in *Mercian Hymns*, XXV; there the accident that hare-lipped her face is briefly touched upon. 'The Stone Man', first of two 'Soliloquies' from *King Log*, includes what may be an oblique allusion to his father's profession, and there he employs the word 'summon' to combine a policeman's power of arrest with a poet's power of recall.[11] At the heart of Geoffrey Hill's poetry is a meditation upon the relationships between authority and suffering. It is characteristic of his work that such a meditation should be accompanied by reflections upon the conducting of that meditation in poetry, upon a poem's power to invoke pathos by touching on pain. Thus, a secondary but no less important preoccupation throughout his work is the struggle – treated almost entirely in impersonal terms – of self-concern with self-censure in poetry.

Geoffrey Hill was thirteen in 1945, a year in which the study of organised barbarism gained new subjects. The often admired feelings of identification with victims, of pity, or righteous anger, are scrutinised in much of Hill's work. Furthermore, his sense of poetry's place in the world involves a belief in the inevitable culpability of utterance, requiring of the poet strenuous efforts to resist. It is through attention in and to detail that Geoffrey Hill locates one of the poet's powers of resistance; and this is a reason why his poetry requires and rewards very close reading. The poem's formal construction itself may be felt to act as a defence not only against bad or dubious feelings, but against the weaknesses and dangers in right feeling: the risk, for example, that right feeling about a subject may slip into feeling right about it, slip into self-righteousness.

Both Geoffrey Hill's parents left school at the age of thirteen. Although there was no academic tradition on either side of the family, there was a care and concern for education as a way of 'bettering' oneself. His literary education has, inevitably, enlarged the range and scope of his language; it has not, however, removed him from the childhood and local substratum of his mother tongue. In his poems the elaboration of a poetic diction remains in complex relation with colloquial speech. The origins of words, and the history of their development, form points of return for Geoffrey Hill as he seeks to embody in his lines responses to the history of men's acts. In a society where conflicts of interest have been class conflicts, and these registered in ways of speaking, Hill's attention to language has included awareness of matters individual, social, political, and also religious.

When writing about poetry, Hill has frequently adopted Christian concepts for literary ends; he has considered language 'fallen'; the post as one who may 'redeem the time'; the good and finished poem 'transfigured'.[12] Thus, maintaining the vocabulary of spiritual life (inherited for poetry largely from the Metaphysical poets, Hopkins, and T.S. Eliot), he reconsiders the dilemma of relations between culture and religion in what is, for the most part, a secular age. The power of true religious poetry may be felt to derive from an authority which, not being of the world, is not tainted by earthly power. Yet the spiritual life also has a history, and Geoffrey Hill's poetry of religion examines the likeness and unlikeness of, for example, secular and divine love, or spiritual witness and self-regard.

Among his contemporaries, Hill is the poet whose work most shows a love of poetry and an admiration, even awe, of other poets. His own poetry abounds in elegies for them, in imitations of poems in other European languages, and – in his earlier work – of poets such as William Blake and the America Allen Tate. His poetry has developed within an elaborate interrelation of sources and poetic allegiances: some are to part of a recognised tradition of poetry in English, others to writers (Tommaso Campanella or Charles Péguy might be examples) not widely known in this country, or extensively read in their own. Hill's poems and essays have on occasion taken for subject the fates of poets – from St. Robert Southwell to Osip Mandelshtam – who have been persecuted by their societies. He has explored the changing context in which poetry as a power has found itself with regard to state power, and, consequently, with regard to readers. To read the work of Geoffrey Hill is to become involved in one part of that changing context, and, it is the belief of those who have written contributions for this book, to discover much pleasure and instruction there.

During the course of my work I have received encouragement, advice, and assistance from people too numerous to name. I thank them all. I must also thank Geoffrey Hill for his helpfulness and, in particular, for providing page-proofs of *The Lords of Limit*, which proved invaluable. Without the guidance and support of John Skelton from the Open University Press I should not have been able to see my way or bring this work to a conclusion. It is my hope, first and last, that the reader will find enjoyment and insight in what follows.

Peter Robinson
March, 1984

I

1

Early poems: journeys, meditations and elegies

Henry Hart

In 1954, as a young poet about to leave Oxford for a lecturing post at Leeds, Hill defined his poetic programme in an open letter published in *The London Magazine*. 'There does seem to be quite general agreement', he said, 'that each artist, young or old, must work out his own salvation, must cut his own path; and that only those with the most strength and the most courage are likely to get to the end.'[1] This combination of qualification and tough assertiveness is either the boast of a young graduate still unsure of his principles, or the pledge of a poet who will remain committed to his vision no matter what his peers might say or do.

In fact, Hill's pronouncement reveals much about his work done at Oxford, and prophesies the direction it would take afterwards. From 'An Ark on the Flood' to *The Mystery of the Charity of Charles Péguy*, his poems depict combatants who pursue salvation with a tenacity which often brings destruction to victor and victim alike. Early and late, he offers up for judgement many examples of 'heroic' enterprise and, in the ambiguities and paradoxes of his lines, poses an ambivalent response. His is a poetry of irresolution before inflexible resolution, which struggles towards action but only to win pyrrhic victories. The guilty collusion of poet with politician and saint with soldier in inflicting great harm in the service of noble causes is Hill's most lasting theme. The poet's task, he argues, is to atone for mistakes and crimes, both past and present, personal and public. His triumphs, when they come, are in the judicious poems themselves – in their wary articulations of defeat.

At Oxford, Hill's poems moved in parallel trajectories, but from a common source. They could be meditative or elegiac, lyric or epic in scope, but they all dramatised some aspect of the devoted man's (and normally the devoted poet's) effort to unify his life or art with his vision of perfection. Hill declared in his 'Letter from Oxford', 'the poet, maybe, hunched in his mackintosh on the top of a bus in the Banbury Road, sits apart from the crowd. Or he follows in the wake of a vision of life that goes before him and which he cannot grasp, a cloud by day and a pillar of fire by night.'[2] Moses, in this fanciful collocation, is also Tantalus doomed to grasp for promised fruits he cannot have. Hill's view of the poet changes little over the years. In a later essay he says: 'The poet will occasionally, in the act of writing a poem, experience a sense of pure fulfilment', but this should not be 'misconstrued as the attainment of objective perfection.' No matter how much 'a poem is shaped and finished, it remains to some extent within the "imprisoning marble" of a quotidian shapelessness and imperfection.'[3] Twenty years later he is still Tantalus unrequited in his pool.

Most noticeable in the early poems is Hill's uneasy alliance with traditional spiritual exercises. The poems are obsessed, as he says of Robert Lowell's early works, with 'the rich European ... legacies of revelation and self-revelation'.[4] But unlike Christian meditation, which directs the mind away from the world towards 'at-one-ment' with God, Hill's meditations return to earth to examine its imperfections with scrupulous vigour. In 'Genesis', for example, his persona begins beside the ocean 'Crying the miracles of God', withdraws into a mythical order beyond creation's violence, and then, after some vacillation, returns 'To flesh and blood and the blood's pain.'[5] Ishmael and Ahab in 'An Ark on the Flood' depart from a world where 'barns remained unfilled and everywhere/The orchards blackened and began to rot,' and sail to a visionary mountain which they associate with a transcendent God. Here

> the shadowing breeze
> Lifts its dark head above the waves of grass;
> Wringing from rough such calm
> That, as on mountains once, so we upon
> The stiff crest of the waves could walk dry-shod,
> Drowning the sea in surf of timbrels loud,
> Nor pass that peak, nor find our vision gone.[6]

This sublime moment, however, recalls the 'Calenture' of John Donne's 'The Calme' – the tropical disease in which delirious sailors believe that the sea is a green field. After the storm has passed in Donne's poem,

> Onely the Calenture together drawes
> Deare friends, which meet dead in great fishes jawes:
> And on the hatches as on Altars lyes
> Each one, his owne Priest, and owne Sacrifice.

(In Hill's poem too, 'The priest is fettered to the sacrifice'). Convinced he can walk on 'the waves of grass' (like Christ), Ahab drowns. Ishmael, similarly credulous, dies on earth where (in a parody of the vegetation gods, Demeter and Dionysus) he becomes a corn stalk entangled in vines. Both return to earth after pursuing delusions of transcendence. 'The Revelation', 'Prospero and Ariel', 'Gideon at the Well', 'To William Dunbar', and 'Saint Cuthbert on Farne Island'[7] all record passing moments of revelation in which the hero finds his apocalyptic expectations painfully rebuffed by mundane facts.

By making his outward journeys symbolic of inner ones, Hill skilfully fuses the spiritual exercise with the myth of the heroic quest, and alters both in the process. While the goal of meditation is to die from the world and, through an intensification of memory and imagination (composition of place), prepare the soul for a colloquy with God, Hill's quests aim to awaken moral perception and to re-create, linguistically, the world as it is. Because these quests so often terminate in death or silence, Hill turns to the pastoral elegy for consolation. But here too he takes what he needs. When his heroes die and the pastures wither (as is customary in pastoral elegies), the dead are not transmogrified into stars, or geniuses of the shore, or Platonic forms. They are resurrected as vegetation or the poet's words. Journey, meditation, and elegy all trace a rhythm of death and renewal. Hill draws on their traditions and criticises them at the same time.

While insisting on the 'inner light' of perception, Hill sought rituals to embody it. With Blake, whose *Jerusalem* and *Songs* he reviewed in *The Isis*[8] as an undergraduate, he revered (and feared) the imagination as a type of Christ who revealed, remade, and judged the world. Because Christ's passion for reformation was bloody as well as Utopian, Hill's attitude towards communion vacillated. At the end of 'Genesis', for instance, it is embraced with qualifications:

> By blood we live, the hot, the cold,
> To ravage and redeem the world:
> There is no bloodless myth will hold.
>
> And by Christ's blood are men made free
> Though in close shrouds their bodies lie
> Under the rough pelt of the sea;
>
> Though Earth has rolled beneath her weight
> The bones that cannot bear the light.

In these powerfully rhythmic lines Hill affirms the bodiliness of the imagination, but also elegises those (the metaphorical and literal 'dead') whose bodies cannot abide its 'light'. Christ atones for the weak, but it is not certain whether the weak rise to 'bear the light', or whether they even want to.

Years later, Hill defined this 'blood myth' and 'blood consciousness' in less exclamatory terms, in a gloss on Coleridge's primary and secondary imaginations. The first, he said:

represents an ideal democratic birthright, a light that ought to light every person coming into the world. In the event, the majority is deprived of this birthright in exchange for a mess of euphoric trivia and, if half-aware of its loss, is instructed to look for freedom in an isolated and competitive search for possessions and opportunity.

The dead under the world's 'rough pelt' (its bestial fur and battering waves) are those who have sunk into blindness.

Therefore the secondary imagination, the formal creative faculty, must awaken the minds of men to their lost heritage, not of possession but of perception.[9]

Christ in 'Genesis' is a 'secondary imagination', as are his militant apostles who, after communion, seek to 'ravage and redeem the world' and, like John, 'to bear witness of the Light, that all men through him might believe' (St. John, 1.7).

In these early poems the mind's divine light cuts and scars as much as it cures. It can 'ravage' the world, which is why in 'An Ark on the Flood' – whose epigraph asserts: 'the imagination of man's heart is evil from his youth', (Genesis, 8.21) – the journey aims to salvage an original, innocent vision on Ararat. Or it can bring the pain of responsibility and guilt. A brief lyric from Hill's second year at Oxford (1951), written in neat, rhyming quatrains, identifies both the light from the star of Bethlehem and the spear that pierced Christ's side with the 'light that ought to light every person coming into the world':

When the sharp star was seen
That pierced each naked eye
And left its scar between
The thin ribs of the sky

Some men could not forget
What had so touched the mind;
But, for all that, the threat
Took thirty years to find

Its execution here . . .

The light inflicts a spiritual wound (in sky and mind) and calls for a redemption that never comes:

He had no quick release,
And, when the others died,
Still cried out for the peace
That had been prophesied.[10]

Although 'Good Friday' is not as tightly woven as some of the other poems ('Genesis', 'Merlin', 'God's Little Mountain'),[11] it demonstrates Hill's early skill with mythopoesis, with taking a traditional story and fashioning from it another whose implications are overtly psychological.

When Hill plunged into the quick of personal wounds and perplexities, he did so armed with myths and rituals. From the start he took a stand against spontaneous confessionalism in favour of stately, impersonal formality. He wanted to build durable poems out of ephemeral experiences rather than 'applaud each broken or complacent confession' as it came.

> Yet that does not alter the fact that, as a person, I am perpetually engrossed in my own dogged and nuzzling neuroses ... I should feel justified in putting into print a poem in which I speak of all these, provided that I had spent myself in tracking down to a point, to a purpose, that purpose being to try to make a poem of enduring worth.[12]

To release the mind's passions willy-nilly would be suicidal, destructive to others, and make bad poems. Hill agreed with Yeats that 'the passion of the verse comes from ... holding down violence or madness – "down Hysterica passio". All depends on the completeness of the holding down, on the stirring of the beast underneath.'[13] Like his mentor he would muster great storms and then master them.

No wonder, then, that the characters in his early poems often choose sleep, violence, and death as the 'quick release' from mental turmoil, and that only Christ-like martyrs persist. The 'contemplative way' impels fiery passions and icy withdrawals ('the hot, the cold'), mountain climbs 'at the Pitch that is near Madness' (in a phrase of Richard Eberhart, a poet Hill imitated at the time[14]), and often tragic falls. Defeat, as a result, can come as partial relief:

> Now Ahab is himself. Though lost and drowned,
> Pitting his bones against the chalky tide,
> He holds his peace ...

Having lost freedom and consciousness, Ahab has 'passed through negative stages to his positive rest'.[15] He is in Blake's Beulah, the 'married land', at one with inertia and flux – like Péguy, 'at one/with the fritillary and the veined stone' (p. 27) after falling at the Battle of the Marne. To 'rise to a discovery of true personality', Hill says in an essay, is to make oneself vulnerable to the 'moral ideal', and 'the effect on us of the moral ideal is not simply admiration; it is confusion; it is accusation; it is judgment'.[16] Hill's graveyards are full of lapsed idealists who have found peace from moral anguish in death.

Symbols of fire and ice (and clusters of images associated with them) abound in these poems. Many come from *The Waste Land* and *Four Quartets*, as well as Yeats's 'Byzantium', so many, in fact, that Hill did not collect most of the early poems in his first volume. The 'pentecostal fire' which blazes in 'midwinter spring', and the remembered world which burgeons from April's 'dead land' of 'broken images', rise among the blossoming hedgerows and icy pools of Hill's 'Pentecost'[17] and 'The Bidden Guest'. Yeats's imaginary flame 'that no faggot feeds' and which 'cannot singe a sleeve' appears in nearly every poem. 'Pentecost', published in 1952, is a good example of Hill's early meditative style, and a rare one since it depicts a reconciliation between antagonisms. Hill envisages the apostles transposed to an English landscape:

As hedge-root, though unpromising,
Flowers powerfully, so, when men heard
The night around them strangely spring
Into a quick of blossoming,
The bramble-flame, the crooked feet of the bird,

They turned to revelation based
Upon the stolid bone and brain.

The 'bramble-flame' cleverly unites Christ's painful dying (crowned with thorns) and the Holy Ghost's utterance at Pentecost. It reveals a paradox of the imagination – that it works most intensely when it dies from the world. But there is nothing otherworldly about the experience. Hill describes Pentecost in terms of blossoming hawthorns and growing hedge-roots. The Holy Ghost is corporeal, a vegetal efflorescence. 'Every part of the Universe, is body; and that which is not body is no part of the Universe', Hobbes declared,[18] whose *Leviathan* substantiates 'Genesis' and 'An Ark on the Flood' (and 'An Ark on the Flood' develops Hobbes's manifesto to the limit, by making everything bodily – Autumn has a mouth, a vine has udders and knuckles, a river skin and jaws, the ocean a belly and back, a fire hands, and a well lips).

Hill rejects ascetic withdrawal as a permanent condition, but not without first being tempted by it. In 'To William Dunbar' he expresses fondness for the Scottish Chaucerian and his timeless world of symbolic swans and fictionalised lovers, but consigns them to a 'world forgotten', 'remote,/ ... From the thin trammels of mortality.' In lucid, rhythmic lines he states his differences with the medieval Christianty of his precursor:

To such a mercy few of us attain:
Swans dwell apart like Troilus in his sphere,
And not by sufferings, even, do we gain
Power, such as theirs, to bring the heavens near,
But win our faith from all who knew the clear
Fulness of vision. Here, on Bewdley Bridge,
I think of you, as of my heritage.

Pondering on a bridge near his hometown in Worcestershire, the poet decides that the otherworldly life, because it does not include 'Fulness of vision', is an enchantment to be resisted.

In another of his most beautiful early poems, 'Saint Cuthbert on Farne Island', Hill again expresses ambivalence towards ascetic contemplation, and to its alternative (also saintly and ascetic) of worldy evangelism. The poem opens with an expansion of vision in a dark night, but focuses on personal destiny. Rhyming quatrains, now fused into octets, draw the conflicting contraries into a suave music:

And so he studied, seeking his own way,
And found a rough sea-bitten island. There
He meditated deeply night and day

> Upon the image of his own despair . . .
> To keep the soul, not body, in repair . . .

The retreat 'for the spirit's good', however, convinces him that working in society is preferable. He resolves his dialogue between soul and body ambiguously:

> So, knowing now for certain that there could
> Be no new way without its new remorse,
> He drew his mind beneath a solemn hood
> And stopped the stars in their unthinking course.

After the monkish withdrawal, the meditation continues. The stars are extinguished or, paradoxically, internalised where their 'unthinking course' illuminates the mind's perplexities.

Cuthbert is a typical hero in that he remains 'in uncertainties, Mysteries, doubts', but unlike Keats's hero of 'negative capability', he is always 'reaching after fact and reason.'[19] Although resolutions occur in these early poems it is more common for opposites to be suspended in an air of glittering irresolution. As a poet, Hill tries to heal the 'diremption between perception and utterance, energy and effect', as he explains it in 'Redeeming the Time', through his own meticulous craftsmanship.[20] 'The Bidden Guest' perhaps best summarises Hill's sense of diremption, of the failure by the meditator to communicate his private vision (the heart's Pentecost) to those committed (or pretending to be committed) to traditional symbols of the church. The 'candles', or church-goers, are inflexibly opposed to the inspiration (the wind) of new revelations, although they 'stir' in the presence of old ones:

> The starched unbending candles stir
> As though a wind had caught their hair,
> As though the surging of a host
> Had charged the air of Pentecost.
> And I believe in the spurred flame,
> Those racing tongues, but cannot come
> Out of my heart's unbroken room;
> Nor feel the lips of fire among
> The cold light and the chilling song . . .

After communion, Hill confesses, 'The heart's tough shell is still to crack'. Withdrawn in the heart's 'interior castle' (as St. Teresa described it), the meditator struggles to gracefully return, but fails. Like the guest in Matthew's parable bidden to the marriage of Christ and his people, he is expelled from a ceremony he would rather participate in. Instead of communing with Christ or his community, he communes with his failure to do so.

The alienated communicant reappears in 'Prospero and Ariel' and 'Gideon at the Well', but in different guise. Here, in the former, spring's efflorescence only accentuates the meditator's wintry confinement:

Now the beaked crocus breaks its shell;
The frost has eased out of the ground,
Out of the rigid pines. But still
In stubborn seams the light is bound

That striking out from its chill lair
Blazed high about me.

Icy withdrawal has brought with it an inner Pentecostal blaze, represented by
Ariel, as if to compensate for the lack of light outside. In a baffling array of
metaphors:

Ariel shrills and beats the air;
I shall not quench his light. For though
Half-choked in Lethe, he'd still flare,
Tarring that dark flood's undertow.

While Prospero frees Ariel in *The Tempest*, Hill puts him to work paving a
road to hell. He is another Lucifer, exiled from heaven, who will build over
the 'dark flood' of pain, lethargy, forgetfulness, and death a Pandemonium
where he and his phantasmal comrades must endure.

Hill repeatedly accosts those who fail to base revelation 'upon the stolid
bone and brain'. Gideon craves signs of supernatural miracles but fails to
achieve the much more modest miracle of leaving winter's barrenness and
accepting spring's abundance. Seasonal change, which reflects God's transfor-
mation of the fleece from dry to wet and then from wet to dry (in Judges,
6.37), occurs without any corresponding change in 'Gideon at the Well'. Like
Prospero (or Eliot's persona at the beginning of *The Waste Land*) he is 'sealed'
in a private hell while flowers bloom menacingly around him. The passionate
eloquence he associates with Pentecost has dried up, as has his ability to
establish contact with others: 'still my tongued heart, rough and dry,/Can
find no respite from its thirst.' But Hill's afflicted hero is not wholly defeated:

Being sealed and chosen,
I raise my staff: the armies move,
As out of rock, as floods unfrozen.

Gideon battles the demons within, rather than the Midianites without, and
partly conquers them.

The demons return in force in 'I See the Crocus Armies Spread',[21] another
meditation which aims to purge meditative iciness. But this purge is also a
pyrrhic victory. The renewal of feeling does not bring God or heaven any
closer; it merely reveals to the mind the painful organic cycles of the world:

The crocus, narrow-helmeted,
Sprung from a dragon's tooth, renews
The battle it was born to lose
Though from its face the snows have fled.

The earth labours with the dead
To bring their buried strength to light.
The flower is drawn into the fight.
The fever gathers to a head.

I see the crocus armies spread
Around the sun. I see them fall,
With spears broken, by the wall,
Though from their face the snows have fled.

Five warriors remained after the battle which arose from Cadmus' dragon teeth, and with these Cadmus founded Thebes and ruled it prosperously. Similarly, the crocuses (which in the later version, 'Veni Coronaberis', symbolise love) scatter corpses over the earth but win their battle with the snow. Although Hill's vision is tragic (all die in the wars of the crocuses), his refrain stresses that the momentary cleansing of perception is a positive gain. 'Poetry – excites us to artificial feelings – makes us callous to real ones', he wrote, quoting Coleridge, many years later.[22] Here he depicts the artificial world broached and invigorated by new feeling.

These visionary warriors, on their many forays into the world with senses bared, struggle to give up their apocalyptic hopes but never quite manage. In 'The Revelation', for example, the narrator, prompted by St. John of the Cross's *The Dark Night*, departs from his 'blind' 'house of the senses' to obtain grace,[23] but he expects the world to be transformed as it is in the other St. John's Revelation. He cannot possibly be satisfied, and concludes, bitterly, that the inner nightmare is merely a reflection of the outer one:

once beyond those walls I did not doubt
My heart would quicken and my tongue renew.

And it was true I trod accustomed ground,
My eyes no longer blinded by the glare
Out of that kiln of darkness. Yet I found
The world was not transfigured nor laid bare,

Nor pierced with singing voices. I who had come
Strenuous through fire stood, now, against the light,
Encountered shapes and shadows that were dumb.
My heart, though it died not, lay cold and quiet.

Communion on 'accustomed ground' again fails. The world is as it was, a silent shadow-play at the back of Plato's cave. In 'The Revelation', orthodox Christian transfigurations and apocalypses are purged. Emptied of its old beliefs, the mind lapses into a quiet disillusionment, where with a cold eye it gazes upon 'things as they are'.

A similar purification occurs in the brief, quietly articulated lyric, 'Summer Night',[24] where a night-walker, traversing the mystic's *via negativa*, witnesses the heavens stripped of their hallowed images. Eternity, he implies, has foisted upon time an enchanting mask of linguistic fictions, but as night passes into day:

> Overhead move the tense stars
> Stripping off such disguise
> As 'this will be' and 'this was.'
> There is not another moment to lose.

In the last line Hill makes a mellifluous and resonant plea for action in the immediate present.

Elegies were a natural choice for a poet whose meditations struggled to make the past present. But Hill remained iconoclastic, condensing the traditional patterns of pastoral elegy into a few quatrains and satirising all forms of memorial as he did so. Rather than lament the deaths of people he knew, he elegised literary heroes (Ahab, Ishmael, Hamlet, Merlin, King Arthur), other poets (Isaac Rosenberg, William Dunbar), fictitious characters (Jane, John and Captain Richard Fraser), and past symbols, both sacred and profane. In these poems tradition or culture is a field, graveyard, or museum full of cultivated dead things. To interpret the present the mind must be rooted in the past:

> As the firm emphasis of Spring
> Falls on old stems that have begun
> Fresh growth, so these new graces cling
> Close to the root, interpreting
> The silence of the seed and of the sun.
>   ('Pentecost')

The 'stems' (language-users, whether readers, critics, poets, or ordinary speakers) derive from roots (linguistic, historical) the energies and materials necessary for new growths. Hill's lines enact what they profess. They gracefully transform lines from Yeats's 'Sailing to Byzantium' which, in turn, authorise such appropriations: 'Nor is there singing school but studying/Monuments of its own magnificence'.

Since 'not only the best, but the most individual parts of his work may be those in which the dead poets … assert their immortality most vigorously', the new poet, as Eliot argued, must cultivate a knowledge of the past. Poetry, from this point of view, is naturally elegiac and demands 'great difficulties and responsibilities'.[25] Stated metaphorically:

> The earth labours with the dead
> To bring their buried strength to light.
> The flower is drawn into the fight.
>   ('I See the Crocus Armies Spread')

Hill's attitude towards the dead, however, was not always reverential. Tradition, as he explained in his 'Letter from Oxford', was full of grand, humiliating ghosts whose monuments made young poets' imitations seem superfluous:

> One might think that the great strength and appeal of Oxford lay in its tradi-
> tion; that an awareness of this would grant a sense of peace and security. But
> one has found tradition as cold a shadow here as in Westminster Abbey. There
> is small comfort in being crowded out by ghosts. Under the chill salty-smelling
> stone of the great Tudor gate-houses, beneath the high rows of portraits in the
> halls, thin-lipped prelates, all evil-looking old men, you are brow-beaten by the
> past.[26]

Hill was later to write that in Jonathan Swift 'a sense of tradition and
community is challenged by a strong feeling for the anarchic and the preda-
tory',[27] an *aperçu* which could apply to him with equal relevance. These
tensions find exemplary expression in 'An Ark on the Flood', which imitates
(and lampoons) great elegies of the past (Milton's 'Lycidas', Robert Lowell's
'The Quaker Graveyard in Nantucket'), but also diagnoses the crippling in-
fluence which such poems can exert. From the start Hill's style 'is a recogni-
tion and a resistance; it is parenthetical, antiphonal, it turns upon itself',[28] as
is Milton's in 'Lycidas': 'Milton is here testing the acoustics of the pastoral
elegy. The poem is an elegy which is also, to some extent, about elegy.'[29] In
'An Ark on the Flood', Ishmael passes by many sirens (the elegiac voices of
the past – Virgil, Donne, Milton, Melville, Shelley , Lowell), but without the
craftiness of a Ulysses to avert them. The acoustics of past elegies menace
him at all points, 'Drowning the sea in surf of timbrels loud,' and, to a certain
extent, drowning his poem:

> Old bones are brought to light and, where we dwell,
> The echoes have not died
> Of those who went beneath the clamouring sea.
> But Ishmael's ears are crippled to that sound,
> (O starry mouths amid the oozes drowned)
> The harp hangs silent from the windless tree.

This is elegiac magniloquence which, ironically, regards the dependence on
magniloquence as paralysing. Ahab's vision has deserted him, and he can no
longer chant of 'Traditional sanctity and loveliness' in the old ways. Never-
theless, Hill writes a visionary romance about the death of romantic vision
and a powerful poem about poetic impotence:

> Dark Ahab cannot fling
> The water's tumbled hair from his drowned eyes;
> Thick drool of salt and sand has quenched his mouth;
> Though once he sang of Beauty and of Youth
> Not trumpets, now, could rouse him where he lies.

For Lowell, who elegised his drowned cousin in 'The Quaker Graveyard',
comparing him to Ahab, death was also irrevocable:

    ask for no Orphean lute
To pluck life back. The guns of the steeled fleet
Recoil and then repeat
The hoarse salute.

While Lowell wrote a distinct, compelling poem, full of searing vignettes of the whale hunt and sea, Hill remained trapped by archaic rhetoric; although he composed from this rhetoric ten exquisitely rhymed and metred stanzas, symmetrically framed around a tragic peripety, the first fifty lines tracing the heroes' journey towards the visionary mountain and the last fifty their descent from it.

Milton's grand style and its gestures of transcendence, however, appear in purified form. Hill articulates his temptations in order to exorcise them. He calls Milton's transcendentalism 'hollow' and 'sleepy':

        And the ark
Rises, now, to the rimmed and hollow calm

That is the sleeping crater of the storm;
Grazing this mountain-valley of the seas
Where whales and herds of billowy narwhal pass
In silence ...

The lines recall Milton's apotheosis in 'Lycidas' where the deceased rises to become a 'Genius of the Shore':

So Lycidas sunk low, but mounted high,
Through the dear might of him that walked the waves,
Where, other groves and other streams along,
With nectar pure his oozy locks he laves,
And hears the unexpressive nuptial song
In the blest kingdoms meek of joy and love.
                        (11.172–7)

Hill associates this with the 'Grand Armada' chapter of *Moby Dick* where the whale hunters experience a moment of Platonic vision. The water is 'to a considerable depth exceedingly transparent' (like Emerson's 'transparent eyeball') allowing the sailors to gaze at infant whales 'still spiritually feasting upon some unearthly reminiscence'.[30] This elicits from Ishmael a speech even more windblown than Milton's:

    amid the tornadoed Atlantic of my being, do I myself still for ever centrally
    disport in mute calm; and while ponderous planets of unwaning woe revolve
    round me, deep down and deep inland there I still bathe me in eternal mildness
    of joy.[31]

For Hill, Milton and Melville are stars whose influence stultifies. The line '(O starry mouths amid the oozes drowned)', with its 'straddled adjectives', echoes Milton's 'Blind mouths' (l.119) and 'oozy locks' (l.175), but isolates them in parentheses without transforming them. That no wind or inspiration invigorates the Aeolian harp at the end is a confession of failure but, paradoxically, an indication of release. The elegy is ambiguously triumphant; it buries elegiac assumptions (heavenly marriages, starry apotheoses) while memorialising the styles in which they were previously embalmed. The final silence represents a truce in the young poet's battle with the mighty dead.

This interpretation can be substantiated by Hill's own gloss on Keats's odes, which 'return upon themselves' and also echo Miltonic cadences and diction:

> It is, of course, a frequently observed fact that the first word of the final stanza of Keats's 'Ode to a Nightingale' ('Forlorn! the very word is like a bell') echoes the last word of the preceding stanza ('Of perilous seas, in faery lands forlorn'). The echo is not so much a recollection as a revocation; and what is revoked is an attitude towards art and within art. The menace that is flinched from is certainly mortality ('Where youth grows pale, and spectre-thin, and dies') but it is also the menace of the high claims of poetry itself. 'Faery lands forlorn' reads like an exquisite pastiche of a Miltonic cadence: 'Stygian cave forlorn' ('L'Allegro', 1.3); 'these wilde Woods forlorn' (*Paradise Lost*, IX, 910).[32]

Hill warns that 'We perhaps too readily assume that the characteristic Romantic mode is an expansive gesture', and observes that 'a "tortuous and strenuous argument, whose structure torments the reader" is equally a paradigm of Romantic-Modernist method'.[33] In 'An Ark on the Flood', Ishmael, the archetypal poet, directs his readers towards an 'expansive' moment on a mountain summit but, at the end, falls among tortuous and tormenting vines. The poem offers 'objective correlatives' for its own procedures.

Hill's heroes attack the dead and their splendid artifice because, like the Gorgon's snakes, they threaten to turn them to stone. A poem written two years before 'An Ark on the Flood', 'God's Little Mountain', again shows how mystical perception, when its objects are the 'stars' of tradition, can paralyse rather than liberate. Simple, declarative sentences, deftly metred quatrains (in which all four lines rhyme or half-rhyme), and a mythical narrative of mountain ascent, however, counterpoise the visionary defeat with a poetic success:

> I waited for the word that was not given,
>
> Pent up into a region of pure force,
> Made subject to the pressure of the stars;
> I saw the angels lifted like pale straws;
> I could not stand before those winnowing eyes
>
> And fell, until I found the world again.
> Now I lack grace to tell what I have seen;
> For though the head frames words the tongue has none.
> And who will prove the surgeon to this stone?

Moses on Horeb (the 'mountain of God', Exodus, 3.1) envisaged God speaking to him from a burning bush; Hill's climber, similarly expectant, observes the heavens dismantled in silence. The voices of past 'gods' are dead, their angelic images reaped like wheat. The poetic 'stars' ('the gods whose knees we clutch'[34]), from whom a Pentecostal influx is anticipated, exert a destructive pressure. The heavens – the wheat fields – winnow him, rather than the opposite. In this version of Last Judgement, dead poets and their angelic images judge the living poet and humble him. Eliot claimed that the poet 'must inevitably be judged by the standards of the past ... not amputated ... not judged to be as good as, or worse or better than, the dead'.[35] Here a 'winnowing' judgement amputates 'the really new' from the old. A partial healing of the 'diremption between perception and utterance' is effected by the poem itself, through its eloquent diagnosis of failure, but still a surgeon is beckoned at the end.

Part of Hill's ambivalence toward the dead must have derived from his immersion in traditional Oxford course work ('I worked very hard at the orthodox English Language and Literature syllabus of that time', he said in an interview[36]) and his simultaneous effort to write new poetry. *The University of Oxford Examination Statutes* of 1950 decreed that students of English Literature prepare to translate Books IV and VI of *The Aeneid* (Aeneas's meeting with the Sibyl appears in 'After Cumae' and later in 'Offa's Journey to Rome') and passages from *The Anglo-Saxon Chronicles, Aelfric's Homilies, Beowulf,* and *Sweet's Anglo-Saxon Reader* (the latter two provided Hill with events and a title for *Mercian Hymns*). Hill chose a course in tragedy, which began with Aristotle's *Poetics* (tragic plot, with its peripety and catharsis, provided a blueprint for many of Hill's poems). From the Middle English period Hill read Chaucer, Langland, and Gower. Texts were taken from Shakespeare, Spenser, and Milton (and adapted in 'Prospero and Ariel', 'For Isaac Rosenberg', 'An Ark on the Flood', and 'Genesis'). From the beginning scholarship posed enchantments and perils for Hill the poet. When he says, 'it's at least to the credit of Oxford that it didn't kill' my 'devotion to modern poetry',[37] he acknowledges a menace struggled with and overcome.

While Hill reacted passionately for or against the dead, he remained remarkably dispassionate toward most of his immediate contemporaries, many of whom he could read in Oscar Mellor's Fantasy Press pamphlets.[38] 'They were either Empsonian in the most arid sense, writing cerebral conundrums' or 'they were narrating amorous adventures and travel anecdotes in language that was the equivalent of painting-by-numbers.' He told his interviewer: 'I really cared for neither of those alternatives.' Instead, he sought the 'fusion of intellectual strength with simple, sensuous and passionate immediacy' in the Metaphysical poets,[39] and in the Americans, Allen Tate, Robert Lowell, and Richard Eberhart. He wanted a 'richness of language' in which 'history and politics and religion speak for themselves'.[40] When he wrote of 'amorous adventure' or 'travel' it was with tradition pressing on every line.

But if tradition was not attacked or mourned it was frequently lampooned.

The elegy 'For Isaac Rosenberg'[41] mocks traditional memorials while employing them to commemorate the hero. In a series of sardonic smiles and half-smiles Hill surveys sentimental rites of remembrance and grandiose public funerals, '... men who mourn their hero's fall,/Laying him in tradition's bed', and notes how his two princes succumb to the formalities they denounce:

> When probing Hamlet was aware
> That Death in a worn body lay
> Cramped beneath the lobby-stair –
> (Whose mystery was burnt away
> Through the intensity of decay) –
>
> It followed, with ironic sense,
> That he himself, who ever saw
> Beneath the skin of all pretence,
> Should have been carried from the floor
> With shocked, tip-toeing drums before.
>
> With ceremony thin as this
> We tidy death; make life as neat
> As an unquiet chrysalis
> That is a symbol of defeat:
> A worm in its own winding sheet ...

Hill, it would seem, also succumbs to tradition – to Richard Eberhart's elegy, 'The Groundhog', which describes how the poet 'seeing nature ferocious' in the dead animal probes its mystery in the 'seething cauldron of his being', and to Dylan Thomas's 'The force that through the green fuse drives the flower', which ends:

> And I am dumb to tell the lover's tomb
> How at my sheet goes the same crooked worm.

But Hill's elegy, more than those of his predecessors, reflects on elegy with witty sarcasm. It concludes that, like all formal ceremonies, it provides a way of ordering and giving shape to events which might otherwise be chaotic, like the chrysalis which wraps the 'dead' worm in a 'thin' silken gloss, and insures its metamorphosis into a butterfly.

One of the best early elegies, 'Merlin', again takes an ironic look at rituals of remembrance, this time in the context of Arthurian heroes. Hill shrinks the traditional pastoral elegy into two quatrains, with each of the four lines assiduously rhymed or half-rhymed, and emphasises the vegetal ontogeny of the dead, who are 'the husks of what was rich seed' and, transformed, become the 'pinnacled corn'. That the locusts have covered the 'long barrows of Logres' like a tide, suggests their apocalyptic destruction, but the dead, as in 'The Distant Fury of Battle', remain more alive and rapacious than the living. Their ghosts, which traditionally feed on blood, come back to prey on the blood-thirsty predators (the locusts), who are in fact bloodless. Predator and prey reverse roles. The corn to be harvested feeds on the corpses of those who were supposed to harvest it. The new heaven and new earth is no holy city of church spires but the 'pinnacled' corn field. The knights who traditionally restored fertility to the king's domain by killing dragons, now fertilise the soil with their own deaths. Culture (in the museum's 'raftered galleries of bone') is dead unless ploughed back into the loam.

Not all Hill's early elegies end with such vigorous vegetal resurrections, but most reflect on conventions of elegy with similar irony. A trilogy of short poems on a fictitious Fraser family, 'In Memory of Jane Fraser', 'The Tower Window', and 'Captain Richard Fraser, Aged 24 Years',[42] confront death in a mood of sardonic gloom. The pastor's sheep-fold, in the first, has turned into a snowy waste land. The whole landscape resembles a beggar's corpse 'blue with cold' and wrapped in 'a cold shroud'. Against this personification of death, Jane Fraser remains vigilant ('Like a strong bird above its prey'), but to no avail. She tries to kill death, like Donne in his 'Holy Sonnets', but inevitably submits to it. Predator and prey reverse roles, and reverse again when the deceased preys on the living with grief: 'Her body froze/As if to freeze us all, and chain/Creation to a stunned repose.' Spring arrives, but only minimally. In the 1953 version:

> She died before the world could stir.
> In March the ice unloosed the brook
> And water ruffled the sun's hair.
> And a few sprinkled leaves unshook.

The impossibility of leaves 'unshaking' is rectified in the later version, which ends:

> And water ruffled the sun's hair.
> Dead cones upon the alder shook.

In both cases, however, spring's recrudescence hardly alters winter's 'stunned repose'.

A memorial to John Fraser, 'The Tower Window', encourages similar expectations of timeless permanence, and recalls the customary ways of achieving them, but only to parody them. The poem lacks the simple, sensuous details and plot of 'In Memory of Jane Fraser', but again demonstrates a deft use of rhyming quatrains:

> Some men have flowered on death.
> Before the guns, at the fire's mouth,
> Having grown big with faith,
> They have cried all at a breath.
>
> Of these are symbols made,
> As Honour; Love; and faiths decreed.

> Old bones are shelved; old ghosts laid;
> Still the transfigured words abide.

> But Fraser, at his death, was dumb.
> Now, where few men come,
> He has an unquestioned claim,
> Like furniture in a room.

Fraser possesses the right of any man to be remembered, but few, besides Hill, remember him. Unlike Arthur, Merlin and Rosenberg, he has not been transfigured into those august symbols laid 'in tradition's bed'. Nevertheless, he persists in a room of his own.

Captain Richard Fraser, in a companion piece, suffers a less ambiguous fate. In contrast, he has 'flowered .../Before the guns'. A gravestone transfigures him, but mainly 'To point the irony of grief' and mock the ineffectuality of funerals:

> Jane Fraser, now, take back your son
> To Bentley Grange where he was born,
> And see him huddled among clay
> With every due observance done.

> There is a stone where deeds still show
> Old scars above, the new below,
> Though where his limbs lie trodden down
> No sun can ever come or go.

The carved gravestone, a mimesis of Fraser's scarred body, recalls his heroic last stand at Powick Bridge, but offers a bleak reward besides the 'pinnacled corn' of 'Merlin'.

Early and late, Hill reflects on elegiac dispensations in poems rich in irony and ambiguity. He courts formality, but simultaneously mocks it. He remarks in an essay on Allen Tate:

> 'Form', for the modern poet, is indeed both triumph and concession ... The ideal of 'form' dismisses the legend of the 'mad' disruptive poet, and affirms the social value of the Respectable Artisan, who may be entrusted with such small necessities as the vote and freedom of speech. The poet looks with an ambiguous eye upon his own creation.[43]

Like Tate, Hill seeks to pattern chaotic energies rather than pretend they do not exist. He pits cherished Christian beliefs against biological and geological facts, and remarks on their relation. He supplicates earth's energies, and the dead to direct them, but resists them in the act of transforming them. Hill's obsession with the dead is really his obsession with tradition and history, whose organic and seasonal cycles he ritualistically observes in nearly every poem. Meditations, often disguised as mythical quests, follow the natural rhythms of withdrawal and return, rising to intense perception and passionate articulation and falling back to the silent, recalcitrant earth. When moral perception fails, and when the vanity of the artist's attempt to act as conscience and 'unacknowledged legislator' of his race asserts itself, Hill rises to challenge these defeats by writing of them winningly. After Oxford he continued to ceremoniously dismantle ceremony, and, as in 'For Isaac Rosenberg', with new energy 'make life as neat/As an unquiet chrysalis/That is a symbol of defeat'. Geoffrey Hill's concluding words about *The Mystery of the Charity of Charles Péguy*, that the poem is a 'homage to the triumph of his "defeat" ',[44] reverberate back through all his work. Rosenberg and Péguy, both poets who died in the First World War, are as if one, although thirty years separate their elegies. From his Oxford poems to his most recent books, Hill has fashioned splendid chrysalides in a world of baffling and painful metamorphoses.

2

For the Unfallen: a sounding

Jeremy Hooker

To adapt a phrase from 'Of Commerce and Society', Geoffrey Hill in *For the Unfallen* is a poet who exposes the muddle of Europe's dreaming. I may perhaps be excused for beginning boldly and generally, by abstracting, from parts of this poem, an overview of his apprehension of the history to which the poems are, in part, a highly critical response; density and complexity must come soon enough to an argument that tries to remain faithful to the very concentrated poetry in this book and at the same time to say something useful about it.

In 'hollowed Europe' there are no innocent beliefs, no pure motives, no unambiguous ideals; all are corrupt from their implication in commerce and warfare, ambition, egotism and duplicity. Geoffrey Hill is acutely sensitive to the corruption as it is manifested in language, infecting words themselves. 'Vision', for example. In Europe

> Statesmen have known visions. And, not alone,
> Artistic men prod dead men from their stone.
> ('Of Commerce and Society, IV')

So, a word commonly used to describe the highest artistic and religious attainments is given its actual, compromised value, naming a commodity of those who, like the 'Apostles' at Versailles, look out on a world whose god is commerce and where even the sea has been turned into a machine that serves it. 'Visions', in Geoffrey Hill's Europe, are that by which the people perish.

'Artistic men' are another dangerous sham: undignified ambitious displacers of the dead from the celebrity which they themselves covet. In the context of values established by the book as a whole, the antithesis between 'artistic men' and 'dead men' is between bought, self-deceiving fabricators of conventional images or muddled dreams, and an absolute but unknowable truth. The dead are like the sea, and Geoffrey Hill's metaphors habitually associate them with it; for although the sea is exploited, domesticated, converted in 'II, The Lowlands of Holland' to land on which Europe's representative history occurs, and although, after carnage, it is made 'decent again behind walls', the sea remains both 'Archaic earth-shaker, fresh enemy', drowner of Babel, as in 'V, Ode on the loss of the "Titanic"'. For Geoffrey Hill, the sea is also a metaphor for what is, like Jehovah, outside all human knowledge, beyond language and the muddle of all dreams, the absolute that with utter indifference judges and silences men.

Geoffrey Hill has perceived in Keith Douglas, 'the kind of creative imagination that approached an idea again and again in terms of metaphor, changing position slightly, seeking the most precise hold'. Douglas, he continues, 'approaches an idea repeatedly through metaphor, as if seeking the absolute definition of experience'.[1] It is quite clear that Geoffrey Hill himself has this kind of imagination. The interpreter of his metaphors should then approach them in a no less exploratory spirit, aware of the slight changes, resisting the temptation to be wiser and simpler than the poet and to formulate in cruder terms what the poet at his most subtle can perhaps only intimate, or unparaphrasably reveal. A further difficulty with the sea and the dead in *For the Unfallen* is that while they have particular meanings in different poems, they also represent the absolute, and are in that sense the silence against which the poems themselves submit to be judged. It is this, more than his preoccupation with Christian and pagan motifs in *For the Unfallen*, that justifies the claim that Geoffrey Hill is a religious poet. No one in recent times plays serious word-games better, but his art is not self-referential; it is a 'sounding' of history that starts from a position of respect for history's reality.

For Geoffrey Hill, art is so compromised by its commerce with social and egotistical dreams and ambitions that it can be trusted with reality only at the same time as it exposes its own untrustworthiness.

> Many have died. Auschwitz,
> Its furnace chambers and lime pits
> Half-erased, is half-dead; a fable
> Unbelievable in fatted marble.
>
> ('Of Commerce and Society, IV')

Auschwitz: there is no more dangerous name for a poet to invoke. But if we recognise the danger, we do so partly because of the quality of Geoffrey Hill's moral intelligence. He, more than any other recent English poet, has made us sensitive to the subtler forms of poetic self-regard, to the ways in which, for example, the desire to shock may be complacently parasitic upon the human suffering with which we are to be shocked. To adopt the metaphor Geoffrey Hill used in the comments on 'Annunciations' which Kenneth Allott included in *The Penguin Book of Contemporary Verse*, (a metaphor defining an idea which is already present in *For the Unfallen*), Auschwitz could easily be a food at 'the poetry-banquet', poet and reader relishing its taste on their tongues. Here, however, it is not for 'conspicuous consumption', or, like the stained-glass saint of 'In Piam Memoriam', 'A feature for our regard'. Or rather it is not only this, because the poem in naming Auschwitz admits that it is, inevitably, partly this. 'Many have died': the simple statement is all that can properly represent the enormity of the fact. Furnace chambers and lime pits have been 'half-erased', and now the meaning of Auschwitz is 'half-dead'. For those who did not suffer because of it, who did not, in suffering it, earn the right to speak the meaning in the name, Auschwitz is not only fabulous and unbelievable but 'fatted marble' – monument to a sacrifice at once vicarious and relishable. Geoffrey Hill's achievement here is to return some of the original obscenity to the name, but without allowing the complacency of supposing that we ourselves can avoid obscenity in naming it. What is at issue here is the difference between a spectator's view of evil and a man's knowledge that he too is defiled.

Geoffrey Hill's scepticism is Conradian in its focus on the very values – vision, art, imagination – on which Romantic art has based its claim to transcend or transfigure reality, resolve contradictions, and reconcile opposites. He knows that there is no barbarity of which the imagination is incapable: a knowledge which he expresses most fully, and most personally (though still obliquely), when he conflates the imagination of the poet in childhood with the bloody, luxurious, and tyrannical Offa of Mercia.

Transactions between different kinds of power give the same word contradictory meanings, and language not only reflects the muddle and divisions of a people and their history, but may contribute dangerously to further moral, social and political chaos. The ironies of this for the poet, the person who believes in words and in a sense lives by them, may be seen if we recall the relation between the language of Luther's bible, and the language of nature in the German Romantic poets, and Hitler's intoxicating rhetoric of blood and will and messianic leadership.[2] The imagery of blood and the dialectic of sacrificial act and victim which inform much of *For the Unfallen*, show Geoffrey Hill's repeated, if often oblique, approach to this particular history, and his understanding that it is above all the most valuable words that are the most dangerous. But his awareness of the imagination's capacity for corruption and duplicity is not confined to the present century or to the poet as its agent. 'Requiem for the Plantagenet Kings' is the first of the series of poems about England that forms a major part of his achievement, poems in which he simultaneously creates resonant images of a land soaked and ingrained with history and reveals the muddle of England's dreams. It casts an equally ironical eye on the self-image of the warring medieval kings:

> At home, under caved chantries, set in trust,
> With well-dressed alabaster and proved spurs
> They lie; they lie; secure in the decay

Of blood, blood-marks, crowns hacked and coveted,
Before the scouring fires of trial-day
Alight on men ...

The effigies are the work of artistic men, who have 'dressed' them well: their skills and techniques are proper to the material and the form, but they also provide the kings' flattering self-images, which conceal their reality. The alabaster kings are a lie, secure in that which is usually felt to be at the root of all our insecurities, 'decay of blood'. They are secure in a lie that has been made possible by the omission of signs of their actual bloody careers. But for how long? Until 'trial-day'. But is it possible that Geoffrey Hill, ironist and sceptic, really believes in Judgement Day? It is possible; what is certain, however, is that the book is haunted by a strongly felt need for a measure of man's worth that is absolute and terrifying, outside all his lying and comforting systems of self-evaluation. It is again the sea that is associated with Judgement:

Before the scouring fires of trial-day
Alight on men; before sleeked groin, gored head,
Budge through the clay and gravel, and the sea
Across daubed rock evacuates its dead.

Only the sea and the dead remain unmoved by the lies and the dreams which the living construct on earth.

A primary meaning of 'for the unfallen' is 'for the living'. The reader of the book may then not unreasonably suppose that, since he has yet to 'fall', the book is dedicated, in some sense, to him. The title also signifies those who are before the Fall: thus including all his readers and none of them. A writer like Geoffrey Hill who is so suspicious of his art, and therefore watchful over what moves him and moves in his own poetry – his means of persuasion – is not going to give the reader any excuse for complacency. And so we find that the poem from which the title is taken, 'To the (Supposed) Patron', is particularly unsettling; (it is also, incidentally, unusually schematic).

Is the reader to assume that he is Geoffrey Hill's patron? In a sense he certainly is, since without readers poetry wouldn't be published. And if he is also inclined to be a little patronising, that would be consonant with our usual attitude to the people we pay to entertain us. We may take it, then, that 'To the (Supposed) Patron' will treat, however obliquely, the relation between the poet and the reader, or perhaps the world of which each is a part. The patron is not, like Richard Crashaw's '... (supposed) Mistresse', a Platonic Idea, but, 'Prodigal of loves and barbecues', lord of the poetry-banquet. Love is a word at the feast.[3] The patron is also a casual perverter of the Christian ethic, for whom 'the lilies' and 'the rewards' are identical. He is 'a connoisseur of blood' (a phrase from 'Of Commerce and Society, IV' in which much of the meaning of the book is concentrated) who relishes 'the inside-succulence/Of untoughened sacrifice'. He has artificers working to sof-ten and refine reality for him:

> That no mirage
> Irritate his mild gaze, the lewd noonday
> Is housed in cool places, and fountains
> Salt the sparse haze.

By these means 'His flesh is made clean'. He is 'unfallen', therefore, because preserved by his power from all contact with reality. His artificers have prepared (at some personal cost: his bronze agents 'drink desert sand') his view of life, and have even made death 'idyllic'. Is this what we pay our poets to do for us? Geoffrey Hill's answer at this stage would be, perhaps, yes, in view of his keen sense of the distance between all forms and degrees of artistic order and the realities of suffering and evil.

'To the (Supposed) Patron' is not, I think, one of his better poems; it is too neat, too knowing. It does however contain a fine example of how the poet 'hearing words in depth ... is therefore hearing, or sounding, history and morality in depth'.[4] In 'There are many/Tremulous dreams secured under that head' the word 'Tremulous' subtly invokes the over-refined nervous artistic sensibility which is familiar in the literature and well-to-do society of Europe, particularly since the Romantic movement; while 'secured', with its connotations of graft, placemanship, complacency and imprisonment, com-pels recognition, in its cynical valuation of the 'Tremulous dreams', of their defining context. Such moments are common in Geoffrey Hill; his poetry is full of 'soundings'. Nor is it only history and morality that he 'sounds', for he has, like T.S. Eliot, a special gift for choosing the word or image that reveals a suspect (usually sexual) psychological motivation for an ostensibly pious or disinterested attitude or action. He can, in fact, match the Eliot of 'Gerontion' at revealing the prurient. The line 'The Pities, their fingers in every wound', from 'A Pastoral', is a particularly disturbing example from this first book.

For the Unfallen begins with 'Genesis', and 'Picture of a Nativity' is placed at its centre. The former is one of several poems (others are 'The Turtle Dove' and 'The Troublesome Reign') with a rhetoric powerful enough to suggest why, in order to counteract its intoxicating effects, Hill should have developed Coleridge's 'drama of reason' in such an acute form;[5] rhetorical power of this order, without scepticism, would stifle all moral intelligence. For example, echoes of Yeats, Blake and Coleridge are all audible in 'Genesis', yet the poem has an equivalent rather than an imitative power. It also has 'soundings' of rhythm as well as words, the most striking of which occurs in the often quoted lines:

> By blood we live, the hot, the cold,
> To ravage and redeem the world:
> There is no bloodless myth will hold.

And by Christ's blood are men made free . . .

Or rather it is usually the first three lines that are quoted, when the ambivalence of Hill's attitude to Christianity may be seen in 'To ravage and redeem the world'. But if we stop here we are left with a statement lacking the curiously antiphonal 'voice' that continues and qualifies it. For the first three thumping lines have a preacher's eloquence, but the fourth is a little boy's, with the rhythm and rhyme of Blake's 'The Chimney Sweeper' in *Songs of Innocence*:

And by came an Angel who had a bright key,
And he open'd the coffins & set them all free.

Geoffrey Hill is far from incapable of a 'solemn music' (to use Edmund Blunden's description of Wilfred Owen's 'Strange Meeting' which Hill quotes in his essay on Keith Douglas) but he is keenly aware of the need not to be mastered by the rhetoric of traditional poetic styles. The effect of sounding voices of innocence and experience side by side in 'Genesis' is to make the poem mock its own use of such rhetoric, yet it is more poignant, more questioning, for this.

At the beginning of 'Genesis' the poet, or the 'I' of the poem, is located in the metaphorical geography that will recur throughout the book: between sea and land, God's Creation and the imagination that will recreate it in human terms, glimpsing an absolute, immeasurable 'order' but defining the human relation to it by images and myths, composing a world: 'the works of God' in section V nicely points a moment at which the original divine Creation becomes man's bookish formula.

There is, of course, no such thing as 'pure' creation: the saint of 'In Piam Memoriam', 'Created purely from glass', is 'Of worldly purity the stained archetype'. Man cannot know the Creation without his language, myths, fables, systems, artefacts; nor can he create purely, without mixed motives or the imposition of a pattern on experience. He can, however, believe in, or sense, a reality that is not his patterns or dreams, and a comprehensive understanding of all things as they are, all suffering. This apprehension, which is essentially religious, and perhaps also the foundation of the religious attitude, will then make him both keenly aware of the ingenuities, limitations, and mixed motives of the human mind as creator of its self-protective world, and open to intimations of the irreducible reality by which it is judged. That which is 'pure', irreducible, absolute, innocent of art, man's measure instead of his measurements, haunts *For the Unfallen*. Here, Geoffrey Hill's metaphorical 'place' dividing the Creation or reality, God's works, from the works of man is the sea's edge. This is where the sea evacuates its dead in 'Requiem for the Plantagenet Kings', where the sea casts out its dead in 'Metamorphoses, V', where the old gather the dead in 'The Guardians', where Doctor Faustus stumbles on the Harpies' 'dead feast'. There are other examples, and the location recurs often enough to define Geoffrey Hill's early imaginative world; on this shore he is a poet of the tensions between art and reality, nature and revelation, the lies of the living and the truth of the dead.

Wallace D. Martin has noted the recurrence of the 'sea-burial' of 'Genesis' throughout *For the Unfallen* and connected Geoffrey Hill's use of the theme with T.S. Eliot's in *The Waste Land*.[6] It is important to see this connection, and also the occurrence in several poems of imagery of 'sea-change', which shows the presence of *The Tempest*, albeit a more shadowy and enigmatic presence than it is in Eliot's poem. But the most important literary influence on Hill's use of imagery and symbolism of the sea in his early work is – audibly – 'The Dry Salvages', just as his absorption of *Four Quartets* as a whole shows in his embodiment of historical, philosophical, and moral concerns in places and elemental settings. There is, not surprisingly, no single poem in *For the Unfallen* that attempts anything on the scale of the sustained passages concerning the sea in 'The Dry Salvages', but the presence of sea and shore is sustained by the book as a whole, and in several important points Hill's use and apprehension of the sea are similar to Eliot's. There are important differences between them, too, and Hill's literary debt to Eliot does not amount to imitation.

The sea surrounds man's world with an 'otherness'; it erodes his securities. Non-human, it nonetheless helps negatively to define man's shortcomings. The sea brings out in both Hill and Eliot a capacity for invoking awe by force of its reality that is irreducible to the scale of human meanings, but also provides their moral imaginations with a powerful symbol. Each looks out, as it were, from the shore, but with a view of the sea that undermines a landsman's complacency, contrasting all the truths he rests on with the absolute reality that negates them. For Hill, as for Eliot, the sea is a destroyer; it is littered with wreckage, and 'tosses up our losses'. Eliot identifies it with 'time not our time', not the timeless moment, but endless recurrence, suffering and waste without end. Facing the sea's power to destroy and to waste, its indifference, its temporal endlessness, in effect its representation of Creation as a succession of meaningless lives and deaths, he wins from near despair his most difficult affirmation of faith and hope. For Eliot, the end 'To the drift of the sea and the drifting wreckage,/The bone's prayer to Death its God' is 'Only the hardly, barely prayable/Prayer of the one Annunciation.'

For Hill too the sea is closely associated with the dead. 'Wreaths' begins:

> Each day the tide withdraws; chills us; pastes
> The sand with dead gulls, oranges, dead men.

His is indeed a sea that *chills*. On the face of it he has not the barest consolation; no 'hardly, barely prayable/Prayer'; no hint of a scheme of values beyond man's, in which 'dead gulls, oranges, dead men' weigh differently in spite of the blind force that equally 'pastes' the sand with them. Here indeed Death is God – and for this reason, if for no other, there is a kind of consolation, for at the sea's edge man's self-importance, his deification of himself and his illusions, come to an end. That which 'chills us' also stimulates Geoffrey Hill's imagination, and much of the poetic power of *For the Unfallen* comes from the zest – the relish, even – with which he depicts the sea as destroyer of the living and indifferent preserver of their remains.

The opening lines of the second part of 'The Death of Shelley' ('Of Commerce and Society, III') show Geoffrey Hill at once at his most Eliotic and his least consolatory:

> Rivers bring down. The sea
> Brings away;
> Voids, sucks back, its pearls and auguries.

The 'pearls and auguries', echoing *The Tempest* and perhaps also *Prometheus Unbound*, suggest preserved wisdoms and foretellings of the future; but these the sea 'Voids, sucks back' – actions of a completely empty, involuntary, and mechanical natural function. The lines are a good example of how Geoffrey Hill offers a positive meaning with one hand and takes it back with the other. They also exemplify the opposition between the language of nature and the language of culture; already evident in *For the Unfallen*, this will become a prevalent, more complex and subtler, strategy of his subsequent books. It is the *presence* of the sea in *For the Unfallen* that breaks the claustrophobic spell of muddled dreams, and, because it is all that man is not, symbolises the Judgement he does not dispense, but is subject to.'

'Picture of a Nativity', though a relatively weak poem, and perhaps only coincidentally at the centre of the book, is nevertheless central to Hill's metaphor of sea and land. As I understand it, 'A dumb child-king' is both the child at the dawn of consciousness and man face to face with Creation, as in 'Genesis', at the beginning of his myth-making; the sea and the spoils of the sea are Creation, with its 'slack serpents' and 'beasts/With claws flesh-buttered' initially 'innocent' of man's interpretation and use of them for his own purposes, to represent something in himself. Then 'Artistic men appear to worship', arriving to bow down, and perhaps also simulating reverence, but in any case, recognising 'Familiar tokens', believing 'their own eyes'. Not seeing the 'bestial and common hardship', they make instead a picture or myth. The effect of this, to borrow the language of 'In Memory of Jane Fraser', is to 'chain/Creation to a stunned repose'; man not only pictures his god but gives birth to him, with a self-centred vision and art that divides him from Creation. I take the last verse to be a picture of the effect of this Faustian arrogance on man's apprehension of the supernatural. At any rate, Geoffrey Hill is not a poet who believes what he sees; like Thomas in 'Canticle for Good Friday' he looks from Christ's 'deliberate blood', the myth according most closely to his apprehension of the truth, to the 'unaccountable darkness', his allegiance to the unknown which no myth can account for.

In the second of 'Two Formal Elegies':

Here, yearly, the pushing midlanders stand
To warm themselves; men, brawny with life,
Women who expect life. They relieve
Their thickening bodies, settle on scraped sand.

Here the shore is clearly a metaphor for the known world, safe and familiar. Beyond, 'The sea flickers, roars, in its wide hearth.' In this instance the sea, associated as in 'Requiem for the Plantagenet Kings' with the fires of Judgement Day, assimilates the fires of Auschwitz too. Geoffrey Hill asks whether it is good to remind people, 'on a brief screen,/Of what they have witnessed and not seen'. The question is complicated, however, by a further question, asked throughout the book as well as in this particular poem, about the ambiguous nature of sacrifice. Before approaching this, it should be helpful to look again at Geoffrey Hill's relation to his art.

From the beginning, conflict between aestheticism and morality has been an energy as well as a recurrent theme in Geoffrey Hill's work. The conflict has helped to make his poetry perhaps the least 'innocent' of our time – innocent, that is, of unconscious corruption. *For the Unfallen* embodies a keen awareness of the 'fallen' nature of its words and devices, indeed of poetry. A first step towards understanding the book (and I here refer to the book as a whole instead of singling out the more difficult poems, because its themes and exploratory metaphors give it an imaginative unity) is a recognition of the way in which Geoffrey Hill perceives words to be fallen and art corrupting.

He is an artist with an extreme suspicion and even, at times, a horror of art. He sees artistic men with a knowledge like Thomas Mann's in *Doctor Faustus*.[7] Hence his fascination with those men and women of words (Simone Weil and Bonhoeffer, for example) who transcended words, and with poets like Mandelshtam, Celan and Péguy who made good their poetry in their lives and deaths. Their words may be on the menu at the poetry-banquet but the poets themselves do not sit at the table; indeed their truth is 'tasteless'. Lacking the specific historical challenges of these witnesses, Hill in his poetry has developed a moral intelligence that both uses and exposes aesthetic devices. His horror of art does of course have an occasion in the ease with which highly cultivated people have become instruments of genocide, but it has more radical and widespread causes too. The poet is only one example of artistic men; all men are artistic in that they are makers of images and systems, self-creators, makers of their material world and its culture, logic and dreams, makers in their own image of the gods they worship and serve. Artistic men become gods in a world of their own making, based on their appetites, desires, self-delusions; they make themselves demons and beasts. Given this apprehension of the power of the imagination, it is not surprising to find Geoffrey Hill developing a demonology and an angelology in *For the Unfallen*.

This aspect of his work may owe something to Cartesian dualism, as interpreted by Jacques Maritain, and considered in Allen Tate's essays 'The

Each poem guilty of original sin?

Symbolic Imagination' and 'The Angelic Imagination'; an interpretation which – stated briefly – traces the confusions and divisions of the modern mind to Descartes' infliction on man of a separation of intellect and will from feeling. This is a large subject, and its mention here is meant only to be suggestive; support for its relevance to Geoffrey Hill, however, may be had from the glimpses his work – especially his later work – frequently affords of a passion for unity that his sceptical intelligence prevents him from embracing.[8] In his poems Geoffrey Hill's mind continually circles the unity of Christianity; only, unlike Christian poets for whom the paradoxes of their religion contribute to its comprehensiveness, for him the double meanings keep open a divided mind. Man's broken unity, within himself and between him and his world, which is a principal cause of his dangerous muddled dreams and self-projections, begins to emerge strongly as a theme in *For the Unfallen*, particularly through the figures of beasts, demons, angels and gods that haunt it.

To approach the same subject differently: Geoffrey Hill's poetry begins where Yeats's 'The Second Coming' ends,[9] with the rough beast reigning from the cradle of the west. There are several versions of the birth of a beast-god in *For the Unfallen*. A beast-god that is articulate, eloquent, highly artistic. He sits at the head of the table at the poetry-banquet, master of the languages of nature and of revelation, which he uses for bestial ends. In his use of the same languages, Hill exposes the beast-god and his mastery.

For the Unfallen, this least innocent of books, is much concerned with innocence. The word has potent religious and Romantic meanings whose contradictions Geoffrey Hill brings out. In 'Holy Thursday', for example, child and nurse walk 'Weaving their innocence with guile'; but they must 'suffer innocence to fall', that is, presumably, arrive at the knowledge of their fallen nature; and the she-wolf lies 'innocent of desire'. In two verses, then, a rather Blakean guileful innocence has been juxtaposed with a theological innocence, and the innocence which is only possible to the beasts because they lack the human being's knowledge of good and evil. More generally, it may be observed that innocence in Christian terms is not a state of being without sin – the only sinless states are non-human, natural and supernatural – but the state of the redeemed who have first to know their sinful nature. Given Geoffrey Hill's awareness that the beast-god, the god of this world, man's apotheosis of part of himself, is a master of all poetic tricks, rhythmic as well as verbal, which overwhelm the moral intelligence represented by 'the drama of reason', it is not surprising that there is much play on the various meanings of 'innocence' and related concepts such as the 'clean' in *For the Unfallen*. Innocents are victims, victims of ignorance or sacrificial victims, and the ambivalent theme of sacrifice faces one way to the martyr and the other to the birth of the beast-god.

The first section of 'Doctor Faustus' concerns the birth of a god from blood of sacrifice. As the title of the section, 'The Emperor's Clothes', suggests, there is really nothing there; man is naked, but the powers he deifies are sinister and menacing:

A way of many ways: a god
Spirals in the pure steam of blood.
And gods – as men – rise from shut tombs
To a disturbance of small drums . . .

The Yeatsian 'Spirals' adds to the suggestion that this emanation from man is out of control. The final verse of the third section serves as the book's epigraph:

A beast is slain, a beast thrives.
Fat blood squeaks on the sand.
A blinded god believes
That he is not blind.

The rough beast of 'The Second Coming' is terrifying because it has the demonic power of man's divided nature. With its 'lion body and the head of a man', it links brute power to intellect and will; with 'A gaze blank and pitiless as the sun', it has a capacity for destruction unchecked by the union of feeling and moral intelligence that makes man human. Hill's beast-god is born of blood-sacrifice, and makes man a beast in his projection of part of himself into omnipotence. The implication of a blinded god who believes that he is not blind is as terrible as Yeats's image. 'Fat blood squeaks on the sand' is one of the most sinister and suggestive lines Geoffrey Hill has written. It combines the voluptuously relishable but disgusting associations of 'Fat blood' with the animal and sterile associations of its other components, and suggests also blood being trodden underfoot. In the middle section of the poem, Doctor Faustus, 'Having stood hungrily apart/From the gods' politic banquet', (the poem's extremely concentrated images may here suggest the rise of Hitler and Adrian Leverkuhn's detachment from it in Thomas Mann's novel), stumbles upon another banquet, the Harpies' 'dead feast'. The artist in his Faustian attempt to transcend the murderous limitations of his time finds only another part of man's broken unity, as Adrian Leverkuhn falls prey to the demons of morbid sex and death. It is a comfortless conclusion to find, in a poet so sceptical of the art he deploys with consummate skill, a 'transcendence' of the duplicity of words which intimates, at this stage, no resolution or reconciliation of opposites, but knowledge of an unendurable reality.

8

King Log revisited

Gabriel Pearson

King Log once seemed to bristle almost aggressively with perverse and arcane features. Not all have disappeared: some initially strange enigmas have merely become familiar enigmas. The volume in its entirety with its armature of sections, headings, appendix ('King Stork') epigraphs, ceremonies of naming its own formal procedures ('Song', 'Poems Regarding ...', 'Fragments', 'Soliloquies', 'Fantasia', 'Meditations', 'Songbook') still seems an austerely defensive structure, not easily invaded, governed by difficult and arbitrary conventions and by a grim purposefulness which expects to be mistook. The critic enters the poet's castle, having given his little tinkle or sounded his annunciatory horn, with some foreboding that he is to be humiliated or scorned. His host's ostentatious punctilio (his acknowledgments, his 'essay', his 'notes', his footnotes, his 'amended version' – to 'be regarded as a necessary penitential exercise' –) is not reassuring: a kind of attentiveness is proposed which he fears he may not measure up to. Still, as Hill has in fact enlarged his castle from volume to volume (and added some convenient offices: the essays, remarks in interviews) the whole structure has become considerably more habitable. *The Mystery of the Charity of Charles Péguy* can only be reckoned almost luxuriously spacious, by contrast to the cramped accommodation of the earlier volumes.

Mercian Hymns began this enlargement. Prose – however tightly organised – succeeded verse: a more intimate geography grounded a less guarded personal history. Offa became a kind of dance of self and other, historic time and personal time, power and poesis, polity and personal passion. I say 'dance' because none of these components is privileged or foregrounded. All are held in one focus, yet each, by a delicate tact, kept intact, not blurred or reduced, the one to the other, but not abandoned, either, to wilful or wishful concatenation. This simultaneous layering and composing of discrete elements, of self and other, conscientiously woos yet resists any final glamour of resolution. So, the very last of *Mercian Hymns* preserves a vision of merging which does not allow itself to form:

> And it seemed, while we waited, he began to walk to-
>   wards us   he vanished
>
> he left behind coins, for his lodging, and traces of
>   red mud

'To' and 'of' by virtue of their position in the row become rhyme words of a kind: it is a skeletal prepositionality which survives the dissolving away of the corpus of language. Similarly, the first sentence intends ('towards us'), hovers upon us, fails into typographic space, 'vanished' upon a gush of type and leaves us with bare and discrete *residua* (his coins, the mud of his dyke) but also in syntactically equivocal phraseology: 'for his lodging'. Is that where he lodges himself or where we have to lodge him? Finally, the 'traces of red mud' are those of any man, or man as such, since 'red mud' is what 'Adam' means. We have to make the best of Offa's remains, his objects ('coins') and its apposition ('red mud'). And Hill's work is markedly a poetry of apposition,[1] units of meaning which form chains of elements, where each element resists the tyranny of the syntactical energy which constituted it by a disconnective thrust that twists and shakes the chain almost, but not quite, to pieces. The procedures of *Mercian Hymns* help to render visible the same habit of language in 'Funeral Music', the sequence which stands at the heart of *King Log*, and which proposes the Wars of the Roses as a kind of historic testing ground, recondite enough not to engage our automatic responses but still sufficiently potent to challenge imaginative sympathy.

In 'Funeral Music' Hill's sentences are likewise remarkably hospitable to appositional figurations which turn upon unsettling discordances, oppositions that they complicate rather than clarify or amplify. Almost any passage of 'Funeral Music' will serve as illustration, but this, from the second poem is a rich and illuminating instance:

> We meditate
> A rueful mystery; we are dying
> To satisfy fat Caritas, those
> Wiped jaws of stone. (Suppose all reconciled
> By silent music; imagine the future
> Flashed back at us, like steel against sun,
> Ultimate recompense.) Recall the cold . . .

The 'wiped jaws of stone' sit queerly enough with 'fat Caritas', the apposition signalling a new phase of feeling, escalating from controlled derision to chilling horror, from sardonic explanation to the enigma of some atrocious aftermath. The verbal texture itself seems to evolve abruptly across the line-break from the organic vocables of 'fat Caritas' to the savagely inorganic 'jaws of stone'. 'Caritas' appears to petrify before our eyes into the mask of an Aztec demon. Yet the Latin form, 'Caritas' has already operated a kind of linguistic petrification of the English form 'Charity'. The line of transformations only reaches back to its living original, the word 'love', at the end of the last poem, and that only in the oblique form of the vocative:

> Then tell me, love,
> How that should comfort us . . .

Against this disruption, this acute change of tone and texture, the metaphorical scheme works independently towards an equally unsettling unity organised around a trope of feeding and feasting. The word 'satisfy' evokes the notion of 'satiate' (one 'satisfies' one's hunger) and the fatness and 'wiped jaws' image a gourmet banquet and cannibal feast rapidly dispatched. Hill has protested that his humour has not been much noticed,[2] and it surely is humour of a black kind that flickers about the association of 'fat Caritas' with 'fat cat', cleaned-up and piously neat about the chops having bolted the family canary. 'Wiped' carefully does not specify the subject or the agent. It is wiped like a film wipe. 'Caritas' is never quite caught with its victim's gore in its whiskers. Indeed, we are all implicated, by the movement of the line in a conspiracy, victims and torturers alike, to maintain the hygenic alibi of our particular version of 'Caritas'.

The most conspicuous disruption (indeed, it fairly shouts at us) is the line break itself. A fracture opens at the point of maximum syntactical sensitivity between 'Caritas' and 'jaws of stone' (as if that were the gape of those jaws) and, more acutely sensitive still, between the demonstrative and its noun. The demonstrative actively points our mental gaze at the object sundered from itself by the line-break. The chasm is deepened more abysmally by the unsettling switch from singular to plural (its movement the reverse of *Mercian Hymns* XXX, from 'coins' to 'red mud', though here 'traces' also half-carries across something of the plurality of 'coins'). Yet again, there is a kind of tension between disruption and unity. A species of vowel-music plays across this chasm: the sequence of 'i' sounds in 'dying', 'satisfied' and 'wipe' encloses in a kind of acoustic parenthesis the flat 'a's' of 'fat' and 'Caritas'; these are, in turn, superceded by the dark-toned 'o's' of 'those', 'stone' and, reaching into the parenthesis proper, 'suppose' and, out of it again, 'cold', yet reviving the 'i's' of the earlier sequence in the phrase, 'silent music'.

One acknowledges of course that such demonstrations of acoustic properties are often specious and at best impressionistic. However, I think one can isolate something like a genuine effect here, a kind of aural backing, itself a performative counterpart, to the phrase 'silent music' which this phase of the poem invites us to 'suppose' as reconciling that which is not reconciled in the chain of apposition. Music is very much in the air of this passage, seductive, sedative, lulling our moral vigilance. The imperative outside the parenthesis braces us to 'recall' what the parenthesis itself tries to resist and contain: that cold climate of outrage and carnage in the view of which any illusions of 'reconcilement' merely deepen the sense of atrocity.

The phrase 'silent music', cannot strike the inner ear without instantly calling up the phraseology and religious and aesthetic argument of Eliot's *Four Quartets*. That poem loomed over the immediate post-war period and inevitably cast its glamour or shadow over any poetic sensibility then struggling to formulate itself. Hill's generation is precisely the one most likely to be affected. When we bear in mind his religious preoccupations, the influence of *Four Quartets* was likely to be peculiarly formidable. *Four Quartets* is a kind of practical education in the poetics of the post-Symbolist tradition, a summation as well as a demonstration. Its theological argument is co-extensive with its poetic practice, organised by the musical analogy. This analogy is infinitely fertile, infinitely seductive. It dissolves the most resistent linearities of the discursive mode, bending them back upon themselves, making them answerable to the logic of metaphor and myth. In the timeless image, the tough contradictions of history are reconciled. It is a musical Hegelianism, the antinomies of experience resolved and transcended in the higher term, which is the very form of their expression. Perhaps not all this is felt consciously, but it is intuited, and not with exaltation only, but a kind of despair. *Four Quartets* threatens impasse. In fact, it has simply been overgrown and outgrown by familiarity, critical commentary, the movement of literary history itself which it threatened along with other histories to supercede. Its moment has itself turned historical. Rather like Offa, it began 'to walk to-/ wards us' and, partly at least, 'vanished'. We find ourselves living in post post-Symbolism. It should therefore be no surprise to find Hill conducting a quiet, loving divorce from Eliot: behind the phrase 'silent music' lurks an almost silent process of disengagement.

It seems then that behind 'silent music' trembles the insidiously incremental phraseology of 'Burnt Norton':

> Words after speech reach
> Into the silence. Only by the form, the pattern,
> Can words or music reach
> The stillness, as a Chinese jar still
> Moves perpetually in its stillness.
> ('Burnt Norton, V')

Here we have, both stated and enacted, the transposition of words into music and music into the silence which grounds it. If, as Thomas Mann said, 'art is a cold sphere' (with as much emphasis one must suppose on *cold* as on *sphere*) then the cold of this circularity is of a different kind from that which 'Funeral Music' asks us to recall:

> Recall the cold
> Of Towton on Palm Sunday before dawn,
> Wakefield, Tewkesbury . . .

The names single out an irreducible and chilling litany of the scene of slaughter. There is no transcendance here. Indeed, the poem refuses to end on a resolving flourish, finishing up distraught and untidy with a demand to recall berufflement and mess:

> Recall the wind's
> Flurrying, darkness over the human mire.

This is much closer, one might think to earlier rather than later Eliot. Reconciliation links itself explicitly to the Christian redemptive scheme, where poetry becomes a sacrament, 'the impossible union' of spheres of existence:

> Here the impossible union
> Of spheres of existence is actual,
> Here the past and the future
> Are conquered, and reconciled . . .
> ('The Dry Salvages, V')

I suspect that the spell-like incantation of Eliot's words here is potent enough to have seeded the word 'sphere', with its long-founded musical association ('harmony of the spheres') in the last section of 'Funeral Music':

> Each distant sphere of harmony forever
> Poised, unanswerable.

To this 'unanswerable' poise, 'Funeral Music' appears to attempt something like an answer, or at least answer-back. There is a discrete and regretful repudiation of Eliot's aesthetic sacramentalism, that consoling dissolution of historical contraries into a figuration on the ground of the redemptive scheme:

> These men, and those who opposed them
> And those whom they opposed
> Accept the constitution of silence
> And are folded in a single party.
> ('Little Gidding, III')

It is a beguiling passage, with its quiet, grave equivoque on 'constitution' (as political institution, and as both the production of silence and the being constructed by it) and the subdued oxymoron of 'single party', where unity and division are brought into the closest possible conjunction. It is the extreme persuasiveness of these exquisite feats of phrasing that constitutes part of the unanswerability of *Four Quartets*. The evocation of Eliot involves then a considerable homage, even piety, as well as a dissent and an adjuration. One obvious form that this takes is the bracketing off of 'silent music', its relegation to a purely subjective hope, a wistful dream, a flashing image:

Subversive punctuating

(Suppose all reconciled
By silent music; imagine the future
Flashed back at us, like steel against sun,
Ultimate recompense.)

Within the parenthesis, itself a suspension of the logic of suffering, we have again a series of appositions: 'all reconciled', 'the future flashed back at us', 'ultimate recompense'. Here the terms of the apposition do not conflict with each other: they make a series of smooth transitions from 'all' to 'ultimate', from totality to finality. These terms embrace the middle term which is itself a reflexive image: 'imagine the future/flashed back at us'. The image unpacks the content of 'imagine': that is what imagining is, making images of ourselves for ourselves: realising a self only in the transition from one to the other. Noticeably, the reflexive image is not tranquil or stable. Its flash is a kind of optical illusion – as they say, a *blinding* flash, where the emphasis may be just as heavily upon disablement as illumination. Moreover, it returns us to the field of battle, to armour in the dawn, which is going to disappear into the comprehensive darkness at the end of this section: 'darkness over the human mire'. Interestingly, the field of the actual also opens (even within the parenthesis) into the mode of simile rather than metaphor, while the phrase 'steel against sun' insists on conjunction and opposition, rather than fusion. But in any case, the parenthesis proposes itself not as the 'ultimate recompense' but as someone's dream of such a thing. This is dramatic utterance, the silent equivalent of those 'mutterings, blasphemies and cries for help', which the poet hears as punctuating 'the ornate and heartless music' of his poem. True, he explicitly rules out 'any overt . . . dramatic structure'. But this still allows for 'dramatic' utterance. At least, we can say that this 'ultimate reconciliation' is qualified and relativised as a desperate vanity, entertained by a soul in its attempt to hold on to its identity in the act of slipping into 'the human mire', itself an angry travesty of incarnation. Thus, far from resolving the reality of suffering, the evocation of 'silent music' has to be read as part of condition of suffering, the torment of illusion, which some religious systems hold as its very essence.

Hill's determination not to entertain that 'ultimate recompense' as any more than a subjective fantasy, manifests itself 'in the very density of the medium',[3] as the maintenance, in their painful discreteness, of the phases of anguish, recoil, rage, desperate hope. His people, or personae, struggle from utterance to utterance, phrase to phrase, the chain of appositions charting, in its twisting, the trajectory of their unreconciled human nature. But dissent, though inevitably always of a respectful kind, from Eliot becomes explicit a decade after the composition of 'Funeral Music' in Hill's inaugural lecture of 1977. The argument there turns about the relationship of 'anxiety' and 'sin', and Eliot's presumed position that in

a secular age we experience anxiety until we learn to read ourselves aright and know that we act and suffer as creatures of sin. Even so, I maintain that something has eluded Eliot, eluded him 'in the very density of the medium' ... It seems to me, however, that in determining the order of priority between 'sin' and 'anxiety' 'the kind of pleasure that poetry gives' is to be experienced through contact with the force-fields of these conflicting yet colluding entities.[4]

The 'force-fields of ... conflicting yet colluding entities' applies precisely to the qualities that I have been trying to identify in 'the very density of the medium' in Hill's own writing. The danger is that the very ambition can become a theme rather than a mode of writing. 'Collusion' then may be viewed as a kind of strategy to avoid this danger. The poet has both to yield, in his practice and yet conscientiously resist. In this instance, there must be some measure of sympathetic collusion with Eliot's kind of musicality; its insidiousness must be not merely signalled, but actively undergone. (To say it is 'transcended' is to risk the wrong kind of emphasis.)

In his own critical writing, Hill permits himself a much more censorious account of the Eliotic surrender to the ineffability of music:

In the essay 'Poetry and Drama' Eliot speaks of 'a fringe of indefinite extent, of feeling which we can only detect, so to speak, out of the corner of the eye and can never completely focus ... At such moments, we touch the border of those feelings which only music can express'. As Eliot well knew, however, a poet must also turn back, with whatever weariness, disgust, love barely distinguishable from hate, to confront 'the indefinite extent' of language itself and seek his 'focus' there. In certain contexts the expansive, outward gesture towards the condition of music is a helpless gesture of surrender, oddly analogous to that stylish aesthetic of despair, that desire for the ultimate integrity of silence, to which so much eloquence has been so frequently and indefatigably devoted.[5]

There are arguably two kinds of 'music' at issue here: one, the total musical form in which linearity is resolved into simultaneity (though there are problems with this, since music is itself a linear mode); the other, a kind of tone-music which touches evanescent moods and fugitive emotions. Eliot I suspect has the latter in mind, and in this is close to Yeats and mainstream Romanticism.[6] It leads Eliot into what Hill regards as a reprehensible dualism, which pitches 'pure' against more discursive or utilitarian operations of language. Hill is suspicious of Eliot's 'ascetic rule to avoid poetry which could not stand the test of strict dramatic utility', bridling perhaps too fiercely at the term utility, (though such a formulation does tend to slide into a genre of wiseacre prating from which Eliot is not always immune when on his professional rostrum):

That 'poetry' which is excluded on utilitarian grounds, is, I would argue, that very element which could master the violence of the conflict and collusion between the sacramental and the secular, between the dogmatic exclusiveness of 'sin' and the rich solipsistic possibilities of 'anxiety'.[7]

Here once more we find 'conflict' and 'collusion' and the evocation of a play of imagination that could permit not merely their clash but their positive interplay. If I jib at 'master', wondering upon what fulcrum such mastery could be exercised, it is because Hill has supplied more modest and humane terms, 'contact' and 'focus' to convey the idea of touching without immersion, and of holding together in one imaginative moment without triumphant fusion, terms granted their own resistant integrity.

Yet 'Funeral Music' itself in its own title appeals explicitly to the analogy of music. Hill asserts that he 'was attempting a florid grim music broken by grunts and shrieks'. In any case, the rest of *King Log* is sprinkled with musical terms; the term 'song', in some combination, occurs four times in titles in this volume. Arguably, 'song' overturns the analogy with music by directing attention to the age-old combination of words-and-music. Indeed, the term performs an inversion, for words have to be both themselves and substitute for the absent music. I find, too, a marked shift away from the musical analogy (words-as-music) in the notion of a 'broken' music 'punctuated' by other kinds of noises – human, natural, animal and instrumental. Eliot's music continually apprehends the silence into which it dies. It is a sort of figuration of that silence. Hill's music sounds against a disorderly chaos of noise. In 'Funeral Music, 1', 'Psalteries *whine* through the empyrean' (like fractious infants, beaten dogs or cringing beggars). In 3 'A field/After battle utters its own sound' and souls can gasp:

> Among carnage the most delicate souls
> Tup in their marriage-blood, gasping 'Jesus'.

'Jesus' here is not only the invoked saviour, but an execration, a scream of pain or for help – even, taking up the force of 'tup', the cry of release in orgasm. However, episodically, we do encounter what may pass as moments of transcendance or paradisal silence:

> On those pristine fields I saw humankind
> As it was named by the Father; fabulous
> Beasts rearing in stillness to be blessed.
> The world's real cries reached there, turbulence
> From remote storms, rumour of solitudes,
> A composed mystery.
>
> ('Funeral Music, 6')

Again, the appositional operation is in full force, as 'real cries' are substituted, in turn by 'turbulence from remote storms', and 'rumour of solitudes', to compose themselves in 'composed mystery'. We can hardly escape the sense in 'composed' of 'made up', as well as that of 'composure' of face or demeanour. Either way, such composition (we see it actually building across the sentence) is both reassuring and suspect, suspect because reassuring. This indeed is the passage in which we have the only obvious allusion to the fable genre from one instance of which the whole volume takes its title. The Aesopian fable is traditionally the vehicle of shrewd, worldly wisdom; yet its talking animals are also prelapsarian and figure a world in which the schism between man and the creatures has not yet occurred. Hill's volume engages with this fabular world obliquely, even suspiciously. It fastens on one of the more ferociously theological of the fables. The two-legged frogs, who protest against their ineffectual ruler King Log, are like parodies of men, blithely skittish, jumpy, inclined to self-advertisement and overweening. This turns King Stork, the real authoritarian monarch who replaces King Log, and devours them, into a fisher of frog-men, an ironic anti-type of the dove of the Holy Spirit. Men perversely will seek rulers and will want to turn them into gods. Their itch for monarchy does not allow them to know when they are well off, under the supine rule of King Log. On the other hand, their discontent with such inert rule is also a kind of perverse glory. And God could be charged with a peculiarly malign sense of humour in punishing them for it. But again, men are both impudently inquisitive and yet rejoice in arrangements which, log-like, don't make any demands upon their moral sympathies. Either way, man is a bad lot, in a bad plight, wooing his own destruction from images of his own making, which he turns into his terrors and punishment. This fable images this image-making, but in naively graphic terms.

Hill pauses here to consider the childlike, wooden yet eloquent world of the fable. It is a toy domain, erected against the terrors of night and of abandonment. Implicitly, it is a model for all art-work, all artifice, including the verbal artifice that in this passage encompasses and composes it. (Where 'composed' can also sound like a child's game: brick set upon brick.) Yet this composition is shadowed, doubled, by the terrors it is constructed to appease or banish: 'A hawk and a hawk-shadow', as the seventh poem in the sequence phrases it. The terms of this 'composed mystery' are only innocent in this charmed moment of 'pristine' communion between parent and child (always itself a communion with the parent's own childhood, the child still within him.) Those 'pristine fields' are shadowed by the battle fields of the sequence, with their obscurely savage yet resonant names: 'Wakefield', 'Towton', 'Tewkesbury'; which take us back to the poem we have been examining:

> ... some trampled
> Acres, parched, sodden or blanched by sleet,
> Stuck with strange-postured dead.

The casual randomness of 'some' is a sardonic counterpart to the gestural solemnity of 'those pristine fields'. Hill is influenced I would guess by some lines in the king's opening speech in the first part of Shakespeare's *Henry IV* where 'those' and 'fields' and 'acres' also figure in close proximity:

> Forthwith a power of English shall we levy ...
> To chase these pagans in those holy fields
> Over whose acres walk'd those blessed feet,
> Which fourteen hundred years ago were nail'd
> For our advantage on the bitter cross.

These lines too have a kind of wooden piety, medieval in feel, in which careful, childlike, inelegant exposition, not afraid of repetition and earnest chime, serves as a guarantee of naive and humble piety. This pious mode is challenged and reduced to a species of child's play by the competing rhetorics engendered by the historical situation of Henry's reign. His wish to redeem and die in Jerusalem finally reduces itself to a solemn simulacrum: he dies in the 'Jerusalem Chamber' and his career – despite the brilliant interlude of Henry V and Agincourt – is to lead his 'power of English' to those very fields which 'Funeral Music' explores.

It is clear that the 'pristine fields' of childhood are a privileged, magical space, a quiet interlude, in which the energies of the poetry itself seem temporarily laid at rest. Yet 'there' 'the world's real cries reached', however magically composed as a 'mystery'. 'Turbulence' carried, from storms however 'remote'. Similarly, words like 'field' and 'cries' carry across the spaces of the poem as verbal particles, highly charged and mobile, carrying complete sets of negative and positive charges, which mirror, echo or reverse each other's polarities across the entire sequence, achieving sometimes a coincidence which goes well beyond the semantic chiming and clashing of normal ambiguities and puns. 'Field' for instance repeats and transforms itself in such terms as 'ground', 'dwelling-place', 'worldly place', 'region'; sometimes these are bonded together by rhymes such as that between 'ground' and 'sound', by virtue of which the 'field' cluster connects with the 'noise' cluster in the seventh poem:

> 'At noon,
> As the armies met, each mirrored the other;
> Neither was outshone. So they flashed and vanished
> And all that survived them was the stark ground
> Of this pain. I made no sound, but once
> I stiffened as though a remote cry
> Had heralded my name. It was nothing . . .'

This reworks with elaboration and variation earlier motifs, such as this from 3: 'A field/After battle utters its own sound'. However, in the later passage, this sound has been localised and internalised, lodged in the sensorium of the protagonist, though still experienced as an alienated approximation of his own name (never, of course, uttered in this sequence). What this dying man almost manages to will into being is the medieval dream of the natural sign, the name which will participate in the essence of the thing named, not just be assigned to it arbitrarily. That sacramental fusion of name and substance does not happen ('It was nothing . . .'). What we are left with is echo ('*remote cry*' recalling the 'remote storms' of 6), representation in the codes of various ceremonious utterances ('heralded'), and beyond that a continuous chain of substitutions, displacements – what Hill had referred to in the passage about Eliot as ' "the indefinite extent" of language itself', which seems co-terminous with the field of human suffering and desire. For Hill cannot himself ground his language in some final set of terms (I skirt around the jargon of the ultimate 'Signified'). The medium is wholly flawed, but can be partially redeemed by a kind of writing which itself confronts, and, in a manner, 'realises' this indefinite extent in a determinate form. Hill is suspicious of his own medium to the point of paranoia; yet he remains committed to the notion that it is all that he had to work with, despite its endemic liability to illusion and consolatory fantasies of power and control. The protagonist of 6 having set up the child's fabular and wooden world against 'abandonment' finally opts for abandonment:

> I believe in my
> Abandonment, since it is what I have.

I would hazard that this poem establishes a parallelism between art-language as a defensive and childlike dream of power, and two false (or at least self-serving) forms of fidelity such as might assuage terror at the moment of death or serve as posthumous justification:

> Some parch for what they were; others are made
> Blind to all but one vision, their necessity
> To be reconciled . . .

Some desire only the continuation of their own identity; others want to participate in some unity (God, or the universe, or the Marxist vision of human liberation). Both are versions of the quest for paradise or Utopia. The protagonist 'believes in' his 'abandonment' because that is what he 'has'. 'Abandonment' offers no final solution, no ultimate term. Simultaneously active and passive, 'abandonment' exhibits the polarised valences with which Hill's poetry is charged. In the passive sense, his protagonist is abandoned by God, by parent, by his fellow men, by reason, by life itself. But there is also an active self-abandonment: to death ('And so it ends. . .'), to the realm of language, to the uncomposed mystery of our actual historical being.

It remains true nonetheless that in Hill's vision of history this 'worldly place'(8) is characterised as 'no-man's dwelling-place', a 'vacuous/Ceremony of possession' (1), where even the subject of that 'possession' dissolves in short order from a presence into an appearance and beyond that simply into some instance or exemplum in a theory or creed:

> Not as we are but as we must appear,
> Contractual ghosts of pity; not as we
> Desire life but as they would have us live,
> Set apart in timeless colloquy:
> So it is required; so we bear witness,
> Despite ourselves, to what is beyond us . . .
> ('Funeral Music, 8')

Here the punning play between formal and colloquial language enacts the disparity between the life we have (had) and the significances which are ascribed to us by theologians, ideologues, historians and romancers. The 'common man/Of death', 'mystified' in more senses than one, shrugs and says it 'is all beyond me.' Hill, too, is in the process of producing a 'Poetry' which 'Unearths from among the speechless dead' such a one as Lazarus, or the unowned, unnamed voice of 'Funeral Music', and parades him for posthumous honours and decorations:[8] another of 'The tongue's atrocities', which extends beyond the dialect of poets to every kind of significance-mongering. Against this, 'the indefinite extent of language' offers a kind of protection, adumbrating something like the shape of human desire ('as we desire life') against all mysteries, however composed. Paradoxically, this decomposition is itself a composition and one which acknowledges that the trajectory of desire is to be traced through those successively assumed and abandoned forms of artifice that threaten to imprison it and to which it resorts out of terror and anxiety.

This goes some way towards explaining Hill's penchant for self-consciously formal, even decorative and ceremonial artifice. His whole volume seeks to display itself as one emblem ('King Log') elaborated in a series of devices and exempla. It aspires to be a single meditation. Its failure to achieve this becomes itself an expressive device, a scrupulous enactment of constraint and limitation. Finally, it is another form of broken music or fractured design. These ornate ceremonial forms and gestures open up between them, by virtue of their elaborate figuration, a kind of space in which desire, suffering, history can find their silent voice. This confers on the poems themselves an extremely equivocal status. Each becomes a 'trap for meditation'[9] which has been escaped from. Each poem wears the air of having been superceded and rendered obsolete by a moral awareness of each imaginative act as a travesty or falsification. From this point of view, elaborate formality may be seen as a form of owning up. It acknowledges that art's structures readily participate in ploys of power and control. This is at least how I construe features of *King Log* which otherwise I find, frankly, antipathetic: the self-important fussiness about titles and epigraphs, the self-conscious dwelling on the terms of art. I would argue however that these function as a conspicuous display of the boundaries of artifice by offering themselves as a virtual parody of the completeness of formal closure.

This expressive function of ritual and ceremonial form ('vacuous ceremony of possession') applies particularly to poems like 'Annunciations', where, as Hill himself has indicated, a phrase such as 'Our God scatters corruption' ('Annunciations, 2'), reads in two totally opposite senses: 'The "germ", I think, is the key phrase in line 11. "Our God scatters corruption" = "Our God puts corruption to flight" or "Our God disseminates corruption".'[10] It is not difficult to sympathise with Kenneth Allott's admission that he could 'understand "Annunciations" only in the sense that cats and dogs may be said to understand human conversation ...'. There is indeed a sense in which such systematic self-cancellation is unconstruable, leaving us to attend to matters of form and tone. At best we might posit a kind of Freudian dialogue, in which competing unconscious impulses jockey for supremacy by insisting on 'the antithetical meaning of primal words'.[11] What is dramatically exhibited is the extreme unprincipledness of poetic form as such, cheerfully condoning a 'vacuous ceremony' while maintaining every appearance of formal composure. The case of 'September Song' is no less equivocal. Much critical labour has been expended to show how it escapes the charge of condoning by profiting (for its subject matter) from the atrocity it 'sings'.[12] Such demonstrations lay it open to an infinite regress: critic and poet get kudos from showing awareness in the poem of the danger of getting kudos from this 'ultimate' subject. The faultiness lies in trying to align the poem too squarely with moral virtue. It would be better, in my view, to admit that the enterprise is inevitably equivocal, and cannot win its way to some sure moral ground which it is not, in any case, the function of literature to secure. The interest of the poem is that it walks the knife-edge, that it performs the dare. Whether it comes off or falls off is not in principle determinable. Life, art, delight in nature have all, as it happens, survived Auschwitz and that fact alone points to the fluctuations and limits of the human capacity for moral response. I read 'September Song' as itself enacting an inevitable callousness, or at best intermittency, of moral imagination; we live in a universe where knowledge of atrocity and the blitheness of song go on co-existing. This view of the poem, however disagreeable, seems to me true to our experience of reading it or hearing it read. Its victim is not and cannot be redeemed. The essence of the atrocity is that the victim has been erased, wiped, annihilated and no form of commemoration of that erasure can serve to render it less complete, though it may momentarily assuage our sense of helplessness. For that, again, is what atrocity is and does to its victims, and to us. To say or feel anything less or more is to fail to take its measure. Hill, it seems, does with this poem what he describes his childish self as doing in *Mercian Hymns* VII, when he 'sidled away from the stillness and silence', after battering a ditchful of frogs to death. Calling it 'Song' releases it to exhibit its moral beggary.

This account makes the poem its own ironic object. However, within the frame of the poem the same sense of the limit of artifice can often take the form of an irritable or angry return of the poet upon himself. 'Fantasia on "Horbury"' considers the Reverend John Bacchus Dykes, a nineteenth-century hymnist, with a mounting sense of disgust at adding one more version to the sequence of accounts that claim to account for his difficult humanity:

> Consider him thus animated,
> That outworn piety and those plush tunes
> Restored for the sake of a paradox
>
> And the too-fashionable North. Or, again,
> Consider him catspawed by an indolent poem,
> This place not of his choosing, this menace
>
> From concave stormlight a freak suggestion . . .
> These heads of nettles lopped into the dust . . .

The *mise-en-scène* sounds like some visit to his rectory, but I take 'this place not of his choosing' to be also the place of the poem as well as the weather, the time of day, the mood that occasioned it. The lopped 'heads of nettles' seems to image the poet's own activity as an idle violence, indifferent to its object, angry and ashamed of itself for being so, given over to gusts of aimless satire and not far removed from that slaughter of the frogs already alluded to:

> ... Coagulations of
> frogs: once, with branches and half-bricks, he
> battered a ditchful; then sidled away from the
> stillness and silence.
>
> (*Mercian Hymns*, VII)

The whole of 'Fantasia on "Horbury"' exhibits an oddly, aimless, irritable demeanour, with its trailing dots, slurred rhymes ('place' and 'menace'), its febrile puns ('Consider him thus *animated*'). But above all it is Hill's own poem that is doing the catspawing, and we have to read it in the light of the accusation it makes against itself. It is not surprising to find in Hill's critical prose a consistent preoccupation with Coleridge. Coleridge is the Romantic poet most given to using his own poetry as a total ironic object: 'Dejection: An Ode' manages to be the poem which Coleridge's dejection does not permit him to write. Hill quotes, with intrigued emphasis, 'one abrupt entry in Coleridge's 1796 Notebook: "Poetry – excites us to artificial feeling – makes us callous to real ones"'.[13] The callousness of art-work is then a recurrent concern, even an obsession. There are of course other ways to come to terms with it than turning the poem into an object of distrust and accusation. But that is the tendency of many in *King Log*, so much so, that I have been sometimes tempted to wonder whether 'Log' is not also a headless pun on 'logos', and whether it is not the incarnated 'Word' itself which is on trial, charged with the heavy complacency of its moral inertia, its predatory desensitising of our capacity for moral outrage. This is how 'The Word' comports itself in 'Annunciations, 1':

> The Word has been abroad, is back, with a tanned look
> From its subsistence in the stiffening-mire.
> Cleansing has become killing, the reward
> Touchable, overt, clean to the touch.

'The Word' is amusingly like those wealthier academic colleagues of the late 'Fifties swanking back from their holidays in Greece and attracting some disgruntled odium. But if it's the poem we are talking about, then its clean, formal lineaments are viewed as life-denying, murderous: 'Cleansing has become killing'. 'The Word' is

> Now at a distance from the steam of beasts,
> The loathly neckings and fat shook spawn ...

where again we seem to have those battered frogs or something very like them quivering behind the queer mingling of disgust and fascination. 'Neck-ings', it should be noted, is another 'Fifties term. It is what was done in the back of cinemas before the 'Sixties moved the action more radically indoors and upstairs. There is in this a strong strain of what Robert Lowell has called 'a puritan's too literal pornographic honesty',[14] though always mitigated by corroding self-satire and acute feeling for the creaturely life thus stigmatised and victimised. Thus the humanist in the poem of that title:

> These
> Lips debate and praise –
> Some rich aphorism;
> A delicate white meat.
>
> The commonplace hands once
> Thick with Plato's blood
> (Tasteless! tasteless!) are laid
> Dryly against the robes

The delicate movement here admirably captures the wincing precision of the painted figure. The bracketed 'tasteless! tasteless!' can be read as the human-ist's own response to connecting blood with the propounder of the bloodless Ideas, or be a lament by the hands themselves for their lost capacity to taste. As often, the predatoriness of art, or any ideal form, connects with an image of eating. But this food has been carefully pre-digested. Its whiteness partici-pates in the whiteness of the paper on which the humanist has lavished the blood of print, in commentary upon the bloodless texts of Plato.

Some such scheme seems to operate in the third of 'Three Baroque Medi-tations', 'The Dead Bride'. The bride again seems to be 'a delicate white meat' to her poet-husband's lust for sublimation:

> So white I was, he would have me cry
>   Unclean!' murderously
> To heal me with far-fetched blood.

It is hard not to see that 'whiteness' again as the whiteness of the page, the 'far-fetched blood' as ink which – again a murderous agent of cleansing – splatters and defiles. 'Murderously' is situated ambiguously within the sen-tence: each could be seen as murdering the other. The point of view, however, is much more that of the victim-bride's; it is virtually her monologue. Her creaturely immuneness to 'The Word' also struggles to accommodate it, as though she were the virgin of a vampire-like annunciation, a supernaturally maculate conception:

> I writhed to conceive of him.
> I clawed to becalm him.

It is as though matter, the matrix, the receptacle, as we find it in the account of the Demiurge in Plato's *Timaeus*, were precisely a kind of womb of the active and disorderly kind described in the last section of that influential and very strange work ('On women, birds, animals, reptiles and fish'):

> ... the matrix or womb in women ... is a living creature within them that longs to bear children. And if it is left unfertilized long beyond the normal time, it causes extreme unrest ...[15]

The bride's dream 'of my father's/House' seems like her version of a reciprocal 'male' receptacle, analogue to 'His sacramental mouth', that must also stand for the 'Heavenly Mansion' on the 'Annunciation' level of the poem. Ambiguity between the levels is maintained by the fortuitous or well-founded coincidence of the capital letters of both 'House' and 'His' with the formal capital of the line-beginning. The 'matrix' seems itself to become tongued, literate, poeticised by this strange and murderous intercourse:

> His sacramental mouth
>
> That justified my flesh
> And moved well among women
> In nuances and imperatives.

Yet, at the poem's end, it is 'The Word' that is murderous, its 'Love' which is execrated:

> This was the poet of a people's
>   Love. I hated him. He weeps,
> Solemnizing his loss.

There is some move here beyond the impasse of poem as its own ironised object: the bride is given her own, though posthumous, voice. Moreover, the title of this group of poems, '... Baroque Meditations', invites us to view all three poems as consciously stylised and figured in a pre-Romantic and pre-Symbolist mode. This leads into the devotional and baroque modes of *Tenebrae*; it is not the side of Hill's work I much enjoy but I can see it has its own experimental and developmental logic.

The other move Hill makes is the more spacious and daring one which opens into the wider and freer régimes of *Mercian Hymns* and *The Mystery of the Charity of Charles Péguy*. In *King Log* it consists in the creation of a further space within the volume which behaves like a fictional model of the entire volume and dramatises Hill's own presence within it under the mask of Sebastian Arrurruz. There is a palpable self-mockery about the name. Hill's suspicious poetic personality is here lampooned in the 'Sebastian', the patron saint, as it were, of his volume, *For the Unfallen*, whose martyrdom, or at least the picture of whose martyrdom, is a metaphor for 'fine art' (that poem is also a homage to Henry James, most intricately crystalline of artists). The other component of the name becomes the English 'arrowroot', which recalls the 'little flutter of ... arrows' of 'The Martyrdom of Saint Sebastian', but is also the anti-diarrhoetic root, denizen, in powdered form, of the medicine chest, until the 'Fifties, sovereign against flux. 'The Word' in 'Annunciations' had returned 'From its subsistence in the stiffening-mire'; as though its sojourn had indeed helped to arrest the dissolution and flow of the phenomenal world. Sebastian Arrurruz is a characterization of the poet as crystalline stiffener: precious, dedicated to artifice, obsessional annotator of a life and love, turning his own life into an art work. We cannot tell whether the 'you' of the poem is real or an imaginary muse: she seems not to be identical with Arrurruz's wife, to judge by the oblique tentative figure delineated in 'To His Wife'. Arrurruz himself is a partially comic account of a kind of 'Decadent' writer, post-Romantic, pre-Modernist (he dies in the year of *The Waste Land*), a dandy, an exile and an exquisite. His own poem take the mannered and intricately wilful mode to the edge of absurdity:

> Oh my dear one, I shall grieve for you
> For the rest of my life with slightly
> Varying cadence, oh my dear one.
>   ('Coplas, ii')

Here refinement and sentiment turn into the very cadence named by the lines. Or again, the sorrow of lost or exiled love is transposed into 'a workable fancy' and thereafter indeed deftly worked with a self-consciously mannered grace. Hill is interested in the artfully mannered personality deliberating its own gestures, like the notables of 'Funeral Music': 'The voice fragrant with mannered humility' (1), where we can also hear 'manna'd' and perhaps 'manor'd':

>   Old petulant
> Sorrow comes back to us, metamorphosed
> And semi-precious. Fortuitous amber.
> ('The Songbook of Sebastian Arrurruz, 4')

Arrurruz is semi-precious, yet the extreme irony of the mask also permits a release: into the prose, albeit mannered prose, of two of these pieces, but also into a translucent, sensuous poetry, which can operate without the ironic double of its self-scrutiny. A poem like 'A Song from Armenia' is so purely embedded in its fictional context that it cancels itself back to an unembarrassed directness and sensuousness of statement that Hill had not achieved before:

> A drinking-fountain pulses its head
> Two or three inches from the troughed stone.
> An old woman sucks there, gripping the rim.

This is indeed a long way from 'the ancient troughs of blood' of 'Ovid in the Third Reich', with which *King Log* opens. There is a curious connection with Mandelshtam, who also couples Armenia with Ovid, and who used the Ovidian title 'Tristia', for a volume of his own, which Hill takes up in his title for his poem about Mandelshtam. Here the blood of atrocity and ink returns to water, the atrocious European mid-century is for the time being mislaid and humanity is allowed an unembarrassed intercourse with its world. The fountain 'pulses', the old woman 'sucks' and 'grips'; but none of these actions is compromised or shadowed as travesty or parody. Even what one may term – with due caution – the sexual politics of the volume works through to a kind of equilibrium. The female voice will neither scold, nor answer back with protest or execration. It is permitted (to borrow a word from 'Cowan Bridge', the poem about Charlotte Brontë) to remain 'unmolested'. The 'mother-matrix', no longer prone to the assaulting 'Word', is restored within the carefully walled paradise of Arrurruz's 'Songbook' – and with only a trace of resistance – to an autonomous, uncontained, limpid sensuousness:

> Why do I have to relive, even now,
> Your mouth, and your hand running over me
> Deft as a lizard, like a sinew of water?

4

Mercian Hymns:
Offa, Charlemagne and Geoffrey Hill

Martin Dodsworth

Mercian Hymns, Geoffrey Hill's third book, looks and feels different from the others. The passionate intensity of meaning that marks the rest of his work is absent here; the tone is often genial and relaxed. Furthermore, the book seems to have been conceived from the beginning as one book – unlike the earlier volumes it is not a collection but a single sequence of thirty prose-poems. If, as C.H. Sisson has said, *Mercian Hymns* is Hill's most 'accessible' book,[1] the reason may lie in these features that differentiate it from the others.

When the book first appeared, however, the poet, conscious that it might be seen as 'a diversion from earlier beliefs, attitudes, procedures', said that he would have liked to stress 'the likenesses, the continuities' between *Mercian Hymns* and its predecessors.[2] Perhaps unluckily for his readers Hill did not go on to say what those likenesses seemed to him to be. The most obvious aspect of 'continuity' must be the concern with government and rule which runs throughout Hill's work, to which the epigraph of his second book, *King Log* ('From moral virtue let us pass on to matter of power and commandment . . .') drew attention, and which inevitably arises in a sequence of poems which, like *Mercian Hymns*, is about the reign of a king – Offa, King of Mercia.

Not that the historical Offa, who ruled from 757–796, is all that Hill is concerned with in his book. He tells us that during early medieval times Offa 'was already becoming a creature of legend', and this seems to be offered as warrant for the characterisation of the king as a creature of myth:

> The Offa who figures in this sequence might perhaps most usefully be regarded as the presiding genius of the West Midlands, his dominion enduring from the middle of the eighth century until the middle of the twentieth (and possibly beyond).

Details of the historical record are used by Hill to suggest the legendary quality Offa's name was later to assume. The means by which this is done are evident in Hymn XIII, the last of three on 'Offa's Coins':

> Trim the lamp; polish the lens; draw, one by one, rare
>   coins to the light. Ringed by its own lustre, the
>   masterful head emerges, kempt and jutting, out
>   of England's well. Far from his underkingdom of
>   crinoid and crayfish, the rune-stone's province,
>   *Rex Totius Anglorum Patriae*, coiffured and age-
>   less, portrays the self-possession of his possession,
>   cushioned on a legend.

Offa's coinage was important as an aspect of his rule. He introduced 'a new type of coin, broader, thinner and heavier than its predecessors, and bearing almost universally the names of the king and the responsible moneyer'.[3] This becomes the model for all subsequent coinage in the Old English period, and even beyond it. According to Sir Frank Stenton, 'the continuous history of the English currency begins in Offa's time'. On some of his coins Offa's head appears, 'coiffured and ageless', as does the inscription 'OFFA REX'. Upon this legend or inscription, the King's head might be said to be 'cushioned'.

However, the title ascribed to the king in this poem, '*Rex Totius Anglorum Patriae*', 'King of the whole country of the English', is nowhere used on Offa's coins; Hill's acknowledgements show him to be too well read in the scholarship of these matters not to have known that he was slighting the historical record here. Yet he does so in order to insist upon another aspect of the historical Offa's reign. The title used is, after all, one that was given to Offa, in a written document, a charter granting land to Archbishop Jaenberht;[4] it was an attribute on which the king was 'cushioned', not in the almost literal sense suggested by the coin, but in one more generalised. Offa's rule was bolstered by his claim to 'the whole country of the English'. Hill's grammar introduces a fine irony here by making '*Rex Totius Anglorum Patriae*' refer both to the king and to his title. Both 'portray' – odd word – 'the self-possession of his possession'. The legend is a legend of possession, the king *is* his legend, and his possession is merely and, if you like, magnificently, 'self-possession', since the extent of his power is bolstered by the effrontery with which he claims (and he was the first to claim it) that his power extends so far – to the 'whole country'.

This is not the end however, of Hill's allusive recreation of the historical Offa in this poem. There is another sense in which Offa was 'cushioned on a legend':

> Whether on his parent's intiative, or (as is quite possible) on his own, he was the
> one ruler of Mercia to bear the name of the great King of continental 'Angel'
> from whom the Mercian kings claimed to be descended. Of the first Offa we
> know little; but in the mysterious ragbag of legendary references known as *Wid-
> sith*, we are told: 'Offa ruled Angel ... with his single sword he fixed the boundary

against the Myrgings at Fifeldor.' We do not know if Offa knew *Widsith*, but we cannot doubt that he knew the legends of his great namesake; nor that they stirred him to fix the boundary against the Welsh.[5]

Because the Anglii are both Englishmen and Angles, the title '*Rex Totius Anglorum Patriae*' serves to evoke Offa's self-possessed exploitation of legend in the pursuit of power; and there is, too, an amused irony at the expense of 'Englishness': this Offa who is so much part of our ideal England as to inhabit an 'underkingdom' somewhere among its geological strata, whose history goes back to the prehistory of the crinoid, actually claimed to come from elsewhere, from continental Anglia.

The Offa in Hill's poem would still be legendary, even without the reference to legend with which it ends. 'Ringed by its own lustre, the masterful head emerges, kempt and jutting, out of England's well.' The rim of the coin is the edge of the well; the coin's silver is the water in the well, which shines with a lustre that is the head's own because the head too is silver, and because it puts the king's mark on the whole coin. But the severed head within a well is part of English folklore; it figures in Joseph Jacobs's *English Fairy Tales* and also in a play with many folklore references, Peele's *Old Wives Tale*, where the head speaks in the well:

> Gently dip, but not too deep,
> For fear you make the golden beard to weep.
> Fair maiden, white and red,
> Stroke me smooth, and comb my head,
> And thou shalt have some cockell-bread.[6]

Hill's poem suggests that the coin itself has been found in a well; the custom of throwing coins into a source of water is itself a superstition. One detail in his sentence encourages reference to Peele's head and its song, and that is the description of Offa's head as 'kempt', that is, combed.[7] In Peele and in the version of the folktale in Jacobs the head asks to be combed:

> Wash me, and comb me,
> And lay me down softly,
> And lay me on a bank to dry,
> That I may look pretty,
> When somebody passes by.

Peele's verses suggest the connection with fertility and self-gratification more clearly than those in Jacobs; Hill's words hint at a 'masterful' sexuality manifesting itself from the 'underkingdom', a power that commands others and yet commands also the man in whom it appears. Here is another meaning for 'the self-possession of his possession'. Since sexuality is partly at least instinctual, it may be thought of as something alien to history; but since it can only appear in historically existing persons it inevitably associates itself with particular times and places. The head on the coin evokes such a meeting of timeless instinct and the man of his time.

The poem begins with an order or an instruction: 'Trim the lamp; polish the lens; draw, one by one, rare coins to the light'. The person addressed here is someone who collects coins, perhaps of this century, perhaps not. The lamp that needs trimming has an antique air, but the lens suggests the assistance of modern technology. The instructions may be given to himself by the collector, or they may be implicit in the 'masterful' look of the head on the coin. There are plenty of possible meanings here; but the one to insist on is that which identifies the collector of coins with the child who figures elsewhere in the sequence, merging with the figure of the king, as at the close of Hymn X, on 'Offa's Laws':

> He smeared catmint on his palm for
> his cat Smut to lick. He wept, attempting to mas-
> ter *ancilla* and *servus*.

A king as well as a child may have a cat called Smut; a king as well as a child may weep in the difficulty of learning Latin, especially if the ownership of that tongue is a token of mastery over maidservant and manservant. The poems are written in the consciousness that a child may be king in his own imagined kingdom and that a king may act out childish impulses ('He threatened malefactors with ash from his noon cigar'). A child's greed for coins, legitimised as the enthusiasm of a collector, may not be so far from a king's greed for power. If that meaning is latent in Hill's poem, however, it is firmly subordinate to others. The compulsion of the collector is no more moralised than the king's compulsion, glimpsed in the multiple meanings of 'the self-possession of his possession'. These compulsions simply are what they are. They combine self-gratification and attention to the world beyond self, they combine pleasure and menace (since, for example, the child's compulsion might become fixation). Both aspects are present in the song from Peele's play: 'Gently dip, but not too deep,/for fear you make the golden beard to weep.' And just as the head in the well is a given in the world of *The Old Wives Tale* so are the natures of king and child given in *Mercian Hymns*.

Since I have spent so long in explicating the meaning of Hymn XIII, it is necessary to emphasise that the poem itself is not a statement about the world so much as a statement *of* it. It does not seek to explain one part of the world in terms of another part, but to present the world as an interrelated whole, without gloss, as it were. 'The arts which use language are the most impure of arts,' Hill has written;[8] language tugs against the poem's pull towards simple presentation, inviting the gloss which in its main current it drives to avoid. Although the poem may be reduced to a series of ambiguous propositions about the relations between Offa, his legend and the life of a child brought up in a land felt in some way still to be his, the poem is in its essence something other than those propositions. It too is self-possessed, a mystery, like the mystery of the severed head, the child's compulsion, the king's self-possession. In its essence it offers itself, simply for meditation.

This view of the poem reflects Hill's own way of speaking about his poetry. The ideas of 'presentation' and 'meditation' are linked for example in his answer to a question propounded by John Haffenden ('But would you resent the criticism that you address yourself to subjects in an ambiguous way?'):

> Yes, I would ... I query the idea that I 'address myself to subjects', which seems to imply some kind of settled policy. It may be that the subjects *present themselves to me* as being full of ambiguous implications, but this is surely a different matter. The ambiguities and scruples seem to reside in the object *that is meditated upon.*[9]

In his poems subjects present themselves for meditation; the essence of meditation is attentiveness to the truth of the way things are. Hill describes his sequence 'Funeral Music' as 'a commination and an alleluia for the period popularly but inexactly known as the Wars of the Roses.'[10] The alleluia, a cry of praise, is the fundamental utterance of *Mercian Hymns*.

It might seem odd that this celebratory eloquence is couched in prose rather than verse, since verse is generally taken to be the form of speech that most does honour to its subject. Since Hill insists on the need for the poet to 'craft' his work meticulously so as to achieve 'a setting at one, a bringing into concord, a reconciling, a uniting in harmony' by 'technical perfecting' – a reconciliation of 'local vividness' and 'overall shape',[11] it is worth pausing to consider the meaning of this paradox of the prose-poem.

The prose-poem is not an English form; its most celebrated practitioners are French: Baudelaire, Rimbaud, Fargue, St.-John Perse. There are prose-poems in English other than Hill's, most notably by T.S. Eliot, but the form remains alien. One would expect its adoption to be an act of deliberate choice. Hill's account of the matter is ambiguous. In the acknowledgements to *Mercian Hymns* he cites the selection of six prose hymns from biblical sources translated into Mercian dialect which are to be found in *Sweet's Anglo-Saxon Reader*. (He alludes to the first of these in Hymn VI). He also cites the 'Latin prose-hymns or canticles of the early Christian Church' as 'a less immediate precedent'. This gives the impression that a deliberate choice of form was made by the poet, to connect it with writing of Offa's own kingdom and with the biblical prose-poetry of praise and commination. Yet in the interview with John Haffenden which I have already quoted, Hill avoids a direct answer to the question why he 'chose to write the sequence in the form of prose-poems', although it would have been a simple matter to refer once more to Sweet and the Latin canticles.

The reason, I think, is that the prose-poem signifies something other and more than the references to the original 'Mercian Hymns' and *The Penguin Book of Latin Verse* imply. Just because the prose-poem is a paradox, it insists on our taking poetry seriously in Hill's own manner. Poetry becomes something spiritual, not a matter of external phenomena like rhyme or rhythm, or even of a particular kind of diction; it is not a form but a quality, a quality of rightness. 'When the poem "comes right with a click like a closing box",' says Hill, quoting from one of Yeats's letters, 'what is there effected is the atonement of aesthetics with rectitude of judgment'.[12] Poetry, then, is not simply a matter of technique; its 'uniting in harmony' transcends aesthetics and enters also, indeed combines with, the realm of morality. To recognise poetry in prose is to recognise the aspect of poetry that, transcending identification with outward signs, is simply and entirely a 'coming right', an 'at-one-ment' which might be likened to the perfect attentiveness of true meditation.

The question is, however, why this form was felt to be especially appropriate for *Mercian Hymns* but not, for the most part, elsewhere in Hill's poetry. Two answers put themselves forward. The first is that prose was especially appropriate because *Mercian Hymns* is a celebration of the poetic nature itself. The climactic moment of the book is one of recognition – recognition of relatedness and of gift:

'Not strangeness, but strange likeness. Obstinate, outclassed
  forefathers, I too concede, I am your staggeringly-gifted
  child.'

It is difficult here not to refer to the fact that Hill's own childhood is partly what the poem is about, and consequently Hill's own gift of poetry. Pressed about this by Haffenden, the poet conceded that there was a correspondence between his own experience and Offa's, 'but I would have thought in a very remarkable way.' He was resisting all the time, he said, 'any assumption that this has anything to do with the "confessional" mode'.[13] In other words, he disowns any suggestion that there is 'special pleading' for himself in the poem. I think that he is right to do so.

The admission of giftedness is wrung from the poet; it is a concession, an admission he would rather not make. It is comic to describe oneself as 'staggeringly-gifted' because it is other people who ought to be staggered not oneself, but comedy is in order because it relieves the pressure of embarrassment. Furthermore, the poet *is* staggered by what he is given: his tribute is to the donors. It is pertinent to remember the words of the philosopher Rush Rhees, quoted in Hill's inaugural lecture at Leeds:

For we speak as others have spoken before us. And a sense of language is also a feeling for ways of living that have meant something.[14]

The moment of recognition in the poem is also a moment of atonement, atonement *with* the 'outclassed forefathers', *with* those from whom the Romantic poet has always felt the possibility and even actuality of alienation: 'Not strangeness, but strange likeness.' The phrase applies as much to literary and spiritual forefathers as to those of the flesh.

Hymn XXIX 'comes right' by contrary and ambiguous motion, which characterises the poet's relation to all kinds of past; the poem is completed in this way:

So, murmurous, he withdrew from them. Gran lit the gas,
  his dice whirred in the ludo-cup, he entered into the
  last dream of Offa the King.

The contrary motion is implicit in the ambiguous reference of 'them', as it is in the move from poetical diction ('murmurous', after all, belongs in one of Keats's best-known lines) to the quotidian 'Gran lit the gas'. Entering the dream of Offa may be something that happens to the child, or it may be something that happened to Offa, dreaming of the future, as primitive dreamers are said to do. The dice might be Offa's and the ludo-cup the child's; this might be a meeting of spirits analogous to that in Berryman's *Homage to Mistress Bradstreet*. The dream, though, is 'the last dream of Offa'; the recognition of the child's likeness to his forefathers means that his isolation as 'a King of some kind, a prodigy, a maimed one', 'dreaming, smug-faced, sick on outings' (Hymn V) is at an end; he is one with his kin, as man and poet. This is one of the poems on 'The Death of Offa'; 'the last dream of Offa' is Offa's last dream before death, and the child's last dream of Offa. In the latter sense, it marks an end to the compensatory fantasies that underlie the identification with Offa's complacent tyranny: 'At dinner, he relished the mockery of drinking his family's health. He did this whenever it suited him, which was not often' (Hymn XIV). In the former, it marks a transfer of power, whereby Offa's intention to speak on behalf of the English nation is passed on to the young poet (whose ability to speak in that fashion is powerfully demonstrated in the iron words of Hymn XXV 'in memory of my grandmother ... in the nailer's darg'). Contrary motion again; and it is the rhythm of prose that assimilates such motion without the stress of verse: one might reasonably compare the end of the sixth sonnet of 'Funeral Music':

> Some parch for what they were; others are made
> Blind to all but one vision, their necessity
> To be reconciled. I believe in my
> Abandonment, since it is what I have.

Prose avoids the characteristically vertiginous line-ending of Hill's verse. Technically, then, it is more appropriate to the celebratory tone of *Mercian Hymns*. The spirit is at one with it.

There is, however, another reason for Hill's choice of prose for *Mercian Hymns*, one that places the book within the line of poetic succession in this century recognised by the poet. It is that of an impersonal poetry arising from a consciousness, aesthetic, moral, and, in so far as may be, religious, that has been formed within traditions at once personal and tribal, literary and more generally cultural. The classic expression of the nature of this poetry is to be found in the criticism of T.S. Eliot.

The form of *Mercian Hymns* does not allude to Eliot's poetry directly, but to the work of a French poet, whom he admired and translated – St.-John Perse. Eliot himself acknowledged the influence of Perse on the style of his own later poems, and his translation of Perse's *Anabase* was in turn, as Roger Little has noted, a formative influence on Auden's prose-style in *The Orators*.[15] Perse is, then, a French poet of special pertinence to English writers.

Anabase is a poem about the life of civilisations; it is, said Eliot, a series of images of migration, of conquest of vast spaces in Asiatic wastes, of destruction and foundation of cities and civilizations of any races or epochs of the ancient East.[16]

Ungaretti, who made the Italian translation of the poem, described it as one of the few examples of modern epic, combining the story of a people's history with a lyrical impulse, 'that is to say, the history of an I, of the Stranger faithful "to his ways by the roads of all the earth" '.[17] St.-John Perse himself said of this poem of many meanings that its subject was:

the poem of solitude in action. Action among men as much as action of the mind, directed towards others as much as towards the self.[18]

Indeed, the poem represents the poet and the man of action in close rapport:

. . . there at the sensi-
tive point on my brow where the poem is formed, I inscribe
this chant of all a people, the most rapt god-drunken,
drawing to our dockyards eternal keels![19]

Mercian Hymns, like *Anabase*, is concerned with relations between the poet and the man of action, between the instinct for creation and that for order. Its prose is hardly identical in nature with that of Perse or even of Perse as translated by Eliot. Hill's book consists of thirty hymns of two to four brief versets each, whereas Perse's is composed of ten long sections framed by an introductory and a concluding song. Perse depends on length for cumulative effect based on repetition of word, phrases and grammatical structures, whilst Hill is succinct. Nevertheless, each uses prose, and for each the basic unit is the 'verset' – Hill uses the word of *Mercian Hymns* in his interview with Haffenden, and it is appropriate because it is equivalent to a 'versicle', and is associated with biblical texts, especially the Psalms. But it is an unusual word; what makes it the right one in the case of *Mercian Hymns* is that it is the word ordinarily applied in discussion of St.-John Perse.

Hill's book is not a simple imitation of or homage to *Anabase*. It alludes equally to Perse's first book *Éloges*, the title of which has special meaning in the context of the *Hymns'* celebratory function: 'Praises'. The first half of *Éloges* consists of poems recalling Perse's childhood days, which were spent in Guadeloupe. The poems are brief compared with the sections of *Anabase*, although they still tend to be twice as long as the longest of the *Hymns*. Hill's book brings together the poet and man of action of *Anabase* and the child of *Éloges* and creates something new, Offa, a specifically English figure opposed to the anonymous/pseudonymous figure of Perse's genius. (Perse's real name was Alexis Saint-Leger Leger; the central figure of *Anabase* is nameless.) St.-John Perse is anglicised, in a fashion at once respectful and considered, especially by Hill's humour and by the sense of history as an inescapable presence everywhere manifest in the *Hymns*. But the base is Persean. Even the strange way of providing titles is part of the Persean debt. The *Hymns* are untitled, just numbered, in the body of the text, but in the 'List of Hymns' that follows them, titles of the kind I have already cited appear. This is like the arrangement of *Anabase* in its English editions, where the sections are also untitled but are given quasi-titles within Eliot's preface. (Eliot had taken them from a note on the poem by Lucien Fabre, published in the *Nouvelles Litteraires*; thanks to his remarking them, they have become virtually canonical, at least for English-speaking readers.)

Titles, though, are in the nature of inessentials, as both Perse and Hill indicate by their treatment of them. What of the *substance* of the poems? Hill's practice resembles that of Perse in various ways, one of the most striking of which has to do with diction. In *Mercian Hymns* the reader is from time to time drawn up short by oddities in usage and choice of words, oddities which have suggested the charge of mannerism.[20] For example: '*Crepitant* oak forest where the boar furrowed black mould, his scent intimate with worms and leaves' (XI); 'They are scattered to your *collations*, moldy-warp' (XII); 'intent to *pester* upon tympanum and chancel-arch his moody testament ...' (XXIV). The italicised words are unidiomatic, and one's sense of this remains even when their justification in terms of the poems' meanings has been grasped. *Crepitant*, for example, takes its force from a Virgilian echo, the description of the golden bough at *Aeneid* VI, 209: 'sic leni crepitabat brattea vento', 'so rustled the foil in the gentle breeze'. The echo is appropriate; the golden bough is commonly supposed to be mistletoe, the sacred plant cultivated on the druidic oak of primeval England. In this poem it presides over a scene that parodies the descent to the underworld made by Aeneas with the aid of the bough. The boar is monarch in the kingdom of the forest, 'intimate with worms and leaves', because his power entails death:

> Swathed bodies in the long ditch; one eye upstaring.
> It is safe to presume, here, the king's anger.

The boar is also the poet whose work of creation involves a journey among the dead in his search for tradition and reaffirmation of its life. The Virgilian hint is just that – a hint; but since Virgil is associated with 'an empire and a language with a unique destiny in relation to ourselves', that is, with the king and poet in western culture itself, the hint is worth taking.[21]

This 'explanation', however, does not naturalise the word in Hill's text; it retains an air of strangeness in spite, or perhaps because, of everything. In this it resembles certain usages in St.-John Perse, as, for example, that of the word *azyme* in the tenth section of *Anabase*, correctly rendered by Eliot in the first edition (1930):

> under the azyme of fine weather, in one great breath
> of the earth, the whole feather of harvest! ...

An even more striking instance occurs in the same section of the poem in the phrase 'l'agriculteur et *l'adalingue*'; even the editor of the works of St.-John Perse for the Pléiade edition felt it necessary to gloss this word. Eliot, who translates the phrase as 'the husbandman, and the young noble horsed', evidently had some trouble with it. In his annotations of the draft version of Eliot's translation Perse remarked of *adalingue*:

The word is not common, I am sorry to say, but I had to accept it here, in all the mystery of its bursting-in and of its fated quality, or more simply of its necessity: for reasons both phonetic and semantic, which forced themselves upon me.[22]

Words like *crepitant* in *Mercian Hymns* work within the semantic economy of the poem, but point beyond that to the 'mystery' of which St.-John Perse speaks, a mystery immanent within the lines about the boar furrowing black mould. Applied to the child-poet-king of Hill's book, they acquire an edge of complex, tender humour which humanises the Persean stamp even as it offers a critique of it.

Perse writes of 'phonetic and semantic' justifications for his use of the word *adalingue*. We suppose that something equivalent to the approximately semantic account of *crepitant* already offered could be given for the French word also. Something more precise needs to be said about the 'phonetic' aspect of Perse's verse and its repercussions for Hill. Its significance for St.-John Perse has been well expressed by Roger Little in the introduction to his edition of *Exil*. Perse, he says:

> makes full use of the unrhymed poem's capacity for flexibility, and while eschewing the rigours of rhyme submits to other, less artificial, more dynamic demands generated from within the poem itself instead of being imposed from without ... The versatile system of rhythmic echoes of phrase, of word, of individual sound gives cohesion to support the interwoven patterns of imagery and narrative.[23]

Little cites the opening phrase of the following passage as an instance of what he is talking about; I have extended the quotation (from *Exil*) precisely because the same process of echo, using different phonemes, continues through it:

> Et ce très haut ressac au comble de l'accès, toujours, au faîte
> du désir; l, même mouette sur son aile, la même mouette sur son
> aire, à tire-d'aile ralliant les stances de l'exil ...

> And this tall surf at the pitch of passion, always, at the
> peak of desire, the same gull on the wing, the same gull under
> way, rallying with spread wings the stanzas of exile ...[24]

Such aspects of the poem test the translator sorely, and T.S. Eliot, no less than Denis Devlin, translator of *Exil*, was duly tested by, for example, this simple phrase in *Anabase*: 'nulle servante sous la tente que la cruche d'eau fraîche!' which he rendered with some noticeable loss of power as 'no serving-maid under the tent but the cruse of cool water!'[25]

In this matter Geoffrey Hill had more freedom. His use of the echo also exploits 'the unrhymed poem's capacity for flexibility', but it does so in the interests of a comedy quite alien to the grandeurs of St.-John Perse. The final verset of Hymn XVII shows the humour, the good humour, with which the echo sounds in *Mercian Hymns*. 'Offa's Journey to Rome' is an imaginary voyage, in one aspect a child's fantasy of triumph, possibly of triumph in defeat:

> His maroon GT chanted then overtook. He lavished on
>   the high valleys its *haleine*.

The incongruous phonetic link between 'GT' and 'chanted', as though the machine evoked a pilgrim's chorus, is precursor to the greater incongruity present in the link between the entirely unheroic and unpaid-for emotional excess of 'lavished' and the heroic excess paid for in lives of the *Chanson de Roland*, the sound of whose horn is evoked in '*haleine*' – the link itself being made possible only by the mediation of the phrase 'high valleys'.

  There are plenty of examples of this device in *Mercian Hymns*. One has already appeared in my examples of the unusual in diction: '... intent to pester ... his moody testament ...'. A touch of satire hangs about the figure in 'He was defunct. They were perfunctory' (XXVII), as it does about 'Attributes assumed, retribution entertained' (XVI), but the note is predominantly genial. Sometimes it is a good deal more than that. The words immediately preceding my last example, for instance, echo each other in a graver way:

> Christ's mass: in the thick of a snowy forest the
> flickering evergreen fissured with light.

Christ's light shines out through the mass, which is a hindrance as well as a help, the mass of forest trees within which both St. Eustace and St. Hubert had their visions of Christ's crucifixion presented shining with light between the antlers of a stag. The vowels of the opening and concluding monosyllable are identical, 'Christ's/light'; between the two, the sequence of phonetically linked words 'thick/flickering/fissured' works dynamically, as an idea of density gives way to one of permeability, letting the light through, as it were. The play of light and sound contrasts with the shuttering abstraction of the following phrase, 'Attributes assumed, retribution entertained' but also gives it a context, and so denies it the possibility of standing for anything other than a part of the way the world is, one moment of feeling in a succession of moments whose difference is an inherent quality of the time in which it is possible to live.

  Hill's imitation of Perse is never idle, though it is never obtrusive either. In form, in style, in sense, *Mercian Hymns* is parallel with Perse; reference to the French poet is unnecessary, and yet when the reader makes it, it yields new and more comprehensive meanings. The book is, as it were, assured of its own independence – the poet will admit no more, for example, than that the prose form alludes to the Latin canticles, and the admission defines limits within which he appears to work – and at the same time the book depends invisibly on the work of another.

  One poem, at least, serves as a commentary on this paradoxical relationship between the English and the French poet. It is the hymn on which I have just been remarking, the sixteenth, titled 'Offa's Sword':

> Clash of salutation. As keels thrust into shingle. Ambas-
>   sadors, pilgrims. What is carried over? The Frankish gift,
>   two-edged, regaled with slaughter.

Offa's power was sufficiently recognised for him to be in touch with Charlemagne, though relations were far from easy. Ambassadors went to and fro between them, and the safe passage of pilgrims was one of the matters on which agreement was sought. All this is alluded to in the verset quoted. 'The Frankish gift' elaborates on history; we know that gifts were exchanged between the two kings, but not that Offa was given a sword. 'What is carried over?' is a question about the traffic across the English Channel, and ships do 'carry' goods. Bearing Perse in mind, however, I find it difficult not to read a quasi-pun on 'translated' in 'carried over'. The question is at once about cultural and literary relations, about the past and the present. 'What is carried over?' What survives when we translate poetry? What survives when Pope imitates Horace, or Hill imitates St.-John Perse? How far is the local culture also part of something larger? All these are adumbrated in the one question of Hill's hymn; and to them all he gives an ambiguous, yes, a 'two-edged' answer. Something survives when we translate poetry, as something survives the passage from generation to generation, from Offa to a child of the 1930s, in the West Midlands; Hill himself is a translator of Ibsen, and will not deny that the labour has some value. But *only* something survives: a great deal is lost: 'he vanished/he left behind coins, for his lodging and traces of red mud' (XXX). Offa's sword, a Frankish gift, is 'regaled with slaughter'. Not all puns are justified by etymology; but 'regaled' nevertheless suggests a coinage for 'made regal' as well as the familiar sense of 'feasted'. The royal power of Offa's weapon, which is a work of art ('the crux a craftsman's triumph') is manifest in the slaughter it performs, not least on the vistas of Perse's 'images of migration, of conquest of vast spaces ... of destruction and foundation of cities', here foreshortened to the visions of a 'staggeringly-gifted child'. Yet the slaughter itself is a 'two-edged' matter. Perse, whose cadences are turned in *Mercian Hymns* to quite other meanings than in his own poems, is nevertheless celebrated by the English poet as donor and man of power. What makes Hill poetically royal is the sword put in his hands: what makes Perse royal is that he is one of those who put it there.

The larger meaning of this relationship is best understood by reference to Eliot and especially his account of Virgil. Like Hill, like St.-John Perse, Virgil is a poet interested in ideas of empire; his hero Aeneas is founder of an empire – it is his destiny. Eliot takes this idea of destiny seriously, as may any poet. *Mercian Hymns* ends with an acceptance of poetic destiny: 'Obstinate, outclassed forefathers, I too concede. I am your staggeringly-gifted child', and what Eliot says about Aeneas could be applied to the poet of Hill's poems; his destiny, he says 'is an election which cannot be explained, a burden and responsibility rather than a reason for self-glorification.'[26] Now according to Eliot, 'Aeneas is egregiously a man of destiny, since upon him the future of the Western World depends'. Eliot plainly feels that Virgil too was 'egregiously a man of destiny', since it was he who gave classic expression to Aeneas' task:

What Virgil proposed to his contemporaries was the highest ideal even for an unholy Roman Empire, for any merely temporal empire. We are all, so far as we inherit the civilization of Europe, still citizens of the Roman Empire, and time has not yet proved Virgil wrong when he wrote *nec tempora pono: imperium sine fine dedi*.[27]

It seems quite probable that Eliot responded as deeply as he did to St.-John Perse's *Anabase* because it too is a poem of *imperium sine fine* – empire without end.

What *Mercian Hymns* does is to insist on the way in which the actual, the particular and historical, intrudes on such visions of empire.[28] It is a book about the child in the man, about the impotent fantasy of the poet, and about 'processes of generation; deeds of settlement' (XXVIII) that intervene between the formulation of an ideal and its achievement. The epigraph to Hill's book, taken from C.H. Sisson, concludes with these words:

Upon 'the law of nature and the law of revelation', Blackstone said, 'depend all human laws.' This quaint language which would at once be derided if it were introduced now into public discussion, conceals a difficulty which is no less ours than it was our ancestors'.

In the magic world of *Anabase* there is no need to reconcile 'the law of nature and the law of revelation'; in Perse's poem the world shapes itself readily to human wishes: 'plough land of dream' – 'the sea at morning like a presumption of the mind'.[29] In the world of *Mercian Hymns* revelation is vouchsafed, but the natural world is reluctant to accommodate it. The difficulty is of such proportions that it is also a joke, the good humour of which overflows into Hill's use of Perse. He does not, after all, deny that it is a great thing to be a poet, or that there is such a thing as a law of revelation. But what Charlemagne grandly assumes comes hard to Offa. That has to be the case for a poet who gave to his inaugural lecture as Professor at Leeds the title 'Poetry as "Menace" and "Atonement"'. There he speaks of 'the menace of the high claims of poetry itself', and of 'a modern literature of penitence', a literature of resistance to the mainstream of ideas, in so far as that involves a 'resistance to sentimental substitution', and a literature of 'active contemplation of minute particulars'.[30] These words describe and explain the complex nature of Hill's response to the imperial and at times imperious dreams of Eliot and St.-John Perse. Offa, who 'fixed the boundary against the Myrgings at Fifeldor', fixes, too, a bound to the dreams of Charlemagne, Eliot and Perse. He is his own man: he inhabits a world less malleable, more constrained than the other two poets could bring themselves to imagine. It is Geoffrey Hill's great gift to speak from within that world and yet not to betray his sense of a 'law of revelation' that challenges the limits of the 'law of nature'.

5

Tenebrae and at-one-ment

Christopher Ricks

The poems of *Tenebrae* (1978), like Geoffrey Hill's version of *Brand* (1978),
put up a profound resistance to a central tenet of Hill's inaugural lecture,
'Poetry as "Menace" and "Atonement"' (also 1978).[1] The poems resist the
tenet, partly because it is the way of poems to resist even the best of tenets,
and partly because this particular tenet does not hold firm. 'Ideally', said Hill,
'my theme would be simple'; but then he allowed the reservations intimated
by the conditional 'would' and the unconditioned 'Ideally' to sidle away:

> simply this: that the technical perfecting of a poem is an act of atonement, in the
> radical etymological sense – an act of at-one-ment, a setting at one, a bringing
> into concord, a reconciling, a uniting in harmony; and that this act of atonement
> is described with beautiful finality by two modern poets: by W.B. Yeats when he
> writes in a letter of September 1936, to Dorothy Wellesley, that 'a poem comes
> right with a click like a closing box' and by T.S. Eliot in his essay of 1953, 'The
> Three Voices of Poetry':
>
> > ... when the words are finally arranged in the right way – or in what he
> > comes to accept as the best arrangement he can find – [the poet] may
> > experience a moment of exhaustion, of appeasement, of absolution, and of
> > something very near annihilation, which is in itself indescribable.
>
> Anyone who has experienced that moment in which a poem 'comes right' must,
> I believe, give instinctive assent to such statements.[2]

One does not blithely accuse Geoffrey Hill of being blithe, but there is a
hopefulness here in the criticism, an unremarked irreconcilability, such as the
poetry of Hill would have had to extend to and attend to. For a start, the
words of Eliot are not at one with those of Yeats. It is impossible to imagine
a testimony which would less fit something's coming right with a click like a

closing box than the pained protracted refusal to click of Eliot's prose, its arriving finally at the word 'indescribable'. So that when Hill concludes that anyone who has experienced that moment must give instinctive assent to such statements, the difficulty is not, as he goes on to posit, the word 'instinctive' but the plural 'statements'. Those of us who are not poets and have not experienced such a moment might be able to imagine a poet's instinctive assent to one or other of the statements, but not to both. Hill's search for at-one-ment has led him to two descriptions of 'this act of atonement', each of which has indeed a 'beautiful finality' in its evocation of atonement as a finality, but the two of which are finally irreconcilable, tonally and totally. There cannot be a reconciling, a uniting in harmony, of Yeats's and Eliot's acts of witness here, any more than there can be of their intransigently inimical poetry. Hill, who has chosen to write criticism in passionate praise of Yeats, has chosen not to write any criticism at all of the poet even more important to his own poetry: Eliot.

One reason for not choosing Yeats's sense of the matter might be that his apophthegm relies upon something prejudicially contrastive which Hill prudently omits: 'The correction of prose, because it has no fixed laws, is endless, a poem comes right with a click like a closing box.' The poet's pains on which Hill broods would be sweetly mitigated if it were the case that poetry had anything as gratifying as 'fixed laws'. But the point is not that Eliot's sense of the creative achievement as something at once ended and endless is the one that must be assented to; rather that Hill does not attempt to set at one these two so different descriptions of the act of atonement.

For Hill's critical argument is unwilling to acknowledge the stubborn resistance put up to its hopes for such atonement and at-one-ment, resistance embodied in the very terms of its hopes. The prose argument may talk of 'the shocking encounter with "empirical guilt", not as a manageable hypothesis, but as irredeemable error in the very substance and texture of his [the poet's] craft and pride'[3]; indeed, the prose argument is at its most poignant, unsurprisingly but revelatorily, when it recalls one of the most deeply-felt poems in *Mercian Hymns* ('It is one thing to celebrate the "quick forge", another to cradle a face hare-lipped by the searing wire.' XXV).

> It is one thing to talk of literature as a medium through which we convey our awareness, or indeed our conviction, of an inveterate human condition of guilt or anxiety; it is another to be possessed by a sense of language itself as a manifestation of empirical guilt.[4]

But the prose argument does talk of these things, not incarnate an acknowledgement that there is not only irredeemable error but also irrecoverable loss. For the word 'atonement' obdurately will not return to its radical roots, to 'at-one-ment'. At-one-ment is simply, and finally, and unanswerably, not a word in the English language; and it will not do to be told that the technical perfecting of a poem is 'an act of atonement, in the radical etymological sense – an act of at-one-ment, a setting at one, a bringing into concord, a reconciling, a uniting in harmony': it will not do to be told this unless, in the very act of telling, it is conceded that there can be no reconciling, no bringing into harmony, of words like 'a reconciling, a uniting in harmony' and the non-word 'at-one-ment'; indeed, more radically despite the etymology, that there can be no atonement of atonement and at-one-ment. For one thing, even if the latter were alive and well and living in our language, it would now be pronounced differently from atonement. (There is the unreality of giddiness in the very sound of the phrase when Merle Brown intones of Hill: 'Such a moment of atonement'.[5]) There are therefore sound reasons for believing that atonement is doggedly and most ironically irreconcilable with at-one-ment. The loss of the ancient concord may be grievous; it must be irrecoverable. When Eliot wrote in 'Little Gidding' that 'Sin is Behovely', the pain was at the admission that though sin is inevitable, an acknowledgement of sin has become as archaic as the arcane and capitalised word 'Behovely'.

The pain from which Hill's prose argument averts its mortal gaze is the one which the poetry of *Tenebrae* and of *Brand*, in its averted conscience, turns against itself.

> Crucified Lord, you swim upon your cross
> and never move. Sometimes in dreams of hell
> the body moves but moves to no avail
> and is at one with that eternal loss.
>
> You are the castaway of drowned remorse,
> you are the world's atonement on the hill.
>   ('Lachrimae: 1. Lachrimae Verae')

There 'at one' refuses to plead that it is or could be at one with 'atonement'. There is an unbridgeable distance between 'at one' and 'atonement'. The quatrain space within the sonnet signals the distance, and so does the acknowledged difference of sound. 'Atonement' here, even while it laments 'that eternal loss', is not to be pronounced 'at-one-ment', not least because if it were it would lose any true uttering of atonement.

So near and yet so far:

> And suffered to remain
> At such near distance
>   ('Canticle for Good Friday')

A sense of loss when 'one' is not quite rhymed animates the elegiac apprehension of what it may be to be 'made one', in Hill's early poem 'Merlin' (1953):

> I will consider the outnumbering dead:
> For they are the husks of what was rich seed.
> Now, should they come together to be fed,
> They would outstrip the locusts' covering tide.

> Arthur, Elaine, Mordred; they are all gone
> Among the raftered galleries of bone.
> By the long barrows of Logres they are made one,
> And over their city stands the pinnacled corn.

For a particular unfulfilment attaches there to 'made one', since the two stanzas do not matchingly turn their off-rhyming monosyllables. The sequence *gone/bone/one/corn* is changed by the one that had gone before; *dead/seed/ fed/tide* was a sequence which had profferred an indisputably full rhyme (*dead ... fed*) at exactly the point in the stanza where 'gone' and 'made one' do not then offer such indisputable fulfilment.[6]

Hill the critic, expatiating and conferring, does sometimes yield to hopes of attaining without miracle the cruelly unattainable; but his art attains, among other things, an exact apprehension of what is for him unattainable. For him, or for *one*? His sentence is unsettled:

> If critics accuse me of evasiveness or the vice of nostalgia, or say that *I* seem incapable of grasping true religious experience, I would answer that the grasp of true religious experience is a privilege reserved for very few, and that one is trying to make lyrical poetry out of a much more common situation – the sense of *not* being able to grasp true religious experience.[7]

One aspect of this is Hill's making lyrical poetry, not out of any perfected at-one-ment of atonement and at-one-ment, but out of the sense of honourably *not* being able to grasp such a perfect concord, such a true religious experience. 'One main reason for this', to apply the praise which William Empson gave to the range of Eliot's 'Marina', 'is the balance maintained between otherworldliness and humanism; the essence of the poem is the vision of an order, a spiritual state, which he can conceive and cannot enter'.[8] Hill turns this into something fearfully consolatory; it may be a mercy that we can only conceive and not enter a vision that might prove a nightmare:

> Averroes, old heathen,
> If only you had been right, if Intellect
> Itself were absolute law, sufficient grace,
> Our lives could be a myth of captivity
> Which we might enter: an unpeopled region
> Of ever new-fallen snow, a palace blazing
> With perpetual silence as with torches.
>
> ('Funeral Music, 4')

> As with torches we go, at wild Christmas,
> When we revel in our atonement
>
> ('Funeral Music, 5')

For poems are themselves torches, and

Heaven doth with us, as we, with Torches doe,
Not light them for themselves: For if our vertues
Did not goe forth of us, 'twere all alike
As if we had them not.

(*Measure for Measure*, I.i)

In hopes of perfect concord, Hill says:

The proof of a poet's craft is precisely the ability to effect an at-one-ment between
the 'local vividness' and the 'overall shape', and ... this is his truthtelling. When
the poem 'comes right with a click like a closing box', what is there effected is
the atonement of aesthetics with rectitude of judgment.[9]

Yet Hill's needing the two forms of the word is itself an admission (insuffi-
ciently an acknowledgement) that this whole business will *not* come right
with a click like a closing box; and the same goes for the use in quick
succession of the different prepositions ('an at-one-ment between ...' and 'an
atonement of aesthetics with'), instead of that perfectly simple conjunction
which would be the conjunction *and*.

To speak of atonement *between* x and y (instead of an atonement of
x and y) is to concede that it is not truly an at-one-ment, since it would
have to be an at-one-ment (a setting at one) of x and y, not between
them. This same untrustworthiness within the etymological plea is be-
trayed by *between* when Hill says, of T.H. Green, that 'a Green lecture
appears as an act of atonement, in the arena of communication, between
the "unconscious social insolence" of the listener and what Coleridge
termed the seeming "assumption of superiority" on the part of the
speaker'.[10]

Hill, who yearns to trust the etymology of atonement, is not willing to be
as imperious as Coleridge:

What is Music? *Poetry* in its grand sense?
Answer.
Passion and order aton'd! Imperative Power in Obedience![11]

All of Hill's work is concerned, in a concurrence with Coleridge, with
reconciliation. *Tenebrae* quotes Coleridge for one of its epigraphs (and as
'STC' moreover) and is close in occupation to 'Poetry as "Menace" and
"Atonement"' where Coleridge explicitly and importantly figures. *Tenebrae*
is at the same time the most ambitious of all Hill's aspirations to atonement
and at-one-ment. The ambition to imagine, at least, the union of sacred and
profane love; the ambition to imagine, at least, the union of English poetry
and European poetry, and of all the conflicting traditions and developments
within English poetry; of England and its empire ('A Short History of British
India'); of Protestant and Catholic: not even all these exhaust the ambitions
of the book and of its masterly sequences. There is the longing to unite
knowledge and wisdom, or to re-unite them, a longing which is responsible
for a reader's thinking that, even more than with others of Hill's books, what
would be better than any critical study would be a truly annotated edition.

Moreover, in its sequences and within individual poems, *Tenebrae* seeks to incarnate the union of the One and the Many, and it is therefore metaphysical poetry. 'Verse properly called metaphysical is that to which the impulse is given by an overwhelming concern with metaphysical problems; with problems either deriving from, or closely resembling in the nature of their difficulty, the problem of the Many and the One' (James Smith).[12]

Yet it is not only the ear which refuses to trust that there could be any perfect consonance of atonement and at-one-ment. For the eye sees the hyphens as forever both holding together and holding apart the elements which seek to constitute the non-word as a word. All punctuation is at once a uniting and a separating. Like mortar, it holds bricks together and holds them apart. When Eric Partridge begins his chapter on the hyphen by saying: 'The hyphen (-) has two main and entirely distinct functions: dividing and compounding',[13] he makes practical sense but only that. The hyphen has the capacity which Hill sees as 'an essential quality of Swift's creative intelligence: the capacity to be at once resistant and reciprocal'.[14] 'Their spades grafted through the variably-resistant soil' (*Mercian Hymns*, XII): there the variably-resistant hyphen at once joins and divides, at once grafts and grafts through.

The hyphen cannot but acknowledge, in the moment when it conceives of two things coming together, that they are nevertheless two not one, just as Hill's need not exactly to spell but to articulate the word 'atonement' differently when he means at-one-ment is tacitly an admission that the two, the same and not the same, will always be magnetically held apart and held together by being like-poles. 'Many of the poems in *Tenebrae* are concerned with the strange likeness and ultimate unlikeness of sacred and profane love' (Hill).[15] A hyphen may articulate strange likeness and unlikeness, conjoining for instance the word atonement and at-one-ment, the latter itself a declared conjunction of its elements.

Likeness and unlikeness meet: 'The Jesus-faced man walking crowned with flies' ('Lachrimae: 3.Martyrium'). Jeffrey Wainwright has said, truly but partially, that 'Jesus-faced' is 'uncomfortably and deliberately close to "Janus-faced"';[16] so it is, but such closeness itself then witnesses to immitigable difference, as it does in such a hyphenation as 'O near-human spouse and poet' ('Elegiac Stanzas'). The closer 'Jesus-faced' is to 'Janus-faced' the more indubitably – from one of the two Janus-viewpoints – it announces itself as other than 'Janus-faced'. The hyphened form is itself two-faced, a 'judas-kiss'. ('Consigned by proxy to the judas-kiss' ('Lachrimae: 6. Lachrimae Antique Novae').) Two-faced, or two-edged: 'What is carried over? The Frankish gift, two-edged, regaled with slaughter' (*Mercian Hymns*, XVI).

So the hyphen is likely to have much to do within a poetry concerned with the strange likeness and unlikeness of sacred and profane love, not least because the hyphen itself may be an acknowledgement of love, the conjunction of two as one, the bringing together of two 'under one' (hyphen: ὑφέν). The head and the body, for instance, as the children's book *Punctuation*

Personified (1824) knew when it exactly located and named the hyphen as the neck. ('Churchwardens in wing-collars bearing scrolls' ('An Apology for the Revival of Christian Architecture in England: 12. The Eve of St Mark').) Metaphysics, the One and the Many, and love, may marry in such articulation.

> Single Natures double name,
> Neither two nor one was called.
>   ('The Phoenix and Turtle')

Neither and both. Or a troth-plight: 'What happens here', said Hill of Spenser's *Amoretti* LXVIII, 'is more solemn than a play of wit; it is a form of troth-plight between denotation and connotation'.[17]

The entry in Johnson's *Dictionary* under 'hyphen' is itself a poem in embryo, aspiring to the best relationships: '*Hyphen*. A note of conjunction: as, *vir-tue, ever-living*.' For the hyphen that divides 'virtue' only brings out that, in its integrity, virtue is indivisible; and the hyphen that unites 'ever-living' carries a conviction about the relation of virtue to everlasting life. Virtue then chiefly lives. Coleridge was not truly attentive to either hyphens or virtue when he issued his rule: 'The rule for the admission of double epithets seems to be this: either that they should be already denizens of our Language, such as blood-stained, terror-stricken, self-applauding: or when a new epithet, or one found in books only, is hazarded, that it, at least, be one word, not two words made one by mere virtue of the printer's hyphen.'[18]

Hill gives salience to his hyphens, tactfully but pointedly, by having the unhyphenated word in the vicinity of its hyphened sibling.[19] In Eliot likewise, the unmelodramatic insistence that comes to settle gravely upon the first half of the compound 'half-look' is a consequence of our having first heard the word 'look', so that a discrimination may be made, a fear acknowledged, without mere alarm:

> The backward look behind the assurance
> Of recorded history, the backward half-look
> Over the shoulder, towards the primitive terror.
>   ('The Dry Salvages')

Hill has learnt from such art.

> High voices in domestic chapels; praise;
> praise-worthy feuds:
>   ('An Apology . . .:3. Who are these
>   coming to the Sacrifice?')

Here is no feud between 'praise' and 'praise-worthy' (the 'high voices' are raised in praise not in anger), but there is some slight antagonism, some distance and distaste, as there is in the strictly unnecessary hyphen in 'praise-worthy'. Or one compound may lop-sidedly refuse to square itself exactly with another:

like carapaces of the Mughal tombs
lop-sided in the rice-fields, boarded-up
near railway-sidings and small aerodromes.
                    ('An Apology . . . : 6. A Short
                    History of British India, III')

There it is natural but futile to try to align '-sided' and '-sidings'.

The pressure in the vicinity, when the transition is from the compounded
to the uncompounded form, may give a particular edge to what might other-
wise have been so unremarked as scarcely to impinge; as when Hill banters
Yeats.

where wild-eyed poppies raddle tawny farms
and wild swans root in lily-clouded lakes.
                    ('An Apology . . . :7. Loss and Gain')

Pretty Coole, the wild swans, especially when followed by 'lily-clouded lakes',
a phrasing which ribs 'the mackerel-crowded seas' of 'Sailing to Byzantium'.
Hill's 'root in' suspects the swans, for all their beauty, of being piggish
truffle-hunters; but then Hill himself is rooted in and has been rooting in
those lily-clouded lakes of Yeats. Again, there are

those muddy-hued and midge-tormented ghosts.
                    ('An Apology . . . : 1. Quaint Mazes')

– a line which has its small sting at Yeats and 'That dolphin-torn, that
gong-tormented sea' ('Byzantium').

Tennyson too is among the ghosts, though likewise for an affectionate
chaffing vassalage, feudal not feuding:

High voices in domestic chapels; praise;
praise-worthy feuds; new-burgeoned spires that sprung
crisp-leaved as though from dropping-wells. The young
ferns root among our vitrified tears.
                    ('An Apology . . . : 3. Who are these
                    coming to the Sacrifice?')[20]

And if we ask, Who taught those new-burgeoned spires to rise? Alfred Ten-
nyson, each lisping babe replies.

Bring orchis, bring the foxglove spire,
    The little speedwell's darling blue,
    Deep tulips dashed with fiery dew,
Laburnums, dropping-wells of fire.
                    (*In Memoriam*, LXXXIII)

It is the 'dropping-wells' which compound the 'spires'. Hill's lines are a
new-burgeoning compound of Tennyson and himself; Tennyson's art is itself,
newly-compounded, a dropping-well of fire. An allusion is a two-in-one, like
a hyphenation. It can return to its roots, and Hill signals this, not only by

using the word 'root' or 'roots', but by using it in the immediate vicinity of
an allusion itself compounded like 'dropping-wells'. On several occasions Hill
avails himself of the junction which a hyphen can effect in this very matter of
roots:

> But when he tore his flesh-root and was gone,
> ('Metamorphoses, V')

> (A slight miracle might cleanse
> His brain
> Of all attachments, claw-roots of sense)
> ('Canticle for Good Friday')

The uncollected early poem 'Pentecost' (*Oxford Poetry*, 1952) is a compen-
dium of Hill's preoccupation with the root-secure or -insecure:

> The sudden putting-on of grace
> Though fresh, new-nerved, is all the more
> Dependent on its neutral base
> That, root-secure through commonplace,
> Has stood the test of strength before.

But this early poem does not altogether trust the commonplace (the 'hedge-
root' to which it later turns), and there is a stretching for something which,
in the bizarrerie of its hyphenation, does not feel like a true fusion at all:

> The surety of growth is where
> Root stem and flower are brought to light –
> Integral as the hawthorn's rare
> True-fusion of deep earth and air –
> Held and expressed in terms of white.

It was not until *The Mystery of the Charity of Charles Péguy* (1983) that Hill
got his rootedness secure:

> Woefully battered but not too bloody,
> smeared by fraternal root-crops and at one
> with the fritillary and the veined stone,
> having composed his great work, his small body,
> (p. 27)

For there 'root-crops' must be at once deeply suggestive and perfectly down-
to-earth ('root-secure through commonplace'); and in obdurately declining to
rhyme with 'stone', 'at one' does not claim any finality of atonement, aware
now that the word's root, the 'radical etymological sense', is not root-secure
but is a forked radish, 'root-crops'.

The Mystery of the Charity of Charles Péguy does effect a true fusion
because it does not strive for a 'true-fusion' (where the very hyphen resists
fusion). The conjunction with 'true-' aspires to running exactly true, some-

thing which a hyphen will both minister to and baulk. This longing for perfect consonance must acknowledge that what seeks to be miraculous may be only fictive:

> Self-wounding martyrdom, what joys you have,
> true-torn among this fictive consonance,
> ('Lachrimae: 5. Pavana Dolorosa')

The consonance, like a hyphen, is fictive; the hyphen in 'true-torn' both clasps together and tears apart the elements.

The Mystery of the Charity of Charles Péguy has in some ways an intent of *entente*. It seeks to imagine (this English poet writing about that French poet) the ways in which England and France were at one in the Great War. This entails seeing the root sense atone/at-one as English and not French. Hill turns naturally to the link which acknowledges differences, two 'under one', a link which may bring not just two words but two languages under one: 'pâtisserie-tinklings of angels' (p. 11). Or:

> you dream of warrior-poets and the Meuse
> flowing so sweetly; the androgynous Muse
> your priest-confessor, sister-châtelaine.
>   (p. 25)

The Muse is androgynous not only as male and female but as English and French; 'sister-châtelaine' (and this is brought home by its being both like and unlike the compound 'priest-confessor' immediately before) accommodates the two languages handsomely, even while recognising that the word 'châtelaine', though socially welcome, remains some corner of an English field that is for ever foreign.

Or there is the exquisite intersection of time and the timeless in the stanzaic transition across a hyphen; the lulled and peaceful sense that there is all the time in the world is enough to pierce the heart:

> and in the fable this is your proper home;
> three sides of a courtyard where the bees thrum
> in the crimped hedges and the pigeons flirt
> and paddle, and sunlight pierces the heart-
>
> shaped shutter-patterns in the afternoon,
> shadows of fleurs-de-lys on the stone floors.
>   (p. 12)

Art, which is gladdened and saddened by such hopes, resists evolutionary optimism. The handbook-account of one kind of hyphenation announces a simple evolution: 'In the life of compound words there are three stages: (1) two separate words (*cat bird*); (2) a hyphenated compound (*cat-bird*); (3) a single word (*catbird*)'.[21] The three stages are elsewhere spoken of as 'degrees of relationship' or of 'intimacy':

> There are three degrees of intimacy between words, of which the first and loosest is expressed by their mere juxtaposition as separate words, the second by their being hyphened, and the third or closest by their being written continuously as one word.[22]

This makes workaday sense, but it is partial. For there may be just as much relationship or intimacy between words side by side as between those hyphened or run together; the nub is not degrees of relationship or intimacy but kinds. To hold the adjacent word at arm's length could manifest a high degree of relationship and even of intimacy. To join two words by a hyphen effects a union, a closeness, to which the two may happily agree or from which the two may strain to break free. This is announced by 'close-' compounds: 'Being close-pressed still kept storms out and storms in' ('Asmodeus'), or 'and kept close-hidden at my heart!' (*Brand*, Act IV).[23]

> churchwardens in wing-collars bearing scrolls
> of copyhold well-tinctured and well-tied.
>   ('An Apology . . . : 12. The Eve of St Mark')

How well 'well-' accommodates itself to the balanced properties and proprieties; how well-tied each compound is, and how well-tied the two of them, with 'well-tied' a succinct and equable contraction of 'well-tinctured'. *Modern English Usage* is a lesser thing than poetry when it insists: 'This possible confusion between adjective and adverb probably accounts for the unnecessary hyphen that often appears with *well* and *ill*'.[24] A special intimacy may be effected by other compounds:

> without vantage of vanity, though mortal-proud
>   (*The Mystery* . . . , p. 10)

– there the link is partly that of an oxymoron, with '-proud' surprised at the audacity of 'mortal-'. Or this:

> But rest assured, bristly-brave gentlemen
>   (p. 24)

– where '-brave' bristles to find itself being given a military French buss by 'bristly-'.

The oxymoron is not the only form of hyphenation to challenge the 'three stages' equanimity, but it is the most unignorable, and Hill can do wonders with it: 'the rooms of cedar and soft-thudding baize' ('An Apology . . . : 9. The Laurel Axe'). Sickening, how imperceptive we usually are about thudding.

One pressing paradox is the apprehension that a great author from the past is both dead and alive. There is an entry in Coleridge's *Notebooks* where (the editor remarks) 'the spacing suggests that there may have been a thought of verse':

> Shakespere, Milton, Boyle, all the
> great living-dead men of our Isle.
>   (Entry 3270)

'Living-dead' is the compacted wisdom of the matter, and I think that perhaps Coleridge was remembering a passage in one of the dead poets whom he revered: Samuel Daniel. Yet Daniel's hyphenation had a reversed emphasis, as was appropriate to its being devoted not, in the first place, to great authors, but to that which is the condition of their greatness: the very alphabet, the letters that became humane letters:

> O blessed Letters, that combine in one,
>   All Ages past, and make one live with all:
>   By you, we do conferre with who are gone,
>   And the dead-living unto Councell call;
>   By you, th' unborne shall have communion
>   Of what we feele, and what doth us befall.
>   (*Works*, 1602)

The rhyme sequence *one/gone/communion*, is itself an act of combining in one, but the incarnation of such combining in one, such setting at one, is the hyphened oxymoron 'dead-living'. *Tenebrae* seeks to set at one 'all the great living-dead men of our Isle'; and it does 'the dead-living unto Councell call'.

Largest of all the reconciliatory aspirations in *Tenebrae*, there is the seeking of that union which Eliot limned as beyond even Valéry (Eliot is everywhere alive in *Tenebrae*, and Hill's art calls up Valéry's):

> Intelligence to the highest degree, and a type of intelligence which excludes the possibility of faith, implies profound melancholy. Valéry has been called a philosopher. But a philosopher, in the ordinary sense, is a man who constructs or supports a philosophic system; and in this sense, we can say that Valéry was too intelligent to be a philosopher. The constructive philosopher must have a religious faith, or some substitute for a religious faith; and generally he is only able to construct because of his ability to blind himself to other points of view, or to remain unconscious of the emotive causes which attach him to his particular system. Valéry was much too conscious to be able to philosophise in this way; and so his 'philosophy' lays itself open to the accusation of being only an elaborate game. Precisely, but to be able to play this game, to be able to take aesthetic delight in it, is one of the manifestations of civilised man. There is only one higher stage possible for civilised man: and that is to unite the profoundest scepticism with the deepest faith. But Valéry was not Pascal, and we have no right to ask that of him.[25]

Hill asks a great deal of himself. 'A Pre-Raphaelite Notebook' was first published with the words 'Adapted from Pascal'; the acknowledgement in *Tenebrae* is that it 'adapts a sentence from Pascal's *Pensées*' (Pensée 96). Originally published sixteen years before *Tenebrae*, this is a poem of atonement, and it repeatedly needs the symbol or mark (something less grand than a symbol, and more mysterious than a mark) by which things are set as or set at one. A hyphen can be what Hill calls 'the precise detail of articulation';[26] and 'the writing of every poem presents its unique problems, of finding the right articulation for the particular moment'.[27] So a single short poem such as 'A Pre-Raphaelite Notebook' may need a variety of hyphened forms. There is the hyphen which most reminds us that a union may be reiteratedly driving or driven in sequence, at once followed by the contrasting unhyphened form:

> Gold seraph to gold worm in the pierced slime:
> greetings. Advent of power-in-grace. The power
> of flies distracts the working of our souls.

The repeated hyphenation yearns for 'unity and simultaneousness' (Coleridge on compounds[28]), but there are cross-purposes such as Hill greeted in exactly the same terms in praise of Shakespeare: 'Shakespeare is perhaps ready to accept a vision of actual power at cross-purposes with the vision of power-in-grace.'[29] Then there is in 'A Pre-Raphaelite Notebook' the hyphen which comprehends the divine acts of issuance and utterance as being simply not imaginable as severance or disjunction, since the hyphen preserves relation-ship even in the act of describing a breach: 'The God-ejected Word'. And there is the hyphen which most admits the incomplete, the prefix 'half-': 'a half-eaten ram'. All of Hill's volumes bring out how a hyphen doubles and halves; *Tenebrae* elsewhere has (very different in their operations): 'half-way', 'half-faithful', 'half-built', 'half-gloom', and 'half-effaced'. The hyphens of *Tenebrae* embody the desire and seeking which are everywhere the poems' explicit energy; a hyphened 'half-' may embody the desire and pursuit of the whole.[30]

Tenebrae is unique and yet perfectly continuous with Hill's earlier work. He has always been a strong (and sometimes idiosyncratic) hyphenator. 'Ge-nesis', the first poem in his first volume of poems,[31] sees the six days of the Creation as one creation, and sees all creation as one ('a repetition in the finite mind of the eternal act of creation in the infinite I AM', in the words of *Biographia Literaria*). 'Genesis' commands its sequence of compounds, from 'The tough pig-headed salmon', through 'The soft-voiced owl' and 'the glove-winged albatross', to 'The phantom-bird'. These work very differently. 'The tough pig-headed salmon' depends not only on the tribute to up-river stubbornness and on the odd accuracy of the physical likening (as if the joining of pig and salmon were vindicated as something much more simply true than either the tragic chimera or the comic child's-book animal strips), but also on the fact that though you can say 'pig-headed', there are things you can't say. 'We do not usually talk of anyone having *an absent mind, a pig head, a chicken heart, a wrong head* or *raw bones*.'[32]

In its context, 'The soft-voiced owl' (in a way that looks 'deliberate' to those who have 'eyes') recalls 'the quiet-voiced elders' of the elderly Eliot, wise old owls. Hill:

>   'Beware
> The soft-voiced owl, the ferret's smile,
> The hawk's deliberate stoop in air,
> Cold eyes . . .'

Eliot:

> And the wisdom of age? Had they deceived us,
> Or deceived themselves, the quiet-voiced elders,
> Bequeathing us merely a receipt for deceit?
> The serenity only a deliberate hebetude,
> The wisdom only the knowledge of dead secrets
> Useless in the darkness into which they peered
> Or from which they turned their eyes.
>
> ('East Coker')

'The glove-winged albatross' in 'Genesis' suggests the unfitting collusion between the victim and its persecutor (there is a different slant on this in Hill's next poem but one, where 'Child and nurse walk hand in glove'). And 'The phantom-bird' is explicitly paralleled by and perhaps identified with 'the phoenix', so that the very hyphen becomes a way in which

> Reason in it selfe confounded,
> Saw Division grow together ...
>   ('The Phoenix and Turtle')

'The phantom-bird' offers a quite different conjunction from those before it in 'Genesis', with its hyphen insisting (since 'phantom bird' would have made perfect sense) upon a linkage which might have seemed needless or forced but which has a compacted reality: 'The phantom-bird goes wild and lost.' Hill's Brand was to ask the deranged and sharp-eyed Gerd about her silver bullet ('They say it works/wonders against demons'):

> And hawks?
> Real phantom-hawks?
>   (Act V)[33]

Those words in *Brand* look not only to the first poem of *For the Unfallen* and its 'phantom-bird', but also to the words of 'Funeral Music, 7': 'A hawk and a hawk-shadow'; and to the words of 'The Pentecost Castle' in *Tenebrae*:

> fulfilment to my sorrow
> indulgence of your prey
> the sparrowhawk the sparrow
> the nothing that you say
>
>   (8)

'The Pentecost Castle', the sequence of fifteen lyrics which begins *Tenebrae*, famously has no punctuation, not even at the end of a poem or of the sequence. It has been argued by W.S. Milne that this sequence's 'unpunctuated tones of innocence (true innocence which has incorporated the facts of experience and transcended them) compromise the "worldly" punctuation of the succeeding sequences' ('Lachrimae', 'An Apology for the Revival of Christian Architecture in England', and 'Tenebrae'), and that Hill 'sets up an idealistic artifice of poetic voice at the beginning of the volume which the succeeding, punctuated sequences are "placed" or compromised by, through comparison'.[34] There can be no doubt of the contrast of the totally unpunctuated and the heavily punctuated sequences: but there is some sentimentality in Milne's feeling no qualms about 'innocence', both in the world and in Hill's poetry.[35] That is, to speak innocently, as Milne does, of 'the lack of punctuation indicating an unchecked flow of the living spirit' (as against 'the succeeding poems in the volume' which are checked 'by what Hill ... called "the inertial drag of speech"') is to avert one's eyes from the fact that the unchecked flow of the living spirit may manifest itself as, for instance, murderousness.

Anyway, every device of the poet, every technical or formal disposition, is an axis and not a direction; its flow of spirit runs between two points, along such and such a line, but not necessarily in this as against that direction. The very quality which makes for such-and-such can in other circumstances make for the exact opposite. 'The thing that causes instability in another state – of itself causes stability – as for instance wet soap slips off the ledge, detain it till it dries a little & it *sticks*' (Coleridge, *Notebooks*, Entry 1017). Hill shares in 'Hopkins's ambiguous, ungraspable "world-wielding" force ("... something that makes, builds up and breeds ... something that unmakes or pulls to pieces ...")'.[36] It may be ungraspable, but the hyphen tries to seize upon it, as Hill does when he turns the 'ambiguous, ungraspable "world-wielding"' to this: 'the word-monger, word-wielder, is brought to judgement'.[37]

'The Pentecost Castle' does not just have no punctuation; it has un-punctuation or non-punctuation. Yet two of Eliot's deepest remarks about punctuation and technique (and 'we cannot say at what point "technique" begins or where it ends') press upon Hill's sequence. First, that 'verse, whatever else it may or may not be, is itself a system of *punctuation*; the usual marks of punctuation themselves are differently employed'.[38] Second, that in a poem punctuation 'includes the *absence* of punctuation marks, when they are omitted where the reader would expect them'.[39]

> If the night is dark
> and the way short
> why do you hold back
> dearest heart
>
> though I may never
> see you again
> touch me I will shiver
> at the unseen
>
> the night is so dark
> the way so short
> why do you not break
> o my heart

(11)

This poem is and is not punctuated, or rather is both non-punctuated and punctuated. It is punctuated because verse, with its lineations sketching its lineaments and with its stanzas taking a stand, is itself a system of punctuation. It is non-punctuated because it not only has none of the conventional marks of punctuation but it has an absence of such marks where the reader would have expected them.

> marked
> visible absences, colours of the mind,
> ('Terribilis est Locus Iste')

One mark in particular is visibly absent: the question-mark. The question-mark presses upon the poem, wishing to steady the lonely sufferer:

> why do you hold back
> dearest heart
>
> why do you not break
> o my heart

For the double cry (positive and negative) both is and is not a question; it is interrogative in its hunger for an answer, it is exclamatory in its protest, and it is declarative in its stoicism. It beseeches a question-mark, an exclamation-mark, and a full stop; all or none of these. Hill would not have effected his very different poignancy had it not been for the Eliot of 'Marina' and its fog-lifting:

> What seas what shores what grey rocks and what islands
> What water lapping the bow
> And scent of pine and the woodthrush singing through the fog
> What images return
> O my daughter.

Non-punctuation is like non-being and it has its depths:

> depths of non-being
> perhaps too clear
> my desire dying
> as I desire

Yet, as this concluding unstopped quatrain of 'The Pentecost Castle' shows, there is one simple and deep respect in which it is simply not true to say that 'The Pentecost Castle' has no punctuation. W.S. Milne says of the lack of punctuation in 'The Pentecost Castle' that Hill represents 'a condition beyond knowing', 'by abandoning those aspects of language which are designed to break down reality into component parts'.[40] But one mark of punctuation which signally breaks down reality into component parts is not abandoned.

For the hyphen ('depths of non-being') both is and is not a mark of punctuation. It is, after all, a mark by which the particular pointing of the language is manifested and controlled, and handbooks of punctuation have for centuries included a discussion of the hyphen. But it is anomalous, since our first thought, and even our central thought, may be that punctuation is a mark of the articulation of word to word, and not within a word. The equivocation of the hyphen is perfectly at one with the way in which 'The Pentecost Castle' both is and is not punctuated (there is what Eliot called 'the disposition of lines on the page', the strongly-felt presence of lineation and stanza, and there is the strongly-felt absence of particular marks of punctuation at crucial points). The presence of hyphens within the poem is, to say the least, a complication of any simple innocence.

> St James and St John
> bless the road she has gone
> St John and St James
> a rosary of names
>
> child-beads of fingered bread
> never-depleted heart's food
> the nominal the real
> subsistence past recall
>
> bread we shall never break
> love-runes we cannot speak
> scrolled effigy of a cry
> our passion its display
>
> (10)

It is the hyphen which threads the rosary of child-beads, never-depleted, and love-runes; it is the hyphen which brings home what it is to conceive of 'love-runes we cannot speak', since the human voice cannot speak a hyphen.[41]

If there are brought together the hyphens and the impinging absence of other punctuation-marks, then the question may arise of the absence of hyphens when they are omitted where the reader would expect them, here in 'The Pentecost Castle' or elsewhere. Tennyson was reproved by Coleridge, and attributed the reproof to a poetical mannerism in 'Œnone':

> I had an idiotic hatred of hyphens in those days, but though I printed such words
> as 'glénríver', 'téndriltwíne' I always gave them in reading their full two accents.
> Coleridge thought because of these hyphened words that I could not scan.[42]

The first dozen lines of 'Œnone' included in 1832 'glenriver', 'steepdown', 'tendriltwine', 'cedarshadowy', 'Godbuilt', 'snowycolumn'd', and 'darkblue'; this opening did permit itself 'Far-seen', as if Tennyson either baulked at the odd form 'Farseen' or had run out of resistance to the hyphen.[43] Hill, who writes as if only an idiot would have a hatred of hyphens, is aware of how

a Tennysonian colouring can be given, sometimes banteringly, by declining
– as in Tennyson's 'cedarshadowy' – to furnish a hyphen. As in this Tenny-
sonian landscape:

> and the marsh-orchids and the heron's nest,
> goldgrimy shafts and pillars of the sun.
>   ('An Apology . . .: 11. Idylls of the King')

This is one extremity of the absent hyphen, the Tennysonian passion of the
past becoming a passion of the pastiche. The opposite extremity is not to run
the words together but to let them float free, even compounding their not
being a compound by how they are lineated:

> At dawn the Mass
> burgeons from stone
> a Jesse tree
> of resurrection
>
> budding with candle
> flames the gold
> and the white wafers
> of the feast
>
> and ghosts for love
> void a few tears
> of wax upon
> forlorn altars
>   ('The Pentecost Castle, 4')

Not 'candle-flames', not even 'candle flames', but

>   candle
> flames

– and this within a sequence of lines none of which had hitherto run over.
The candles and their flames both are and are not one; they drift poignantly
apart even in their celebration.

It may be said that to make this much of hyphens is far-fetched and
murderously dissecting ('. . . murderously/To heal me with far-fetched blood':
'Three Baroque Meditations: 3. The Dead Bride'). But the general case for
attention to minutiae in Hill's poetry is corroborated by his own sense that
nothing is beneath notice. 'I would claim the utmost significance for matters
of technique'.[44] As for this particular point of technique, hyphenation, Hill's
revisions of 'The Pentecost Castle' in particular, and of *Tenebrae* more
widely, and of all his poetry most widely,[45] show that he attends meticulously
to this very matter. For 'under the briar rose' (twice in 'The Pentecost Castle,
2') was first published as 'under the briar-rose'; 'my love meet me half-way'
(9), conversely, was first published as 'my love meet me half way'; and
'Splendidly-shining darkness' (13) as 'Splendidly shining darkness'.

Such an adverbial hyphenation in 'ly-' is an insistent one in Hill. Perhaps he is refusing to be intimidated by Churchill, who wrote to Edward Marsh: '*Richly embroidered* seems to me two words, and it is terrible to think of linking every adverb to a verb by a hyphen.'[46] Eric Partridge says roundly that 'an adverb in *-ly* never takes a hyphen, whether before or after a participle, present or past'.[47] But Hill's art is, in its own terms, 'greatly-aloof' from, and 'variably-resistant' to, such a dogma; as an art which is 'splendidly-shining', 'evidently-veiled', 'newly-stung', 'rawly-difficult', 'roughly-silvered', 'truly-chastened', 'blazingly-supreme' and 'nicely-phrased', the one thing it isn't is 'blindly-ignorant' of the handbooks' urgings. Hill praised the poetry of Robert Lowell: 'The writing is deeply-felt and strongly-mannered: the feeling is embodied in the mannerism.'[48] In Hill's own poetry, the deep feeling is embodied in that strong mannerism of adverbial hyphenation. So 'Splendidly shining darkness' became 'Splendidly-shining darkness'.

That is, Hill knows the difference between 'Hearthstones' in *Mercian Hymns* (XXVIII)[49] and 'hearth-stone' in his *Brand* (Act II). He is not oblivious of the strange likeness and unlikeness ('At such near distance') when the 'same' word takes minutely different forms:

> Dawnlight freezes against the east-wire.
>   ('I had hope when violence was ceas't')

>   In dawn-light the troughed water
> floated a damson-bloom of dust –
>   (*Mercian Hymns*, XXV)

>   Then turn your backs on the dawn-light.
>   (*Brand*, Act II)[50]

> Down in the river-garden a grey-gold
> dawnlight begins to silhouette the ash.
>   (*The Mystery* . . ., p. 26)

'Not only is the use of the hyphen a matter of indifference in an immense number of cases . . .' (*OED*, 'General Explanations: Combinations'). Not in poetry, it isn't. 'Car-dealers' are so nearly those other untrustworthy people who deal cards, especially if they are to be found in the company of 'shuffle' and 'carls'; Hill uses the momentary flicker of mis-spelling and mis-hyphenation rather as Robert Lowell did.

>   Merovingian car-dealers, Welsh mercen-
> aries; a shuffle of house-carls.
>   (*Mercian Hymns*, XXVII)

Hill is a poet preoccupied (some would say obsessed) with such minutiae. Coleridge's observation is true for the critic because it is first true for the poet: 'And I must not forget in speaking of the certain Hubbub, I am to undergo for hypercriticism, to point out how little instructive any criticism can be which does not enter into minutiae.'[51]

> When the sky cleared above Malvern he lingered in his orchard; by the quiet hammer-pond. Trout-fry simmered there, translucent, as though forming the water's underskin. He had a care for natural min-utiae.
>
> (*Mercian Hymns*, XIV)

The lines are evidence of a care for artistic minutiae too, as in the way the hyphen in 'hammer-pond' permits the eerie juxtaposition of 'quiet' and hammer' to be so tellingly unmelodramatic ('by the quiet hammer-pond'); for the hyphen paces and points the sequence of words so that 'quiet' is un-obtrusively held at a very slightly greater distance from 'hammer-pond' than it would be from 'hammer pond' and yet not so distant as it would be from 'hammerpond'.

When Hill refers to 'Ash-Wednesday feasts', he remembers the hyphen which Eliot had and which even Eliot's best critics sometimes fail to remember. In *Tenebrae*, Hill offers 'Two Chorale-Preludes', not, as John Peck has it, 'Two Chorale Preludes'[52] (the two poems are both two and one; their autonomy is preserved, and the hyphen does the more than trick). Hill might ask, chasteningly, what Andrew Waterman means by distinguishing the adverb 'selfchasteningly' from the noun which he uses three pages later: 'the poetic self-chastening'.[53] *Self-* is perhaps Hill's most frequently needed hyphenation; it is certainly the form which dominates *Tenebrae*, *Brand* and 'Poetry as "Menace" and "Atonement"'.

Compounds with 'self-' at once incarnate the utmost singleness of a hyphenation and strike at its roots, since they turn the doubleness upon itself and make the matter perversely one. Hill's distrust of self-expression,[54] and of every such 'self-inspiring self-deceiver',[55] even when sitting 'in gaunt self-judgment on their self-defeat',[56] is responsibly desperate for a contrasting honourable word of self. He finds it in selfhood. 'Selfhood is more vital, recalcitrant, abiding, than self-expression.'[57] It is in the poet's acknowledgement of 'irredeemable error in the very substance and texture of his craft and pride ... that his selfhood may be made at-one with itself'.[58]

For selfhood, unlike 'at-one', is indeed one, and it has no room for even the best-intentioned hyphen. *Tenebrae* brings this home when 'selfhoods' are threatened by splits and by hyphened faceting:

> Moods of the verb 'to stare',
> split selfhoods, conjugate
> ice-facets from the air,
> the light glazing the light.
> ('Two Chorale-Preludes: 1. Ave Regina Coelorum')

The ice-facets are not conjured from the air, but are learnedly conjugated;

the selfhoods do offer at least a vision of integrity, unsplit, refusing the violent scholarly yoking.

> Already, like a disciplined scholar,
> I piece fragments together, past conjecture
> Establishing true sequences of pain.
> ('The Songbook of Sebastian Arrurruz, 1')

No less painful, and no less true though never above suspicion, are the sequences which are pieced not from fragments but from wholes. Hill is much more sceptical of multiple hyphenings than are his critics.

Yet the critic's mannerism is caught from the poet, even if he is not only more sceptical than they are but more sceptical than his much-loved Hopkins. Hill permits himself neither the callisthenics of 'Amansstrength' at one extreme, nor the self-advertisement of 'drop-of-blood-and-foam-dapple', of 'wimpled-water-dimpled, not-by-morning-matchèd', or of 'Miracle-in-Mary-of-flame'. Yet Hill greatly admires Hopkins's indeflectibility.

> Our hearts' charity's hearth's fire, our thoughts' chivalry's throng's Lord.
> ['The Wreck of the Deutschland']

> ... I cannot entirely agree with [Elisabeth Schneider's] suggestion that 'the effect is arbitrary and labored'. The method, I would accept, is arbitrary and laboured but the effect is one of hard-won affirmation.[59]

But it was not simply the fact that Charles Péguy's title had been *Le Mystère de la Charité de Jeanne d'Arc* that made Hill call his poem *The Mystery of the Charity of Charles Péguy* rather than *Charles Péguy's Charity's Mystery*. Hill admires Hopkins and does otherwise. English ought to be kept up. And so should the English distrust of compounding compounds.

> I wake
> To caress propriety with odd words
> And enjoy abstinence in a vocation
> Of now-almost-meaningless despair.
> ('The Songbook of Sebastian Arrurruz, 11')

'The phrase "now-almost-meaningless"', said Jeffrey Wainwright, 'is hyphenated to point up its accession into cliché, though here a cliché restored to hint at the real despair of the poet – the possibility of no longer, through the contraction of valid speech, being able to say anything meaningful'.[60] Such hyper-hyphenated phrases are not to be trusted, though this awkwardly has to include the fact that you can't trust them to be false either. You must simply exercise 'A busy vigilance of goose and hound' ('Asmodeus: II'). Especially when near such a lithe paradigm of doubled-hyphenation as this:

> I am shadowed by the wise bird
> Of necessity, the lithe
> Paradigm Sleep-and-Kill.
> ('Three Baroque Meditations. 1')

Necessity, the tyrant's paradigm, is winged by hyphens.

Even, or particularly, the grandest of these turns may be twists:

> Whose passion was to find out God in this
> His natural filth, voyeur of sacrifice, a slow
> Bloody unearthing of the God-in-us.
> But with what blood, and to what end, Shiloh?
>   ('Locust Songs: Shiloh Church, 1862 . . .')

Brand has its comic preposterousness:

> that Fear-and-Trembling School
> has taught you very well!
>   . . .
> high-stepping Meek-and-Mild!
>   (Act I)[61]

Tenebrae more darkly declines to adjudicate between the authentic and the inauthentic, pressing the reader to take the responsibility of response to such finely judged withholdings as : 'Stupefying images of grief-in-dream' and 'this is true marriage of the self-in-self' ('Tenebrae'). Those last three words, that last one word, might not ring like a true marriage.

In his essay on *Cymbeline* (a text with 'a strong taste for hyphens'[62]), Hill refers to 'James VI and I, the unifier and pacifier'.[63] Divinely rightly unhyphenated, James VI and I was something of a metaphysical as well as political feat, and when in his Jonson essay Hill quotes Coleridge, the form used is again evidence that the handbooks on punctuation have (as Eric Partridge insisted) a point:

> The *anachronic* mixture of the Roman Republican, to whom Tiberius must have appeared as much a Tyrant as Sejanus, with the *James-and-Charles-the-1st* zeal for legitimacy of Descent.[64]

James-and-Charles-the-1st? That looks to be at once a succession and a simultaneity, unifying and pacifying. There is likewise something happy, a touch of the trouvaille, in its being the United Committee of Framework-Knitters which moves Hill to invoke such knittings as 'time-signature', or to this sequence:

> To do justice to the quality of his seeing [Hopkins's, of Wordsworth] one must refer again to Richard Oastler and to the Nottingham framework-knitters. Writers on linguistics employ a term 'stress-pitch-juncture'. ' "Juncture" is that particular configuration of pause and pitch characteristics by which the voice connects linguistic units to each other or to silence' (Seymour Chatman). In this case one requires a modified term, 'stress-pitch-disjuncture'.[65]

When Eric Partridge pondered the way in which, thanks to hyphens, 'a number of distinct entities – apprehended, it is true, as a collectivity or a collective idea – becomes an intellectual, aesthetic, stylistic unit', he found himself gravitating to a unit not intellectual, aesthetic, or stylistic, but religious and metaphysical. The gravity of the instance pricked Partridge to a certain uneasy levity about high-style hyphenation:

> Thus, whereas most of us would write:
>> The ideal of the mystic is oneness with God,
> the stylist would perhaps write:
>> The ideal of the mystic is oneness-with-God.
> If the collectivity be put first, i.e. made the subject of the sentence, most of us would write:
>> Oneness with God is the ideal of the mystic,
> but the stylist would probably prefer:
>> Oneness-with-God is (*or*, constitutes) the ideal of the mystic.
> The relationship of the theory to the practice can be more clearly seen in a sentence no stylist would permit himself:
>> The idea oneness-with-God forms the very basis of mystical philosophy, that of God everywhere-and-in-everything-whether-animate-or-inanimate, the basis of pantheism; and that of God-in-the-form-of-man or, at the least, God-with-the-(better)-feelings-and-the-(superior)-attributes-of-man, the basis of anthropomorphism.[66]

The hope (beyond hope) of setting at one the two soundings of atonement is the impulse of religious consciousness. It was the philosopher F.H. Bradley who furnished one of the great high and dry moments of philosophical comedy when his Table of Contents summarised the arguments of Book I (Appearance) Section III of *Appearance and Reality*:

III. RELATION AND QUALITY
  I.   Qualities without relations are unintelligible. They cannot be found, 26–27. They cannot be got bare legitimately, 27–28, or at all, 28–30.
  II. Qualities with relations are unintelligible. They cannot be resolved into relations, 30, and the relations bring internal discrepancies, 31.
  III. Relations with, or without, qualities are unintelligible, 32–34.

It was Bradley's disciple, T.S. Eliot who perpetrated the comic totality of a related footnote:

> Ultimately, it must be remembered, there are not even relations.[67]

Meanwhile, Eliot's footnote bore some relation to his text.
Bradley hoped to reconcile the Atonement and atonement:

> You can not understand the recognition of and desire for the divine will; nor the consciousness of sin and rebellion, with the need for grace on the one hand and its supply on the other; you turn every fact of religion into unmeaning nonsense, and you pluck up by the root and utterly destroy all possibility of the Atonement, when you deny that the religious consciousness implies that God and man are identical in a subject.
> For it is the atonement, the reconciliation (call it what you please, and bring it

before your mind in the way most easy to you), to which we must come, if we mean to follow the facts of the religious consciousness. Here, as everywhere, the felt contradiction implies, and is only possible through, a unity above the discord: take that away, and the discord goes.

(*Ethical Studies*, 'Concluding Remarks')[68]

It was a great turn, so to retort Ulysses' words as to make the discord go in peace:

> Take but Degree away, un-tune that string,
> And hearke what Discord followes.
> (*Troilus and Cressida*, I. iii)

If, in these highest reaches of philosophy and religion, Bradley is right to insist that 'the felt contradiction implies, and is only possible through, a unity above the discord', it is equally true that at those rare opposite moments of the felt atonement there is implied a discord below the unity. It is this double truth that in Bradley so makes against any complacency of utterance.

Yet 'a unity above the discord' – not obliterating or oblivious of the discord – may, on occasion and by grace, be incarnated by virtue of the poet's hyphen:

> and abstinence crowns all our care
> with martyr-laurels for this day.
> ('Veni Coronaberis')

Like the spiritual Platonic old England which Coleridge revered, Hill, when he rests, rests in not on his martyr-laurels:

> Platonic England, house of solitudes,
> rests in its laurels and its injured stone,
> ('An Apology . . .: 9. The Laurel Axe')

But mostly there is little rest; rather, there is what Hill in 1954, precariously hyphening, called 'the tight-rope over the jaw-hole'.[69] His poems are some versions of what *The Mystery of the Charity of Charles Péguy* compactly calls 'militant-pastoral'. They are 'variably-resistant' to criticism.

'Any-mad-versions of an Author's meaning now a days pass for animad-versions.' Hill might agree with Coleridge.[70] But as a child his first recorded word was 'jam-jar'.[71]

6

Hill's 'version' of *Brand*

Adrian Poole

'The voice of a Savonarola': so Strindberg described what he and his generation heard in Ibsen's dramatic poem *Brand* (1866).[1] What those first ears seem to have thrilled to was the lash in the voice of the eponymous Lutheran pastor, who believes himself to bear the savage word of redemption. A modern and Norwegianless reader is unlikely to be as promptly roused by a voice of such caustic conviction. What, if anything, can such a reader hear? And how might Geoffrey Hill's 'version' help him to hear it?[2]

Though his poem was unconcerned with a literal stage, Ibsen grounded the matter of Brand's vocation in the inherent drama of voice. That drama is born in the lapse between the voice that calls and the ear that hears, between utterance and audition. Even the most solitary utterance is normally heard by at least one pair of ears, those of the utterer, and Ibsen's poem is as interested in how Brand sounds to himself as in how he sounds to others, in the kinds of rapture and deafness with which his voice is hailed and ignored by his own and others' ears. How far may Brand be thought to succumb to the power of his own voice? How far does he succeed in convincing himself and others that a voice more and other than his own speaks through him? One of Ibsen's first English translators observed of Brand that he was 'a man who believes the voice within him is the only thing he has a right to listen to', and that there are other voices to which 'in his ever narrowing mind' he remains wilfully deaf.[3] There is more than one voice in Ibsen's poem; while Brand's voice demands to be heard, that demand turns out to entail a tragic refusal to listen.

Ibsen's poem ends, dramatically, with an unidentifiable and unembodied 'Voice' that seems to answer Brand's final cries with the words 'He is the God of Love', or 'God is Love!', or (closest to the Norwegian) 'He is *deus caritatis*'.* The reader hears this voice clearly 'above' (Oxford) or 'through' (Ewbank, Meyer) the thunder of the avalanche that buries Brand. But does Brand himself hear this 'Voice'? Probably not. The avalanche intervenes between the asking and the answering, so that the auditor unscathed by avalanche assumes that *he* hears what Brand's deafened, buried ears cannot. Geoffrey Hill's version of Brand's final appeals is notably more agonised and protracted than the others against which I have compared it. The Oxford translation gives Brand three lines and two questions:

> Answer me, God, in the jaws of death:
> Is there no salvation for the Will of Man?
> No small measure of salvation . . . ?
>
> (Oxford, p. 250)

This is Hill:

> Tell
> me, O God, even as your heavens fall
> on me: what makes retribution
> flesh of our flesh? Why is salvation
> rooted so blindly in your Cross?
> Why is man's own proud will his curse?
> Answer! What do we die to prove?
> Answer!
>
> (p. 160)

One of the many virtues of Hill's version is that it makes the most of the critical moments in Ibsen's poem in which an answer or response is uttered too late. I am reminded of the deceptively quiet conclusion to Hill's poem ' "Christmas Trees" ': 'We hear too late or not too late.'[4]

Ibsen's first play, *Catiline*, opens with the words:

> I must! I must! Deep down within my soul
> A voice commands, and I will do its bidding; . . .[5]

It would be surprising to find Hill uninterested in or by Ibsen's ferocious, tormented idealists, and in particular by 'a man of genuine zeal and messianic fervour, a life-defender, and a life-destroyer', to use Hill's own description of Brand.[6] Nor would one be surprised to find his interest quickened by the

---

* I have compared Hill's version with three other translations. The first quotation above is from the translation by Michael Meyer (London, 1967), hereafter referred to as 'Meyer'. The second is from the translation by James Kirkup in collaboration with James Walter McFarlane, in *The Oxford Ibsen*, Vol. III (London, 1972), hereafter referred to as 'Oxford'. The third is from the annotated literal translation which Inga-Stina Ewbank provided for Geoffrey Hill, hereafter referred to as 'Ewbank'.

I must acknowledge a large debt of gratitude to Professor Ewbank for her generosity in allowing me to study her 'literal' and its notes, and also for permission to quote from it.

prospect of animating this man's voice, of finding rhythm and pitch to make it sound the passions and temptations of self-conviction. Weight too, one might say, bearing in mind Hill's comments about 'the inertial drag of speech', that: 'Language gravitates and exerts a gravitational pull'.[7] But the density and pull of the medium through which Brand's call tries to pass is not just that of the language he must use; it is also composed of the resilient, refractory beings to whose ears his voice addresses itself and through whom his call seeks to carry. In an early Oxford piece on François Mauriac, Hill commended the novelist's strength in showing 'the dedicated spirit as existing, not in a sphere of radiance and song, but in a cramped environment of small-town gossip and malicious and petty intrigue'.[8] Hill's own version of the small-town environment to which Brand chooses to dedicate his mission turns out to be rich in words of physical and spiritual constraint and recalcitrance – 'cramped' and (to grasp another word favoured in Hill's early poetry and prose) 'crabbed'. This image, for instance, from the early poem 'Flower and No Flower' would seem to catch the same abysmal complicity of mineral and spiritual that one finds in Ibsen:

> The shadow of a spark
> Deep in the crabbed rock.[9]

In Ibsen's *Brand* there are important differences between the beings who comprise the milieu and medium. There is the 'small town' on the one hand: in Hill's own words again, the 'canting, provincial, sanctimonious, murderously self-righteous society',[10] most prominently represented by the Mayor and the Dean. But on the other, there are those figures too intimate with Brand's essential self to be guiltlessly renounced as 'others': Brand's Mother, his wife Agnes and their child Alf, and his weird shadow-sibling, the gypsy girl Gerd. It is in these raw proximities that the qualities of Brand's voice, virtuous and vicious, are most sorely tested.

It is important to keep the record straight. Hill's version of *Brand* obviously occupies a special and in some ways tantalising place in his work. One must try to do justice to the particular kind of creative labour involved, and unimpertinently distinguish the elements in it for which he is answerable. On the matter of responsibility, Hill is characteristically scrupulous. In 'A Note on the Text' for the first edition, he writes:

> This work makes no claim to be a translation of *Brand*. It is a 'version for the English stage' of a poetic drama which was not intended for the stage. It is based on an annotated literal translation by Inga-Stina Ewbank. She is not responsible for the liberties which I have taken or for the errors into which I may have fallen.

In 'A Note to the Second Edition' Hill distinguishes the 'privilege and responsibility' of the theatre director with similar care. The nature of the claim Hill makes for his work is explicit; it is not to be judged as something turned from one language to another, but as something turned from one kind of text to another, from the page towards the stage. (Indeed, in the first instance, specifically 'the English stage'; one notes that the sub-title to the second edition, published in the US, finds itself forced to bypass the possible collision in the word 'English' – it becomes simply 'A Version for the Stage'.) It is tempting to seek out those moments in Hill's version when he would appear most obviously to diverge from his 'source' (or as one should say, 'sources': immediately, Inga-Stina Ewbank's 'literal'; mediatedly, Ibsen's 'original'). When Brand faces Agnes with a Kierkegaardian choice between himself and the artist Einar, he says: 'For, choosing, you are chosen.' (p. 49) Near the end of the play the Chorus of Invisibles call Brand 'self-inspiring self-deceiver' (p. 154). But it would be unjust to say that these lines were Hill's *rather than* Ibsen's on the grounds that they less obviously correspond to anything in the 'literal' from which Hill was working than they do to things one could point to elsewhere in Hill's 'own' work. At such moments, the characteristic turn Hill gives to a line successfully concentrates hints and nuances that in Ibsen are fugitively dispersed through longer passages or, indeed, the play as a whole. On the question of Hill's fidelity to the 'spirit' of Ibsen, the reader is referred to Inga-Stina Ewbank's invaluable introduction to the second, revised edition.[11]

On the question of its relation to his other writings, Hill is himself helpfully exact about one important aspect of the distinctiveness of his *Brand*, 'the kind of labour' he found himself putting into it. In answer to a question about the possible 'entrancement' of creative activity, he describes the unique state into which the work on *Brand* threw him.

> Labour and excitement combined to induce a state of euphoria, what you would call 'entrancement', a kind of quite falsely mystical ecstasy, which was most interesting to observe in oneself. At the same time, I knew exactly why I was in that state, and I observed myself with interest and not without humour. That's the only time I've ever found myself in that state, and I do not in any way overrate it.
>
> With my own poetry, when I'm able to write it, the process seems a slow, common craftsmanship, an ordinary occurrence.[12]

The distinctions he makes are unusually confident, between the 'state of euphoria' and the assured suspicion, between this kind of labour and 'my own poetry'. To imply that something is other than 'my own poetry' is not necessarily to disclaim it; but the speed and fluency with which Hill accomplished his work on *Brand* are in notable contrast to the kind of difficulty with which he records the composition of his 'own' poetry. Hill concedes that in retrospect *Brand* was 'not an inappropriate play' for him to attempt, but the initial call for the project did not originate with him; indeed he says that he had not read the play until he received the commission. It would be wrong to identify Hill with the play and its matter too snugly, and Hill's own account of the quality of his engagement requires respectful attention.

> I became, almost against my will, fascinated not only by the daunting scale of the demand but also by my own deep and very mixed feelings about it. Both as a work of art and as a portrayal of a certain kind of character it contained a great deal that was hateful. I also became fascinated by certain technical matters ...[13]

There would seem to be a conjunction between the two 'fascinations', where the fascination with 'technical matters' is both a consequence of, and a resistance to the fascination with 'deep and very mixed feelings'. The particular technical matter that Hill goes on to mention is that of metre. Ibsen had sought for a metre 'in which he could career where he would "as on horseback" ', and Hill says that he 'enjoyed the challenge of having to move rapidly from farce to ecstasy'.[14]

To illustrate the skill involved in some of these 'technical matters', one might begin by admiring the precision in the choice of two small words: 'smudge' and 'blare'. The 'smudge' comes from Einar in the passage in Act I succeeding Brand's confrontation with the two young 'butterflies', the artist and his girl Agnes. Einar is rhapsodising about the renewed prospect that lies before them now that the forbidding Brand has left them to go their own heedless way.

> What a picture! Such harmony
> of sky with sea and sea with sky;
> deep azure lit by silver streaks,
> suffused with golden lights and darks,
> out to the far horizon's edge,
> the boundless main! And, look, that smudge
> of smoke – the steamer coming in,
> the very ship we go to join.
>
> (pp. 14-5)

Comparison reveals that Hill has made a tiny conflation of two distinct entities, the 'dark smoke', and the 'black spot' (Ewbank) or 'black dot' (Oxford) or 'black speck' (Meyer), of the steamer. Hill's refusal of 'spot', 'dot' or 'speck' in favour of the precise imprecision of 'smudge' manages at the same time to credit Einar with a promising eye for painterly detail and to admit an objective element of realistically vulgar imperfection into the 'picture'. And although Hill would seem in general to keep literary echo and allusion at bay in this work, there is the faint echo from a line of Hopkins that he has elsewhere admired ('And wears man's smudge ...').[15] The title of this poem does in fact find its way into Brand's mouth much later on – 'God's grandeur'. Einar's voice seems here to find a momentary and unexpected weight in the word 'smudge'.

The word 'blare' occurs in Brand's Act II monologue after the death of the man who has killed his own child. Meditating on the future of the two sons who have watched him die, Brand rises to this generalised exclamation:

> Where did it all begin, and why,
> eternal culpability?
> What answer blares from the abyss?
> 'Remember who the father was'.
>
> (p. 29)

The other versions emphasise Brand's dissatisfaction with the answer to his question by making him call it 'hollow'. All three use this word, though the Oxford translation goes furthest in making it 'like an echo's/Hollow mockery' which 'reverberates from the abyss' (Oxford, p. 109). The 'literal' here provides Hill simply with: 'Why? Hollow answer from the abyss'. A 'blare' is an auditory smudge offensive in its proximity as Einar's 'smudge' was reassuringly remote, controlled by the eye. But both choices lend a precision of apprehension to the voice, as curiosity and outrage clutch for grip. Both choices cleave close to the blurred, inexact contours of the sight and sound they purport to signify, and in so doing they carry a small pleasure and pain that a good actor will feel invited to make something of. There is relish and distaste for the voice to find in such words as 'smudge' and 'blare'.

As Hill suggests, one of his primary general decisions concerned metre.[16] Ibsen had shortened to iambic and trochaic tetrameter the pentameter line of the satirical narrative poem out of which the 'dramatic' *Brand* was fashioned, and Hill seems to have been attracted by the advantages of a sensibly contracted line, usually with three stresses, but often extended to four, and trimmed to two. Along with the choice of varied but persistent 'rhyme' (the term covers a wide range of effects), this establishes a permissive but distinct ground of constraint on the voice. Some of the voices in the drama are happier within these constraints than others. When Brand's Mother is telling him about the savings she has hoarded, her voice makes itself at home by the glee with which it smacks home the pulses of a line:

> But carry it on me?
> I'm not mad! It's at home,
> all snug in wad and bag.
> (p. 38)

That last line catches with succinct, exemplary relish the whole tenor of a way of life. Her son, by contrast, often finds himself restless and at times near desperation as his breath struggles to escape from these measures. Here, for example, he is railing at the Mayor in Act V:

> You'd take a metre-rule
> to measure the sublime
> measureless universe,
> visions of fire and ice,
> those blazingly-supreme
> powers that radiate –
> the focus, Man's own heart!
> I can't ... I can't go on ...
> (p. 125)

His wife is also tormented by the impossibility of escape 'from breathing this fierce air' (p. 107).

Closely related to these basic measures are the various other elements

through which Hill gives body to the voice, makes it pause and strain against
the physical and spiritual obstructions that thwart its drive for fluency. The
voice has to make its way through and round the crassness that finds outward
expression in words that register the difficulty or impossibility of physical
motion, words such as 'trudge', 'crouch', 'clamped', 'rooted', 'stuck'. There
is a pained crudity in some of the final words of Brand's Mother:

> Why does God leave a soul
> stuck like this in the flesh ...
> (p. 45)

This has the nerve to make God sound like a careless surgeon, in contrast
with the more courteously traditional query that Oxford gives her: 'Why was
my soul housed in this flesh, ... ?' (Oxford, p. 123)

Not only does Hill take advantage of the continual punctuation of line-
endings, he also uses to the full the marks that suggest the catches and
abruptions that divide the flow of a voice. One can admire, for instance, the
meticulous punctuation of the following lines in which Brand's voice weighs,
with a solemn and painful compunction, the encroaching figure of his Mother:

> Who is this who comes
> so slowly: who climbs
> with such anguish; who bends,
> so, her head; who stands
> gasping for breath; who drags
> her body in its rags
> as if it were a hoard
> of precious, secret greed; ... ?
> (pp. 35-6)

As she 'stands/gasping for breath', the colon, semi-colons and commas make
him pause to catch his own. One of the sharpest intakes of breath in the play
is marked by a comma in a speech by Agnes, when she says that now she
knows what 'those grim/words' mean:

> 'He who sees
> Jehovah's face, dies.'
> (p. 106)

It is noticeable that 'now' is a word that frequently attracts a comma. (One
might compare the line in 'The Turtle Dove': 'As though needing no ques-
tions, now, to guess ...'[17]) Thus when Brand says at the end of Act I: 'My
way is clear, now' (p. 19), his voice seems to respect a doubt and a difficulty,
ostensibly overcome – as 'My way is clear now' would not. Near the end of
Act II, he says, similarly: 'I see, now, the true goal' (p. 47).

What I have called 'precise imprecision' also distinguishes the technical
matter of 'rhyme'. It would seem foolhardy to try and match with any exact-
ness Ibsen's own rhymes (mainly couplets, with some variation). Hill estab-
lishes the principle that every line-end should meet its match, but the quality
and regularity of these unions is open to wide and continual variation. In the

following passage from Act II, the mild distances in time and sound between 'while' and 'still' or 'fear' and 'hair' seem self-forgetfully supportive of the more absorbing consonances between 'singing', 'glistening', 'gazing' and 'listening'. Brand has been arrested by the quietly waiting figure of Agnes:

> Has she sat there all this while?
> What is it she can hear?
> Is it singing in the air?
> In the storm, as we drove
> on through the wild sea-wave,
> she sat, so rapt and still,
> wholly without fear,
> with the spindrift glistening
> upon her brow and hair,
> gazing and listening,
> yes, listening with her eyes
> to secret harmonies!
>
> (p. 33)

Much of the time the bonds between 'rhyme' words are fleeting and easily soluble, the congruities unworryingly temporary. But there are moments when more is at stake, as when Brand ends a line calling man an 'animal' and defers for five lines the response, 'And yet He is merciful.' (p. 22). When the Spokesman for the local folk is asking Brand to stay, the two commonplaces he voices are given substance by the effort with which the rhyme words attend to each other over the unusually large distance of eight lines (in the theatre the ear would indeed have to quicken to catch this):

> You practise what you preach, . . .
> Don't leave us in the lurch, . . .
>
> (pp. 30–1)

These would sound quite differently if the gap between them was closed. One notices that Hill uses the deferred rhyme to create and do justice to gravities, as for example in the parting between Brand and his Mother in Act II:

> MOTHER   Why does God leave a soul
> stuck like this in the flesh
> where your heart's dearest wish
> makes your soul die?
> Stay by me, Pastor,
> in my last hour
> and help me out.
> But until then
> let me hold on
> to the things I've got.
> *Exit*
>
> BRAND   (*follows her with his eyes*):
> Yes, your pastor will stay.
>
> (p. 45)

This is one of the critical moments of deferred response which I alluded to earlier. The Mother does not wait to hear her son's answer, and the appeal and defiance in her final lines are suggested by her ability to leave the word 'die' hanging in the air. It only meets its match with Brand's 'stay' after she has gone. When it does, Brand is repeating the word she has herself used: 'die?/Stay ...'. There is here a grim acknowledgement of identity between mother and son; Brand also repeats his Mother's word 'Pastor', though without the capital letter, and with a possessive pronoun. I note that Hill has his Brand choose not to use the response 'your *son*' here, as Inga-Stina Ewbank's 'literal' does.

Much of the painful, intimate strife which Hill finds in the exchanges between Brand and his Mother, and his wife Agnes, works through these tiny details – the command of possessive pronouns, the appeal and rebuff of rhyme. The most dramatic of all deferred responses in the play occurs at the close of Act III. Brand's line 'So judgment is given ...' (p. 81) has to wait for twelve lines before Agnes concedes its answer: 'I dare to give to Heaven.' (p. 82). That unprecedented distance between 'given' and 'Heaven' marks the distance between husband and wife, and predicts the severance to which the death of the child condemns them: a 'diremption', to borrow a word from Hill in another, but not unrelated context.[18] One might also take the opportunity of observing how faithful to the Ibsen of the later prose plays is such an acute vigilance over the minute details of speech, into which large passions are cramped, and through which they are waged.

Various things may happen at the other extreme when rhyme-patterns converge. First, there is much ingenious mirth in the shameless levity with which the rogue of a Mayor can rhyme 'porridge' and 'marriage', as he condoles with a man for the death of his wife:

> It's an ill wind they say ...
> she'll need no more porridge.
> (*to the man who is leaving*)
> Forget about marriage; ...
> (p. 21)

In the mouths of the more humble locals such as the Spokesman or indeed Brand's Mother, commonplaces may offer protection and meagre relief for lives numbed with need, but the unscrupulous opportunism of the Mayor turns all such colloquialism into vacuous platitude. The role of the Mayor is a gift for an actor; consider the bravura twirl with which he urges Brand to clear off:

> The world's your oyster
> from now on, Pastor.
> (p. 64)

Or the ludicrously pompous rhyme with which he pretends to admire Brand's stoicism in bereavement:

> You seemed, though, so imbued
> with Christian Fortitude ...
>
> (p. 96)

There is a vicious ease in the propensity of rhyme for self-congratulation, and
even the scrupulous Brand is lured by its satisfactions. For instance, there is
a mutually confiding regularity to the line-chimes in the self-consciously vir-
tuoso couplets of 'moral satire', which Brand addresses to Einar in Act I. At
least, he *begins* by addressing Einar, but he rapidly becomes so absorbed in
listening to himself, it would seem, that he becomes oblivious to Einar's
presence. Any dissonance his speech admits points confidently to an incon-
gruity extrinsic to his own words:

> Sin if you dare, but have the grace,
> at least, to be fulfilled in vice.
>
> (p. 11)

But the natural gravitation of these lines is inwards, towards one another,
and they find themselves falling into uncommonly pure unions:

> Throughout this nation I observe
> such littleness and loss of nerve.
>
> (p. 11)

No wonder that when Brand stylishly concludes with:

> Above the worst, beneath the best,
> each virtue vicious to the rest.
>
> (p. 11)

Einar greets him with 'Bravo, Brand!' Hill here seems to highlight what is
only a hint in Ibsen by making Einar's consciously ironic applause retrospec-
tively 'place' the theatricality of Brand's speech. Elsewhere, in his essay 'Re-
deeming the Time', Hill has some keen points to make about the danger of
excluding 'the antiphonal voice of the heckler'.[19] But one should also remem-
ber the scope for comedy in such moments, when the focus of a speech is
abruptly altered by the way an unbargained-for auditor asserts his or her
presence. In *Mercian Hymns* there is a charming surprise in discovering in
the first Hymn that the public tribute one had thought unanswerably monu-
mental has not after all fallen on deaf ears: ' "I liked that", said Offa, "sing
it again." '[20] There is a quite different pained relief in the surprise in Hymn
X, when a question finds itself answered by an unexpectedly familiar voice
that shrinks it to a child's qualm:

> What should a man make of remorse, that it might
>   profit his soul? Tell me. Tell everything to
> Mother, darling, and God bless.[21]

There are a number of moments at which Hill makes Brand seem to
succumb to the charm of his own voice. There is a dazzling, triumphant ring

to the couplet which Hill restores in the revised edition, when he makes
Brand try to clinch the superiority of his own God to Einar's:

> But mine is young: a Hercules
> not fourscore of infirmities.
>
> (second edn, p. 16)

This is worth balancing against another restoration at the end of Act I, when
Hill extends Brand's apprehension of the wild girl Gerd by an added couplet.
The first version reads:

> Her spirit struggles to be heard;
> flawed music from a broken reed.
>
> (p. 18)

This noticeably endows Gerd with more of a distinct *will-to-be-heard* than
the judicially contemplative image of Ewbank's 'literal' does ('Lost is your
way and lost your soul .../A harp with a cracked frame.'), or than the Oxford
or Meyer versions do. But in the revised edition, Brand finds it in him to
answer that appeal with a couplet that lays the struggle momentarily to rest:

> Yet God in his strange mercy draws
> such souls to Him, out of their flaws.
>
> (second edn, p. 23)

There does not seem to be any mention of God's mercy in the other versions.
(Meyer omits what would seem to be a difficult, cryptic couple of lines in the
Norwegian.) It is possible to feel that the 'mercy' has been drawn out of the
'music', and that these quietly gracious lines are themselves drawn out of
Brand by a rare grace.

Gerd draws another line out of Brand in the closing speech to Act I, when
Hill has his Brand linger for an extra line over the last of the three 'trolls'
that Brand intends to slay so that 'mankind shall breathe again'. (One of my
very few cavils with Hill is that he overdoes the word 'troll', which seems to
me inevitably outlandish and undemonic in English.)

> Madness wanders from itself
> half shadowing the other half; ...
>
> (p. 19)

Gerd does shadow Brand through the play, but of the three women in his
life, it is Agnes rather than Gerd or his Mother in whom he encounters most
fully the substance of an other self. Agnes is the one person to the root of
whose being Brand's call carries, and who lives through its issue. Much of
the murderous marital entanglement of Ibsen's later prose plays is fore-
shadowed here: the fugitive tenderness, the numbing complicity, the heart-
arresting compulsion. Hill magnifies the impact that Brand has on Agnes
when at the end of their first confrontation in Act I, she exclaims with awe:
'When that man spoke/he burned!' (p. 15). (In the other versions, he merely

'grew'.) But he also heightens the impact she has on him. In the passage from Act II already cited, in which Brand is stopped by the image of her rapt attention, Hill makes him mark that arrest with three urgent questions. The Oxford version is calmly contemplative: 'See how she sits' (p. 113). And Hill slightly but distinctly deepens Agnes's rapture by withdrawing the single physical gesture that Ibsen gave her, 'shaking' (Ewbank) or 'wiping' (Oxford) the sea-spray from her brow. He makes Brand apprehend a perfect immobility: 'so rapt and still'. (Brand will later echo the phrase, in inversion, in Act IV when he uses it of his own attitude in the face of his child's death (p. 103).) In Agnes's subsequent vision, Hill singularises the 'voice' she says she hears crying 'through the emptiness' (p. 34). The Norwegian has plural voices, it would seem, and of different kinds, some 'ringing' and others 'interpreting' (Ewbank). The possibility that Agnes catches a glimpse of a state from which he is debarred is further enhanced by the beautiful lyric passage in Act III, when he asks her to watch over their child. Again there is a contrast between rage and stillness, as Brand turns yearningly from his own condition

I'm like a castaway
crying in vain among
the spars of a great wreck.
(p. 61)

to the stillness and tacit responsiveness uniting mother and child:

Sometimes his mother's face
hovers over that hushed place,
is received, is given back,
as beautifully as a bird
hovers, and hovering, is mirror'd
in the depths of the lake.
(p. 61–2)

Hill concentrates much of Brand's longing into the word with which he closes his appeal to Agnes:

O Agnes, guard him well,
in quietude.
(p. 62)

Ewbank's 'literal' here offers Hill the plainer 'silence', while Oxford just has 'Watch over him well' (p. 137), and Meyer 'Take good care of him' (p. 62). 'Quietude' is not the same as 'silence'; 'quiet' is a word to tense the ear elsewhere in Hill's poetry – 'O quiet deed!' in 'The Bidden Guest',[22] or in ' "Christmas Trees" ', the line preceding one already quoted:

Against wild reasons of the state
his words are quiet but not too quiet.
We hear too late or not too late.[23]

There is, however, one moment in the play which most vividly places in retrospect Brand's admiration – even envy – for Agnes's possible access to a state of grace from which he is excluded. It occurs after her death, at the start of Act V, when he delivers an anguished lament for his failure to find atonement in the power of music:

> What have I made? Not music, not
> music! Cries wrung from music's throat!
> Splayed chords of discord, a groan
> rising in the place of praise, the organ
> stormed, faltered; as if the Lord sat
> in the empty choir, raging and quiet,
> rebuking with His presence the voice
> of thanksgiving and sacrifice.
>
> (p. 122)

Both Oxford and Meyer enthrone the Lord God 'high in the choir' and give him a decisive, physical gesture: '... with one wave/Of his hands angrily rejected' (Oxford, p. 202); 'cast it down in His wrath' (Meyer, p. 90). The auditor whom Hill has Brand imagine, though unelevated, is more mysteriously inaccessible. Where previously the image of Agnes ('rapt and still', 'in quietude') offered Brand the prospect of an answer to the storm and the rage, now he is left alone to face the paradox of an empty choir filled with a presence that is at one and the same time 'raging and quiet'.

I would suggest that Hill 'improves' on Ibsen's Agnes, in that he gives her qualities of resilience and dignity that Ibsen himself gave to some of his later 'prose' women, but which in the relatively early *Brand* are muffled by a prompter surrender to the will of the male. I am thinking in particular of the agonized exchanges between husband and wife in Act IV, after their child has died, which foreshadow in some respects the terrible Act II of *Little Eyolf*. Hill accords his Agnes the power to make her pain speak through the very force of her restraint. The 'withers' and the 'quiet' of the following speech pick up other incomplete 'witherings' and unachieved 'quiets' elsewhere in the play:

> Be patient with me. The hurt
> I had was deep. It will smart
> for a while. But pain
> withers. I shall be quiet soon.
>
> (p. 84)

The manner, and equipoise, of their marriage is recognisably different from Ibsen's; they are more on a level, and Hill's Agnes has a self-respect that demands respect from her husband. Her 'Know me for what I am' (p. 85) is as much a challenge as it is a plea.

The crisis of this marriage occurs at the end of Act III, when Agnes agrees to sacrifice their child, condemning him to certain death so that Brand can follow his call. Hill has noted, albeit wryly, that this was the passage with which he concluded his own work on *Brand*.[24] Whatever his reasons, it is certainly possible to conclude that there is a consummating equity between the broken voices at the end of this act, an equity which serves to measure the terrible inequity between the two voices that close the play itself at the end of Act V. These are the final lines of Hill's Act III:

AGNES   (*lifts the child high in her arms*):
          That which you have dared
          to ask of me, O Lord,
          I dare to give to Heaven.
          Accept my sacrifice.
          Now lead me through your night.
          She goes into the house.
          BRAND *stares for a while into space; bursts into*
          tears; clasps his hands over his head; throws
          himself down on the steps and cries out:
BRAND: O Lord, grant me your light!

                                                    (p. 81–2)

Comparison with the other versions makes it clear that Hill has tilted the angles of these desperate lines through the possessive pronouns: 'my sacrifice', 'your night', 'your light'. His Agnes affirms a claim even in the act of renunciation by opposing 'my sacrifice' to 'your night'. Brand hears this challenge, and we understand that his own final line, which seeks to quench Agnes's 'night' with 'light', is as much an answer to Agnes as it is an appeal to God. But Agnes is already out of hearing.

In his *TLS* review of Hill's *Brand*, Kenneth Muir described Hill as 'a fine poet, but not noticeably dramatic in style'; he then commended the way in which Hill had 'successfully altered his style to suit a theatre audience'.[25] Poets may have to go out of their way to be noticed for being dramatic, but the poet of *King Log* and *Tenebrae* has by no means gone out of his way in *Brand*. The grammar and syntax of drama are fundamental to Hill's writing. Hill has himself suggested that 'lyric poetry is necessarily dramatic'.[26] His own poetry is necessarily dramatic in so far as it is deeply informed by the sense that all utterance is answerable, and that it is the condition of human speech to be denied the last word.

7

The Mystery of the Charity of Charles Peguy

Jeffrey Wainwright

'*Ah, les mots, mon vieux, les mots!*'[1]

Take that for your example! But still mourn,
being so moved: éloge and elegy
so moving on the scene as if to cry
'in memory of those things these words were born.'[2]

After the long, shifting account of Péguy in this poem, what are we to take
from him? What sense is to be made, for what will he, who 'commends us to
nothing', serve? The concluding moment of the poem is when we expect
summary, a considered gesture, at least the ceremony of closure even though
it might resemble stiffened custom and a bellowing 'with hoarse dignity into
the wind'. Hill's tone, directed at his own contemplation as well as that of
the reader, concedes little. 'Take that for your example!' mingles defiance, the
clean blow, with surly dismissal. But take what? Take it how? Take Péguy and
his end as an instance, a case to demonstrate some point? Or take him as
exemplary, a model? There is no ready dénouement. The stanza edges towards
a close for the poem's complex meditation in an almost sidelong fashion,
motivated or affected towards its 'cry', the sounds of 'éloge and elegy', eulogy
and lament sliding the words against each other, the French word hinting at
the danger of fulsomeness. The way these words work is entirely character-
istic of the poem, and the eventual concluding 'cry', set as a quotation, retains
the apparent guardedness of a phrase which is 'found' to be appropriate:
'"in memory of those things these words were born."' But it is in fact a
much more certain phrase, and one that embodies a central concern
of the poem in its conjunction of '"those things these words"'. The line asserts

that these now living words bear upon 'things', have a bearing upon them. The poem relates to 'things', the world outside itself, specifically the life lived by Charles Péguy for which it is a work of celebration and sorrow, the genres of 'éloge and elegy'. Nonetheless, although this is asserted, even yet the poem could be words into the wind, carrying at best the euphony of 'éloge and elegy'. Hill's whole poem travels over these two possibilities: circumstances in which the self-sufficiency, the given facts of the world, events themselves, are moved by words, and circumstances – poetry itself may well be one – where words seem without real object and yet are 'moving'. *The Mystery of the Charity of Charles Péguy* is a poem about the potencies of words, their direct issue, their distant weights and attractions, their formation of memories, images and ideologies, their sounds and resonances – about what kinds of things can be done with words.

Phrasing that conjoins 'things' with 'words' echoes that of J.L. Austin's book of lectures *How To Do Things With Words*,[3] and the implications of Austin's ideas are painstakingly taken up by Geoffrey Hill in his essay 'Our Word Is Our Bond'.[4] Austin's interest is in the ramifications of what he calls 'performative utterance', that is the use of words in which 'the issuing of the utterance is the performing of an action – it is not normally thought of as just saying something.'[5] For Austin the 'performative utterance' is an act, and as such stands as a commitment in regard to the things to which the words refer: 'Accuracy and morality alike are on the side of the plain saying that *our word is our bond.*'[6] Thus, when *The Mystery* ... begins with the grim and nearly satiric evocation of the murder of Jean Jaurès amid the bathos of his café supper, the event gives rise to speculation about the part played in this by Péguy's rhetorical attacks upon Jaurès' pacifism. We have a clarification of the issues, a philosopher's crisp identification of questions:

> Did Péguy kill Jaurès? Did he incite *Péguy's rhetorical attacks on Jaurès*
> the assassin? Must men stand by what they write
> as by their camp-beds or their weaponry
> or shell-shocked comrades while they sag and cry?

Did Péguy's utterance constitute, in Austin's terms, a 'perlocutionary act', that is, that his words got someone to do something – as, for instance, closing a door? But through this stanza the questions become less than crisp as the verbs 'incite', and then especially 'stand by', reverberate with their multiple associations. In 'plain saying' does 'stand by' your words mean: (i) be responsible for; (ii) support, stick up for; (iii) guard; (iv) await inspection; (v) be ready to shoot? The verb will cover the comic military cliché 'stand by your beds!', and the support in desperate circumstances for 'shell-shocked comrades while they sag and cry'. It is not easy to comprehend, plainly, what is being asked. And yet this opening section also shows the flowing of the blood that comes of what the poem later calls 'the metaphors of blood' (p. 21). In metaphor, in the spoken and written word, the blood is painless as it spouts; but it can be made real, as by the archetypal political rhetoric of Shakespeare's Mark Antony who puts a tongue in each of the 'poor dumb mouths', the

'ruby lips', of Caesar's wounds and who saw how his trope, in the words of
'*The Mystery* …', 'spoke to the blood' (p. 15). 'In Brutus' name' was there
incitement or over-susceptibility to metaphor?[7] Yet in the whole of the sug-
gested context here, such scrupulous worrying over 'performatives' might
seem beside the point in that all these events, together with their characters
and their intentions, are part of a grotesque and endlessly repetitive perform-
ance:

> History commands the stage wielding a toy gun,
> rehearsing another scene. It has raged so before,
> countless times; and will do, countless times more,
> in the guise of supreme clown, dire tragedian.

The words perform, they are performed, their performance is but part of
history's theatre, now before us in the continuous performance of the cine-
matograph:

> The brisk celluloid clatters through the gate;
> the cortège of the century dances in the street;
> and over and over the jolly cartoon
> armies of France go reeling towards Verdun.

Everything is representation.

Hill's Péguy, like Jaurès, and 'the cortège of the century', is caught behind
glass, on view, still on guard, standing by, bull-headed, and still defending
his 'first position to the last word' as through amid realities, as though there
is some such thing as truth. (Péguy held to truth as an absolute, spoke of his
projected *Cahiers* as *le journal vrai*, and emphasised this commitment by
references to *le vraiment vrai*.) Here he is 'Truth's pedagogue', a naïve idealist
full of contradictions: 'raw veteran', 'Footslogger of genius', 'skirmisher with
grace/and ill-luck', and so a proper figure for our scorn. The tone in this part
of the poem is of wry mockery – even an indulgent patronising that extends
to the cartoon armies of Péguy's fallen comrades, 'the old soldiers of old
France' who 'crowd like good children wrapped in obedience', the *enfants* of
a thousand stricken war-memorials. The wit and word-play ('Dying, your
whole life/fell into place') are distancing and self-protective: who would want
to be implicated with such a man? He can also be accommodated by the
conventional celebrations of tourism, represented to us through the guide's
rote:

> '… this is the wall
> where he leaned and rested, this is the well
>
> from which he drank';

and by statue, 'brave mediocre work/ … cornered in the park'. But across
the grain of this mockery stand the words: 'still Péguy said that Hope is a little

child.' Hill's line here is open, without any of the surrounding ironies. Its slightly awkward rhythm, close to plangency, and the somewhat pedantic inclusion of 'that', makes the line near a rather simple-minded affirmation, an effort to keep faith. The allusion is to Péguy's *Mystère: Le Porche du Mystère de la Deuxième Vertue*:

> Faith and Charity are going somewhere,
>   going purposefully,
> But Hope is like a child, who is not
>   interested in getting to its destination,
>   but is interested in the way itself.[8]

We have 'History' in command of the world, of 'such things' as are shown; but here, faintly, we have the voice that strives to stay aside from the performance, that is without destination, that can do nothing, and yet *is* – 'embattled hope'. If we are seduced past this to any of those accommodations, then Péguy now mocks us.

Resisting the given world requires a vision of something else. In the third section of the poem Hill evokes the lineaments of Péguy's vision, in which this 'Joseph' provides a dream of old France, rural, peaceable, simply religious, living in a steady round of physical and mental labour mutually respected, and, like Joan of Arc (whose spirit suffuses the whole) militant yet not militarist. The strength of Hill's account lies in his suggesting exactly those kinds of details and images that go to make up an indistinct and yet powerful consciousness of attachment and ideal:

> Yours is their dream of France, militant-pastoral:
> musky red gillyvors, the wicker bark
> of clematis braided across old brick
> and the slow chain that cranks into the well
>
> morning and evening.

Here Hill is colouring a version of the 'matter' of France in a similar way to the lustrous images of his portrait of 'Platonic old England' in 'An Apology for the Revival of Christian Architecture in England':

>   Trees shine
> out from their leaves, rocks mildew to moss-green;
> the avenues are spread with brittle floods.[9]

Such images are the real nuclei of the attachments upon which any more conscious articulation or history depends. The lines from *The Mystery ...* continue into such a history:

>   It is Domrémy
> restored; the mystic strategy of Foch
> and Bergson with its time-scent, dour panache
> deserving of martyrdom.

Hill's lines here cut deeper into a complex of notions in which Joan of Arc's native ground blends with the 'militant-pastoral' army of 1914. In achieving this, they perform the very process of memory Bergson describes: 'we feel vaguely that our past remains present to us'; 'a persistence of the past in the present'.[10] Within this animation, in the 'mystic strategy of Foch/and Bergson', two configurations of *élan* are conjoined: that positive quality of attack, of the spirited seizure of the initiative that obsessed French military theory at the start of the Great War in reaction to their supine humiliation of 1870; and Bergson's life principle of *l'élan vital*, the vital, and original, impetus which he opposed to mechanistic and determinist theories of life and evolution. In this phrase Hill catches exactly the ironies of this complex, playing the supposed, on-the-ground actualities of 'strategy' against the other-worldly connotations of 'mystic'. Indeed, by all accounts, the very particulars of Péguy's death, leading his section across a field towards the enemy, upright in a hail of bullets, exhorting the advance, must make him appear the embodiment of such a spirit, at once heroic and quixotic.[11] The contradictions of this moment are returned to time and again in the poem – Péguy, like his men, 'covered in glory and the blood of beetroots.' In one sense it is for 'musky red gillyvors, the wicker bark/of clematis braided across old brick' that Péguy dies.

Yet potent as it is, *real* as it is, the vision is always seen as a fable. This is explicitly stated, but the irony is carried in other ways too. There is a court-yard, 'crimped hedges', pigeons:

> and sunlight pierces the heart-

> shaped shutter-patterns in the afternoon,
> shadows of fleurs-de-lys on the stone floors.

That tongue-in-cheek enjambment across stanzas teases the reader by leading first into sentiment, the affect of the scene, before removing into mere physical description. Also, while the whole poem makes use of French words, phrases, and loan-words, their presence in Section 3, which presents the first version of Péguy's vision, is particularly richly apparent: *archive, domaine, discourse, echelon, cadre, panache*, in addition to the evocative place-names. In English a liberal use of French words and loan-words flourishes the diction, poses it in a particular way that makes us sense the striking of an attitude. The doubts about the substance of this fable are carried partly in these verbal effects, and, as they accrue, come to face *le vraiment vrai*:

> . . .
> is this not true? Truly, if you are wise,
> deny such wisdom . . .

The immediate, insistent truth is that of 'this world', the lean kine of Joseph's dream, the world long ago taken by 'the lords of limit and of contumely'. And it is in this world that Péguy lives, amid the labours and acerbities of controversy: Dreyfus, the '. . . unsold *Cahiers* built like barricades,' the attack on Jaurès, the desperate farce of the murder. Giving himself to the given, this world of street battles, proof-reading, and the tying of parcels, Péguy seeks to redeem it, to transcend it. His entanglement in the whole rhetoric of Jaurès's assassination, however, shows how difficult such transcendence is. Instead it seems it is only mortal pride that he achieves, and the appropriate bathos of his end recurs, this time across a yet more drawn-out enjambment:

> So, you have risen
> above all that and fallen flat on your face
>
> 5
>
> among the beetroots ...

[handwritten marginal note: I also move from the vaguely metaphorical to the literal and literal in a drawn out enjambement.]

The way in which that phrase straddles the two sections mimes the way in which the different responses to Péguy and his attitudes and circumstances persistently overlap and flow into one another. No sooner is one perspective established than it dissolves, and the qualification and the strength of an opposing view come into focus. This is the process of this fifth, middle and longest section of the poem, which returns, far less ironically, to Péguy's vision of 'old France', but yet sees its qualities and possibilities constrained and corrupted. Again, but this time with greater gravity, the meanings impressed by the images of his ideal homeland are traced out in all their deeply sensuous power. It's 'landscape and inner domain' are joined – the outer and the inner, the real, the earth, the conditioned, with the deepest imaginings of the ideal, grace, the unburdened, the free. It is the process of the mind that can achieve this transfiguration, 'the working/of the radical soul'. In this phrase, once more, is the remarkable and characteristic clustering of meaning, with the unelevated noun-participle denoting straightforward, regular activity and labour, and the adjective and noun 'radical', and 'soul', going in apparently different directions – the one downwards to the root (as the succeeding stanzas confirm) though also with political, indeed iconoclastic connotations; and the other upwards towards the ethereal, the heavenly. 'Radical' anchors 'soul', 'soul' irradiates 'radical', and its 'working' connects with a whole series of opposites: the 'sun-showers', hedgers and ditchers become seraphim, 'in a bleak visionary instant', become the 'winged ogives' with the 'criss-cross-trodden ground'. The potency of landscape working through that 'radical soul', '– instinct, intelligence,/memory, call it what you will –', is that it can be internalised. This works subliminally, at a barely perceived level of consciousness where images and associations form indissoluble significance. Here this potency is not only acknowledged, but its sensuousness suffuses the lines:

> Landscape is like revelation; it is both
> singular crystal and the remotest things.
> Cloud-shadows of seasons revisit the earth,
> odourless myrrh borne by the wandering kings.

This deep investiture of feeling and thought in place, in the earth, and the composure that might come of it, derives by specific allusion from the passage in Péguy's own long poem *Ève*, the eighteen stanzas that have the refrain 'Heureux ceux qui sont morts ...', the first of them beginning:

> – Heureux ceux qui sont morts pour la terre charnelle,
> Mais pourvu que ce fût dans une juste guerre.[12]

The phrase will be echoed again in French, but here Hill writes, 'after' these lines:

> Happy are they who, under the gaze of God,
> die for the 'terre charnelle', marry her blood
> to theirs, and, in strange Christian hope, go down
> into the darkness of resurrection ...

The dictionary gives the meanings of 'charnelle' as 'carnal, fleshly ... sensual'.[13] Earlier, in Section 2, the sensuality was displaced into the cheaply diminished 'sun-tanned earth'. But here the word emphasises a physicality to the attraction – 'marry her blood/to theirs,' – that is consummated in burial, the word in English evoking of course 'charnel ground'. This 'investiture', however, does not entirely derive from Péguy's poem, but coincides with a concern previously evident in Hill's work, for instance in *Mercian Hymns*, IV:

> I was invested in mother-earth, the crypt of roots
>   and endings.

In fact, the whole working between place and history through 'instinct, intelligence,/memory,' especially with its recognition of the vivid persistence of the child's memory, is common to both poems. The particular details of the country are known as they are in child's-play; and it is into this old intimate familiarity that the dead, 'in strange Christian hope, go down':

> into sap, ragwort, melancholy thistle,
> almondy meadowsweet, the freshet-brook
> rising and running through small wilds of oak,
> past the elder-tump that is the child's castle.

Poignantly, the child's tin soldiers, and those 'scarred most sacred', put us in mind of the adult legions lost among the haystacks and streams of this same landscape. But it is now an old country, worn and antique, preserved but bygone, and its sorrows quiver with an erect but hopeless dignity:

> ... proud tears,
> proud tears, for the forlorn hope, the guerdon
> of Sedan, 'oh les braves gens!', English Gordon
> stepping down sedately into the spears.

The word-play, 'guerdon'/'Gordon', 'Sedan'/(Sudan)/'sedately', echoes one defeat with another, and while it does not take to the advantage of satire, nonetheless signals a withdrawal from the world whose elegy has just been so beautifully and sympathetically made. Swiftly, then, the myths of this same world are dissolved as the aura of Péguy's idealisations gives way to a sketch more familiar from another version of *la France profonde*, that of Zola's *La Terre*, a world of

>   familial debts and dreads,
>   keepers of old scores, the kindly ones
>   telling their beady sous ...

For all its magnetism, Péguy remains crucially alienated from this myth-world and its religion, and looks from 'its truth and justice, to a kind of truth,/a justice hard to justify.' Truth, justice, the ideal over-riding absolutes that Péguy saw at stake in the Dreyfus affair, and that he sought to manifest and further in all his labours as writer, printer, proof-reader, salesman of the *Cahiers*: these words play before our eyes, echoing back to the 'juste guerre', and beyond to the ideal goal of Péguy's work, and of this poem, which must itself be 'le mot juste'.[14]

The sixth section takes up the word immediately:

>   To dispense, with justice; or, to dispense *the moving of a*
>   with justice. Thus the catholic god of France, *comma*
>   with honours all even, honours all, even
>   the damned in the brazen Invalides of Heaven.

How to do things with words! The simple dispensing with that first comma effects the instant transition by which the ideal of Péguy's nation becomes part of the reactionary ideology embodied in the persecutors of Dreyfus. The 'labourers cap in hand' stand now before 'the catholic god of France'. The play with words is here at its most sardonically intense, a grim exchange of meaning, neat about-turns whereby things are brought round to the sanguine convenience of those 'lords of limit and of contumely'. But the word-play directed here is only part of the entire fabric of that with which the poem is composed. If words are to be regarded as action, as 'bonds', and not as 'just saying something', then the clarity of what is said, Austin's 'plain saying', is obviously of vast importance.

In his discussion of Austin in 'Our Word Is Our Bond', Hill eventually subscribes to the philosopher's principle of commitment to the words one utters; but he finds him worryingly complacent about the complexities that surround the achievement of 'accuracy' and 'plain saying', and too confident of his own capacity for transparent exposition, despite the sense that Isaiah Berlin attributes to him of 'the complex and recalcitrant nature of things'.[15] Hill's effort, in his essay, is to direct attention to that complexity and recalcitrance, and its inevitable implications for language. So, 'the very idea of a "transparent" verbal medium is itself an inherited and inherent opacity. Where there is "semantic content" it is most likely that there will be semantic "refraction", "infection" of various kinds'.[16] Hill quotes Coleridge: 'our chains rattle, even while we are complaining of them'.[17] Thus, the aphoristic flourish with which Austin concludes one part of his argument, 'our word is our bond', is itself capable of varying ambiguity: 'bond' as 'reciprocity, covenant, fiduciary symbol', and also as 'shackle, arbitrary constraint, closure of possibility'.[18] Hill writes: '"Our word is our bond" is an exemplary premise, but if we take it in the positivist sense alone we take only part of its mass and weight. "Our chains rattle . . ." is the inescapable corollary for any writer who takes up Austin's stringent sentiment.'[19] So the radical working with words, their 'mass and weight', 'refractions' and 'infections', working in 'the crypt of roots and endings', means working with the most fundamental senses of constraint and freedom, necessity and possibility, finality and hope. The *word-play* which is so basic to Hill's method acknowledges the forces of each side of these dichotomies.

Ambiguity, in one respect is the flexing of the determinations of language. Its play with us, as we seek to use and deploy it, demonstrates the frustrations of our own interventions towards meaning. In this respect, the word binds, ambiguity is the function of 'shackle, arbitrary constraint, closure of possibility'. Literature might be seen as being able to turn this, together with other kinds of the common features among words, to advantage, since within its fictions it can exercise what Roland Barthes calls 'creative transgression', with the play among words delighted in as 'defections from the semantic system'.[20] This might give us the pleasurable nihilism of a Feste, his lady's 'corrupter of words', in his confusion of Viola:

> FESTE: Why, sir, her name's a word, and to dally
> with that word might make my sister wanton.
> But, indeed, words are very rascals, since
> bonds disgraced them.
> VIOLA: Thy reason, man?
> FESTE: Troth, sir, I can yield you none without
> words; and words are grown so false, I am
> loath to prove reason with them.[21]

Such a view of literature, at any rate, if not of language at large, as cheerfully divorcing words from any bond or troth, might well have appealed to J.L. Austin, who, in a manner somewhat by the by, lights upon poetry for instances of where performatives need not 'be taken "seriously" . . . I must not be joking, for example, nor writing a poem.'[22] Austin would presumably not have wished to deprive the poet and his reader of their *jouissance*, but would in turn expect them to acknowledge his argument that 'a performative utterance will, for example, be *in a peculiar way* hollow or void if said by an actor on the stage, or if introduced in a poem, or spoken in soliloquy.'[23] Accepting this, and so the playful fictionality of his utterance, offers a certain liberation to the author of the kind Hill associates with Sir Philip Sidney's dictum that 'the Poet he nothing affirmeth, and therefore never lieth'. Further, by 'faining notable images of vertues, vices, or what els', the poet, Hill suggests is 'generously propositioned': 'If he will accept that his art is a miniature emblem or analogy of res publica rather\ than a bit of real matter lodged in the body politic there is much scope for the exercise of serious and refined example.'[24] *CL. p - 143*

However, if obsession with ambiguity and the play between words, and between words and things, might lead in these ways to an acknowledgment of how we are conditioned, it can also, as Hill's essay and this poem show, lead to other possibilities, difficult though these may be. The sounding of words and their reverberations, from the constant reminder of their contiguities presented by the half-rhymes and rhymes of *The Mystery* ..., to their multiple ambiguities ('must men stand by what they write') presents opportunity for suggestive connection. This is effected not by what Jonathan Culler calls 'an unseemly rush from word to world',[25] but by exploring the ways in which, as John Crowe Ransom puts it, 'the density or connotativeness of poetic language reflects the world's density'.[26] This exploration seeks to delineate relations between word and world, and to sense and reveal the immanence of sentiments and ideas through words. This 'fathoming of words as "heavy bodies"' (Hill is speaking of, and using, Hopkins's phrase here)[27] does not become merely the juggling of nuances, or, in Paul Ricoeur's term 'a case of vagueness'; rather it is a polysemic understanding which constitutes, as Ricoeur says, 'the outline of an order, and, for that very reason, a counter-measure to imprecision'.[28] It will provide 'a kind of truth,/a justice hard to justify.'

Concluding even part of an argument – inevitably not without some rhetoric – and so setting oneself within some 'kind of truth', immediately opens up a different kind of problem. In *The Mystery* ..., Dreyfus's judges dispense 'a justice hard to justify'; indeed, they dispense with justice altogether: '"A mort le Juif!"' Regarding this we have every reason for indignation, and then an articulate human despair, and then, by the worth of this mortification, a sense of moral redemption that is ultimately superior and self-regarding. Righteousness, alienation, even martyrdom, bring here, as in Hill's 'Lachrimae' sequence,[29] their own improper rewards:

> We are the occasional just men who sit
> in gaunt self-judgment on their self-defeat,
> the élite hermits, secret orators
> of an old faith devoted to new wars.

The violence of virtue, 'the wrath of the peacemakers', the self-inflicted-wounded, 'ecstatic at such pain', make their contribution, and

> Once more the truth advances; and again
> the metaphors of blood begin to flow.

Faced with a figure like Péguy, with his stubborn commitment to absolutes, his vulnerability and worldly defeat and self-defeat, we are eager to bestow the cachet of martyrdom. The idea of eventual, transcendent victory in the realm of 'higher things' consoles and provides meaning for his life. But this

consolation is suspect, the righteousness of martyrs is exposed and even Christ's salute is unlooked for. The remainder of the poem focuses principally upon the war, and so upon Péguy's death and the sufferings of the soldiers at large. His colleague Daniel Halévy, in his biography of Péguy, wrote of the young soldiers of 1914 that 'they were going to die. They consented to that but not meaning that their death was some incident in a butcher's shop. They wanted it to be a sacrifice illuminated by a certainty.'[30] The lines from Péguy's *Ève* offer such a certainty, and 'we still dutifully read "heureux ceux qui sont morts."', but the tone now is more sceptical. Bergson developed a theory of 'duration', a qualitative concept rather than the quantitative one of chronological extensity, a concept of process, of evolution, that he saw as denying determinism: '*we endure* and are therefore free'.[31] A less philosophical notion of what it is to 'endure' is picked at through the specific word and its root in these lines from Section 7:

> Drawn on the past
> these presences <u>endure</u>; they have not ceased
> to act, suffer, crouching into the hail
> like labourers of their own memorial
>
> or those who worship at its marble rote,
> their many names one name, the common '<u>dur</u>'
> built into <u>duration, the endurance</u> of war;
> blind Vigil herself, helpless and <u>obdurate</u>.

The longing must be that something of them will prove durable in purpose or memory as, 'flesh into dust', their 'dreams of oblivion' replace paradise. The quest to attach meaning is yet more desperate through the eighth section, where the ironies of 'pour la patrie' are painfully evoked, though without ready satire. Rather there is a real, regretful texture in the overblown pretensions of 'la France' to gather all her fallen children to the nation's 'august plenitude'. What can be held onto as 'the mind leaps/for its salvation' diminishes to a most abstract point of faith, barely grasped:

> Whatever strikes and maims us it is not
> fate, to our knowledge.

Eventually, it comes down to the ideal of self-abnegation: 'Say "we/possess nothing; try to hold on to that."'

As the soldiers' 'last thoughts tetter the furrows,' a dreadful simplicity and reduction appears through the poem. Thoughts, aspirations, love – 'mother, dad,' – become a spattering across the pocked field. All through the poem we have seen the mind at work in the world, in the matter of ethics, language, ideology, attachments, visionary possibility. In the final section of the poem, all those intricacies of living that Péguy had fought over in his life and writing, and on which he finally turned his back with the stoic, or ironic, acceptance of the barest choice ('"Rather the Marne than the *Cahiers*."') – all these reduce to the simple distinction between life and death:

At Villeroy the copybook lines of men
rise up and are erased. Péguy's cropped skull
dribbles its ichor, its poor thimbleful,
a simple lesion of the complex brain.

And what is this human substance? *Ichor:* (i) the ethereal fluid, not blood, supposed to flow in the veins of the gods; (ii) (in transferred and figurative use) blood; a fluid likened to the blood of animals; (iii) (in pathology) a watery, acrid discharge from certain wounds and sores. (*OED*) This contradictory matter of the self soaks into the earth, and what it truly is, what Péguy finally gives, 'having composed his great work, his small body,' is a mystery. In the involved sentence over this and the succeeding three stanzas in Section 10, Hill approaches the meaning of Péguy's death. A sequence of adjectival clauses build towards the centrally placed main clause, which is, after that expectation: 'he commends us to nothing'. Péguy's testament, as the sentence moves on from that point, is wordless, 'the body's prayer,/the tribute of his true passion' for 'the Virgin of innumerable charities.' However great that work is, or however slight a trickle into the soil, he gives his all, whether in token of the Virgin's endless love of human beings, or of the tinkling of beady sous into countless collecting boxes. If Péguy managed such a resignation – at least ' "Rather the Marne than the *Cahiers*." ' – then he leaves us no conviction of apotheosis of any kind, no certain commendation. Deprived of such ready meaning, the possibility hovers that 'moving' as they might be, the words of the poem float in their own element, without connection in the world of 'things': 'Encore plus douloureux et doux', the actualities of human pain rendered into the abstractions of 'affliction'. Throughout the poem the density, self-awareness and sensuous richness of the language has anticipated this possibility and formed its own critique. What is exemplary is this proceeding engagement in language, if not the destination, then 'the way itself'. This corresponds to the poem's portrait of Péguy, for he is exemplary in that he presents recalcitrant complexity, ambiguity, contradiction. The way is that of the footslogger, the pedagogue, the stubborn vigilant, doing his stint – no panache, no élan, but movement by inches. It is the complexity, ambiguity, contradiction of *things*, and of the *words* that would do things properly. Hill has done his Péguy justice: 'the ethical and the esthetic are one';[32] his great poem is 'a bit of real matter lodged in the body politic'.[33]

II

8

War and the pity

Jon Silkin

In Blake's poem 'The Tyger' the last but one stanza reads:

> When the stars threw down their spears
> And water'd heaven with their tears:
> Did he smile his work to see?
> Did he who made the Lamb make thee?[1]

'Thee' is of course the tyger, and here Blake is not so much offering the reader a manichaean God, responsible for the creation of not only good but evil also, as recording his perplexity at having to confront the image of one with the image of its opposite. The creatures are not reconciled but face each other in mutual, terrifying recognition, but the terror is as much Blake's as it is the two creatures'. The complexity and directness of this kind of response is part of the character of Hill's achievement in *For the Unfallen* and *King Log*. It is what Merle Brown recognised in *Double Lyric*,[2] and Charles Tomlinson before him in his essay 'Poetry Today'.[3] Hill's strength, not his lyric gift, extends across two adversary positions in a self-auditing compaction.

Thus, with Wilfred Owen for instance, the two modes that Owen could not always bring into one poem are pity and anger; pity for the sufferer and anger for those who are the agents of the suffering. When these constituents are not together, the responses run the risk of dilution;[4] where Owen brings them into qualifying interaction, he writes some of the best poems of this century. If this claim seems large, I ask the reader to consider the way in which such a complex set of irreconcilable responses are brought into direct relation with each other in the poem 'Insensibility', or to consider the complex blend of irony and compassion in 'Strange Meeting'. It is my contention that Hill produces his best poetry in *King Log* when he is engaged in expressing conflict of a comparable intensity and for which he found, after his own fashion, a remarkable strength and directness which neither compromised nor was compromised by ironic subtlety and delicacy.

To help us consider how this doubleness evolved, here is a judgement Charles Sisson makes in his essay on Hill:

> They [Hill's explanations concerning *Funeral Music*] seem to imply a notion of the sequence as artefact, as something worked towards and which suggests a growing distance between the poetic impulse and the words which finally appear on the page – a gain in architectonics, perhaps, but at a price which is so often paid, by all but the greatest writers, in a loss of immediacy ... *Funeral Music* bristles with lines and phrases of indubitable directness.[5]

So, the touchstone here is directness. In 'The Stone Man', the first of 'Soliloquies' from *King Log*, there is the beautifully direct recreation of 'My father':

> My father scuffed clay into the house.
> He set his boots on the bleak iron
> Of the hearth; ate, drank, unbuckled, slept.

And in the fourth of 'Four Poems Regarding the Endurance of Poets', 'A Valediction to Osip Mandelshtam', we read:

> A few men glare at their hands; others
> Grovel for food in the roadside field.

That is much more than merely 'direct', but it is direct. Two books beyond these poems, in *Tenebrae*, there are the rhymed sonnets 'An Apology for the Revival of Christian Architecture in England', headed with a quotation from Coleridge's *Anima Poetae*: 'the spiritual, Platonic old England ...'. In '2. Damon's Lament for his Clorinda, Yorkshire 1654':

> The tributaries of the Sheaf and Don
> bulge their dull spate, cramming the poor bridges.
>
> The North Sea batters our shepherds' cottages
> from sixty miles. No sooner has the sun
> swung clear above earth's rim than it is gone.

Like other poems in this collection, this is 'as simple as [Rosenberg's] ordinary talk',[6] and for that we must be glad. It is direct, especially in those last two lines quoted, where 'swung' kinetically enacts the sun's circular transit: huge and swift. But where in the quotations from the earlier *King Log* the direct-ness comes in the character of the expressed experience, for which there is no finer, more delicate intermediary than directness, the simplicity in this later quotation from *Tenebrae* – excepting perhaps that of the 'sun' – is one of

style. There is nothing to compose from conflicted response into directness.
There is no apprehension.

It is as though Sisson's exemplary advice has been misconstrued. Where
before there was directness – more than Sisson allowed – there is now simpl-
icity alone, which is a lesser achievement. Where there was conflict and
coadjutant power, there is now often brilliant paradox. The tensions have
been eased away by a use of paradox. And where in *King Log* we had conflict,
we now have brilliance enriching itself with beauty:

> Platonic England grasps its tenantry
>
> where wild-eyed poppies raddle tawny farms
> ('7. Loss and Gain')

and

> the squire's effigy bewigged with frost,
> and hobnails cracking puddles before dawn.
> In grange and cottage girls rise from their beds
>
> by candlelight and mend their ruined braids.
> Touched by the cry of the iconoclast,
> how the rose-window blossoms with the sun!
> ('13. The Herefordshire Carol')

It is striking and it is brilliant. Wit in that eighteenth-century sense of 'quick-
ened imagination' is there, but it is there to illuminate itself rather than to
help into difficult existence the conflicted life of another or other beings.

Between *King Log* and *Tenebrae* there was the 'quite quickly' written[7]
Mercian Hymns. This contains a more fictionalised account of conflict (Offa's
tyranny) than, for instance, 'September Song'. There, the naked substance of
suffering and its contingent carefully offered pity is no closer to reality, it
might be objected, than the fiction of Offa's tyranny, Hill's creation, which
he bases on history. Yet the sense of the victim in 'September Song', the
victims in 'A Valediction to Osip Mandelshtam', as well as the predator-
victims in 'Funeral Music', all suggest something more and stronger than a
fictionalised account – fact impresses fiction. The sense of this pain, this woe,
and these complex responses, in a poetry that matters both to the people of
whom the poems are made, and to the poet who makes the poems, is almost
everywhere palpable.

In *Mercian Hymns* I feel that the conflicting responses from which many
of the poems in *King Log* were made are temporarily in abeyance. There are
exceptions, the beautifully tender XXV:

> I speak this in memory of my grandmother, whose
> childhood and prime womanhood were spent in the
> nailer's darg. . . .

It is one
thing to celebrate the 'quick forge', another to cradle
a face hare-lipped by the searing wire.

The difference between *Mercian Hymns* and *Tenebrae*, as opposed to *King Log*, may be understood by comparing *Tenebrae* with Hill's first book, *For the Unfallen*. Both are preoccupied with style, and with a writer's experience in relation to what is avowedly not his experience. Both are in part made from this complex of conditions. But if *King Log* has been Hill's watershed so far, the difference between the first and fourth volumes with regard to rhetoric is that in *Tenebrae* beauty is triumphant, beauty that is the rage of art; whereas in *For the Unfallen*, despite the archness, the rhetoric, prickly and at times brittle though it is, seems a constituent of the poet's argument with himself. The rhetoric cannot help itself; but also, since it cannot, it might as well (as Hill has elsewhere suggested) make the best of itself. Rhetoric, as Hill indicated in his essay 'Redeeming the Time', is not something to be ashamed of.[8] It is not a meretricious adjunct to true poetry, but, as it is in the first two books, a consented-to expression of conflicting attitudes, of doubleness. The best poems in *King Log* have had removed the patina which overlay some of the poems in the previous collection; there the rhetoric is a direct product of the conflict and doubleness, so that the focus is, as a consequence, sharper than before. This makes these poems in *King Log* – those I shall be discussing – amongst the best of our post-war period.

The Second World War and the questions raised by it were still being struggled with in his poetry. The past – the camps, combat, torture, exile, even the 'simple straightforward death' – could not be relegated to the past. History is not in that way done with. 'September Song', a poem centred on an anonymous victim of a camp, and 'Funeral Music', a poem that arises in part out of the Battle of Towton (one ferocious product of the Wars of the Roses) are both in different ways poems of present history. If the soul is immortal, its body's acts are so also – those largely evil as well as those principally good. The slate may not be wiped clean.

Forgiveness is only a somewhat different matter, for forgiveness, in offering love to the offender, works to recognise, not delete, the act. This is why charity – 'Caritas' – even if it is 'fat', is so important a figure in Hill's 'war' poems. The contradiction is one on which I have touched in discussing Owen's compassion and anger. Where Owen is all compassion he risks being both too dulcet and self-indulgent, as though the response of compassion provided him with a fully satisfying feeling which was, however, in danger of offsetting the emphasis on his fellow-sufferers. The related risk was that of dissolving the guilt of the reluctant killer in an anodyne compassion, which the intrusion of anger would not however permit.

Hill's 'fat Caritas' ('Funeral Music, 2') operates with a similar double function. Yes, charity (love) is required, and yes, forgiveness in also necessary. But we must remember that charity begins in another's misfortune: it is not there for the benefit of the one who gives it. If it grows fat on another's

action is immortal, the soul is too.

misfortune, let it slim by attempting to reduce the misfortune. Similarly with forgiveness. Forgiveness does not erase the evil act but, on the contrary, recognises its existence and then offers love. To use an adjective from Rosenberg's playlet *Moses*, it is 'all-eyed': 'Like naked light seizing the all-eyed soul.'[9] And this is why, in case I seem to be making of him a 'war' poet, Hill's poems are at once 'platonic' and palpable; the ideal (real) act stands behind the one actually committed. The platonic act is love (and justice) but only, as Hill indicated, 'If we lived in an ideal world'.[10] The function of charity is at once to offer what is necessary and to expose what the world in this respect is deficient in.

*   *   *

Of the forty-one poems in *King Log*, twenty-one are preoccupied with war or violence. I set out below some of the recurring preoccupations in these poems.

1 The relation of pity to the victim; the relationship between innocence and the suffering victim; and the (supposed) innocence of the one giving pity.

2 The acknowledgement of the role of the poet, tacit or otherwise, in the poem he or she creates and in which the writer's pity is explicit.

3 The recognition of the damned, and the relationship between them and the poet.

4 All these seen in the contexts of war, or oppression.

'September Song'[11] involves many of these concerns, and so does 'Ovid in the Third Reich', although in a more mediated way because of the fiction the poem uses – the fiction of Ovid speaking as if he were in exile within the Third Reich. We can add to these: 'Shiloh Church . . .', the third of the 'Locust Songs'; 'Funeral Music' itself; 'Four Poems Regarding the Endurance of Poets'; and the second of the 'Three Baroque Meditations'. *For the Unfallen* has several poems that work towards some of these concerns; although 'Of Commerce and Society' is the sequence most evidently concerned with what becomes in *King Log* Hill's flesh-and-soul commitment to an exploration of the individual's relationship with violence. The best of the poems in *King Log* work out of a doubleness of contradiction inherent in the relationship between the individual and violence, the rhetoric thus produced being of the drama of such conflict. The suffering artist will deplore the violence in himself and in others, but the burnishing of style which is done as the artist works on this painful material affords the writer a compensatory pleasure. Something of this contradiction is expressed by Shelley in 'The Triumph of Life':

> 'See the great bards of elder time, who quelled
>
> 'The passions which they sung, as by their strain
> May well be known: their living melody
> Tempers its own contagion to the vein
>
> 'Of those who are infected with it – I
> Have suffered what I wrote, or viler pain!
> And so my words have seeds of misery –[12]

'Ovid in the Third Reich' opens *King Log* and stands therefore as admonitory spirit to the reader of the book; the poem uses many of the concerns and self-admonishing responses with which the other poems are composed. The poem is concerned with inner exile. Ovid was thought to have been exiled from Rome because he knew something that might, or would, embarrass Augustus. In Hill's poem, Ovid is both exiled from Rome and exiled to within the Third Reich. But Hill is also paralleling the condition of Rome with that of the Third Reich (as Simone Weil did).[13] By placing Ovid in the latter context, he indicates how far many poets, aspirants towards, or occasionally receptors of, the ideal, are exiles within the condition of their societies. They may also condone the acts of their societies. That, at least, is a reading of the poem's premises.

The poem uses a number of the poet's devices (we all have our devices) – the pun, the refurbished cliché: 'Innocence is no earthly weapon' and 'I have learned one thing: not to look down/So much upon the damned.' (I prefer the earlier 'Too much',[14] because it is more pointed and abrasive). But most of all, the poem utters an awareness of how, in the eyes of the divine, the damned have as much right to the whole abject condition of oppression, and an understanding of it (since they are its creators) as we, the allegedly innocent, have in our supposed role:

> They, in their sphere,
> Harmonize strangely with the divine
> Love. I, in mine, celebrate the love-choir.
> ('Ovid in the Third Reich')

Coleridge distinguishes between primary and secondary imagination. Something of Plato's cave inheres in the distinction:

> The primary imagination I hold to be the living power and prime agent of all human perception, and as a repetition in the finite mind of the eternal act of creation in the infinite I AM. The secondary I consider an echo of the former, co-existing with the conscious will, yet still as identical with the primary in the kind of its agency ...[15]

For Hill, divine love is the primary act and we, in secondary echoing act, form – each of us – a part of God's 'love-choir', even if it is the poet who continues to 'celebrate' the choir. Love is the attribute of God, and our love can, it appears, only be an imitation of his.

In 'Shiloh Church, 1862: Twenty-Three Thousand', the subtitle refers to the number slaughtered in this battle of the American Civil War. But where Allen Tate in 'Ode to the Confederate Dead' contemplates a vista of the slain ('Row after row with strict impunity'),[16] Hill recognises the original continental inhabitant – 'the damned red-man' – following on from whom the Calvinist 'tribe' divides and destroys itself, and the Indian, in the sight of God: 'a slow/Bloody unearthing of the God-in-us.' 'Unearthing' suggests not only a removing from this earth of one another, but also a digging up of what ought to be sacred, as if by killing each other we unburied the dead. The line also suggests a patient excavation of all that is atavistic and destructive in our natures, what had better remain buried if it cannot be denied its activity. The slain and their battle-field are indeed unearthly.

> A field
> After battle utters its own sound
> Which is like nothing on earth, but is earth.
> ('Funeral Music, 3')

'Shiloh Church ...' concludes with 'But with what blood, and to what end, Shiloh?' The ambiguous role of the church as a constituent in an ambiguous struggle serves to underline the question. For 'end' yields at least two meanings: 'termination', and 'purpose'; and in doing so indicates that termination need not include teleology. Consider the bitter lines in Owen's 'Exposure':

> Therefore, not loath, we lie out here; therefore were born,
> For love of God seems dying.[17]

Owen's soldier enlists for a moral end, but that purpose seems likely to be overtaken either by bitterness at the experience of war, or else by death. A similar play on the two meanings of 'end' (purpose and termination) occurs in 'September Song': 'Things marched,/sufficient, to that end.'

Hill's use of language, and choice of words, has been noticed – often, one feels, to the detriment of his themes. The compressed language is intimately bound up with what it is conveying. This is true of many poets, but true to an unusual degree with Hill in *King Log*. It is true in another sense. The language itself is unlike most other current writing, and there is an unusually self-conscious pointing on the part of the poet to the language. This is not because he wishes to draw attention to it for its own sake, but because the language both posits his concerns, and is itself – in the way it is used – an instance of them. His use of language is itself an instance of his moral concerns, and, at the same time, the sensuous gesture that defines them. It is therefore difficult to speak of his themes without coming first into necessary contact with his language.

Hill's use of irony in *King Log* is ubiquitous, but it is not, usually, of the non-participatory and mandarin sort. It articulates the collision of events or brings them together out of scruple and concern, and for this a more or less regular and simple use of syntax is needed, and used. 'September Song' begins:

> Undesirable you may have been, untouchable
> you were not.

A concentration camp victim. There is 'play' even in the subtitle 'born 19.6.32 – deported 24.9.42' where the natural event of birth is placed, simply, beside the human and murderous 'deported', as if the latter were of the same order and inevitability for the victim; which, in some senses, it was. Even here, the zeugmatic wit is fully employed. The irony of conjuncted meanings between 'undesirable' (touching on both sexual desire and racism), and 'untouchable' (which exploits a similar ambiguity but reverses the emphases) is unusually dense and simple. The confrontation is direct and unavoidable, and this directness is brought to bear on the reader not only by the vocabulary, but by the balancing directness of the syntax. This stanza contains one of Hill's dangerous words – dangerous because of its too-frequent use, and because these words sometimes unleash (though not here) a too evident irony:

> Not forgotten
> or passed over at the proper time.

'Proper' brings together the idea of bureaucratically correct 'as calculated' by the logistics of the 'final solution' and by the particular camp's timetable; it also contrasts the idea of the mathematically 'correct' with the morally into-lerable. It touches, too, on the distinction between what is morally right, and what is conventionally acceptable, and touches incidentally upon the way in which the conventionally acceptable is often used to cloak the morally unac-ceptable. It is one of Hill's grim jokes, deployed in such a way that the laughter is precisely proportionate to the needs of ironic exposure. It is when the irony is in excess of the situation that the wit becomes mannered. But here it does not. So the poem continues, remorselessly:

> As estimated, you died. Things marched,
> sufficient, to that end.

One feels the little quibbling movement in 'As estimated, you died', as, with-out wishing to verbalise it, Hill points to the disturbing contrast between the well-functioning timetable and what it achieved. 'Things marched' has the tread of pompous authority which is immediately qualified by the painfully accurate recognition that just so much energy was needed, and released, for the extermination. 'Sufficient' implies economy, but it also implies a conscious qualification of the authoritarian tread. The quiet function of unpretentious machinery fulfilled its programme, perhaps more lethally so because 'quiet' and efficient. One also notices here how the lineation gauges, exactly, the flow and retraction of meaning and impulse, and how this exact rhythmical flow is so much a part of the sensuous delivery of response and evaluation. It is speech articulated, but the lineation provides, via the convention of verse line-ending, a formal control of rhythm and of sense emphasis by locking with, or breaking, the syntactical flow. Thus in the third stanza, the syntax is broken by the lineation exactly at those parts at which the confession, as it were, of the poem's (partial) source is most painful:

> (I have made
> an elegy for myself it
> is true)[18]

The slightly awkward break after 'it' not only forces the reading speed down to a word-by-word pace, in itself an approximation to the pain of the confession, but emphasises the whole idea. By placing emphasis on the unspecifying pronoun 'it', Hill is able to say two things: that the elegy was made for himself (at least, in part) since in mourning another one is also commiserating with one's own condition:

> When we chant
> 'Ora, ora pro nobis' it is not
> Seraphs who descend to pity but ourselves.
> ('Funeral Music, 5')

But 'it' may also refer to the whole process: I have made an elegy for myself, as we all do, but I have also made an elegy on a 'true' event. True imaginatively, true in detailed fact; both, for someone other than myself. Thus he is also to point to the difficulty of the poet who wishes, for a variety of reasons, to approach the monstrousness of such events, but has compunction about doing so. He tactfully touches, for instance, on the overweening ambition of the poet who hitches his talent to this powerful subject, thereby giving his work an impetus to which it may not be fully entitled, since only the victim herself would be entitled to derive this kind of 'benefit'. But he also modestly pleads, I think, with 'it/is true' that whatever the reasons for his writing such an elegy, a proper regard for the victim, a true and unambitious feeling, was present and used. I hope enough has been said here to point to Hill's use of irony at its best, and to indicate that the tact with which he uses language is not a convention of manners which he is inertly content to remain immersed in, but an active employment of the convention as it co-operates with his scrupulousness. The scrupulousness, like the pity, is in the language. The theme permeates it.

In the final stanza the concentration is upon the living – us – who cannot now, 'after such knowledge',[19] assume the selves which we were. No growth is possible, as it is possible in a season of 'mellow fruitfulness'; which season contrasts in us now with the skeletal remains of the camp prisoners. For us, Hill appears to suggest, where before the autumn fruits were (as for Keats in 'To Autumn') plump and acceptable, they now appear to 'fatten' in overproduction – an obscenity. Yet in reverse association, the fattening brings to mind ideas of being fatted for sacrifice. Thus Keats's subsidiary point in the fourth stanza of 'Ode on a Grecian Urn': the 'smoke of harmless fires' will sting the eyes and provoke harmless tears for other than harmless acts. In the concluding line of 'September Song', 'plenty' denotes not only the plenitude of harvest, therefore, but also the abundance of suffering and, for both the victims and us, degradation. The tone-mixture in this line is complex; we hear lamentation, irony and indignation.

The first of the eight unrhymed fourteen-line poems of 'Funeral Music' opens with: 'Processionals in the exemplary cave,' – presumably Plato's. In the philosopher's cave we are permitted to see shadows, imitations of the ideal, and this whole is a parable of the imitative condition which we human creatures are in. We at best aspire to the ideal, and our actions are the imperfect replication of ideal forms. This, presumably, is the basis of satire, the exploiting of the discrepancy between the conduct of the one satirised and the norm from which he or she departs. What is unclear, in the first poem, is whether the fire that 'Flares in the pit' places the reader back in Plato's cave, or whether this is some pit in which executions are taking place, for whatever 'necessities' of state. Even if the latter is the case, the effect of 'ghosting upon stone' is to refer back – through the execution of the perhaps rather 'nice', perhaps somewhat self-regarding martyrs – to the ideal and its shadow. The poem, at any rate, sets up the way we are to background the ideal and thus read the other seven poems.

Poems 2 and 3 refer us to the Shiloh-like slaughters of Towton, each side dependant on the other to consummate ('Tup' in 'Funeral Music, 3') their mutual destruction. The 'marriage-blood' of the dying is so expressed as to remind us that, potentially, these were human beings with the capacity for procreation; they are now married not to a mate, but to their mutually inflicted death, and to Christ. But negatively so, for it is not a marriage in a willing assent to the living deeds of the good life but, on the contrary, to dying ('For I have murdered where I should not kill'[20]) and to that which stands contrary to Christ's code of pacifism.

'Funeral Music, 7' concentrates the moral vision of all eight poems within the vision of the battlefield; it has some of the didactic power of *Everyman*, and some of its power of lament:

> Methink, alas, that I must be gone
> To make my reckoning and my debts pay,
> For I see my time is nigh spent away.
> Take example, all ye that this do hear or see,
> How they that I loved best do forsake me,
> Except my Good Deeds that bideth truly.[21]

Here is Hill's poem:

> 'Prowess, vanity, mutual regard,
> It seemed I stared at them, they at me.
> That was the gorgon's true and mortal gaze:
> Averted conscience turned against itself.'
> A hawk and a hawk-shadow. 'At noon,
> As the armies met, each mirrored the other;
> Neither was outshone. So they flashed and vanished
> And all that survived them was the stark ground
> Of this pain. I made no sound, but once
> I stiffened as though a remote cry
> Had heralded my name. It was nothing . . .'
> Reddish ice tinged the reeds; dislodged, a few
> Feathers drifted across; carrion birds
> Strutted upon the armour of the dead.

Our being martial has a part of its rationale in vanity. The more we give conscience the slip ('Averted conscience') the more we are vulnerable to those consequences we thus ignore. 'A hawk and a hawk-shadow' is an ironic pointer to the cave equation: we are the imperfect versions of the ideal predator, whose shadow we are. But the hawk's shadow is real enough, a sign of the immanence of our mutual predatoriness which in fact achieved reciprocal destruction. There is honour, even glory: 'Neither was outshone'. Yet in vanity we mirror each other; and in the moment of the mirroring, which is also ('flashed') the moment of ignition, we fight, blind to each other ('dazzled'), destroy each other, and vanish. The virtue of this poem is that the account is not only moving but further fleshed by the strange, alien presence of 'I': 'I made no sound', 'I stiffened', thought I heard 'my name'. A survivor, a witness? Whatever identity 'I' has, it is as a person of actual, true, moral power that the figure lives. And it is this person's being so alive that makes the morality of the first part the more convincing, poised delicately as it is between moral vision and event. 'It was nothing', for no one is left, either in conscience or in living fact, who can call his name, and the 'stark ground/ Of this pain' offers a basis for 'nothing'. The carrion birds that strut on the armour of the dead reflect the vanity of the warriors. But the birds are themselves seen as being as foolish (and predatory) as the warriors – as incapable of perceiving how they are observed, in a performance of what they would not dare to do were these soldiers alive. The witness is saved from appearing self-righteous by a posture that expresses perception, humility and bewilderment. Understanding is what flows through and bathes the witness, and not judgement. But the overarching drama is didactic, for both the birds and the dead soldiers mirror the essential dialectic of vanity which, as it is martial, produces destruction. Like the warriors, the birds reveal a predatory blindness to their own 'carrion' condition. By making most of the poem the supposed narrative of one who testifies, the poet avoids the danger of appearing single-mindedly didactic. The devastation points to the ideal judgement.

The concluding poem in this sequence unfolds an ambiguous vision of pity:

> Not as we are but as we must appear,
> Contractual ghosts of pity . . .

We are obligated ('Contractual') by the professed norms of our society, and by those of the ideal 'beyond' with which or with whom we have 'timeless colloquy ' – however much this may work against the less scrupulous life we might have preferred. And these moral norms require a 'fat Caritas': 'fat' because it is fed on the expense of others' suffering. Thus Blake makes the Devil declare in 'I heard an Angel singing':

> I heard a Devil curse
> Over the heath and the furze:
> 'Mercy could be no more
> If there was nobody poor,

'And pity no more could be,
If all were as happy as we.'
At his curse the sun went down,
And the heavens gave a frown.[22]

The heavens require compassion from us. 'As we must appear' therefore yields two meanings: inasmuch as we feel obligated to offer pity, we at the same time dissemble as though we gave what in fact we withhold. One is reminded of that epigraph from Ovid's *Amores* which Hill prefixes to his 'Ovid in the Third Reich': 'she only is disgraced who professes her guilt'. But the other meaning is, simply, that pity is what we *must* give if as a community we are to survive, morally, or otherwise. Rosenberg, in 'Dead Man's Dump', perceived this necessity as much as Owen did in 'Strange Meeting'. It may be, Hill's poem continues, that our vanity and its contingent suffering will procure no different resonances in 'eternity'; but though this provides no comfort for us, it is required that we should not be other than aspirants of love. ' "I have not finished" ' may be what we cry at death; and the more we desire to be such aspirants the greater will be the pain of perceiving that 'I have not finished'. Death takes me and 'I am finished'; morally, normatively, I have never finished. The handling of the pentameter in these poems exactly reflects a poise that treads between a metronomic norm and a life-yielding fluctuation from that norm. The analogue of Hill's metric is delicate and scrupulous.

The 'Four Poems Regarding the Endurance of Poets' do not touch on combat but on the victim helpless to do other than comply with his or her captors, as the covering title indicates. The four poets are each victims of tyranny – an indication of the complexion of Hill's attitudes; and they act as an index to a substantial portion of his verse, in the 'Sixties. All four are ranged in contained opposition to their oppressors. Tommaso Campanella (1568–1639), an Italian philosopher, poet and Dominican priest, sought to stir up a movement against the Spanish domination in southern Italy. Thirty years of imprisonment followed, during which he wrote advocating a utopian form of theocracy based on natural religion, which should unite humanity into one family. Miguel Hernandez was incarcerated by the Franco régime and allowed to die in prison. Robert Desnos, a victim of the Nazis, died in Terezin, a camp that was designed to contain artists, in 1945. And Mandelshtam perished – probably in a transit camp: 'it seems likely to have been in Vladivostok at the very end of 1938'.[23] That all four were poets is not because Hill is simply looking after his own, though that is also the case, but because the poet, in the nature of his or her production, is of the essence of a potential and – in these cases – actual resistance to oppression. They approach, in Hill's estimation, the ideal good. Russian culture has always recognised this potential, as English culture has failed to; which is why, in the main, poets can be subversive in the English world with impunity. A further and final point is that it is death, not the régime, which silences each of the four poets. And so, it is for the acts of language that Hill's poets opt, and not for silence.

The sacred word is perpetual testimony. Yet testimony will not properly fit the poem for Desnos, 'Domaine Public'; rather, savage hilarity, farce, the vitality of sophisticated resistance and defiance:

If the ground opens, should men's mouths

open also? 'I am nothing
    if not saved now!' or
'Christ, what a pantomime!'

Here is a fecund delight in outdoing, with an exaggerated and luminous decay, the voluntary decay of 'the Fathers' (one kind of piety) and the moral decay implicit in the captors' activities.

For reading I can recommend
    the Fathers. How they
cultivate the corrupting flesh:

toothsome contemplation: cleanly
    maggots churning spleen
to milk.

There is the now familiar doubleness in 'corrupting'; the flesh corrupts in its decay – in this instance through incarceration; but also, the earthly flesh is ever in danger of corrupting with its lusts the pure soul. That, however, is almost a side-show. The principal gathering of the poem occurs with the next stanza, and it is 'to milk' that affects it. For 'cleanly', applied to the activity of maggots, indicates the thoroughness of 'churning'; rather in the sense that Housman in Poem XLIV of *A Shropshire Lad* exclaims :

Shot? so quick, so clean an ending?
    Oh that was right, lad, that was brave.[24]

– though without Housman's affirmation and single-mindedness. This is not paradox, but the seeing of something that is 'cleanly' (which ought therefore to be affirmative) and loathsome; the reader is asked to participate in two opposed ways at once, but not invited to balance them out. Decay is loathsome; there is no ambiguity in that, and Hill underlines with this notion of such a voluntary piety the enforced decay of camp citizens. The disgust is strong and just, but there is, however, no lessening of the dignity of the poet who is undergoing this decay.

Flesh in both its moral and physical corruption contrasts with the innocence and purity of 'milk'. The decay looks like milk, and is not. With all this, we are prevented, even so, from too neat a dichotomy either way, in that the flesh of the victims is, in this context, innocent (if physically in decay) and the captors' flesh appears in fine fettle whereas their souls are not. Yet though the poet may be 'saved' morally (and not physically), each of us – the poem indicates – resurrects and each is to be judged. There is a sense of an evenhanded justice in all this, but the sardonic tone suggests some resentment at the prospect. All this and judgement too? Can justice and farce co-exist?

As I have already suggested, 'Tristia ...', the poem concerning Mandelshtam, shows how direct *and* fully creative Hill can be:

> A few men glare at their hands; others
> Grovel for food in the roadside field.

Without discursive comment the phrase 'glare at their hands' contains the image of suffering, and the aggression engendered in those who suffer, whether it is directed at their captors or at their own physical condition. 'Glare' also communicates the poet's pity for these creatures, and, on this occasion, the pity is allowed to pass without demur. Hill also registers admiration at their courage – in these circumstances aggression would require courage.

It is not possible to produce a single stanza from the second of 'Three Baroque Meditations' and serve properly the culmination towards which this poem works:

> In darkness outside,
> Foxes and rain-sleeked stones and the dead –
>
> Aliens of such a theme – endure
> Until I could cry 'Death! Death!' as though
> To exacerbate that suave power;
>
> But refrain. For I am circumspect,
> Lifting the spicy lid of my tact
> To sniff at the myrrh.

If foxes, stones, and the dead are 'Aliens of such a theme', what is the theme? Is it 'Flesh of abnegation'? Or are all three aliens to light, that is, to the heartless conduct of the lamp – society's lamp? If they are aliens in this guise they are aligned with darkness, but only in the ironic sense that they are potentially or actually part of death, as they are also a part of the actual poem. Or perhaps foxes, stones, and the dead are all withdrawn from the minimal *regard* of the lamp. At any rate I conjecture that the reason why the 'I' of the poem does not protest '"Death! Death!"' is that, the unspeakable word being uttered, the poet would tactlessly point up his own death. Who is he to stir up that 'suave power'? Yet the self-protecting 'tact' is referred back against the poet's self, and this self-critical pressure is the more emphasised through the *transferred* adjective 'spicy'. Being thus transferred, the condition of the word forms a kind of synecdoche and so assists in compaction, which is an essential ingredient in the power of the poem. The lid is said to be 'spicy' because one is tempted to lift the lid and sniff admiringly, and with pleasure, one's own tact ('myrrh'). Tact is self-preservative and a sufficient balm to one's ego. The poet would thus be courageous in the face of death, if he could; but he is sufficiently tactful about his own condition to defer candour. It is worth remarking, in conclusion, that the furies who 'bask' their claws have the same degree of composed clarity and evaluative power – in play – as the prisoners who 'glare' in the Mandelshtam poem do. But where the word 'bask' is comic, the modest caricature inhering in 'glare' produces an utterly direct and complex perception of others' suffering, as I have tried to suggest.

I come, I think, full circle. In pointing to the strength and directness of the Mandelshtam poem, and to the second of the 'Three Baroque Meditations', and the poem concerning Desnos, I would like to indicate once again the difference between these poems and those in *Tenebrae*. The directness of the poems from *King Log* comes from the kind of complexity that finds itself having to experience conflict, and listening to oneself reporting that experience. The subject of the experience, another person's suffering, is not diminished by having the poet record his presence because the poet is also qualifying the very language with which he responds. But by *Tenebrae*, it is as though the condition of such conflict and its demanding directness are no longer bearable. The condition of conflict has been resolved into the lesser condition, as I see it, of paradox. It is the kind of paradox that not only simplifies contradiction, but enriches itself with the striking and the beautiful; it is the paradox that occurs in religious poetry – the poetry of religious and secular love – which there engages Geoffrey Hill's energy.[25]

9

'How fit a title…'[1]: title and authority in the work of Geoffrey Hill

Hugh Haughton

There is something obstinately archaic about Geoffrey Hill's poetry. The traditional diction, the elaborately formal architecture, the urge towards magniloquence, the relish for oxymoron and paradox, even the consummate finish and authority of the poems, seem to speak from the past – as well as of it. All suggest a disconcertingly anachronistic writer. And as for his choice of subjects … medieval wars, an Anglo-Saxon monarch, recusant martyrs, Asmodeus, the Spanish Counter-Reformation, a Victorian vicar who composed hymn tunes, a Cornish sculptor, the Gothic revival, and now the life and work of a visionary Catholic patriot of Old France, killed in the Great War. Such preoccupations do not score high on contemporary appeal. In fact, 'An Apology for the Revival of Christian Architecture in England', the title Hill uses for his sequence exploring Victorian revivalism, must be one of the most immediately unappealing poetic titles in the literary history of recent years. It might even tempt the modern reader into classifying its author as a deviously nostalgic revivalist of outmoded poetic and theological architecture, a poet of whom it might be said, as Charles Rosen said of Brahms, that he 'made music out of his openly expressed regret that he was born too late'.[2] Wallace Stevens once called poetry 'the scholar's art',[3] but few poets have exploited the arts of scholarship to the degree that Hill has, in digging up semi-forgotten mystics and martyrs, unfashionable poets and theologians and wars. These are the obscure figures who compose the 'Processionals in the exemplary cave'[4] of his poetry.

Yet if Hill's poetry reverberates with traditional diction, and draws on material that is often archaic and arcane, it addresses the reader with the kind of formal violence and hermeneutic ellipsis more often associated with the aggressively modern. The poems habitually engage with what his fictional Spaniard calls 'The long-lost words of choice and valediction',[5] and in particular with those of the 'durable covenant'[6] of Christian theology and iconography; but they do so with the sceptical self-consciousness of a modern intellectual in the teeth of such resonant rhetoric. There is an element of historical pastiche in all Hill's poetry, even at its most original; of tortured pastiche. His powerfully immediate sequence on the desolating civil violence of the Wars of the Roses, 'Funeral Music', rings with the stiffened, rinsed-out rhetoric of Shakespeare's *Henry VI* plays; it reads like a Tudor chronicle play mercilessly condensed into sonnet-form, a sonnet-form stripped of its rhyme like a monument defaced.[7] Both *Mercian Hymns* and *Tenebrae*, too, contrive to speak of English history in forms and idioms borrowed from that history. The first is written in a style that partly simulates that of an erudite Anglo-Saxon royal chronicler and hymnodist, and the second involves, among other things, a series of elaborate imitations of Counter-Reformation songs and sonnets, and Pre-Raphaelite idylls. Historical pastiche of this palpable kind draws attention to the way in which the historical past is necessarily fictive, in whatever degree, and a source of, as well as subject to, rhetorical contrivance and the consolations of poetry.

One of Hill's most tortuous poems is *called* 'History as Poetry', and seems to call the whole process into question.

> Poetry as salutation; taste
> Of Pentecost's ashen feast. Blue wounds.
> The tongue's atrocities. Poetry
> Unearths from among the speechless dead
>
> Lazarus mystified, common man
> Of death.[8]

As a salutation this, for all its mutilated eloquence, is somewhat baffling. The 'Poetry' that 'History' is figured as is hedged about with suspicion, despite the riddling allusions to both resurrection and salvation (the 'salut' in 'salutation'), and the pentecostal promise of the gift of tongues. In the course of the poem, the idea of unearthing Lazarus as poet-historian comes to seem at best double-edged, at worst a travesty. The 'gift' of tongues becomes a 'knack'; Lazarus undergoes not resurrection but a 'resurgence' (a journalistic cliché) and is dramatised as 'mystified', that is, not only 'bewildered' but the victim of mystification (we must suspect a conjuring trick). The apparent unanimity of the close, where we hear of 'The old/Laurels wagging with the new', makes the wearers of the bays appear suspiciously like gossips with 'wagging' tongues. And when we learn that the 'knack of tongues' is 'unanswerable', this must confirm our sense that the 'fortunate auguries' the poet conjures from the earth of ash, loam, dung and bone, are highly questionable. Treating history as poetry may make the past pastiche. The slipperiness of the title's equation of the two seems to be demonstrated by the slipperiness of the key word 'as', which is assimilated so polymorphously within the first sentence. It is first seen as reversible ('poetry *as salutation*'), and then passed through '*taste*', '*ashen*' and '*feast*', each time with a different phonetic emphasis. One comes away from the poem with an ironic sense of the factitious nature of a poetic transformation of history and the 'wounds' of the dead, and also of the rootedness of speech in a world of bodies (tongues and wounds in such intimate proximity) where physical atrocities are committed as a result of acts of language. But one also comes away with a sense of the intimate association of poetry with the historical past – not only of the tongue's atrocities, but a mouthy resonance born out of what another poem from *King Log* calls the 'Half-recognised kingdom of the dead'.[9]

I think it can be argued that the fraught anachronism of Hill's poetry represents the imaginative pull of the past for a poet obsessed above all by the persistence of what has been lost, and the impossibility of reappropriating it: the idea of continuity – and the stark fact of distance.[10] 'History as Poetry' alerts the reader to the poet's distrust, his sense of possible violation and travesty of 'those best dead',[11] and what I have called his 'fraught anachronism' is a paradoxical resistance to the specious glamour of the 'timeless moment' (to which even Eliot succumbed), and the inertia of 'traditional appeal' – indeed the appeal of tradition.[12]

This poem speaks of Lazarus as the 'common man/Of death', but it has to be admitted that the common man is not common in Hill's poetry as a whole. In fact even in this poem the phrase 'common man/Of death' seems to confer a heroic or honorific title upon the mystified corpse. Such resonant titles are common in Hill's work, and play a notable part in the rhetorical drama of his poems. In fact 'entitlement' might be said to be critical to Hill's literary imagination, in its search for propriety of utterance in a world of excruciating improprieties and historical extremity. Hill's is undoubtedly an extreme historical imagination, drawn to situations of maximum moral and civil conflict – the fate of the Jews in Europe, the armies of the Plantagenet kings, the 'holocaust' of the Battle of Towton, the endurance of poets, prisoners and martyrs, the Crucifixion ... Yet he is also as a poet committed to an extreme formality, the idea of 'Poetry as salutation' or an act of 'witness' (a word he often uses[13]). The situations he writes of are ones in which the authority of the state, of religion, and the individual moral conscience, are tested – and the situation he writes out of, if I can put it that way, is one in which the authority of poetry, of Hill's own art, is itself tested. In both situations the questions of entitlement and authority are intimately allied.

The American one-volume edition of *For the Unfallen, King Log* and *Mercian Hymns*, published in 1975, is called *Somewhere Is Such A Kingdom* after a poem of John Crowe Ransom's,[14] and draws its epigraph from Hobbes's *Leviathan*:

> Sometimes a man seeks what he hath lost; and from that place, and time, wherein he misses it, his mind runs back, from place to place, and time to time, to find where, and when he had it ...[15]

The 'somewhere' of the collection's title, set beside the 'sometimes' of the epigraph, give pointed emphasis to the 'place and time' mentioned by Hobbes in this passage (which comes from his account of the 'Discourse of the Mind, when it is governed by designe', defined as 'nothing but *Seeking*, or the faculty of Invention'). Taking the deliberate conjunction of title and epigraph as a composite suggestion – as is evidently Hill's governing design – we find a distinctive identification of poetic 'Invention' with 'Seeking' for lost material on the one hand, and an association between voluntary memory and the appeal of a distant 'kingdom' on the other. The calculated resonance of this association indicates something disconcertingly concerted about the design of Hill's poetry: a Hobbesian identification of memory and imagination and a commitment to history as the site of lost authority. Though the passage Hill quotes is studiously unpolitical in sentiment, Hobbes's own title looms over it with unmistakable political implication, one effect of which is to cloud the innocence of the title of Ransom's witty fable of civil harmony and civil tongues. Hobbes's grimmer fable of political authority might have aptly borne Ransom's title.

Hobbes continues, where Hill breaks off his quotation:

> that is to say, to find some certain, and limited time and place, in which to begin a method of seeking.[16]

This may give us a clue to Hill's methodical search for appropriate historical sites and prototypes for his poetry – his need to locate his poems in, or derive them from, specific historical circumstances, usually of political or religious extremity. All his poems confront loss. *For the Unfallen*, his first book, is a fastidious book of the dead, crowded with images of mass casualties – the Jews in Europe, the anonymous victims of the Wars of the Roses, Drake's navy, the unlucky passengers on the Norman 'White Ship' and the *Titanic*. It is obsessed, above all, by the burden of surviving; the 'unfallen' of the title names the living only as those who have not fallen. Yet if the book is clearly an attempt to work through the historical predicament of Hill's generation after the Second World War, often by reference to historical precedent, it does so in a curiously timeless mythological idiom, without specific circumstantial inflection. It is only with *King Log* that Hill develops his characteristic stance of meditating on a certain 'limited time and place' – a particular voice, picture, text, or historical idiom giving him a point of purchase for his historical imagination in some 'long-sought and forsaken ground'.[17] Since *King Log* the bulk of his poems describe specific historical predicaments; but where in *King Log* Hill is most interested in the intellectual caught up in political atrocity in prison or on the battlefield, his most recent books, *Tenebrae* and *The Mystery of the Charity of Charles Péguy*, concentrate on men of the past themselves remarkable for their loyalty to a vision of past religious culture, men such as those radical conservatives Pugin and Péguy.

There's a remarkable statement in Hill's interview with John Haffenden which throws some light on the later Hill's idiosyncratic conception of poetry as history, and his vision of an earlier kingdom:

I think there's a real sense in which every fine and moving poem bears witness to this lost kingdom of innocence and original justice. In handling the English language the poet makes an act of recognition that etymology is history. The history of the creation and debasement of words is a paradigm for the loss of the kingdom of innocence and original justice.[18]

Though Hill is here adapting a description of Hopkins's sermons, and it is not clear whether this 'lost kingdom' is theological (referring to a prelapsarian 'original justice') or historical ('etymology is history'), there is no doubt that this mythical paradigm has a hypnotic appeal for the poet – perhaps because of its inherent ambiguity. Yet nothing in Hill's actual portrayal of English or continental history confirms the reality of 'such a kingdom'. Quite the contrary: it is most conspicuous for mass conflict, authoritarian brutality, and war; debased words and lost innocence. The substance of the poems refutes the paradigm while bearing witness to its rhetorical appeal, the appeal of a past authority. 'What I dare not', confesses a voice in 'Funeral Music⁴', 'is a waste history/Or void rule.' Bleak realities of human 'waste' on the battlefields of the Wars of the Roses lie behind the refusal to accept a 'void rule' by this speaker, and it is some such vision which sustains Hill's persistent need to seek out 'rule' among the devastations of history. It is a measure of his temperamental conservatism that this 'rule' has increasingly come to be identified with something lost rather than still unfound, and that it bears the archaic title of a 'kingdom'.

A distinctive feature of Hill's attitude towards the past is his persistent recourse to established literary titles. This is straightforward enough in his characteristic use of generic terms like 'ode', 'requiem' and 'hymn', which declare allegiance to the codes of literary tradition. What is more unusual is his pleasure in taking over titles from individual works of earlier writers. A note to *Somewhere Is Such A Kingdom*, for example, tells us that: 'The title of this book is the title of a poem by John Crowe Ransom' and then adds (with elaborate scruple) 'I gratefully acknowledge the debt'. Such ceremonial acknowledgement advertises the poet's conscientious book-keeping as well as his cunning book-making. Though it is common for writers to create titles from quotations or from allusions to earlier writers, few, if any, can have so consistently appropriated their titles for both sequences and individual poems. The first poem of his first book brazenly asserts the title of the first book of the bible: 'Genesis'. 'Holy Thursday', the third, takes its title from another, but anti-Mosaic, poet of genesis, William Blake; and of course it is a title Blake uses twice for the contrary poems in *Songs of Innocence and Experience*. 'Solomon's Mines' appropriates the title of Rider Haggard's popular historical romance (though uncharacteristically drops Solomon's own title of 'King') to explore the sinister romance of history. 'Metamorphoses' obscurely invokes Ovid's title to preside over Hill's twistedly gnomic metamorphoses; one of these, 'The Re-birth of Venus' gives a second birth to a Botticelli title and makes his innocent marine goddess a 'sea-scoured temptress', and another takes the title of Sir Henry Newbolt's once popular ballad

'Drake's Drum' to offer a form of imaginative reproof to Newbolt's breezy vision of the enduring submarine life of England's naval heroes. 'Elegiac Stanzas: On a Visit to Dove Cottage' applies Wordsworth's 'Elegiac Stanzas, Suggested by a Picture of Peele Castle, in a Storm, Painted by Sir George Beaumont' to Hill's own ambiguously elegiac response to the Romantic poet's Dove Cottage, and rhetoric of sublime ejaculation ('O Lakes, Lakes!/O Sentiment upon the rocks!'). Two other poems in *For the Unfallen*, 'Doctor Faustus' and 'Orpheus and Eurydice', reproduce famous titles (of Marlowe and Gluck among others) at the same time as they refer to legendary heroes. And, of course, 'The Martyrdom of Saint Sebastian', Hill's first picture of the transformation of martyrdom into art, is the title of countless Renaissance paintings, and in particular the 'priceless' masterpiece attributed to the Pollaiuolos in the National Gallery.[19] In almost all these cases, Hill's use of established titles bears upon the root-preoccupation of *For the Unfallen* as a whole: the difficulty of proper commemoration of the dead, and the treacherous process whereby 'pains' are translated into 'fine art', (to use the terms of the last-named poem), so that losses are transformed into gains (as Wordsworth tried to do in his stanzas on Peele Castle, written after the drowning of his brother). 'A Pastoral' is the subtlest study of this potentially treacherous commemoration through art, with its 'evergreen names' – and titles:

> Here are statues
> Darkened by laurel; and evergreen names;
> Evidently-veiled griefs; impervious tombs.

King Log, certainly Hill's most intellectually sceptical and discomforting work to date, makes less use of established titles than the earlier and later books. Apart from 'Funeral Music', which suggests a number of musical precedents, the few titles he does use have a specific biographical meaning. 'Domaine Public' and 'Tristia', in his sequence 'Four Poems Regarding the Endurance of Poets', use titles of collections by the poets they formally commemorate, Robert Desnos and Osip Mandelshtam.[20] Of Mandelshtam's second volume of poems the critic Clarence Brown has written: 'The book that begins with a poem written from inside another's work, Racine's *Phèdre*, also bears the title of another man's book, Ovid's *Tristia*' – suggesting a rather intriguing parallel between the Russian and the English poet.[21] The other instances are more obscure. 'Fantasia on "Horbury"' is Hill's own title, but it includes the name of the most famous hymn-tune of the Reverend John Bacchus Dykes (the J.B.D. of the sub-title), the obscure biographical subject of the poet's elliptical memoir; and 'The Stone Man' uses the title of a brief memoir by Charles Causley of the equally obscure Cornish sculptor Burnard, whose childhood stirred analogies with Hill's own, later to be summoned back more directly in *Mercian Hymns*.[22] It is an ironic confirmation of the poet's need to draw upon prior title and earlier writers that his most apparently direct and least historical sequence of poems, containing what seem the most personal lyrics he has allowed himself to write, 'The Songbook of Sebastian Arrurruz', depends on his invention of 'an apocryphal

Spanish poet' from whom he can then borrow his title.[23] This most sensuous English poet needs the mask of scholarship.

In *Mercian Hymns* Hill adopts a solemnly self-mocking mask of scholarship once more to explore his own and his region's early history. The title, a note tells us, 'is a suggestion taken from *Sweet's Anglo-Saxon Reader*'. In fact Sweet has a short section called 'Mercian Hymns' consisting of Anglo-Saxon interlinear glosses on set pieces of the Vulgate.[24] No doubt this title evoked strong territorial memories in the Worcestershire poet when he read English at Oxford, and Hill's marvellously original sequence – a 'moody testament' (XXIV) that elaborately intertwines Latinate scholastic wit and pungent vernacular observation – redeems the unfulfilled promise of Sweet's title. These are 'Mercian Hymns' in a full sense, hymns about and to Mercia, not simply native glosses on a canonical Latin text.

Tenebrae, Hill's next book, is the one in which he draws most systematically on earlier titles and the language of Latin Christianity. The book itself (and title-poem) derives its name from Holy Week services in the Roman Catholic Church, and may allude to musical settings of the psalms used in the services, such as those of Gesualdo. Certainly the title-poem, originally part of a cantata text, has something of the abrupt chromatic plangency and broodily polyphonic texture of Gesualdo's music. The first extended sonnet-sequence in the book, devoted to English Counter-Reformation martyrology and the devotional literature of tears, also bears a Latin title with musical and devotional associations. It is the magnificently ornate title of Dowland's 'Lachrimae, or Seven teares figured in seven passionate Pavans', which Hill associates in an epigraph with the title of St. Robert Southwell's 'Mary Magdalen's Funeral Tears' – thus associating the careers and art of the recusant poet and the composer. The sequence is effectively a virtuoso imitation of Dowland's sombre five-part pavans, in the form of seventeenth-century divine sonnets. Some of the individual sonnets bear Dowland's titles, such as 'Lachrimae Antiquae Novae', which might be taken as a description of Hill's renewal of the music and literature of tears; others those of other contemporary works, the 'Pavana Dolorosa' of Peter Philips, and *The Masque of Blacknesse* of Ben Jonson who modelled 'new heavens in his masquerade'. This constellation of titles from one period sets up complex cultural reverberations among the sonnets. Though each sonnet is an impassioned spiritual exercise on the Passion, it is at the same time an exercise in an historical reconstruction of the elaborate aesthetic culture of the time, with its court masques, baroque meditations and intricate consort-music, exploring how an artist constructs and construes the *language* of 'passion' in relation to the 'celestial worldliness' of his conventions. Hill's titles here have a smack of a holy Madame Tussaud's about them, but they touch upon his grander concerns – in particular the way a language of transcendence is deployed in, and compromised by, particular historical circumstances and conventions, riddled with worldliness.

The other extended sonnet-sequence in *Tenebrae* revives the title of Augustus Pugin's theologico-architectural manifesto of 1843, 'An Apology for the Revival of Christian Architecture'. Pugin's fighting title sounded a high trumpet-call for the Gothic revival, but it has acquired a somewhat ironic, almost Quixotic resonance at the head of Hill's thirteen studies in revivalist nostalgia.[25] In reviving an irreparably dated title, and a literary idiom which is brilliantly redolent of glassy Victorian medievalism, Hill seems to be investigating the ambivalent resonance of the title and language of 'Christian' England in the nineteenth-century, with its dreams of medieval order and realities of exploitation. Individual sonnets borrow titles from influential medievalist poems by Keats and Tennyson, 'The Eve of St Mark' and 'Idylls of the King'; while others *seem* to quote established titles, such as 'A Short History of British India' and 'The Herefordshire Carol'.[26] Such titles, in association with the fastidious, high-toned pastiche of the sonnets themselves, evoke the rather stuffy, icily decorative ethos of an English dream of the English past. In the context Hill provides for them the titles speak of Victorian fictions of the past such as are expressed in the period's versions of Gothic, folklore, medievalism, and the romance of the country house. Hill's mannered sonnets re-enact and petrify a *language* of the past largely invented by the Victorians, and which can be said to be less their inheritance than their legacy.

Hill's latest long poem, *The Mystery of the Charity of Charles Péguy* – a tribute to the life and art of the visionary populist poet and Catholic traditionalist who died for his 'militant-pastoral' dream of Old France – continues Hill's queer tradition of deploying established titles, but in a different key. It adopts an English translation of the title of Péguy's most widely known work and simply substitutes the poet's own name for that of his saintly protagonist Jeanne D'Arc. This is not pure mannerism, since, in adopting a title from the literary canon, Hill is effectively canonising Péguy, who stands to the English poet in much the same relation as Jeanne to the French one. Hill's title is either cumbersomely eloquent or teasingly ambiguous, depending on whether you take 'Mystery' to be a theological or rationalistic category (as something beyond explanation, or something to be explained). In fact it could refer to two near-antithetical genres: a quasi-medieval mystery play such as Péguy's poetic dramas ('History commands the stage' proclaims the first stanza) or a detective mystery 'whodunnit' ('Did Péguy kill Jaurès?' asks the fourth). Hill's poem has something of both. As patriot, war-poet, mystic, ideologue and martyr, Péguy is a cunningly estranged French mask for Hill – a substitution for Offa – enabling him to write a great First World War poem (for I believe it is that) nearly seventy years later. Throughout the poem, ritual and travesty, the grotesque and the dignified, heroic and phoney idioms, play off against each other ('low tragedy, high farce, fight for command'[27]), as they do in the title. The poem enacts the black tragi-comedy of poetic decorum faced with modern warfare and modern civilisation, by focusing on the peculiar decorum and savage incongruities of the career of Charles Péguy, and exploring the realities of the writer's rhetorical and moral authority.

Hill's titles evoke precedent and appeal to traditional aesthetic decorum, then, in a peculiar and expressive way. One of the most striking aspects of this is the sheer number of titles which declare what Hill, speaking of his passionate love of music, has called his 'envy of the composer'.[28] Setting aside the musical allusions in 'Lachrimae', the poet has written hymns, variations on a theme, chorale-preludes, songs (indeed a songbook), a carol, a fantasia, funeral music and a requiem – though he has not yet written a fugue like Celan, or quartets like Eliot. One effect of this is to make good Hill's implicit claim to the title of composer. Another is to emphasise the artfulness of art in relation to the 'real cries' and crises to which it corresponds:

> Music survives, composing her own sphere,
> Angel of Tones, Medusa, Queen of the Air,
> and when we would accost her with real cries
> silver on silver thrills itself to ice.
>
> ('Tenebrae')

The formal autonomy of music as a sensual and intellectual figure is, it seems, a paradigm of art's capacity to transcend its own occasion, but it may also betray the brute truths of experience. Hill's formal fastidiousness is instrumental and investigates the satisfactions it proposes. It does not offer transcendence, for all its 'fictive consonance', since Hill's own music reverberates with semantic dissonance and unresolved ambiguity. The artist is indeed a 'Self-seeking hunter of forms' as one of the 'Lachrimae' sonnets suggests.[29] Poet and composer seek out a real self in hunting forms, yet this is also self-seeking in a pragmatic or narcissistic sense. The formality of Hill's titles respects this perpetual paradox of poetic forms, and for all their claustrophobic decorum represents an impressive scepticism in the face of art and their own artfulness, their own title to poetic authority.

Yet Hill in another sense is a great respecter of titles. His poems bristle with them. Music is celebrated as 'Angel' and 'Queen' in the above quotation, and the language of earthly and heavenly hierarchy, status and authority permeates Hill's own music from his first poem to his latest. In the poems there is nearly always a kingdom somewhere.[30] It is this basic trope that enables him to combine his portrait of the artist as a young man with historical celebration of Anglo-Saxon Mercia in *Mercian Hymns*. The opening hymn is a mock-heroic fanfare of titles celebrating Offa's power and status:

> King of the perennial holly-groves, the riven sand-
> stone: overlord of the M5: architect of the his-
> toric rampart and ditch, the citadel at Tamworth,
> the summer hermitage in Holy Cross: guardian of
> the Welsh Bridge and the Iron Bridge: contractor
> to the desirable new estates: saltmaster: money-
> changer: commissioner for oaths: martyrologist:
> the friend of Charlemagne.

The phrase 'overlord of the M5' may seem bathetically modern after the archaic grandeur of 'King of the perennial holly-groves', but, as with most of the writing in the sequence, it eludes final classification.[31] After all 'overlord of the M5' is strictly comparable to 'architect of the historic rampart and ditch' (described by Christopher Brooke as 'one of the great engineering achievements of the dark ages'[32]), or 'guardian' of the world's first iron bridge, a conscious symbol of Britain's Industrial Revolution. The poet's initial epic address obviously appeals to the king's not entirely disinterested aesthetic sense – ' "I liked that," said Offa, "sing it again." ' – since it confirms his carefully engineered self-image and the claims of local patriotism. Yet Hill's grandiose titles are not simply satirical: they celebrate accumulated achievement even as they ironise it. There is a touch of phoney 'historic' rhetoric and what T.S. Eliot called 'Bovarisme' about the whole invocation, but there is also a memorable civic resonance which wittily suggests the complex cultural inheritance of the region. In fact it is a perfect instance of Hill's claim that 'etymology is history'.[33] The reader is made to hear the interaction of social history and linguistic usage in such 'perennial' words as 'estates' (an economic history of England might be written around this word) or the still current but now incongruous title of 'commissioner for oaths', as well as in local names like 'Welsh Bridge'. We may experience Joycean incongruity as we read, but we cannot help being impressed by the cunning composite mirage conjured up by the poet's playful rhetoric: the mirage of a continuing historic identity of Mercia presided over by Offa ('a name to conjure with', II). As in the poem as a whole, the effect here is to evoke the complex political stratigraphy of the rich 'variably-resistant soil' (XII), what George Eliot in *Theophrastus Such* called 'the speech of the landscape' or 'a piece of our social history in pictorial writing'.[34] For Hill this is a 'speech' shot through with the language of administration and authority.

Mercian Hymns explores the hiding-places of the poet's own power by means of the conceited identification of his childhood self with the most ruthlessly effective king of Anglo-Saxon Mercia. It is as if he had added Sartre's *L'Enfance d'un Chef* to Wordsworth's *Prelude*. The book seems to equate the Romantic 'growth of a poet's mind' with the development of a domineering political genius. His 'dream of Offa the King' (XXIX) enables Hill to equate the historical founding of a kingdom with the finding of it by himself as a boy, and with his later rediscovery of it and mastery over it through the right-royal conceit of *Mercian Hymns*. Offa, whom Hill has called his 'image of a tyrannical creator of order and beauty',[35] is, like the poet, a great respecter of titles, but he creates his own title ('*Offa Rex* resonant in silver', XI) and his own currency ('Coins handsome as Nero's').

Neither king nor kingdom in *Mercian Hymns* suggest anything remotely like a 'lost kingdom of innocence and original justice'. The book is certainly fascinated by the romance of origins – 'the crypt of roots and endings' (IV) – but it never loses sight of guilt and injustice, the *Realpolitik* of *Leviathan* and the egotistical sublimations of childhood. Curiously, the heading 'Offa's

Kingdom' is reserved for a hymn exclusively devoted to the poet's own child-hood, its names its only purchase in the Anglo-Saxon past (VII). Here 'king-dom' is, for once, purely metaphorical. After evoking the sinister glamour of the schoolboy hero's violent acts of aggression against a ditchful of eel-swarms and frogs, and against his friend Ceolred 'sniggering with fright', the poet celebrates the boy's intense, desolate sense of solitary power, as a kind of imaginative initiation or epiphany:

> Then, leaving Ceolred, he journeyed for hours,
> calm and alone, in his private derelict sandlorry
> named *Albion.*

The spacious roll of the final phrase ('private, derelict sandlorry named *Al-bion*'), with something of the conscious magnificence of the pentameter, is faithful to the absurd grandeur experienced by the child, and it spells out his enamoured equation of the wrecked lorry's trade-name with the ancient poetic name of the kingdom itself – Albion. From such fantasies of power and verbal magic his 'dream of Offa the King' grows, with its entranced sense of terri-torial identity with 'the long-unlooked-for mansions of our tribe' (IV). This is intensified, no doubt, by his memory of the coronation of George VI when he was three (III) and his experience of the nation at war (evoked in XXII). Hill's fascination with a 'kingdom', interiorised through 'childsplay' (II), not only enables him to take Offa's title as his own, but to question the origins of his need for poetic mastery and authority. If, as Harold Bloom has said, *Mercian Hymns* is 'a kind of "Prelude"-in-little',[36] it also offers a disturbing critique of the Romantic poet's transcendent account of the sources of ima-ginative power, and places it in a landscape inscribed with history and culture, not a pure realm of innocent 'nature'.

'The language of poetry', writes Hazlitt, 'naturally falls in with the lan-guage of power'. The remark forms part of Hazlitt's troubled reflections on Shakespeare's *Coriolanus*, but was clearly written with the political apostasy of Wordsworth and the Lake Poets fresh in his mind (the date is 1817).[37] Faced with the swing to conservative monarchism among contemporary writers, and stung into recognising that 'Shakespeare himself seems to have had a leaning towards the arbitrary side of the question', the libertarian sceptical Hazlitt is driven to give a political interpretation to Coleridge's distinction between 'understanding' and 'imagination', making the first a 're-publican faculty' and the second an 'aristocratic' and 'anti-levelling' one. He goes on to characterise the 'principle of poetry' as inherently hierarchical:

> It shows its head turretted, crowned, and crested. Its front is gilt and blood-stained ... It has its altars and its victims, sacrifices, human sacrifices. Kings, priests, nobles, are its train-bearers, tyrants and slaves its executioners. – 'Carnage is its daughter.' – Poetry is right-royal. It puts the individual for the species, the one above the infinite many, might before right. A lion hunting a flock of sheep or a herd of wild asses is a more poetical object than they ... There is nothing heroical in a multitude of miserable rogues not wishing to be starved, or com-

plaining that they are like to be so ... The love of power in ourselves and the
admiration of it in others are both natural to man: the one makes him a tyrant,
the other a slave.

So Hazlitt, the faithful supporter of the French Revolution, is led to fear that
it is the very 'logic of the imagination' to think like Burke rather than like
Tom Paine, and to see 'the history of mankind' as 'a romance, a mask, a
tragedy constructed upon the principles of *poetical justice*' rather than a
struggle for the Rights of Man.[38]

Hazlitt's impassioned and self-lacerating simplifications are very much of
their time, but they touch upon a discomforting paradox of the imagination
that is pertinent to our own, and especially so in relation to Geoffrey Hill's
fascination with the 'right-royal' language of title, hierarchy, and subordina-
tion. Offa is not a bad personification of Hazlitt's 'Coriolanus-factor', and it
is an ironic joke that Hill attributes to him two 'Defense[s] of the English
People' since Milton's two pamphlets with this title provide a critique of
monarchical titles, and a defence of the English people against an English
king.[39] One of the best poems in *For the Unfallen*, 'Solomon's Mines', gives
a brilliant account of Hill's scholarly romance with the past:

> Anything to have done!
> (The eagle flagged to the sun)
> To have discovered and disclosed
> The buried thrones, the means used;
>
> Spadework and symbol; each deed
> Resurrecting those best dead
> Priests, soldiers and kings;
> Blazed-out, stripped-out things.

Historical scholarship here seems to figure as a claustrophobic historical rom-
ance, fired by a vision of 'buried thrones'. The speaker's attitude towards
these seems suspended between professional impatience, historical resentment,
and a glamorous sense of discovery – depending on how you read that first
phrase, 'Anything to have done': 'anything to get this over and done with',
'anything to be done with this historic stuff', or 'anything to have done it,
and actually achieved something'. The poem suggests the way the dogged
exercise of 'spadework and symbol' both resurrects 'those best dead', and
seems to undo or exhaust what it sets out to understand, those 'blazed-out,
stripped-out things'. The poet's ambivalence hinges on the two ways we
might understand the words 'those best dead'. They can refer to 'the best
among the dead, the élite, such as priests, soldiers, and kings', in which case
poetry would indeed be right-royal – or imply 'those who are best left dead',
leaving open whether it is best for them or us. The last verse accentuates the
poem's protest against the oppressive appeal of 'that strong land', whatever
that is: is it simply the past? Or specifically King Solomon's mines? Or what
Walter Jackson Bate has called *The Burden of the Past* for the modern

writer?[40] Or the draw of superseded hierarchies and archaic kingdoms? However the reader interprets Hill's cryptic fable, the rest of his verse might be seen as a protest against that protest. The poet had certainly not 'done with' the blazed-out, stripped-out things, with Offa's 'Muse of History' (X), or the history of the Muse. '1. Quaint Mazes' in the much later 'An Apology for the Revival of Christian Architecture in England' ends with a vision of 'the rood blazing upon the green', which turns the Puritan destruction of the old roods of medieval England into an affirmation of the burning persistence of the symbol being destroyed.

The epigraph to *King Log* quotes Bacon's category of 'power and commandment', and much of the book can be seen as an investigation into the relation between what Hazlitt calls 'the language of poetry' and 'the language of power'. The 'King' of its own title *King Log* announces the problematic appeal of titular authority for the poet and connects up, in the course of the work as a whole, with Ovid's 'Reich', the 'ritual king' of 'Funeral Music', the 'imperious theme' of 'Annunciations', the 'half-recognized kingdom of the dead' of 'The Stone Man', and the 'majesty of man' invoked in 'Three Baroque Meditations':

> Do words make up the majesty
> Of man, and his justice
> Between the stones and the void?

The words of *King Log* are suspended in the space of this question – between the stony and petrifying domain of political violence, and the empty space of metaphysical questions. The historical situations represented in *King Log* do not allow the reader to grasp any harmonious alignment of civic, religious, and poetic authority. It is left open whether the words of man's 'majesty' (which the *OED* defines as 'the dignity, or greatness of a sovereign') define man, or merely invent a dignified fiction, a 'majesty' that is only made up in atrocious circumstances to justify power, or justify resistance to it.

The dramatis personae of Hill's poems are intellectuals and poets for the most part, but also men who wield executive or judicial power, or are the victims of such power. On the one hand there are the ambiguous, suspect, and compromised figures like Ovid, who sings 'the love-choir' though faced with the 'troughs of blood' of the Third Reich; the 'word-perfect' humanist whose hands were once 'thick with Plato's blood' but now sits blandly at 'the Muse's table'; and the three scholar noblemen of 'Funeral Music' (whose titles are of course given in full at the poem's opening), who are both men of letters and men of arms, poets or patrons but also men of political authority with power over life and death.[41] On the other hand are the four poets commemorated in the 'Four Poems Regarding the Endurance of Poets', who as political prisoners and exiles are victims of such authority, whether like Campanella in Renaissance Italy, or Mandelstam in Stalinist Russia. Hill handles the predicaments of this last group in a rather chillingly elliptic idiom that is as foreign to English as the poets he remembers, a kind of stilted international baroque, presided over by 'glutted Torment', a 'Blind Sun', 'the

Fathers', and 'Tragedy' – damagingly sealed-off from the particular lives and political contexts that are his starting-point.[42] His characters are all trapped between brutal earthly authority and a remote, rather inhuman heavenly one, but the poems are more successful in evoking the grim worldly dominion of a certain rhetoric of otherworldliness, as in 'Annunciations' or 'Funeral Music', than in imagining a political or moral alternative. We hear nothing of the Utopian vision of Campanella, his revolutionary politics, 'City of the Sun' or the eloquent moral credos and defiant proclamations of his sonnets; nothing of the Mandelshtam of his wife's great memoir,[43] and nothing of the energetic surrealism of Desnos. The 'majesty' presented in *King Log* is claustrophobically terrible. Only in 'The Songbook of Sebastian Arrurruz', where the poet dispenses with the language of hierarchy and title, and replaces it with the ironic idiom of a 'scholar' concerned with a neutral 'propriety', is there any room to breathe, and in 'September Song' where having room to breathe, in a world that has known 'patented terror', is itself cause enough for celebration. The word 'patented' there is a reminder that the atrocities remembered by the poem were 'authorised' by the German state, and given legal title like other routine modern inventions.

My point is that while Hill is continually drawn to the 'language of power' and entitlement, he consistently subjects it to a paradoxical or critical counter-pressure. 'Annunciations', for example, announces its 'dubious' and twisted theology in something like a grand style:

> Our God scatters corruption. Priests, martyrs,
> Parade to this imperious theme: 'O Love,
> You know what pains succeed; be vigilant ...

Yet these priests and martyrs parade to an 'imperious' not an 'imperial' theme, the otherworldly rhetoric struts with the assertiveness of an earthly charade, and the speaker's confident boast about divine vengeance on corruption ('Our God scatters corruption') unwittingly lays itself open to the contrary interpretation, that his God broadcasts corruption.[44] Such rhetoric, the poem implies, is itself corrupting, and for all its tyrannical insistence on vigilance, not vigilant enough. Though I think the poem frustratingly obscure – mainly because it fails to locate its theological drama in a plausible historical situation or idiom – it shows Hill's characteristic connoisseurship about the worldliness inherent in high language and high places. In using the resonant language of divine authority here, he insinuates its possibly brutal coerciveness (in the name of 'Love') through his unrelenting play on telling ambiguities. Similarly in the more precisely located poetry of 'An Apology for the Revival of Christian Architecture in England', which seems to celebrate Pugin's or Richard Oastler's vision of feudal harmony – 'the spiritual, Platonic old England' of the epigraph – Hill carefully distances himself from unambiguous celebration of the Platonic idea of England and the old 'religion of the heart'. 'Platonic England grasps its tenantry' ('7. Loss and Gain') and 'Religion of the heart ... rejoices in old hymns of servitude' ('1. Quaint Mazes'). Such phrases, with their exhilarating traditional diction, and cunning exploitation of a roomy and dignified pentameter, conjure up an eloquent dream of feudal harmony. Yet, at the same time, 'servitude' remembers the legal oppression of 'serfdom', not that 'service' which we almost hear and which was said to be perfect freedom. Coleridge's myth of a Platonic order is shown to be rooted in aristocratic title to, and ownership of, the land – the grasping physical pressure of the verb ('grasps') comments on the treacherous idealism of the epithet. In such ways Hill resists the glamourisation of the English past that is his starting-point and inspiration. 'Tenantry' and 'servitude' remember a legal history that the Pre-Raphaelite fiction tends to forget.

The kind of Christian architecture that most interests Hill the poet, at least in *Tenebrae*, is paradox. Paradox subjects the 'language of power' to a different kind of critique by inverting its power-relations, typified by the address to the 'Crucified Lord' of 'Lachrimae'. Yet Hill's virtuoso deployment of this device gives us an insight into the power gained by these rhetorical inversions, makes us see into the queer psychology of mystical paradox. There is a vivid case of this at the end of '6. Lachrimae Antiquae Novae', where the speaker proclaims: 'Dominion is swallowed with your blood'. This must mean 'I suppress (swallow) my desire for dominion as I take the Eucharist', but it can also mean something like 'I participate in dominion by drinking your blood' – a brilliant instance of having your dominion and swallowing it. There is an eerie 'triumphalism' here, akin to that seen by Nietzsche in his analysis of the biblical axiom 'he that humbleth himself shall be exalted' which the philosopher interprets as 'he that humbleth himself wills to be exalted'.[45] In the title-sequence 'Tenebrae' there is a comparable effect, when the phrase 'This is the Lord Eros/of grief' uses the line-break to play out the ambivalent drama of reversals. At first, the lordly title the poem confers on Eros seems diminished by its association with grief, and then grief appears magnified by the title of lordship, evoking a vulnerable magnificence and magnificent vulnerability. But Hill does not leave the matter there:

> This is the Lord Eros
> of grief who pities
> no one; it is
> Lazarus with his sores.

The second line-break enacts a second peripeteia, converting that magnificent erotic grief into a more selfish-seeming pitilessness (of a recognisably lordly kind). The climactic final line can then be read in two ways: as a triumphantly asserted claim to status; or as a Christian reduction of the pagan Eros of the classical world into a grievous object of charity. However we read the disconcerting doubleness of these paradoxical titles, we cannot miss the poet's fascination with the power generated by such inversions – turning Lord Eros into Lazarus and vice versa.

There is a notable political example of this kind of paradox in '"Christmas Trees"', the poem on the German theologian Dietrich Bonhoeffer, imprisoned for his complicity in the plot against Hitler:

> Bonhoeffer in his skylit cell
> bleached by the flares' candescent fall,
> pacing out his own citadel,
>
> restores the broken themes of praise ...

The poet restores or recognises Bonhoeffer's commanding autonomy in a situation of apparent defeat and subjection at the hands of an authoritarian state, and does so in part by conferring the title of 'citadel' upon his cell. The primary meaning of the term is 'a fortress commanding a city, which serves both to protect and keep in subjection' (OED), and the effect of Hill's use of it here is to give a commanding moral authority to the imprisoned pastor and to his 'quiet but not too quiet' words. Though Bonhoeffer is portrayed as a restorer of broken themes, like so many of the figures in Tenebrae a representative of traditional Christian values, the authority of 'his citadel' is a metaphoric one, and exemplary rather than executive. A counter-example to 'Ovid in the Third Reich', it represents a victory in defeat – for once, a paradox with no moral ambiguity.[46]

The language of authority and asserted title is inevitably a political matter. God, destiny, history, even the classics, are appealed to in order to justify 'power and commandment' – in order to *authorise* the assertion of political will. There is a peculiarly poignant instance in 'Funeral Music'. The third poem in the sequence opens with what seems a triumphant invocation of divine will at the outset of the day's battle:

> They bespoke doomsday and they meant it by
> God, their curved metal rimming the low ridge.

The poem closes with voices simply 'gasping "Jesus"', an exhausted exclamation that grotesquely associates the sighs of the wounded on the battlefield with those of the marriage-bed ('their marriage-blood'). The initial 'by/God' combines a routine formula for intensified emphasis ('by God, they meant it') and a consciously rhetorical appeal to God to justify their violent assertion of human power in war. The trajectory from such initial confidence and rhetorical magnificence to that last worn-out cry, half-curse and half-prayer, a kind of involuntary admission of human powerlessness, might be taken as a grim epitome of man's need for religious language.

'4. A Short History of British India (II)' from 'An Apology ...' presents a more complex case of an authorising utterance, this time an apologia for British imperialism in the nineteenth-century:

> Destiny is the great thing,
> true lord of annexation and arrears.
>
> Our law-books overrule the emperors.
> The mango is the bride-bed of light. Spring
> jostles the flame-tree. But new mandates bring
> new images of faith, good subahdars!

Destiny, like necessity, is the tyrant's plea, and here Hill catches the absurd bravura of imperial bluff. There's a touch of both club-room cliché and Churchillian bow-wow about the rhetoric ('Destiny's the great thing'), with its phoney appeal to some portentous 'Destiny' to underwrite the policy of imperial expansion and annexation as its 'true lord'. The previous sonnet in the sequence had spoken of 'fantasies of true destiny that kills/"under the sanction of the English name"', thus giving a ringingly hollow inflection to 'true destiny' and that 'sanction'. Here, British law-books under the same sanction, over-rule the native emperors, and their 'new mandates' implicitly over-rule the Hindu architecture of wayside shrines and the old sanction of Krishna and Radha. 'Good subahdars' provides a telling instance of the politics of entitlement in Hill's poetry. Originally a native Indian term for a local leader or governor, it was annexed by the British to mean 'a native commandant of a company of sepoys' (*OED*) in the imperial army. Its use here ('good subahdars') exhibits the good humour of conscious patronage towards inferiors. 'Mandates' and 'law-books', 'destiny' and the 'sanction of the English name', are all eloquently invoked by the speaker to justify and impose the British title to India, indeed the title 'British India' itself. The effect, however, is frigidly pompous beside the idiom of 'The mango is the bride-bed of light.' The 'But' that follows this both reveals and conceals the unspoken historical violence exerted upon native Indian culture in the name of such titles. At the same time, however ironically Hill poses the rhetoric of imperialism here, he also recognises its particular kind of authority; 'true lord of annexation and arrears', like 'overlord of·the M5', rings out with a historic and histrionic note of grandeur, accentuated by the Elgarian swell of the pentameter – however suspect that grandeur might be. You could call this a study in 'imposing rhetoric'; and that of course is precisely what it sets out to do, impose.

Much of Hill's poetry hinges on such suspect grandiloquence. We see it as early as his description in 'Requiem for the Plantagenet Kings' of those 'fired, and for good,/To sound the constitution of just wars'. The note of flawed authority, or cracked eloquence, plays a crucial part in many of Hill's most memorable and characteristic performances from first to last. There's an unusually vivid and unusually personal example of this in *Mercian Hymns* XXII, which describes the poet's earliest experiences of political authority and national identity as a child in war-time Britain:

> At home the curtains were drawn. The wireless boomed
>   its commands. I loved the battle-anthems and the
>   gregarious news.

The child instinctively respects such public rhetoric, but, ironically, perceives the wireless itself as the source of the boomed commands, not the speaker. It is in the sheltered privacy of his blacked-out home in war-time that the young Hill/Offa paradoxically learns a 'gregarious' sense, listening to the news and martial music relayed by the BBC. Hill's readers may regret that it is only here in *Mercian Hymns* that he directly engages with the modern technology of government, and the new media for representing 'matters of power and commandment' like the radio – though words like 'battle-anthems' and 'gregarious' send us back into the remote past. *Mercian Hymns* is paradoxically Hill's most archaic and modern work, that in which he most systematically explores the origins of his romance of kingship, and most humorously and critically exposes it. Under its studied mask of impeccable scholarship, it remains an astonishing portrayal of the poet's quest for poetic authority – and meditation on the disturbing analogies between the language of poetry and the language of power. It is still the best guide to the exemplary cave of Hill's poetry, and the richest clue to the elaborate repertoire of his oppressive kingdom, its 'crypt of roots and endings' (IV), and dreams of ' "menace" and "atonement" '.[47]

I suggested earlier that Péguy might be seen as a substitute for Offa, another remote double for that inveterate 'martyrologist' Geoffrey Hill. *The Mystery of the Charity of Charles Péguy* is, after *Mercian Hymns*, the most systematic and extended poem of transferred title, as well as having something of its circumstantial gusto and grotesque panache. Where Offa had a political title to a historical kingdom, Hill's native territory of Mercia, Péguy acquires, in the course of Hill's poem, a literary title to his native region of the Beauce through his creation of a compelling 'fable' of the landscape of France in the prolonged, eccentric, and compelling visionary harangues published in his *Cahiers*. It is of them that Hill writes:

> The proofs pile up; the dead are made alive
> to their posthumous fame. Here is the archive
> of your stewardship; here is your true domaine,
> its fields of discourse ripening to the Marne.
>
> Chateau de Trie is yours, Chartres is yours,
> and the carved knight of Gisors with the hound;
> Colombey-les-deux-Eglises; St Cyr's
> cadres and echelons are yours to command.
>
> Yours is their dream of France, militant-pastoral . . .

Though the French poet's 'command' is exerted over 'fields of discourse' only, Hill's commanding text celebrates this command as a 'true domaine', and Péguy's 'stewardship' is made potent by those fields of discourse which, like real fields, are described as 'ripening to the Marne'. The name 'the Marne' indicates both the river and the battlefield, relating those fields of discourse not only to farmland and farming but to the future war ('militant-pastoral' indeed), where that discourse will come to terrible fruition in the Battle of the Marne, in which Péguy died, 'covered in glory and the blood of beetroots.' Having conferred the title of steward on the French poet, Hill's text effectually translates the earlier fanfare to Offa's political power into a celebration of

Péguy's literary power, in appropriating through his writing a public domain and historical landscape: 'Chateau de Trie is yours, Chartres is yours,' and so on. The 'domain' the poem explores is a field of discourse, a field in a particular landscape, a field of battle (the poem portrays Péguy as embattled well before the war), and an 'inner domain' occupied by 'images/of earth and grace'.[48] 'Domain' here is a version of Hill's 'kingdom', and implies 'lordship', the peculiar authority with which the poet seeks to invest the image of the poet, as well as 'inheritance'. The poem as a whole enacts the battle for an inherited rhetoric within the unprecedented context of the modern world, and the mass violence of the First World War in particular. If Péguy is a tragi-comic victim of that war, he is also, as the poem's starting-point makes clear, in some degree responsible for it, at least on the evidence of his attacks upon the pacifistic, progressive internationalism of Jaurès. If Hill's poetry seeks to confer authority upon the exemplary figure of the poet, it also imposes a corresponding moral responsibility.

The inherited 'inner domain' of the poem about Péguy, and the idea of a 'lost kingdom' throughout Hill's work, seem at one level to represent the kingdom of poetic eloquence. This is both the 'right-royal' language of Hazlitt's polemic, and the challenge represented by Wallace Stevens's argument in 'The Noble Rider and the Sound of Words'.[49] More than the American poet, Hill consistently subjects the urge towards magniloquence to the com-promising pressures of historical power-relations and consequences of civil violence. That is, he refuses to allow poetry an autonomous domain of its own, separable from the attrition of circumstance, but also refuses to abandon the poem's proper urge to transcend its own occasions and speak with its own authority and proper dignity. This has often led Hill to explore the occasions of other poet's utterance and adopt their titles and rhetoric as his own – thus perhaps licensing him to transcend his own limiting circum-stances, and mask his own need for authority. His adopting W.H. Auden's phrase 'O Lords of Limit' for the title to his collected essays is a beautiful confirmation of my argument, I suppose. Yet Auden's haunting and witty phrase, conjuring a grandly absurd title for the focus of limitation, acquired a noticably more lordly and magisterial ring at the head of Hill's book of essays.

T.S. Eliot, in his essay on Marvell, lamented the separation in the middle of the seventeenth-century, between 'magniloquence' – which he defined as the 'deliberate exploitation of magnificence in language' – and 'wit'.[50] We could see Hill's masterful and mannered struggle with traditional poetic dic-tion and archaic political and religious title as an attempt to analyse the fundamental 'Bovarisme' of man's urge towards magniloquence, with all the intellectual wit at his disposal – but also, at some level, an attempt to redeem magniloquence by wit.

The fable invoked by the title of *King Log* embodies a fateful paradox for Hill. The story it refers to describes the protest of a community of frogs against the ineffectual rule of their log king, who neither lives up to his title nor asserts his kingship. This leads to his replacement by King Stork, a real authoritarian monarch, who then proceeds to devour them. The fable proposes two unacceptable kinds of authority, though it seems to imply that we should prefer a comfortable and tolerant political inertia to autocratic or totalitarian assertiveness, to Leviathan in fact. Yet much of Hill's poetry must be read as a protest against the indignity of King Log, and seems to yearn for real authority and real title, the kind of transcendence embodied in a language of kingship derived from the past and earlier power-relations. Only Christianity could effectively justify such a language; thus its privileged position in Hill's own rhetoric. But Hill is too intelligent and humane a poet to succumb to the appeal of King Stork (the title he ironically gives the Postscript to *King Log*, as if the concluding essay and 'reparation' amounted to another and more authoritarian mode of discourse). Though he is fascinated by his glamorous rhetoric and grand style, he continues to scrutinise it with wit and scepticism. His problem of poetic authority confirms him in a double-bind like that implied by the fable, but fortunately for us, that has fired a poetry of memorable resonance that restlessly questions its own title. We might apply to Hill what he has written of W.B. Yeats:

> The poet is hearing words in depth and is therefore hearing, or sounding, history and morality in depth. It is as though the very recalcitrance of language – and we know that Yeats found the process of composition arduous – stood for the primary objective world in one of its forms of cruelty and indifference . . .[51]

And though we may lament Hill's more than 'indifference' to the 'new images of faith' and current power-relations, current political battles, we have to recognise that his recognition of the relationship between traditional poetic tropes and history illuminates the present as well as the past. No other English poet this century has generated such a powerful and disturbing sense of history in his work. If part of the work's own authority strikes us as anachronistic, it may be that that will help to liberate us from anachronistic authority. This is plenty. This is more than enough.

10

Hill and the dictionary

Henry Gifford

From the beginning Geoffrey Hill has been a philologist, rather in the sense that Emily Dickinson can be so described. He would not, I think, assent to her awestruck claim 'A Word is inundation, when it comes from the Sea', nor has he ever been in a position to say with her 'for several years, my Lexicon – was my only companion'[1] – the comma and the dash, like little gasps, betokening a wonderment on dangerous ground between the arch and the ecstatic. Yet of him it is true, as Emily Dickinson wrote of herself, 'The Poet searched Philology'.[2] Although their purposes and situations are not the same, one basic resemblance does exist. Emily Dickinson was, as Hill a hundred years later is today, a religious poet by inclination, and like him displaced, being unable to give freely her credence to the Christian doctrine that her own family and neighbours took for granted.

We have to concede that a good poet never takes conceptual terms for granted, since it is in the nature of his art to find out meanings for himself. Even if he could have the certitude of Dante, he would still need, as Dante needed, to prove his certitude by experiencing it through a journey of the imagination. Both Emily Dickinson and Hill have been unable to achieve that happiness. They show their disquiet, their unwilling scepticism, in a painfully ironic play upon words. In poem number 501, she affirms and retracts at the same time:

> This World is not Conclusion.
> A Species stands beyond –
> Invisible, as Music –
> But positive, as Sound –
> It beckons, and it baffles –
> Philosophy – dont know –
> And through a Riddle, at the last –
> Sagacity, must go . . .

Sagacity (all too much for Emily's comfort, her own distinction) draws back from passing through that 'Riddle', a dark mystery and also a sieve that sorts out the wheat from the chaff. 'Conclusion' is brought to the poem in a final note of unbelief beyond help:

> Narcotics cannot still the Tooth
> That nibbles at the soul –

In a poem in *Tenebrae* (the title of this collection evokes 'the lone frost's black length' of Hardy's sequence 'In Tenebris'), Hill observes with a deceptive casualness: 'Theology makes good bedside reading.' But the 'good reading' serves only to induce a drowsy oblivion:

> Some
> who are lost covet scholastic proof,
> subsistence of probation, modest balm.
> ('An Apology . . .: 10. Fidelities')

Laying aside the book, 'we close our eyes to Anselm and lie calm', dropping off now that Anselm has done the trick for us – and also, the phrase can imply, with regard to the first original thinker of Christian scholasticism, accepting our blindness, like that of Milton, who, in Gray's Pindaric ode 'The Progress of Poesy', 'closed his eyes in endless night.'

Poets in our time, even since the First World War, when the language of politicians at home was seen by men at the front as derisively out of touch with experience there, have been aware that words are on trial as never before. The brutal manipulation of words in order to seduce the masses in Hitler's Germany and Stalin's Russia, and the sheer difficulty of finding any terms to express the impersonal horrors of the Second World War, made speech, the cardinal human achievement, no longer secure.[3] Geoffrey Hill, in common with the majority of the world's inhabitants today, has grown up to the knowledge that the old sanctions have been obliterated. As a student and teacher of English literature, he is given the uneasy privilege of being able to frequent a world differently constituted from ours, when the moral vocabulary seemed to rest on a durable basis, so that such a work as Johnson's *Dictionary of the English Language* was designed also to be the treasure-house of a civilisation. Only for the last few decades have poets in Britain, as somewhat earlier in the United States, become, perforce, grammarians – the word used 'in the more extended sense' of 'philologist' by Lewis and Short to translate the Latin *grammaticus*. Cicero defines *grammatici* as those who are 'interpreters of the poets'. When a mind unusually sensitive to the mounting atrocities of human behaviour comes to spend the main part of its working life in what today the majority look on as a forbidding museum, with stiff turnstiles for admission to the further galleries, there will be many painful recognitions. A poet is original to the degree in which he senses the future in the present. His engagement with the writing and linguistic usage of the past is singularly

direct. What Eliot said in 'The Dry Salvages' about 'Something that is prob-
ably quite ineffable' underlying the most deeply aware experience has its place
here:

> The backward look behind the assurance
> Of recorded history, the backward half-look
> Over the shoulders, towards the primitive terror.

Hill already shows the awareness I have described in *For the Unfallen*,
where his 'Requiem for the Plantagenet Kings' is set opposite the first of 'Two
Formal Elegies' written 'For the Jews in Europe'. The Plantagenet kings are
now, safely it would appear, sealed in funereal decorum:

> At home, under caved chantries, set in trust,
> With well-dressed alabaster and proved spurs
> They lie; they lie; secure in the decay
> Of blood, blood-marks, crowns hacked and coveted,
> Before the scouring fires of trial-day
> Alight on men . . .

But the 'fires of trial-day', when the sea gruesomely 'evacuates its dead', have
already been burning in Auschwitz, and the kings are resurrected as Sir Walter
Scott and his admirers had never realised them. If they were 'set in trust', that
trust is broken. They are no longer secure; the careful effect has been ruined.
There they lie, and lying it is – the language that might have been taken to
support the illusion is now exposed. They came to their rest 'Relieved of
soul', but this means 'starkly deprived', as you might be relieved of your
purse, without any hint of relief as an end to trouble. The alabaster has been
'well-dressed', well-tooled by the craftsman, but now seems to have been
sartorially at fault – Savile Row will burn up with the whole world at Judge-
ment Day. And the spurs may have been proved in the sense of 'tested in
battle'; they are no evidence of proven chivalry. As Hill declares in the
following poem about the Jews, 'The wilderness revives,/Deceives with sweet-
ness harshness.' But now we have been taught to recognise the deceit in this
pageant that was meant to hold up while the world lasted.

'Funeral Music', the centre-piece and finest achievement of Hill's next vol-
ume, *King Log*, is an elaborate meditation on the same theme. Hill refuses
'to play down the violence of the Wars of the Roses' or to conceal the hideous
truth that the Battle of Towton in 1461 was, even by modern standards, a
holocaust. For his exposure of the brute facts he has devised an idiom of
'ornate heartlessness' (a phrase used by Ian Nairn to describe 'much mid-
fifteenth-century architecture, especially court architecture'). It is the disparity
between a learned and ornate rhetoric (possibly that of a highly placed cleric
at court), and the crude butchery it conceals that produces his 'florid grim
music broken by grunts and shrieks'. The simulation and the reality are
present in the first poem in the sequence, when it relates the beheading of
Tiptoft, Earl of Worcester:

> The voice fragrant with mannered humility,
> With an equable contempt for this World,
> 'In honorem Trinitatis'. Crash. The head
> Struck down into a meaty conduit of blood. . . .

The ornate in English is usually the latinate, and Hill (like Emily Dickinson) here and in many other places is exploiting the contrast that Shakespeare did in the familiar example of Hamlet's dying words to Horatio:

> Absent thee from felicity awhile,
> And in this harsh world draw thy breath in pain,
> To tell my story.

True, Hamlet does not seek to jeopardise the notion of felicity by the native English bluntness of the second line: he is rather opposing the ease and dignity of the celestial state to the aching struggle below, where a man is reduced to a hurt animal (Hamlet himself at this moment must have been drawing his breath in pain). Tiptoft, demanding three strokes from the axe 'in Honour of the Trinity', 'enjoyed', as Hill remarks, 'a degree of ritual' – he seized the occasion to relish it. The description of a voice as 'fragrant with mannered humility' is itself mannered, like the expression of Gray which Johnson objected to: 'The gales ... seem ... redolent of joy and youth',[4] or even that in Pope's line 'Die of a rose in aromatic pain'.[5]

The calling to account of Latin words, either by confronting them with ugly fact, or showing it as lurking in them when other senses they have are allowed to surface, is something that goes on steadily in 'Funeral Music'. Indeed, it is a main characteristic of Hill's poetry in *King Log*. The fifth poem of 'Funeral Music' gives another striking example:

> As with torches we go, at wild Christmas,
> When we revel in our atonement
> Through thirty feasts of unction and slaughter,
> What is that but the soul's winter sleep?
> So many things rest under consummate
> Justice as though trumpets purified law,
> Spikenard were the real essence of remorse.

The preceding poem provided a bridge to this one: 'a palace blazing/With perpetual silence as with torches.' Now that silence is rudely broken: 'As with torches we go, at wild Christmas ...' The festival is, like everything in their way of life, uncontrolled and tumultuous. There could be wild weather outside, but the word indicates above everything that this is a pagan feast, as it were an orgy in the mead-hall of their remote ancestors. They 'revel in their atonement', ostensibly to celebrate the birth of their redeemer; but this is a continuous monster revel 'through thirty feasts' over as many years, and what they rejoice in is their concord, the being-at-one of a tribal company. Their feasts are characterised by 'unction and slaughter' – 'unction' can have the sense of strong religious feeling, though it accords strangely with the slaughter of the beasts that provide the cheer. It also hints at the last rites at the block, or on a field of bloody battle. Christmas marks the winter solstice, the sleep or hibernation of nature; but this is the soul's winter sleep, not its holiday, and 'winter sleep' could be an apt description of the whole period, from Suffolk's execution in 1450 to Rivers's in 1483.

The three lines that follow bring back the self-ennobling deception:

> So many things rest under consummate
> Justice as though trumpets purified law,
> Spikenard were the real essence of remorse.

We now know that nothing in this pageant can truly rest, and least of all under 'consummate/Justice', even though the style of the pageant might look consummate, like the perfected tombs. To 'purify' bears among others a legal sense, of making an obligation 'pure' by fulfilling its conditions, as Christ would fulfil those of the atonement. But here it is the trumpets (like those 'silver, snarling' ones in 'The Eve of St. Agnes') that are deemed to have 'purified law', the jungle law of these conflicts. Fragrancy returns to the sequence with mention of spikenard – but the assumed 'real essence' turns out to be no more than a perfume, a cosmetic for remorse. Tiptoft's voice was fragrant with a humility that was impure, being tainted, as Hill notes, with 'unorthodox arrogance'. The essential core of remorse is missing in this passage, likewise recording a deceptive show.

Mercian Hymns establishes a different kind of continuity – not simply that of the violence which binds together the acts of Plantagenet barbarism and Hitler's attempted 'final solution for the Jews'. In the *Hymns* it is not a matter of simple resurrection. What Hill had done in the preceding books is aptly summarised by a sentence from 'History as Poetry' (*King Log*):

> Poetry
> Unearths from among the speechless dead
> Lazarus mystified, common man
> Of death.

And this is one of 'The tongue's atrocities', to compel a puzzling resurrection:

> The lily rears its gouged face
> From the provided loam.

In *Mercian Hymns*, where one region's history over twelve hundred years has become a living amalgam of present and past under King Offa as 'presiding genius', the dictionary is put to more complex uses. It is no longer a task of stripping away false eloquence, or riddling confident, superb phrases with other connotations they had hoped to hide. What the *Hymns* require is an act of assimilation, of interplay, some irony and more of delight in proving a continuity like that of 'the perennial holly-groves, the riven sandstone', and of Offa himself:

> 'Now when King Offa was alive and dead', they were
> all there, the funereal gleemen: papal legate and
> rural dean: Merovingian car-dealers, Welsh mercen-
> aries; a shuffle of house-carls.
>
> (XXVII)

The opening words, a 'ritual phrase' of the time as Hill explains, formulate neatly the status of Offa in *Mercian Hymns*, with the interfusion between different periods of history, the past at the elbow of the present. So David Jones had found it when he wrote *In Parenthesis*,[6] about the First World War and his regimental comrades – 'mostly Londoners with an admixture of Welshmen' – and the mingling of their traditions, their 'speech and habit of mind' that 'were a perpetual showing'. Earth, in this particular hymn, 'lay for a while, the ghost-bride of livid Thor'. There is a glimpse of the ancient shire-tree that has been uprooted, but more important for the perpetuation of Anglo-Saxon Mercia than abiding scenery or surviving landmarks – since this is a work of poetry – is the knitting together of two periods by the language: 'Merovingian car-dealers, Welsh mercenaries; a shuffle of house-carls'. The Merovingian dynasty in France had been succeeded by that of Charlemagne – friendship with whom is Offa's final glory in the catalogue of his achievements (I). The hymns perform very often the skilful operation that takes place here. A 'Merovingian car-dealer' is an anachronism disguised by the antiquity of the two components forming the noun. 'Dealers' of various other kinds, corn-dealers or money-dealers, for instance, have been with us for at least three or four centuries. 'Cars' were known long before they became 'automobiles'; the word derives from late Latin, and is akin to an Old Celtic word (not inappropriate here, next to Welsh mercenaries). The 'house-carls' (personal bodyguard of a Saxon king) close the procession in this paragraph, still, it might seem, apart from the others. But they are characterised by the term 'a *shuffle* of house-carls', and so the last knot in the linguistic knitting process is deftly tied. It probably strikes the modern ear as a generic term, like 'a gaggle of geese' (where the group makes itself known as such by their sound). A 'shuffle' can be the movement of feet, uneasy or perhaps reluctant; but it could also refer to the dealing out of cards, which leads back to the Merovingians, and a possible submerged pun whereby 'car-dealer' becomes 'card-dealer'. But another sense of the verb 'to shuffle' is to act in an underhand way, and standing as they do next to mercenaries (hired soldiers whose loyalty to the other contracting party was never too sure in the Italian middle ages), these 'car-dealers' begin to sound like second-hand car dealers, whose professional reputation by and large is an uncertain one.

This work of assimilation, on the surface of language or below it, is constant in the hymns. One more passage out of many that could be used will suffice:

Gasholders; russet among fields. Milldams, marlpools
that lay unstirring. Eel-swarms. Coagulations of
frogs: once, with branches and half-bricks, he
battered a ditchful; then sidled away from the
stillness and silence.

(VII)

This is a poem in which the child Offa has become a twentieth-century boy,
with 'a biplane, already obsolete and irreplaceable', and 'his private derelict
sandlorry'. The 'sandlorry' however bears a name at once current (there were
lorries of this make at the time) and antique (the ancient poetical name for
Britain). His friend is Ceolred, and Dorothy Whitelock in *The Beginnings of
English Society*, a book referred to elsewhere in the notes by Hill, mentions
a man 'at the abbey of Wenlock', who 'saw prophetically King Ceolred of
Mercia among the damned'.[7] The opening paragraph of the hymns, quoted
earlier, is at work mantling over the present with the past. Similarly, the
biplane, 'of heavy snub silver', which Ceolred 'let ... spin through a hole in
the classroom-floorboards', goes to join 'rat droppings and coins', the detritus
of nature and man. Offa, at the end of *Mercian Hymns*:

vanished

he left behind coins, for his lodging, and traces of
red mud.

(XXX)

'Gasholders' (in contrast to the alternative form, 'gasometers', already some
two hundred years old) fits easily into the original world of Offa, as do the
'windshields' of motor-cars (XXI), or the 'schoolyard' and the 'cloakrooms'
(VI). They stand in this poem among 'milldams', from the technology of
Offa's day: R.W. Southern in *Western Society and the Church in the Middle
Ages* has stated that water mills 'spread everywhere in north-western Europe'
during the dark ages, and 'the imperfect statistics of Domesday Book record
the existence of some six thousand ... in 1086'.[8] 'Marlpools' are probably
flooded marl-pits. The gasholders, 'russet among fields', have turned autum-
nal: the water behind the dams and in the pool lies unstirring. Into this
timeless scene there breaks the concealed music of two alliterative lines of
verse in the Old English tradition:

once, with *b*ranches and half-*b*ricks, he *b*attered a ditchful;
then *s*idled away from the *s*tillness and *s*ilence.

The range of diction in *Mercian Hymns* can accommodate 'Thrall to their
freedom, I dug and hoarded' (VI) or 'Swathed bodies in the long ditch; one
eye upstaring' (XI), both of which examples might have been lifted from Old
English poetry; and, at the other extreme, a latinate usage as mannered as
anything in *King Log*:

> He strolled back to the
> car, with discreet souvenirs for consolation and
> philosophy. He set in motion the furtherance of
> his journey. To watch the Tiber foaming out
> much blood.
>
> (XVIII)

'For consolation and philosophy'; the note ('though it is doubtless an excess of scruple to point this out') refers the phrase to the famous treatise by Boethius, whose dungeon at Pavia has been viewed in 'a visitation of some sorrow'. Once again, a highly elaborate phrase, which is almost Jamesian – 'He set in motion the furtherance of his journey' – is brought up against the shock of harsh actuality in plain English: 'To watch the Tiber foaming out much blood.' Consolation and philosophy will be sapped by this tide. A master-mason (as is said of the one who decorated Kilpeck Church in Herefordshire) has been sent 'Itinerant through numerous domains, of his lord's retinue, to Compostela', bringing back 'home for a life-time amid West Mercia' the inventiveness of style seen there for 'tympanum and chancel-arch' upon which he is 'intent to pester … his moody testament' (XXIV). 'To pester' can mean 'to crowd', or 'obstruct'; the 'testament' is his own headstrong act of witness; but the phrase looks forward to the description of what he shows:

> … pale
> spree of evangelists and, there, a cross Christ
> mumming child Adam out of Hell

The evangelists are in holiday mood; Christ is 'cross'. It is impossible for the mind not to brush aside syntax here and see the phantom of a pun: the word 'cross' in proximity to Christ cannot be parted from the idea of crucifixion; and indeed according to the apocryphal gospel of Nicodemus, Christ, after being taken down from the cross, descended to hell which he then harrowed, liberating Adam and Eve with some of the patriarchs. He is 'mumming child Adam out of hell' in the sense of enacting this scene; but to the contemporary ear the association of 'mum' and 'child' is irresistible. It raises another fleeting vision, that of a cross mother with her child, leading him away from the trouble he has fallen into.

Mercian Hymns abounds in wayside felicities, often in the form of a pun: 'the chef … a king in his new-risen hat', (III); 'I wormed my way heavenward for ages amid barbaric ivy', (V, another alliterative line of verse, incidentally); 'The strange church smelled a bit "high"' (IX); 'The Frankish gift, two-edged, regaled with slaughter' (XVI, of a sword: 'regaled' carries the double sense of 'entertained, feasted' and 'gratified by a gift'); 'deciduous velvet peeled from evergreen albums' (XXI); 'Fortified in their front parlours, at Yuletide men are the more murderous' (XXVI: the first word of the following line, 'Drunk', suggests that the Englishman in the castle of his home is fortified further by alcohol); 'He was defunct. They were perfunctory' (XXVII). One of these puns deliberately exploits a false etymology: 'Trout-fry simmered there' (XIV). 'Fry', young fish newly from the spawn, have no connection with the frying pan; but the visual effect is remarkably neat. Prose poems bring their notorious difficulties, and the avoidance of an air of preciosity is the chief one. Hill avoids this hazard by the accuracy of his diction – 'a stringent mystery' (having the sense of 'skill'), as in the *Opus Anglicanum* of XXIII. And it can place beautifully the slipshod or tawdry modern: 'spoil-heaps of chrysanths dead in their plastic macs, eldorado of washstand marble'; or change from high solemnity to the recorded voice of homely prattle:

> I unburden the saga of your burial, my dear. You had
>   lived long enough to see things 'nicely settled'.
>
> (IX)

In *Tenebrae* the language of paradox is often to be heard. Its opening sequence, 'The Pentecost Castle', moves around the anguished contradiction stated in its first epigraph, from Yeats: 'It is terrible to desire and not possess, and terrible to possess and not desire'. Another main sequence, 'Lachrimae', seven poems in sonnet form, sets up the endless counterpoint of Christian meditation, the more painful for the poet's sense of exclusion and unworthiness. Hill had been reading, at this time, Spanish verse, and the last poem in the cycle freely translates a sonnet from Lope de Vega. The epitaph from Robert Southwell (later canonised by the Catholic Church) further emphasises an affinity in style and feeling with the Counter-Reformation: Southwell's own idiom stands close to that of Spanish devotional poetry in that era. '5. Pavana Dolorosa', is weighted with Christian paradox:

> Loves I allow and passions I approve:
> Ash-Wednesday feasts, ascetic opulence,
> the wincing lute, so real in its pretence,
> itself a passion amorous of love.
>
> Self-wounding martyrdom, what joys you have,
> true-torn among this fictive consonance,
> music's creation of the moveless dance,
> the decreation to which all must move.
>
> Self-seeking hunter of forms, there is no end
> to such pursuits. None can revoke your cry.
> Your silence is an ecstasy of sound
>
> and your nocturnals blaze upon the day.
> I founder in desire for things unfound.
> I stay amid the things that will not stay.

The phrasing is once more tense with precision. It works often through negative forms ('moveless', 'decreation', 'things unfound'); through contradictory statements ('Ash-Wednesday feasts, ascetic opulence'; 'self-wounding martyrdom'; 'joys ... true-torn'; 'Your silence is an ecstasy of sound' – sound in rapture that stands outside, is liberated from itself). It also works through a discreet play upon words: 'revoke your cry', meaning recall and retract; 'founder in desire for things unfound' – no etymological link here; 'stay amid the things that will not stay' – the second 'stay' can mean to sustain. The poem is the most elaborate, in this regard, in the sequence, but these devices occur in the others too.

Geoffrey Hill is not a hermetic poet: his verse never becomes impenetrable. At times the learning may present a barrier, which has to be surmounted by patient research in the dictionary. The technical terms are not always taken easily, as in the concluding lines of 'Martyrium':

> Viaticum transfigures earth's desire
> In rising vernicles of summer air.

Readers of T.S. Eliot will remember, from 'Animula',

> Living first in the silence after the viaticum,

even if they had not known previously this term for extreme unction, or Eucharist administered to the dying. 'Vernicles' refer to Christ's face imprinted on the kerchief of St. Veronica. Such baroque touches are made acceptable because the poet is also content to play elsewhere with the very simplest diction:

> Married and not for love
> you of all women
> you of all women
> my soul's darling my love.

Wordsworth complained of another scholar-poet, Gray, that he was 'curiously elaborate in the structure of his own poetic diction', much of which became remote from 'the language really spoken by men'.[9] Hill's strength is that he can return at will to lines as exquisitely simple as those I have just quoted, where the same awareness of the complicated and the contradictory that often makes him 'curiously elaborate' resorts to the most natural and naked of speech. He never fails, even at his richest, to be a poet of 'ascetic opulence'.

11

Hill's imitations

Michael Edwards

Geoffrey Hill's first title, *For the Unfallen*, is already an interesting piece of writing. By referring one to 'For the Fallen', the well-loved Great War elegy of Laurence Binyon, and so to any number of other poems in the genre, it delves the reader into poetry's many-layered process of writing and re-writing, while keeping its distance. More specifically, Binyon's response to the war, his muffling of pain, evil, death in undemanding versions of patriotism, art and transcendence, is exactly what Hill's poetry works against, the nexus of simple affirmations of which he continually takes the measure. The title also involves word-play. As quoted in the concluding poem in the volume, it backhandedly dedicates the book to those who fail to recognise that they are fallen more deeply, and implicated in a fallen world.

All his book-titles, in fact, including that chosen for the single American edition, and many of the titles of his poems, are taken from the works, or liturgies, of others. They display the central and varied presence in his poetry of imitation, whose graph rises from volume to volume. His writings imply previous writings; word-play frequently accompanies this poem-play.

The poems he chooses to approach are characteristically positives from which, in the act of imitation, he withdraws. In the 'Lachrimae' sequence from *Tenebrae*, '2, The Masque of Blackness' and '7, Lachrimae Amantis' demur about art and about religious experience; they are versions of Quevedo's 'Retrato de Lisi que traía en una sortija',[1] and Lope de Vega's '¿Qué tengo yo que mi amistad procuras? ...'.[2] They are also, I believe, two of his finest poems, and at the heart of his work. 'Lachrimae' as a whole derives, as he indicates, from other works. An anonymous sonnet of the Spanish Renaissance, 'A Cristo crucificado', whose strategy of addressing Christ on the cross governs the series, provides recurring details. Dowland's 'Lachrimae', a sequence of intricately interwoven pavans of the English Renaissance, each beginning with the same swelling and falling motif figurative of tears, inspires an equally intricate series of sonnets; three of them open with the phrase 'Crucified Lord', which has a similar rhythm to Dowland's and is likewise figurative – this time of the focal paradox of Christianity. 'Lachrimae' changes its material, however, using it as a point, precisely, of departure, from certainties which Hill finds difficult to recover, and which he is suspicious of recovering, and of wanting to recover. Whereas Dowland moves ascensionally from 'Lachrimae Antiquae' to 'Lachrimae Verae', Hill, beginning with 'Lachrimae Verae', redefines 'true' in terms of his own tough-minded truth-telling, via powerfully affirmed negatives:

> I cannot turn aside from what I do;
> you cannot turn away from what I am.
> You do not dwell in me nor I in you.

Although he closes with 'Lachrimae Amantis', 'lover' too, as we shall see, is considerably disturbed.

The moments of deepest change are in 2 and 7, the two versions. The 'free translation' of Lope de Vega's poem shifts the confession and longing of the original into a self-abrasive, desirous refusal of the sequence's 'Crucified Lord'. Take the beginning:

> What is there in my heart that you should sue
> so fiercely for its love? What kind of care
> brings you as though a stranger to my door
> through the long night and in the icy dew
>
> seeking the heart that will not harbour you,
> that keeps itself religiously secure?
>
> > ('7, Lachrimae Amantis')

There is still the echo, as in Lope de Vega, of the Old Testament cry, 'What is man, that thou art mindful of him?' (less in the classic instance of Psalm 8 than in Job, 7. 17–18, which also asks why God 'shouldest set thine heart' upon man and 'try him every moment'), and also of Christ's words: 'Behold, I stand at the door, and knock', (Revelation, 3.20), along with their context in the letter to the 'lukewarm' Laodiceans (Revelation, 3.14–16). One becomes aware also, however, of the slow, intent, wresting of Lope's poem in a translation deliberately 'wrong'. An address to 'my Jesus', with its assuredness, through any failure, of belonging, is replaced by one to an unnamed lord – an address more eloquent perhaps, and (for this Christian) more moving. The vividness of the emotion is achieved in small details for the ear and the mouth, especially those hard 'c's' in 'What kind of care ...', which catch in the throat and impede utterance. Moreover, where the speaker in '¿Qué tengo ...?' continues to invoke Jesus until the end, Hill's tercets turn aside, to distance the lord, in the last word of the poem, as 'him'. The final move is a change of temporal perspective. The lament in the Spanish sonnet is that the speaker has so often deferred opening the house of his soul to Jesus, through the past; while Hill's poem exists in a present of continuing rejection, where the heart 'will not' – or wills not to – harbour the lord, whose wounds in a later line 'must' bleed anew, and where there is no sign that the 'tomorrow' of the conclusion ' "tomorrow I shall wake to welcome him" ' will ever arrive. There is even another 'mistranslation', the line 'At this dark solstice filled with frost and fire', a version of a moment in the midwinter-spring passage of Eliot's 'Little Gidding': 'When the short day is brightest, with frost and fire'.[3] The change here hints at the absence of any spiritual spring from the darkness in which Hill's poem is situated.

The self-analysis and self-censure have also become more severe, and more modern in the Hill. In his exploration of pseudo-religious emotion in the line 'bathed in pure tones of promise and remorse', one notes by the way a critique of art, which favours such states, and specifically – Dowland still being present – of the 'tones' of music; while the phrase *religiously* secure [my italics] is truly harsh. The poem's achievement is surely the meshing of recognition and refusal, self-knowledge that is both hurt and clenched, complexities of honesty requiring, as Eliot wrote of Blake in *The Sacred Wood*, great technical accomplishment. It is, in its way, a *marturia*, a witness to the truth, not of God but of our unwillingness for God.

The strength of the poem is owing partly to its being the last of a sequence, the whole of which it gathers and reorganises. A feature of Hill's use of other writers' materials is that by placing them in his work he creates new tensions within and around them. The imitation of Quevedo, moved to second place from its original position as fifth in the 'Lachrimae' sequence, intensifies the glance in the opening poem at the shocking ambiguity of art, specified in the crucifix: 'This is your body twisted by our skill'; there may also be a reference to the poem itself: 'This'. For if the version of Lope de Vega's poem is a major engagement with the possibly delusive perplexities of religion, the version of Quevedo's is a major engagement with the certainly delusive ease of art. Quevedo's 'Retrato de Lisi ...' seemingly climaxes in a voicing of the speaker's baffled love, and bitter realisation of the girl's inhumanity; it focuses, however, on a fine conceit, which sees the beautiful girl transformed into the art-work of a miniature as enclosing in that tiny compass all the splendours of the day and of the starry heavens, the gems of the east, the dramas of weather, and even as constituting, concealed from the real sky and the usual sunrise, a new light and a better birth. Hill's imitation gags on that late-Renaissance exuberance:

> Splendour of life so splendidly contained,
> brilliance made bearable. It is the east
> light's embodiment, fit to be caressed,
> the god Amor with his eyes of diamond,

celestial worldliness on which has dawned
intelligence of angels, Midas' feast,
the stony hunger of the dispossessed
locked into Eden by their own demand.

Self-love, the slavish master of this trade,
conquistador of fashion and remark,
models new heavens in his masquerade,

its images intense with starry work,
until he tires and all that he has made
vanishes in the chaos of the dark.
('Lachrimae: 2. The Masque of Blackness')

By a surprising and suggestive move, he filters the 'conceit' of the Incarnation
(a man who is God, a creature the Creator) into Quevedo's conceit about art,
concentrating two aspects of that divine leap i ） the human in the word-
play of 'bearable'. In a language at once lavish and sardonic, he explores (I
take it) responses to incarnation and to the work of art when both have
become idolatrous. As to the latter, Hill's is a relentless decrial, and a stricken
one, where poetry – 'this trade' – is then the servant of self-love, while the
'new heavens' which it produces have as their end fashion and remark, and
as their conclusion the nothingness of disillusion and death. The art-work, a
creation comparable to God's in the Romantic view, returns to the chaos and
dark from which, according to Genesis, creation proceeds.

Much of the power of the poem is in its emphatic and accumulative nam-
ing, which one 'makes prose again' only with hesitation, and about which
one may well be mistaken. There is re-creative art, seemingly, as a 'celestial
worldliness' (an oxymoron whose logic is repeated but also demonised in the
phrase 'slavish master'), perhaps a truly earthed vision of the world made
new, but more likely a desire for a new world fed by merely worldly lusts;
and there is re-creative imagination as the 'intelligence of angels', either an
authentic higher percipience, or just the possibly empty 'angelism' of so many
poets since Rimbaud. There is also the banquet of art as 'Midas' feast' (a hint
from another Quevedo poem[4]), where the hunger for a golden world turns
poeticised reality into stone, querying the Yeats of 'Sailing to Byzantium', and
preparing music as 'Medusa' in the chilling final poem of the volume (an
extraordinary, pared anti-ode to St Cecilia, which only someone passionate
about music and poetry could be moved to write). There is submission to the
dispossessing art-work as being 'locked into Eden' (Quevedo calls the portrait
a 'prison') – an ironic doom for a race, according to Genesis, locked out of
it; and the work of the artist as 'starry', because it fashions and concentrates
a new and heavenly brilliance, but also because its vision is starry-eyed;
perhaps, too, the artist himself wants to be a 'star'.

The reference in Hill's title to *The Masque of Blacknesse* of Ben Jonson and Inigo Jones, extends the idolatry to empire – one better appreciates 'conquistador' – and specifically the British Empire which comes under scrutiny later in the book. Among the delusions catered for in Jonson's masque, in which the daughters of Niger come to Britain to lose their blackness in that superior resplendence, are that Britannia is *'a world, diuided from the world'* and the 'Diamant' in the world's 'ring' (the imagery is also Quevedo's), and that the light of the British monarch is 'scientiall' and 'past mere nature'.[5] Hill parallels those terms, opening his poem's critique to this further – and to all – presumptions of transcendence.

It is a formidable poem, more than merely 'challenging'. It has to be lived through, by writers and readers concerned in any way with poetry as re-creative. It is a scourging of motive, and scores through any reaching for new heavens, or indeed a new earth, any celebration of the value and potency of art, which does not proceed from whatever the opposite is of self-love – love, perhaps. And one's sense of its truth is not diminished but increased by the realisation of its own ambiguity: that this sonnet too is a splendid container, that, to quote the terms of the fifth poem in the sequence, this 'self-wounding' has its own 'joys'.

Other imitations approach transcendence in different terms. *Mercian Hymns* is the most abrupt about it. Thematically, the hymns declare an ironic distance from the 'Mercian Hymns' of *Sweet's Anglo-Saxon Reader*, which are praisings of 'Dryhten', the Lord. Though they are still hymns, they fail to address themselves to God: they cause Offa, the 'overlord' whom they both praise and dispraise, to appropriate them to himself – ' "sing it again" ', he answers antiphonally in I – and so they explore tyrannical selfhood, the 'kempt and jutting' ego of Offa (XIII) as, indeed, of Hill himself and of the reader; and they choose to celebrate such matters as 'Gasholders, russet among fields' (VII), 'the meadow scabbed with cow-dung' (XXII), 'lime-splodges and phlegm' (XXIII). Nor does the volume avoid transcendence merely because it deals with a mundane period of our history. Hymn XXIII turns to the 're-entry of transcendence into this sublunary world' in the later Middle Ages, yet silently opposes, to the 'treacherous' thread of embroidery which 'riddled' that mystery (a pun), the 'reliable' light of oil-lamps, shining not on 'masterworks' but on munching workers.

In 'An Apology for the Revival of Christian Architecture in England' (*Tenebrae*), transcendence and its loss are viewed in terms of national nostalgia, pain for the return home. The sequence, Hill's most searching work on the 'condition of England', includes as its precisely placed second poem an imitation of another Spanish sonnet, 'Llevó tras sí los pámpanos otubre...' by Lope de Vega's contemporary, Argensola.[6] Argensola's poem concerns wasted time and the loss of the object of desire, and concludes descriptions of the hardening of the natural world in autumn with the sight of a 'delaying' lover (his name is Fabius) weeping with shame at his mistress's threshold. The real and emblematic countryside is named as northern Spanish, and Hill seems to have lighted on this hint for the making of a poem not only set in northern England but with England as its subject. The adversity of the late season becomes the autumn of our discontent, and when the brief sun is gone we are said, according to a notion added to the original, to live 'like gleaners of its vestiges', picking, one supposes, at what remains of empire, and of other national splendours. The ending of Hill's poem transforms and complicates Argensola's:

> Why does the air grow cold

> in the region of mirrors? And who is this clown
> doffing his mask at the masked threshold
> to selfless raptures that are all his own?

These are not rhetorical questions, and I am none too sure of the answers. It appears that as well as the lover who, maskless, knows his failure and sinks into the self-regard of ostensibly outward-looking repining; and as well as the poet, no longer modelling new heavens in his masquerade but caught in an equally self-loving contemplation of an unattainable poetic kingdom; there is also the Englishman – the Englishman as lover-poet – cold in a country suspended in mirror-images of itself, but glowing with the self-indulgent raptures of nostalgia.

Hill's title 'Damon's Lament for his Clorinda, Yorkshire 1654' doubtless refers one to another poem, Marvell's 'Clorinda and Damon', where the amorous advances of a shepherdess are met by a shepherd's chaste resolve to redeem the natural objects of pastoral into tropes of Christian piety (flocks into lost sheep, fountains into baptismal waters, etc.). For Damon to lament the shepherdess suggests that, to his witty and successful transfiguration he now prefers Arcadia, as the emblem of unfulfilled longing. By setting the poem in 1654, when Marvell had in fact left Yorkshire and Nun Appleton – which may imply, more simply, that by a similar move Damon has for-feited Clorinda – Hill also introduces another nostalgia, for the lost country house.

Argensola's theme of the lover lamenting his mistress has been made extra-ordinarily more dense and extensive. The reading of Hill's imitation as a poem about historical England is prompted by the title of the sequence, but also by the first poem, '1. Quaint Mazes', whose richer nostalgia and softer irony '2. Damon's Lament for his Clorinda ...' serves to chill. The former layers its nostalgias, beginning:

> And, after all, it is to them we return.
> Their triumph is to rise and be our hosts:
> lords of unquiet or of quiet sojourn,
> those muddy-hued and midge-tormented ghosts.

'They' are the Pugin, Coleridge and Disraeli evoked in the title and epigraphs, intent on the revival of an older England of transcendence. They are also the 'quaint mazes' of *A Midsummer-Night's Dream*, the Renaissance turf mazes transported to Fairy-land; this adds a Shakespearian to a nineteenth-century regret, since Titania describes them as having become 'undistinguishable' through 'lack of tread'.[7] They also suggest the world of Shakespeare himself, and, as the poem advances, the Catholic religion banished in his time, a still older religion of 'sacred well'and 'hidden shrine', as well as the 'trysts' and 'quests' of romance, the country house of the centuries intervening between Shakespeare and Coleridge, the English wood slowly ravaged. And to those losses, and our loss of the masters of those losses, is added regret for a world perfectly named, a vision of 'Linnaean pentecosts' – which, as the Spirit-wind (The Acts of the Apostles, 2) makes the lilac-bush 'blustery' and its tongues of fire cause fountains to 'burn', illuminate objects with their 'pronged light', with the binomial classification, that is, in that most sustained of modern revivals of Adam's naming of the beasts.

It is a marvellous act of recovery, of pious memory; a definitive performance of what the poem calls 'Religion of the heart', the religion of warm imaginative allegiances, to charged writings, places and moments of the past, of reverent pilgrimages in part through the mind, which a literary education fosters, or used to foster. Since Hill's concern, however, is not to indulge in nostalgia but, as he said in an interview with John Haffenden, to draw its graph,[8] the poem is also touched with doubt. These may indeed be 'mazes', and their quaintness, fine and delicate in Shakespeare's use of the word, may also be somewhat picturesque. These healing places and sacramental spots can bind the heart to 'old hymns of servitude', a word Hill opposes in his essay on T.H. Green to its acceptable form, 'fealty'.[9] There is even a hint in the fourth line's oblique recall of the ending of 'Byzantium' ('That dolphin-torn, that gong-tormented sea'), that Hill's ghosts may not be entirely distinct from Yeats's shade, and that his midsummer-night's dream may be ultimately kin to Yeats's All Souls' nightmare of desperate, manic transcendence. 'An Apology ...: 2. Damon's Lament for his Clorida, Yorkshire 1654', the imitation, then suggests the delusion which can be involved in that nostalgia, that return to 'Clorinda'. And although the commemoration of inheritance continues through the sequence, the suggestion is still to be heeded in the final sonnet, where an image of transcendence from the past is allowed to radiate triumphantly at the moment it is most aggressed:

> Touched by the cry of the iconoclast,
> how the rose-window blossoms with the sun!
> ('13. The Herefordshire Carol')

The sonnet begins, 'So to celebrate that kingdom', and such a kingdom appears in various guises in Hill's poetry, as the object of a celebratory but also sceptical search. It is many things, but essentially, according to an expression of Christopher Devlin which Hill quotes elsewhere to Haffenden, 'the lost kingdom of innocence and original justice', to which, he adds, 'every fine and moving poem bears witness'.[10] Hill's work really is for the fallen: it acknowledges both the power and the powerlessness of poetry, that it can evoke Eden but may not usher one into it, being an alluring sign of exile. The awareness of that loss is not, of course, a passivity. It is the motive for modelling a new, guilt-acknowledging justice; for grappling the possibility of knowing God, nevertheless, and of discovering a significant world through art; and also for exploring a new transcendence of locality. We shall observe the latter in *Mercian Hymns*. There are also two engagements, in 'Fantasia on "Horbury"'' in *King Log* and 'Terribilis est Locus Iste' in *Tenebrae*, with Genesis, 28, where Jacob dreams of angels ascending and descending a ladder between heaven and earth, and is convinced on waking that the place where he finds himself is 'dreadful', the house of God and the gate of heaven – fascinated, resistant approaches, from complex distances, to one of the cardinal passages in scripture for linking this world to another.

Isn't it also true, in one light, that all 'fine and moving' poems – whatever their suspicion, or whatever their orientation towards the future – eventually bid to become the lost kingdom, themselves the objects of nostalgia, Edens of imaginative ease, of verbal fulfilment? Here is another significance of Hill's imitations: they 'return' to those places of hazardous repletion, and disturb them.

Nevertheless, one needs to underline the celebration of both the experiences and the poetries which he makes available. Although the originals are sometimes present as the poems he is *not* writing, another and obvious point to be made about his imitation is that he praises certain poems by other writers which he is happy to have come upon, by using them as means to engender poems of his own. He makes them part of the process of his own writing, involving them in the transformation which is arguably the practice of every poem. Like many poets, and especially like Lowell (whose *Imitations* he reviewed with a practitioner's care,[11] and whose influence on him has been extensive and diverse), he creates partly by scrutinising works already there in the world of literature, as he makes word-play by scrutinising words already there in the world of language.

'The Pentecost Castle' (*Tenebrae*) arranges into a new and stanzaically uniform sequence, a number of Spanish poems and songs of the fifteenth and sixteenth centuries concerned (like the Song of Songs which lies behind them) with the relations of sexual and divine love, which it sometimes couples in the Renaissance orgasmic connotation of 'to die'. (Again, Hill discovered the poems in Cohen; one of the wider effects of his imitations is to open English poetry to the poetry of Counter-Reformation Spain.) Although this poem, too, disturbs its sources, Hill has also drawn on them to produce a kind of ballad poetry that is hardly recognisable as having existed in English before. The puzzling title may be announcing this. While it points presumably to St. Teresa of Avila's 'interior castle' of the soul and to the uniting of the disciples with God and with each other at Pentecost, it also suggests the gift of tongues at work in translation and granting new utterance: 'Pentecost Castle' replacing 'Babel Tower'. The poems are therefore both Hill's and not Hill's, almost anonymous, hauntingly impersonal – a novel means, indeed, of procuring impersonality. And one still presumes his commitment to them. The engagement with experiences away from his own provides focus, so that, while miming the various voices, the actors and commentators of the drama, he is telling things as he understands them to be.

Mercian Hymns was also generated formally by the works it imitates – unless, that is, the hymns simply came that way. Rather than merely 'prose-poems', they are an original form, 'versets of rhythmical prose', as Hill himself has called them, with a 'pitched and tuned chant',[12] the versets even occasionally interrupting the syntax. They could have been suggested by an acknowledged precedent, the 'Te Deum', whose rhythmical prose lines are divided into sections; they also recall, as I have already noted, Sweet's 'Mercian Hymns', prose versions of biblical poems which likewise imply both prose and poetry, the sense of poetry in reading them being enhanced by one's memory of them as verses in the bible and especially, where appropriate, in the Missal or Prayer Book. Hill's hymns are then provided with a further visual formality, the ranging of the start of each verset to the left of the subsequent lines, which alludes to one of the ways of printing sonnets.

The hymns are also, in their way, translations. A particularity of Sweet's hymns is that they are not free-standing, but are written as an interlinear gloss on canticles from the Vulgate; the Anglo-Saxon neither merely implies the Latin nor faces it, but combines with it page by page. Hill similarly interlineates our world with Offa's, the two lines, of Mercian and modern, sometimes merging entirely, so that one can read through 'Their windshields dripped butterflies' to 'Their shields dripped blood' (XXI). One thinks of Eliot ('The Chair she sat in, like a burnished throne . . .'), but more of David Jones, since Hill is clearly writing for continuity, almost in the manner of the Mercian translator, or crib-writer, who matched the Latin word for word.

Indeed, *Mercian Hymns* also resembles its 'source' in being bilingual, an interlacing of Latin and Anglo-Saxon. The dual thread of text in Sweet's hymns can be very moving, since it is precisely that doubling which has come to constitute our own language: English is present on a ninth-century manuscript as a glint in the eye of history. We are now all bilingual, as are all our writings. Hill, however, draws attention to the two strands. Sometimes he composes a 'Latin' of singular eloquence: 'Itinerant through numerous domains, of his lord's retinue' (XXIV); but more often a more mysterious 'Anglo-Saxon': 'They clove to the hoard' (XII). This is highlighted in vocabulary: 'burh' (XX), 'wergild' (V); in agglutinations: 'blue-glassed storm-lantern' (XXII), 'classroom-floorboards' (VII); or in metre: 'with branches and half-bricks, he battered a ditchful; then sidled away from the stillness and silence' (VII). And he indicates the presence of this language play, this peering back into the ill-documented and foreign gloom, by setting down what looks like unusually powerful 'translatorese': 'forewarned I have thwarted their imminent devices' (VIII); by perpetrating a seeming mis-translation or scribal error: 'unattainable toys' for 'unattainable joys' (VI); by conjuring a whole poem, the second, from various, punning, attempts to translate the one word 'Offa'.

And are these 'Mercian' hymns only because Mercia is their territory or, as Sweet's, because they are written in 'Mercian'? – not the known Anglo-Saxon variant but a fresh language elaborated for the purpose. It is possible to emphasise Hill's mistrust of language and to miss his undertaking to renew it. The renewal here is achieved partly through various forms of the word-play for which he is well known, particularly rife in this volume, and at one point obliquely discussed. Of men who came to 'caulk water-pipes' it is said in Hymn XII, through a terse apostrophe: 'They are scattered to your colla-tions, moldywarp'. 'Moldywarp' is an Old English and now dialectal word for 'mole'; it is also, less the 'm', an anagram of 'word-play' – and thereby an example of word-play into the bargain. This may merely be an ingenious reading, yet Hill has used a spelling of 'moldwarp' that needs to be searched for among the many spellings listed in the *OED*, and the context supports it. Since 'collations' is another equivoque (both a 'light repast' and a 'bringing together'), as the men are scattered into the soil to feed moles so sounds and meanings are dispersed, then gathered in word-play. As the moldywarp 'throws the earth', moreover, in keeping with its etymology, so word-play heaves the loam of language, disturbing and re-forming it. The two loams are even assimilated: when the opening verset states that the men's spades 'clove to the hoard' it also evokes the Anglo-Saxon word-hoard which is equally being dug for, and the fact that they 'grafted' through the soil means that writing is in question too, since 'graft' derives from the Greek word for stylus. In a poem which delves through the soil of England, in terms of workman, gardener, archaeologist, literary historian, writer, a complex word-play where anagram collaborates with etymology (Hill is a poet who knows his Onions) is enacted and referred to, in a context which relates language profoundly, to the earth and to a process of death and recovery.

'Moldywarp' is one of the ways in which the poetry thinks. Word-play binds the world in its relations, so that a wasps' nest 'ensconced' in a hedge-bank becomes quite appropriately a wrapped 'head' (XV). It mediates between Offa's time and ours, the attendants at Offa's funeral (XXVII) in-cluding 'car-dealers' and 'house-carls'. It superimposes apparently alien areas of experience, saying of children who sport with plunder, fire and destruction in a garden echoing with Anglo-Saxon war and burial rites, that they 'play havoc' (XIX). It snarls varieties and discrepancies of human experience inex-tricably in the space of a few words, entering the meditation in Hymn XVI on courtesy and empire, art and slaughter, sacrifice and murderous intent, to call the Frankish sword presented to Offa a 'two-edged' gift and to locate the craftsman's triumph in its 'crux'. One recalls the line about love in the second of the 'Annunciations' in *King Log*: 'Forever being pledged to be redeemed', which compromises vows and purification with the routines of pawnbroking.

(Has it been remarked that Hill makes many of his phrases unsayable?) By closing with word-play, even to employing, as Christopher Ricks has shown, double-takes of deliberately shocking tastelessness,[13] Hill grasps the potentially most frivolous manœuvre of the fallen word for a teeming creativity at once ludic and grave.

The re-making of English goes further, to the evolving of a language ours and yet not quite ours, for a world similarly elusive. Hill's 'Mercian' re-names things, as 'village-lintels' (III). His idiom digs, like a mole, for strange objects in the earth, 'Ramparts of compost', for instance, 'pioneered by red-helmeted worms' (XV), for 'telluric cultures' (there is play on both words) enriched with 'shards, corms, nodules, the sunk solids of gravity' (XII). It is a dialect which cleaves to numerous linguistic roots, bringing to the surface, with a few words such as 'They ransacked epiphanies, vertebrae ...' (XII), Old Norse, Greek, Latin. It amasses an extreme physicality which includes nevertheless a kind of mentality: 'Coagulations of frogs: once, with branches and half-bricks, he battered a ditchful' (VII) – where strictly the boy battered, not the frogs but 'a ditchful' (and where bricks naturally 'batter' through the prompting of 'brickbat'). And what kind of place is described in Hymn XIX, a 'kitchen-garden riddled with toy-shards, with splinters of habitation'? This garden, which is no paradise in its exposal of detritus and death, seems nevertheless the glimpse of a newly-named earth, both familiar and unfamiliar. Isn't this, in fact, the book's 'transcendence'? In its gardens and its 'numinous but actual landscapes' (William Cookson),[14] it delves into the material, the worldly, the earthy, as the site of aspiration, from which, according to a vertiginous expression of Hymn V, to worm one's way heavenward.

Hill's imitations affect one mainly, however, with a sense of distance. 'The Songbook of Sebastian Arrurruz', a special case since it purports to be a version of an (apocryphal) Spanish poet's *cancionero*, is particularly suggestive. It concludes a volume, *King Log*, several of whose poems rework actual originals from a distance which is polemical. It also ministers distance of a different kind to the reader as it opens and closes: by the shiver back and forth between 'Sebastian Arrurruz: 1868–1922', which places him as, above all else, dead, and the first line of the first poem, with its equally careful counting of time: 'Ten years without you ...'; and by the consigning of Arrurruz's 'now' in the final words of the sequence, 'Of now-almost-meaningless despair', way into the past. For distance is one of its concerns. The feigning of Arrurruz allows the writing of the poems; his name indicates the nature of that writing. If he is a St. Sebastian pierced by the arrows of his wife's leaving him, he also possesses arrowroot (the translation of 'arrurruz'), which is the herb that absorbs arrow poison. (He is to be healed, interestingly, by an unstated interlingual pun, 'arrowroot' having been derived from the Aruak *aru-aru* – heard as the root which cures from arrows – by some seventeenth-century paronomastic.) The question, however, is whether the antidote – language, memory, poetry – works with propriety. Its function will be, not to dispel pain, but to establish 'true sequences' of pain, creating value in both the truth recovered and the 'bleak skill' of the writing which recovers it. Yet Arrurruz is continually aware that language and memory move to betray feelings:

> Oh my dear one, I shall grieve for you
> For the rest of my life with slightly
> Varying cadence, oh my dear one.
>
> ('Coplas, ii')

(The last phrase supplies one of the varying cadences.) He is also aware that in imagination he and his wife become each time 'more stylized more lovingly/ Detailed' ('lovingly' being as unsparing as the 'religiously' of 'Lachrimae Amantis'). The antidote does succeed, but also discloses a slippery inner distance from feeling and a distance of words from feelings.

Hence the idea of imitation, which adds a further distance since the feelings and the approach to feelings in words are those of someone else, who more-over never existed. And hence the idea of translation. Although Hill has stated that he was inspired to create an imaginary poet mainly by Antonio Machado's Juan de Mairena and Abel Martín, Spanish fictions of a Spanish writer, he actually altered the device by inventing not a native but a foreign poet. The original work is doubly unattainable; it doesn't exist, and within the pretence of the writing we meet only a version of it, and an approximate version at that, where 'the finer nuances' (his quip to Haffenden) 'have been lost'.[15] One is conscious that Hill is involved in the common humanity enacted in the poems, yet the activity of reading them differs from reading, say, the statements of a novelist's character, or even the *Cancionero* of Abel Martín. One attends closely to a process of translation operating, as it were, on other, unreachable words, to a gap being bridged and not bridged. As a second 'skill' comes into play, that of the translator, the poems themselves change and withdraw. The process is foregrounded, moreover, and a further remove suggested, when in the seventh poem, 'From the Latin', an unnamed Latin writer is rendered (so to speak) by Arrurruz, whose rendering is rendered by Hill: somewhere is an exact sensuality, wry knowingness about relationship and social occasion, but where, and whose?

'The Songbook ...' follows the 'Three Baroque Meditations' in *King Log*, and these begin with the question 'Do words make up the majesty/Of man ...?' – an overt Empsonian ambiguity where words may either constitute or fake our majesty, and where the tense hesitation is also carried in the broken pentameter and the combination of prosodic and lexical grandeur and vulner-ability in the held-over 'Of man'. 'The Songbook ....' continues the practice of that question, in terms of the adequacy, the appropriateness, of language to experience, from the different perspectives of Arrurruz and Hill. Dying in the Modernist year of 1922, Arrurruz writes an earlier poetry intent on the expression of personal feeling (though not without indirection, since a refer-ence to Mount Ararat in his wife's part of the world implicitly evokes the Ark, which the species entered 'two and two'). Hill, on the other hand, the heir of Modernism, uses the foreign and apocryphal Arrurruz to compose a sequence where feeling is approached through a complexity of screens. They piece together their identical yet different 'fragments' on either side of the decisive shoring of fragments in *The Waste Land*, which appeared in the year of Arrurruz's 'death'.

Of course, the distance is not merely negative: its acknowledgment is part of the honesty of Hill's poetry (honesty, not sincerity), and it makes the achievement of Arrurruz's poems – which are songs, and which do form a genuine sequence, ordered by something other than mere date of composition – all the more striking, a feat of writing and of character. The close references in the two Armenian poems to Mandelshtam's *Journey to Armenia* ('ripe glandular' blooms being an actual quote from Clarence Brown's translation)[16] – references that Arrurruz could not have made and that Hill has bestowed on him – even align the forgotten fictitious poet with one of the great literary martyrs. Out of his particular *misère*, he and Hill have wrung, after all, a new kind of utterance.

That combination of distance and achievement is something to be found quite near the centre of Hill's writing. His is a poetry struck with the difficulty of closing with experience, especially religious experience, and nerved against the ease of pretence. It is a poetry almost of not experiencing, or rather, it is rich with the complex experiencing of the truth of that exclusion. It is also dubious concerning the transcendence of language, and informed about the declension of words themselves from the 'lost kingdom'. Its achievement is to enact experience paradoxically dense, layered, and new, and to create a language, paradoxically, transfigured. Imitation, one might say, compounds the distance and stimulates the achievement.

12

Hill's criticism: a life of form

Eric Griffiths

In 1966, Geoffrey Hill told an interviewer 'I did not have an adolescent love affair with poetry, I have been a poet for as long as I can remember.'[1] If writing poetry and remembering himself are coeval for Hill, then he is denied an introspective return to the origins of his own impulse to compose; he cannot go back behind his poetry to find a self from which it stems, for there is nowhere to go behind the poetry, and no one to go there. This is a poet's version of Adam's predicament as regards accounting for his self:

> For man to tell how human life began
> Is hard; for who himself beginning knew?[2]

All of us come out of a time of infantile amnesia, a clouded start which colours the incompleteness of human self-consideration. When the Emperor Caligula wished to pretend that he was a god, he began by claiming a memory of the wine that wet his lips to start his breathing; Stalin reversed the gambit by fashioning an absence of the past, obliterating childhood photographs and friends, but the aim was the same as Caligula's: to deface the fact that our selves are born in forgetfulness. Much intellectual effort has gone into more respectable attempts to clear up the obscurity of our origins; psychoanalysis, for example, pursuing an entirety of human self-control, heads for the early, unrecalled experience as the solution of our blankness to ourselves. (That Freud sometimes thought it possible that primal experiences might not actually have happened, does not alter the nature of the yield such 'recoveries' of the self are supposed to offer.) The enigma of self-oblivion would be moved out of the way of 'our best hope for the future ... that intellect ... may in process of time establish a dictatorship in the mental life of men.'[3] Freud uses the word 'dictatorship' coolly; he was writing in 1932. Hill has measured the appeal of such offers:

> Averroes, old heathen,
> If only you had been right, if Intellect
> Itself were absolute law, sufficient grace,
> Our lives could be a myth of captivity
> Which we might enter ...[4]

'Absolute law', set against Freud's 'dictatorship', sees and curbs the reach of ambitions for the intellect as the principle of self-explanation, as Wittgenstein did in *On Certainty*: 'It is so difficult to find the *beginning*. Or, better: it is difficult to begin at the beginning. And not try to go further back.'[5] Wittgenstein here is cautioning against the epistemologist's search for the 'foundations' of human knowledge; equally, in his *Remarks on the Philosophy of Psychology*, he is unsure of the grounds of human self-knowledge. Both kinds of dig fall victim to the 'illusion of depth' which they create out of our concepts and practices.

Literary critics also find it hard to begin at the beginning, or to know where the beginning is. 'Where do poems come from?' is a question we are variously required and forbidden to put; the balance incumbent on criticism between respect for a poem's autonomy and regard for the weight of its relations elsewhere often hinges on how that question is pressed. Anti-intentionalists check us in one direction with the threat of illicit inference from the public statement of the work to the private state of the author's mind, for it is as a private inner state that anti-intentionalists, from Wimsatt to Barthes, conceive intention. Their arguments impress only in proportion as the Cartesian philosophy of mind which they assume is impressive. Marxists of all shades of refinement direct us to check a bourgeois tendency to reify the material process of cultural production into objects whose history is occulted by the language of consuming 'appreciation'. Then, if we undertake to bring writing into relation with some ambient or formative circumstance, we must either adopt a consistent theory of that relation, or content ourselves with the casual sense of connectedness which unsystematised terms may provide, and provide with a profusion so exuberant as to be wearisome. Eliot has an armful of terms in *The Use of Poetry and the Use of Criticism*, which does not prevent him from seeming empty-handed when it comes to explanation: 'The poetry of a people takes its life from the people's speech and in turn gives life to it'; 'Poetry was ... deeply affected by the rise of a new social class ...'; '... the expression of the two poets and critics is determined by their respective backgrounds ...'; '... the development and change of poetry and of the criticism of it is due to elements which enter from outside ...'.[6] To be 'deeply affected' is not so much as to be 'determined'; the 'backgrounds' of writing might be less precise than 'the rise of a new social class', and more precise than something which enters 'from outside'. When Eliot writes 'the study of history has shown us the relations of both form and content of poetry to the conditions of its time and place', it is not asking too much to ask what that relation has been shown to be; nor is it intellectual gluttony to be unsatisfied by Eliot's attempt at an answer: 'I can only affirm that all human affairs are involved with each other ...'.[7] The weakness of phrase here brings Eliot's prose down to the nerveless level of chat about other people's *amours*.

Hill has commented on a similar, baffled exiguousness of wording in John Crowe Ransom's criticism:

'A poem', he notes in 1943, 'densifying itself with content ... is about the dense, actual world'. We in turn are bound to observe that Ransom's verbal substance is at its thickest and most suggestive where its 'logic' is thinnest. 'Is about' is a pathetically frail locution to act as the ontological membrane between two such '*dinglich*' clauses.[8]

In contrast to the emaciated gestures of 'involved with' and 'is about', the alternative of theory appears at first beckoning but not eventually inviting, for it turns out to be an alternative tribulation rather than an alternative to tribulation. Raymond Williams has charted the pitfalls of one of the most venerable theories of cultural relation, the marxist 'base'/'superstructure' model. It has a 'figurative element' which is potentially misleading, and which Williams thinks suspect in itself for the purposes of sober analysis; the relation of determination between 'base' and 'superstructure' is often indirect, or involves 'lags' in causal cross-over which are difficult to account for, as they are not regular or predictable; the 'base' has been thought of in 'essentially uniform and usually static ways',[9] against the spirit of Marxian thought. But Williams's own attempt to graft subtlety of cultural responsiveness onto the marxist theory achieves only a conceptual duplicity such as often dogs piety. He wants to 'revalue "the base" away from the notion of a fixed economic or technological abstraction, and towards the specific activities of men in real social and economic relationships'.[10] 'Real social ... relationships', though, cannot be described without reference to those ideological matters which the model assigns to the 'superstructure', just as the 'specific activities of men' require understanding in terms of the agents' self-conceptions of themselves as having certain intentions and not others, acting under some ideals and not others; such self-conception is also superstructural. In order to lend the 'base'/'superstructure' model the pliability needed for plausibility, Williams has imported the *explicandum* into the *explicans*; he brings no succour to the marxist case, for in his reformulation it ceases to be either marxist or a case, and this is not Williams's fault.[11] The central difficulty for marxism as a theory of cultural relation, as for any theory of cultural causality, is its commitment to find a rigorous sense for the word 'determine'. Williams gravely concedes that 'the term of relationship which is involved, that is to say "determines", is of great linguistic and real complexity'.[12] The concession is honest but inadequate, because the problem with 'determines' is not that it is complex but that it is no more than figurative in its application to processes of cultural development, and so cannot lift marxism out of the toils of contestable insight onto the plane of scientific law. If x determines y, then there is a causal relation between x and y, but we cannot establish causal relations in cultural developments with anything approaching the rigour of empirical science because we cannot perform experiments on culture to distinguish causally significant from causally insignificant variables in the process. The title of 'science' hangs loose about marxist criticism, a giant claim to a status for its propositions which they cannot come up to, and which dwarfs those propositions which might have done well enough in a humbler station. Only a decent tact in fact, the courage for unsystematic contact with the materials of consideration, can keep 'determine' in working life for historical discussion. As Wittgenstein says, 'What is most difficult here is to put this indefiniteness, correctly and unfalsified, into words'.[13]

Hill's greatness as a critic lies partly in his ready finding of the right words for the indefinite. His essays close in on the 'idioms of the society which determines the realities' of a writer's situation;[14] but the intimate breadth of his acquaintance with such realities keeps his 'determines' in the language of ethics with a practical wisdom that can sense the writer's resolve within and under the world's determination. His studies of a writer's exercise of choice in the thick of constraint substantiate the 'prevalent ethical emphasis' of T.H. Green's time that 'while we are "unconditionally bound", "necessarily belonging to such a world"', being so bound is not necessarily the same as being in a fix and is most certainly not the same as being a fixer'.[15] Nowhere does Hill make this, his essential act of recognition, more keenly than in the ardent and erudite essay on the style in duress of St Robert Southwell, brought by violence to the paradox of a 'necessary choice',[16] and bringing out of worldy defeat the eloquence of transfiguration. In his criticism, the writer is compelled by language itself, by 'the inertia of language, which is also the coercive force of language'.[17] The melodious airs a writer gives out to others, as the airs he maybe gives himself, are a reflux, however newly-fashioned, of the air he breathes; other people's words, bear on, inspire, and might choke, the finished composition. So the poet as Hill writes of him is far from being that proprietor of the ideal he sounds in Imlac's enthusiastic dissertation: 'the interpreter of nature, and the legislator of mankind ... presiding over the thoughts and manners of future generations ... as a being superior to time and place',[18] and even further from Shelley's less guarded version of Imlac's brag: 'Poets are the unacknowledged legislators of the world'.[19] Hill concludes his collected critical essays with a firm rebuttal: 'But poets are not legislators, unless they happen to be so employed, in government or law ...'.[20] He is alert to how and where writers work, and the way in which 'the nature of a man's occupation, the range of his expectations and the limits of his security' may be 'influential in forming the rhythms and cadences of his speech'.[21]

Sometimes I think his sympathy for the mundane predicament of an artist wrongs his critical sense. It is natural that the poet and lecturer, Hill, should feel for the 'emotional discomfort' of the poet and lecturer, Ransom, in the face of a grudging academic world,[22] but that sympathy exceeds the facts, and so skirts self-pity, when he writes of the 'gross inequality' of the 'respective worldly rewards' of Ransom and T.S. Eliot.[23] If that is meant to suggest that Ransom's work, either as poet or critic, bears serious comparison with Eliot's, it seems to me an absurd suggestion, and the implied resentment that

Ransom's royalties didn't come up to Hill's estimate of his worth is uncharacteristically naïve about the gods of this world and their dealings with achievements of imagination. On the other hand, his epitome of the milieu in which J.L. Austin lived, and which lives in his writing, as 'basically cheerful, hedonistic, preoccupied with business, professional conduct and games-playing but ... also shot through with anger, infelicity, blank incomprehension',[24] has a judicious penetration of the prowess and foible of the Oxford philospher – as shows in the deft glance of 'shot through' (is 'shot' here like the 'shot' of 'shot-gun' or of 'shot silk'?) at the idyllically tranquillised world of the Austin seminar where disasters are always and only exemplary. More seriously, when Hill calls Southwell's period of interrogation and torture at the hands of the Elizabethan establishment 'the most searching of contexts',[25] he discovers his (completely earned) confidence in the acute humanity of even the most worn literary-critical term, as he uses it. It would seem a trivialisation of what Southwell went through if any other critic called it a 'context'; but Hill plots with such care the transformation in Southwell of the contorted experience into the contour of style, that the critical term properly takes the stress of the life it meets, the writing it describes.

This last instance helps to demonstrate the responsible vitality of Hill's conduct in critical language. In his critical practice, Hill implicitly answers the question 'Where do poems come from?' with 'The question really is what they come *between*, and the answer to that is: "other uses of the language, and other users too" '; and in doing so it might seem that he is ranged with those who profess 'intertextuality' as the means and substance of literature. His recognition of the width and depth of field in which literature moves, in fact, distinguishes him absolutely from the gyrating formalisms of the intertextualists. The language whose tugs and eddies he follows from tract to lyric, back through denunciatory pamphlet to panegyric ode, is always actually grounded, and 'grounded', not in the sense of 'explained by its origins' as I previously discussed, but in a sense which can be conveyed in the address of St Robert Southwell to his persecutors, a passage Hill quotes in discussing the ethos and pathos of Southwell's creation:

> And as a cunninge imbroderer hauinge a peece of torne or fretted veluet for his ground, so contryueth and draweth his worke, that the fretted places being wroughte ouer with curious knottes or flowers, they farr excel in shew the other whole partes of the veluet: So God being to worke vpon the grou[n]de of our bodyes, by you so rente & dismembred, will couer the ruptures, breaches, & wounds, which you haue made, with so vnspeakable glory, that the whole partes which you lefte shalbe highlye beautifyed by them.[26]

At the end of the 'chains of signifiers' of the intertextualists, Hill finds a body on the rack; he has never wished to solve the problem of relating literature to history by dissolving history into literature, or into issueless, illimitable discourse. It is true that the history he most often stresses is the history of words but he attends in words to more than an abstract play of 'difference', scanning rather for what R.C. Trench called the 'boundless stores of moral and historic truth, and no less of passion and imagination' accrued in words;[27] though Hill does not have Trench's hospitable fervour over the language, like a housewife laying out a good spread, for the poet, knowing the brutalities and the cussedness of his material at first hand, cannot rejoice in the language so artlessly and whole-heartedly as did the Dean of Westminster.

'The ground of our bodies' remains in Hill's criticism, stubbornly part of the 'edifice of form'.[28] The dealings of writer and world with each other are reciprocally needling, writer and world point each other up, so that it is no diminution of what is due to the world to think of it as the 'background' of compositon, for the metaphor of 'background' implies no distinction of status but only the direction of attention – the figure of the writer is as much 'picked out' by, as against, the 'background'. Hill has preferred 'hinterland' to 'background' as a critical term; he takes it over from D.W. Harding's essay on 'The Hinterland of Thought', which shares many of the concerns of Hill's criticism with 'the area where thought emerges from what is not thought'[29]. Hill shifts the emphasis, though, from the growth of thought in the individual out of physiological motor-sensations and 'postural sets and movements',[30] up into linguistic articulation; he is occupied rather with the emergence of what is composed from what is not composed, the births of phrase amidst the drag and fracas of contending tongues. Harding and Hill are at one, though, in their realisation that 'thoughts are not full-grown from the start but have their origin and infancy',[31] and in their pursuit of what such a realisation implies for criticism: a new understanding of artistic 'mastery'. Harding writes that 'Wordsworth and Shelley ... seem at times to create a complex or subtle effect through what looks like an accident in the words they use';[32] Hill puts it more generally: 'In a poet's involvement with language ... there is ... an element of helplessness, of being at the mercy of accidents ...'.[33]

This 'element of helplessness', the constant share of 'infancy' in the poet's speech, is not an object of explanation for the literary critic, as infantile amnesia is for the psychoanalyst. Oblivion is taken up into the 'stubborn textures'[34] of the memorable artefact, and the critic describes it there not as a riddle or a plight but as the opportunity for shape: 'The contrasting and sometimes barely consistent ideas in these stanzas seem to have reached expression partly through verbal associations that might be called accidental, were it not that they evidently gave openings for important variants of idea and attitude to emerge. ... In this way the partial surrender to the seeming accidents of language has become a means of discovering and releasing partly-formed ideas and attitudes ...' (Harding on 'Adonais').[35] Or: 'His creative gift was to transform the helpless reiterations of raw encounter into the "obstinate questionings" of his meditated art without losing the sense of rawness' (Hill on 'Resolution and Independence').[36] This last example of sharp and compassionate praise is characteristic of Hill as a critic, particularly his grasp of the way in which it is a triumph for Wordsworth not to lose the 'sense of rawness' presented to him in his material, the language he encounters, and I think he gets this major canniness about poems from his patient adherence to the detail of words as a moral response to a given situation. His criticism deals rarely with the complete poem or work, and so rarely succumbs to the ' "cold fury" of appetite for proof of absolute "mastery" ';[37] he preserves undismayed into the light of appreciation the toils through which artistic 'finish' has come. That is, Hill's understanding of composition is thoroughly dramatic; the achieved utterance witnesses to its roots in human needs. This is a reason why he writes so well about Shakespeare. He says of *Cymbeline*: 'In the play's opening scenes the breach of convention and the strained court relations create the original milieu for inflationary panegyric and protestation. The love-cries of Posthumus and Imogen are a lyrical defiance of circumstance and a breeding-ground of error.'[38] Generally, his criticism realises backgrounds as breeding-grounds, pivots on 'original milieu' and 'lyrical defiance of circumstance' (though 'defiance' is a lesser thing than the 'transfiguration' he often finds in writing), but it does so with a flexibility of treatment and wealth of concretion from which no theory of literary genesis could be derived. Indeed, Hill adopts from T.H. Green a suspicion of the derivation of conceptual solitudes from the specific activities of men in language; he quotes Green: 'Man reads back into himself, so to speak, the distinctions which have issued from him, and which he finds in language', and in this 'retranslation' man 'changes the fluidity which belongs to them in language, where they represent ever-shifting attitudes of thought and perpetually cross each other, for the fixedness of separate things'.[39]

This will itself seem suspect to some, either because they scent an 'ideology' of empirical open-endedness, or because they will wonder how, without propositional explicitude and defined concepts, criticism can ever proceed to knowledge of literature, or show that it possess such knowledge. To the first group, little can or need be said; once everything is supposed to be 'ideological', and 'ideological' has been whittled down to meaning 'biased' or 'explicable as defending a vested interest', then, of course, the possibility of study in good faith has been closed, and one cannot attempt a reply to arguments of this type without condemning oneself to accusations of conspiratorial partisanship. The second worry is more serious. When Hill writes of the nineteenth century, for example, that 'the epoch was marked by a drastic breaking of tempo and by an equally severe disturbance of the supposedly normative patterns of speech',[40] there seems to be a real question whether his claim could ever be evidenced satisfactorily. The essay from which this remark comes, 'Redeeming the Time', is phenomenally agile in its moves across a range of citations; nobody could complain that the most learned and luminously intelligent efforts are not made to give the claim substance. The worry is rather that the claim could never be fully backed, whatever the brilliance of the critic's labour; it is a worry about such claims generally in criticism, not about Hill's conduct of this claim. When Frank Kermode writes that Eliot's hypothesis of a 'dissociation of sensibility' which affects European culture between the sixteenth and twentieth century, is 'quite useless historically',[41] he is voicing the kind of disquiet I am thinking of. Eliot is, no doubt, vulnerable, to Kermode's superior scholarship, and there is a sense in which Hill might be even more vulnerable to objection on matters of fact, simply because he makes his claim with a meticulous richness of instance far beyond anything Eliot ever attempts. There is more to Kermode's dismissal of Eliot, though, than a disagreement over the interpretation of facts; it is more that the kind of epochal claim which Eliot makes seems counter to any contact with fact at all, because it is in excess of what facts, however many, could be made to show. Here, it seems to me, we have moved from a debate within history (whether or not a 'dissociation of sensibility' occurred) to a debate about history (whether or not concepts like 'dissociation of sensibility' have any place in the study of history). It would be wrong to commit Kermode to the brisk, positivist line which he took against Eliot in *The Romantic Image* a quarter of a century ago; his position about facts has developed notably since then. Whether or not Kermode would himself still wish to make this objection, it is an astringent point which would clear away much historical argument if accepted; the 'standard of living' argument, for example, about the effects of the Industrial Revolution could be regarded as merely a matter of taste, beyond history's competence, as beneath its dignity, to settle. We would be spared putting ourselves the question whether human history was a record of progress or not, and this would relieve us of the rarely pleasant task of putting ourselves in question.

There would not be much left for history legitimately to be about, and, certainly, the academic discipline of history would have to live officially divorced from the actualities of the historian's life in his own time, with his current allegiances and fears. The possibilities of rigorous demonstration in historical study are too limited for history to proceed without involving itself with views that are beyond its strict competence to prove. History is more than the totality of everything that has happened, it is also what is happening now, and when we contemplate the culture which is the medium of our contemplation as well as its object, we have to learn the skill and contentment of living without proof of the senses we propose to ourselves to make of it. Part of that skill is understanding the complex, and often unsatisfactory, relation between such concepts as 'dissociation of sensibility', and the facts they strive to subsume. Eliot wrote of his own formula: 'for what [the] causes were, we may dig and dig until we get to a depth at which words and concepts fail us',[42] and this is true of other attempts to characterise large cultural formations. With the example of Hill's criticism in mind, we may feel that Eliot's 'dig and dig' congratulates itself too whole-heartedly for spade-work which, in comparison to Hill, Eliot hasn't visibly done. Had Eliot worked as hard as Hill has, he mightn't have been so ready to say that words 'fail us'; at least, he would also have seen that there are times when we fail them, or when language is the substantial register of our failings. The point is still there: trying to unearth the causes of the culture which informs us is like trying to get back behind infantile amnesia; the element of oblivion, bafflement and an attendant partial helplessness is the condition in which we know things about culture, not an obstacle to knowledge. The haul brought back from such researches will not bear scientific examination; that should daunt only those who believe themselves to be engaged in scientific work, such as orthodox Freudians. As Hill writes: 'If we follow T.H. Green's argument, as put forward in his paper "The Philosophy of Aristotle", to place ourselves "outside the process by which our knowledge is developed" is to conceive of an untenable "ecstasy", whereas to recognise our being within the process is to accept our true condition'.[43] The positivist attitude in history is ecstatic in Green's sense, surprising though it is to connect positivists with ecstasy. In the positivist view, the historian handles facts as something extrinsic to himself, but a fuller sense of history requires us to acknowledge that we are in the grip of facts, and that is how we come to be able to grasp them.

Criticism does not provide knowledge; it records, and may deepen, acquaintance. The distinction is rough and tactical, rather than philosophical. Criticism does not provide knowledge of the kind provided by the agreed disciplines of the natural sciences but rather testifies to an acquaintance such as one might have with a person; here the descriptions one would give, the predictions one would make, are never demonstrable as a scientific hypothesis may be demonstrable, but rest on an articulation of particular observations into an intimacy and a cogency which cannot be proved, but which can be, and often is, tried. This admission should not seem humble when it is considered that literature itself is not a body of knowledge, as a science is, and that it is deformed when it is treated by cognitive disciplines, for example, when a sociologist uses a novel as a document. The status of epochal characterisations in criticism, such as Hill's remark about broken tempo in the nineteenth century, is like that of the truths we learn through pleasure about our friends; and it is possible for a critic to demonstrate acquaintance, to show that he possesses the kind of rational contact with his subject which an acquaintance is.

One way this may be done is by a tactful divination of the apt vocabulary for description of a writer's work, a tact which is like the apprehensive gentleness which enables us to know 'the right thing' to say to a friend in particular circumstances. Hopkins shows this tact in a comment on Wordsworth which Hill admires:

> There have been in all history a few, a very few men, whom common repute, even where it did not trust them, has treated as having had something happen to them that does not happen to other men, as having *seen something*, whatever that really was … human nature in these men saw something, got a shock ….[44]

Hopkins is drawn to the word 'shock' for what he wants to say about Wordsworth because he knows Wordsworth so well; it is one of Wordsworth's own words for the experience of vision and recoil upon the self which Hopkins is describing:

Then, sometimes in that silence, while he hung
Listening, a gentle shock of mild surprise
Has carried far into his heart the voice
Of mountain-torrents ...

The potent shock
I felt: the transformation I perceived,
As marvellously seized as in that moment
When, from the blind mist issuing, I beheld
Glory ...

Has not the soul, the being of your life,
Received a shock of awful consciousness,
In some calm season, when these lofty rocks
At night's approach bring down the unclouded sky ...[45]

A concordance could not substantiate the profound correctness of Hopkins's homing in on the word 'shock', for the perfect intuition he shows of what counts in Wordsworth is not itself demonstrable by counting. It is not that Wordsworth uses the word remarkably often but that it appears in great passages which are akin to Hopkins's own critical perception – the poet's words are father to the critic's term. Hill himself shows a comparable genius in his selection of 'gleam' and 'perplexity' as key words in 'Tintern Abbey' which are germinative for the nineteenth century:

'And now, with gleams of half-extinguish'd thought,
With many recognitions dim and faint,
And somewhat of a sad perplexity,
The picture of the mind revives again ...'

The combination of 'gleams' with 'perplexity', the collision of the ideas of 'gleams' and 'perplexity', seems to me something that gets into the very grain of philosophical and critical talk through the nineteenth and indeed into the twentieth century ....[46]

These words come often in Wordsworth – in the 'Elegiac Stanzas ... Peele Castle', in 'The White Doe of Rylstone', throughout *The Excursion* – but Hill's closeness of insight is most vindicated in *The Prelude* where, once again drawn to 'the picture of the mind', Wordsworth again joins the words:

As one who hangs down-bending from the side
Of a slow-moving boat, upon the breast
Of a still water, solacing himself
With such discoveries as his eye can make
Beneath him in the bottom of the deeps,
Sees many beauteous sights – weeds, fishes, flowers,
Grots, pebbles, roots of trees, and fancies more:

Yet often is perplexed and cannot part
The shadow from the substance, rocks and sky,
Mountains and clouds, from that which is indeed
The region, and the things which there abide
In their true dwelling; now is crossed by gleam
Of his own image, by a sunbeam now ....[47]

In such moments of quiet, dictional affiliation, a critic recognises his 'being within the process'; he acknowledges a debt to what has been written before, a debt which can be paid only by being incurred again. His dwelling on the poet's words is his recourse to pleasures experienced in reading which begin the critical activity of question and tribute. Such a capacity for delight, and for fidelity in delight, with the partial surrender to the accidents of gratification which is inherent in that capacity, is at the heart of the critical intelligence.

It can also be asked: 'Where does criticism come from?' In the course of his reply to Wellek, Leavis, while rightly denying that the logic of critical inference is deductive, gives away more than he should in making critical inquiry sound like random sampling: 'The critic's aim is, first, to realize as sensitively and completely as possible this or that which claims his attention ... His first concern is to enter into possession of the given poem ... in its concrete fulness ...'.[48] Leavis's 'this or that' suggests a spree, while 'the given poem' implies a constraint; and neither indicates a consistent and purposeful conduct of attention which will result in that 'utmost consistency and most inclusive coherence of response' he strives for.[49] Hill has given a hint of the source of his own criticism in his assay of the intuitions he comes into while writing poetry: 'the energy of passion attracts information to it'.[50] But this is too modest about the energy of information in his prose. When he writes of Swift, for example, that 'A reader of his correspondence, as of the *Journal* and birthday poems to Stella, comes to accept the real presence, as well as the ritual, of his friendship',[51] the reader is briefly treated to an insightful metaphor ('real presence' and 'ritual') which sparks from the social to the sacramental as it might in one of his poems. For all the decorous scruple of Hill's criticism, he emerges as one of the boldest of critics, indeed, 'swashbuckling' might be a better word. His penitent concessions on matters of detail are sometimes less humbled than they look. He admits that 'in setting the phrase "grammar of assent" in lower case type one is arbitrarily making a metaphor, a metaphor to take the place of Newman's reality';[52] but he keeps the lower case, and has honestly admitted the daring of his typographical change: 'a metaphor *to take the place of* Newman's reality' (my italics) – that would be something. This is not the only moment in his criticism where you feel a careful, but driving will making its way through the resistance of the material and of conventional disciplines to a weighted and focussed personal view.

It is, though, one of the few moments when his criticism is untrustworthy.

I have been trying to show why Hill's adroitness with the figurative in critical language embodies a delicately attuned understanding of the range and limit of the critical activity, but it seems to me, at a moment like this, that whereas in the poems the elaboration of religious quandary through the torque of metaphors achieves writing of the last honesty, the criticism throws clouds of hesitant and impulsive glorification around what Hill supposes the artistic imagination achieves, and does so because of the writing's unsteady reliance on religious metaphors. In the poetry, you feel that the fervour of vigilance about religious longings is his own; in the criticism, the caution seems dutiful, imposed on the desire it checks rather than growing up with it: we witness the spectacle of the unacademic nature trapped in the inexorable toils of academe. Hill resists the 'temptation to claim that a timely encounter with popular colloquial verse "redeemed" Swift as a poet';[53] the inverted commas catch and discard a cant locution but there are no quotes round 'redeem' when it is applied to Hopkins's vocation[54] – not his vocation as a priest (which is not mentioned) but as a poet. Hill tries to face the issue in 'Poetry as "Menace" and "Atonement"':

> It is evident that my argument is attracted, almost despite itself, towards an idea by which it would much prefer to be repelled. But surely, one may be asked to concede, it is more than attraction. Is it not a passionate adherence; a positive identification with the magnificent agnostic faith whose summation is in the 'Adagia' of Wallace Stevens? – 'After one has abandoned a belief in god [sic], poetry is that essence which takes its place as life's redemption.'[55]

Yet the essay, profoundly and richly as it engages with these questions, only enacts its own dilemma. It is not an argument but an agon – in its last paragraph, 'menace' keeps the inverted commas it had from the first, but 'the atoning power of [the poet's] art' has got free of such typographical reserve, not by arguing its way out of the dilemma but by a quiet side-step. The conclusion appears to be that literature, though perhaps not redemptive, is penitential, and, though this has a shame-facedness about it which is preferable to the enthusiasms of Matthew Arnold, I. A. Richards or Wallace Stevens, it is still complicit with their filching of religious terms to which they have no title. What is one to make of Hill's own phrase 'magnificent agnostic faith'? The paradox, 'agnostic faith', is woefully and wilfully contrived, and there is very little 'agnostic' about Wallace Steven's plushy sentence, decked out as it is with 'essence' and 'redemption', except his askesis over capital letters. It surprises me that Hill, who so deeply responds to the work of Simone Weil, work which might aptly be called an instance of 'agnostic faith', and a strong, harrowing instance of such faith – can think Stevens's sentence 'magnificent'. But then, religious doubt and longings of the depth and purity of Hill's demand a language other than that of literary criticism.

A poet who cannot remember a time when he was not a poet discovers a form of self-understanding when, as a critic, he studies his predecessors. He recovers himself, not in an explanation or a theory which puts him at the controls of history (his own or others'), but in an articulate exchange of pleasures. Nietzsche tells half the story of the admiration due to such criticism when he marvels: 'how great is the "plastic power" of a man or a community or a culture ... I mean the power of specifically growing out of one's self, of making the past and the strange one body with the near and present, of healing wounds, replacing what is lost, repairing broken moulds'.[56] This is too hearty and heartening; the experience of critical inquiry into history will also be an experience of the wounded, irreparable, and remote. Human wholeness – whether personal or cultural – is a dream by turns alluring and sinister, a dream of the escaped self, with its history obscured by many blots and passings-over. Yet the self finds ways of talking to the dark world where it was born; this critic stands to this poet in friendship and admonition, as Raphael to Adam:

> ... thy request think now fulfilled, that asked
> How first this world and face of things began,
> And what before thy memory was done
> From the beginning, that posterity
> Informed by thee might know; if else thou seek'st
> Aught, not surpassing human measure, say.[57]

13

Somewhere is such a kingdom: Geoffrey Hill and contemporary poetry

John Bayley

I was once standing in the foyer of the Oxford Playhouse, during an interval, with a friend who placidly observed, in reply to a gloomy comment of mine: 'No, the play's no good, but I just like the theatre'. It is an observation that accidentally tells all about the general state of the arts today. In the cases of painting, sculpture, poetry and music it is the medium itself which appeals to its following. An artist doing 'interesting' or 'exciting' things (fatal twin clichés so often invoked on programmes or in BBC talks, as recently in one by the sculptor Anthony Caro) is drawing attention, in various ways, to the potential of his medium. He and his observers are in an area like so many others today, where technology merges with sport.

Something like this is not so very uncommon in the history of writing and the visual arts, but in general there is a difference between looking at the medium of art and looking through it.

> A man that looks on glasse,
> On it may stay his eye;
> Or if he pleaseth, through it passe,
> And then the heav'n espie.[1]

A puzzled viewer may ask of an art object 'What's it for?'; he would not do so if he took it in not as art object but as a way of looking into the world, as we look into the world of Wordsworth or Cézanne. Everyone interested in art is interested both in how it has been done and what has been done, and in good art the two usually come together: the Madonna moves us because she has been expertly painted. At the same time, she is not painting but a representation of God's mother: and in the same sense *The Prelude* is not poetry but representation of experience lived by Wordsworth. As long ago as 1830, however, Delacroix replied to a viewer who asked whether an object on a canvas was the front of a man or his back: '*Ni l'un ni l'autre – c'est la peinture*'.

Delacroix was no doubt reacting against expectations of an audience conditioned by the classicism of Ingres, but his attitude underlies many of the assumptions about art current since his time, among artists and audience alike. In practice, and with the notable exception of painting, the change does not have a great effect. In the verbal arts, even in poetry, words are there to be seen into; what they reveal cannot be obfuscated, even by a determinedly opaque or pure poetry. The poetry of Rimbaud and Mallarmé is not only wonderful but transparent, though what it reveals may be difficult or tantalising. Art for art's sake is in any case not the same thing as the concentration upon the medium itself. The naïve idea, apparently held in all good faith by such a rigorous scholar as A.E. Housman, that there exists a substance called 'poetry', organically different from its verbal constituents and significances – this idea too is not the same as the present-day preoccupation with the medium. Housman's 'poetry' is different from the poetry on the poetry scene today: the latter is a form of verbal gregariousness, constituting a part of the lifestyle of its following – a sort of muses' discothèque.

Poetry, like *peinture*, tends today to become a thing in itself, to be found in certain places – galleries or magazines – and this is quite different from old ideas about 'pure' or 'absolute' poetry. Poetry today is something we feel we have to have, like community. The result is that it is usually about itself, or exists as itself, irrespective of what it is supposed to be about. Instead of clarifying and intensifying a world which we are looking into, it has itself the status of an art area, 'a poem' being like one of the nominally sculptural objects considered fitting for a civic precinct. Even such a highly skilful and effective poetry as that of John Ashbery, much admired by Harold Bloom, has the distinguishing quality of 'poetry' or *peinture*, an artefact or assemblage in which surface is all, and the promise of interiority a carefully manipulated illusion. The American school of structuralist and post-structuralist criticism takes to this kind of poetry as being essentially at one with the way in which it can be discussed.

Good poets are of course writing today – indeed Ashbery is one – who make nonsense of any generalised judgement about the way poetry appears or presents itself. Not long ago 'poetry', the medium's common denominator, consisted of personal utterance of a fraught kind, descriptions of the self and its predicament modelled on those of Plath or Larkin, Lowell or Berryman. The reader looked through involuntarily – he could do no other – but the experience offered him in the poem usually remained at the level of 'poetry': in revealing itself and the poet, the experience as medium usually created nothing but its own vulnerability, the poetic commonplace, something that had not come off. None the less that inadequacy had *something* in common

with the sublime inadequacy of Wordsworth or Hardy, or one could say
Blake or Larkin as well, and many diverse others – poets with whom we look
through into contingency transformed, a world made not 'poetic', but utterly
different, and itself. Even when such a transformation does not take place, as
it can often do, to look through into the world of any such poem is to
experience an intensifying of perception, a sharpening of meaning, and it is
the sense of an experience which remains with us rather than the sense of a
poem. To adapt R.P. Blackmur's phrase a 'matter in hand' has been seen and
dealt with, even though the process has not added to 'the sum of available
reality'.

That sum is unmistakably added to by Betjeman and Larkin, as by Lowell
and Berryman, even by Ashbery. They do not write 'poetry' but create a
world of words into which we are drawn, by which we know them. In the
case of Larkin the way in which this happens is peculiarly his own, and based
on the kind of paradox which a world of poetry can so well sustain. The
situation in his poetry, the situation with which its multiple personality is
co-extensive, delights by assuring us of two things. First, that we, like the
poet, are not deceived about the nature of things; second, that the glum
accuracy of the poet, with which we collude, is in fact creating a world of
elsewhere',[2] a world that increases available reality as much as those of
Spenser or Keats, Auden or Tennyson do. Deprivation itself is fashioned by
Larkin into 'nutritious images'.[3] Ashbery's poetry does something not dis-
similar, making a new world out of the difficulty of saying just what it is we
normally experience in this one.

These examples reveal what is in any case to be expected: that the poet
'adds to the sum of available reality' by putting himself in the picture, in one
way or another: it may be by methods which recall the sentence from Leslie
Stephen that Thomas Hardy copied out in 1879, 'The ultimate aim of the
poet should be to touch our hearts by showing his own ...'.[4] That seems
naïve in the context of Modernism, but the fact is that Joyce or Eliot, in their
elaborate ways, followed it out almost to the letter. The confusions on which
the techniques of Modernism were intent were also implicit, unconsciously,
in the personalities that employed them. What they needed to think they were
doing was different from what occurred. In the context of Eliot's poetry today
his own thoughts about what the poet needs to be are almost touchingly
comical. 'The progress of an artist is a continual self-sacrifice, a continual
extinction of personality'.[5] He may have needed to think so, but to read him
today is to find his personality. The artist is present, as Henry James knew in
his own context, on every page from which he assiduously sought to remove
himself. Mallarmé would say that time has made him what he truly is; but
that is not the point, for his living personality is present in his work in all its
comedies and contradictions, as much as it is in the incongruities of his actual
life – for example in Wyndham Lewis's story of finding Lady Ottoline Morrell
on her knees before Eliot, saying: 'Teach me how to pray!'.[6]

The absurdities of the living become, with this sort of poet, an abiding addition in what he has turned out to create:

> though I do not wish to wish these things
> From the wide window towards the granite shore
> The white sails still fly seaward, seaward flying
> Unbroken wings
>
> And the lost heart stiffens and rejoices
> In the lost lilac and the lost sea voices
> And the weak spirit quickens to rebel
> For the bent golden-rod and the lost sea smell . . .[7]

The poet appears to surprise his own self absolutely, as Hardy does at the end of 'After a Journey':

> Trust me, I mind not, though Life lours,
> The bringing me here; nay, bring me here again!
> I am just the same as when
> Our days were a joy, and our paths through flowers.[8]

Larkin does the same thing, in his own odd way; for example at the end of 'Dockery and Son':

> Life is first boredom, then fear.
> Whether or not we use it, it goes,
> And leaves what something hidden from us chose,
> And age, and then the only end of age.[9]

All three present a kind of overflowing of the poet's self, which he would only be able to manage in this form. The 'self-delight', in Yeats's sense,[10] finds it proper embodiment in art, creates its own 'elsewhere' through its own realisation. The world in which Wordsworth moves in 'Resolution and Independence' ('I was a Traveller then upon the moor')[11] is an elsewhere created by the surprise of the poet's own being, and quite different from the world which the leech-gatherer inhabits. The poem recognises the leech-gatherer only through the fulfilment in art of the poet's own self-preoccupation, and such a recognition is typical of the way in which poetry works in achieving a total sense of the individual, an achievement synonymous with a certain kind of Romantic poetry. Our response to it vouchsafes a similar kind of awareness in ourselves: the 'bosom returns an echo',[12] not only in Dr Johnson's sense, but because we are establishing through art the existence of another person, an existence transcending any we could get in touch with in life, and yet closely related to that kind of contact.

We make contact not only with Eliot, Hardy, or Larkin in person as the essential reality of their art, but with that other kind of reality which their selves in poetry are investigating or trying to establish, as Eliot is seeking to establish his own self-sacrifice, the extinction of himself in poetry. Larkin becomes himself by being fascinated with the existence of Dockery, the positive that cannot exist in this poetry any more than the leech-gatherer can. Hardy becomes himself in the poems that seek to establish a reality – itself a kind of 'elsewhere' – for his dead wife and his relations with her. In each case the poet lets slip his own being as he could do in no other way.

Post-Derrida formulations about literature and language implicity deny in their functions the possibility of this kind of transcendent self. It is the kind of self with which Romantic poetry is involuntarily associated, and which since Yeats it has been the purpose of some poets deliberately to create. The nature and tendency of the poetry here is more important than its intention. There is no contrast between self and persona; Hardy and Eliot and Larkin become themselves in their poetry, its power to universalise and to move us, to present both a unique and strange dimension of its own (for nothing is as familiarly unfamiliar as to encounter another self in poetry), and to become a part of our own world of being and seeing.

The authenticity, the singularity, of this kind of creation establishes a close relation between poet and reader. For one thing the reader is conscious, as much in the case of Hardy as in the more obvious one of Berryman, that the poet is saving himself by becoming himself in his poetry; and that the reader, in helping him, is a part of the human transaction. This is implicit in the comment Hardy liked about the touching of hearts. In the critical climate of today such a relationship seems ludicrously old hat: an absorbed interest in individuality is regarded almost as in bad taste and improper by those who accept the new way of seeing things. On the poetry scene, the area where what gets written is 'poetry' as such, rather than other worlds to be explored, assertion of the self changes into an observation of the community, a desire to be of it, however brutishly indifferent it may be to its would-be spokesman and celebrant. It might be said that the new community atmosphere in poetry represents a return to pre-Romantic principles, to the impersonal camaraderie of the seventeenth-century poets or the decorous uniformity of the eighteenth-century. It is certainly the case that decorum, in an odd sense, a pervasive conventionality of tone, distinguishes the apparently eccentric or down-to-earth kinds of poetry of today.

Auden's 'All I have is a voice'[13] would seem in this atmosphere an unthinkable, almost a shaming claim. A voice is also a personality, in the sense in which I have been using the word in relation to Hardy or Eliot or Larkin. And a voice, in the context of modern poetry, has become a kind of solecism. Geoffrey Hartman has observed that in the proper reading of poetry we have 'the eclipse of the voice by text', and, as usually happens today, poetry has insensibly accommodated itself to the ways in which criticism wants to 'deconstruct' it. The 'poetry' of today seems to invite the co-operation of the reader in taking it to pieces, as if it was indeed an artefact the poet had made rather than words he had uttered. What Denis Donoghue rather unnecessarily calls 'Graphireading' (from *graphos*, 'writing', as opposed to 'Epireading', from *epos*, 'speech') alters the immediacy of words that are speaking to us into objects waiting for us to adjust and play with. The singular thing about 'voice' poetry is that it never needs to be deciphered: we take in the words as they are spoken, understanding them in terms of unique speech even if we do not translate them as writing. In an important sense the voice does not and cannot offer itself among us and as one of us, because utterance is its own solipsistic completeness. Wordsworth's 'man speaking to men' does so, paradoxically, because he is speaking as if alone: he is not sharing words with them on the page. Criticism has replaced voice by text because what a voice says 'only of itself' is not reducible in terms of text. When we write about what Larkin, for instance, talks about, the discrepancy between the poem and our glosses upon it is obvious, indeed ludicrous. This is not the case with, say, Wallace Stevens, whose poetry as text is shared with his reader. It is a curious thing that the poet of voice (who is also the poet who in his work is making his personality) is essentially far less communicative than the poet read as text. Being and becoming himself he does not have to communicate: he is always more or less his own version of Wordsworth's 'egotistical sublime'.

Herein lies precisely his appeal, his 'otherness' and his 'elsewhere'. The fundamental error of modern critical methods is their assumption that we want to *join* the poet, to be with him by spawning our own solutions to his difficulties and our own textual versions of his text. In fact it is our separation from the 'voice' poet's personality that makes possible the relation with us. He is in every sense different from us, in the same sense as a Vermeer interior is different from its original and from any interior, however similar, that is actually inhabited. David Holbrook's poem 'Reflections on a Book of Reproductions',[14] which is a meditation on this point, could be compared in its own context with Auden's 'Musée des Beaux Arts'.[15] Because it speaks with its own voice, Auden's poem is as distant from us as the picture it describes. Holbrook's, as admirable in its own way, joins simply on to the tones of a hypothetical communal discussion.

*   *   *

I come by a roundabout route to the relevance of this for Geoffrey Hill's poetic achievement. His position among contemporary poets is unique, and to demonstrate the uniqueness it is necessary to look at the kinds of poetry, and the kinds of assumption about it, which occupy the contemporary scene. To begin with, he seems to have neither a personal voice nor the communal substitute for one which occurs in media poetry in any age, with us as with the Georgians, but whose properly contemporary social tone is more self-consciously approved and cultivated in 'poetry' circles today than used to be the case.

Like other highly accomplished poets Hill, though he never sounds contemporary, can seem to adopt a variety of tones, or no tone at all. This power is in one sense his own kind of 'otherness'. Through it he achieves in his own peculiar way the absolute authority of speech which the best poetry must have. That authority is obviously lacking in, say, David Holbrook's poem which I mentioned; its absence there is made a virtue of, as if poetry could afford to be diffident if its ambience was sufficiently humane and civilised, and as if authority in a modern poem was an outdated concept. The fascination of Hill's poetry, especially the later poetry, is in the way he makes it at once completely authoritative and implicitly renunciatory of the authority which its words totally establish. Michael Longley in *The Guardian* (quoted on the *Tenebrae* dust-jacket) wrote that Hill 'makes exquisite, immaculate music.' True, but also deeply misleading. The music exists to draw attention to an absence of music, the authority to the ideal of selflessness and abjectness. In one of his most haunting poems, '"Christmas Trees"' from *Tenebrae*, Hill imagines 'Bonhoeffer in his skylit cell':

> Against wild reasons of the state
> his words are quiet but not too quiet.
> We hear too late or not too late.

The authority of poetry is always 'too late', because it cannot coincide with the fact it seeks to immortalise. It creates an alternative structure outside it, as Yeats did in 'Easter 1916', a structure which in time takes over the event, and can seem to be both creating and denaturing it. We learn, too late, what art does to life, to aspiration and spontaneous idealism, to santify itself. If it is not too late the art has not been 'made'; it can be turned back, 'decreated', into a sense of original contingency and imperfection that goes with original intensity and anguish.

The 'quiet' of art must also contain something that is not too quiet. The irony in the adjective is that it expresses both the inevitable condition of great art and the necessary pre-condition of spiritual awareness, humility and enquiry. Neither the artist nor the saint and martyr must live too much in the idea of perfection. There is, however, a similarity between them, or there can be. Hill's poetry strives to express in the peculiar mode of its own perfection an awareness of how far that is bound to be from the realities it deals with, the realities that struggle and are lost 'among the ruins and on endless roads'.[16] Meticulousness itself conveys its opposite: in spirit, feeling, and diction.

It is illuminating to compare Hill's poem 'Genesis' with Pushkin's poem *Prorok*, 'The Prophet'.[17] In 'Genesis' the act of creation, and its celebration, is also an expression of deep self-distrust and despair at the nature of the physical world. The 'I' of both poems, the prophet, and the creator, is not the poet himself, or any extension of his own person. Nevertheless Pushkin can and does identify with the prophet, because the ecstatic power with which the prophet has been endowed by God ('Like a corpse I lay in the desert, and the voice of God called out to me') corresponds to the self-generated power of the poet's own achievement. He too has had a coal of fire laid in his breast and a serpent's tongue put in his mouth. Pushkin's poem is a perfect example of negative capability, that gift which Keats identified in Shakespeare, and which is so different from Keats's own personal powers as a poet. The poet has put his gift at the service of a theme, the thrilling theme of the prophet's ecstasy in his role as God's spokesman, but the thrill is also in his own powers, just as we feel Shakespeare's own powers expressed by the energies of Coriolanus or the despair of Hamlet.

This dynamic and kinetic relation is quite alien to Hill's art. If he has an 'I', the statements that 'I' makes are stealthily paradoxical, 'shut/With wads of sound into a sudden quiet', like the speaker in 'God's Little Mountain' from *For the Unfallen*. Hill's poetry has the peculiar and often disconcerting gift of suggesting intellectually as well as intuitively the opposite of what it seems to be constructing and creating, as here in 'Genesis':

> By blood we live, the hot, the cold,
> To ravage and redeem the world:
> There is no bloodless myth will hold.

> And by Christ's blood are men made free . . .

That phrase 'the hot, the cold' trips us as we become aware of its implications. A cold-blooded myth is a disturbing conception, but truer the more we reflect on it, for myths are manipulated by those who make use of them, and they are also turned into the quietude and freedom of art. Christ's blood makes men free by giving them not only the warm exemplar of sacrifice but the cold quiet comfort of religion which, like art, gives them freedom from the weight of their quotidian and material being. Hill's poetry is full of such concealed oxymorons, phrases and lines of deft and harmonious construction which open, on re-reading, to reveal a continuing preoccupation with the weak dissolving flux of existence. It is this which the spirit must receive, and yet cannot receive through the egotistical sublime of verbal arrangement.

The paradox haunts Hill's poetry, giving a peculiar air of perpetual expectancy, awaiting the unvouchsafed mystery, the miracle that can never take place. This poetry seems to know that as the stone is rolled away, and the words 'He is not here. He is risen' are uttered, then art takes over and we are safe in the solidity of ideas and dreams. Such knowledge embodies itself in a disquieting exaggeration of the normal weight of art ('Your silence is an ecstasy of sound/and your nocturnals blaze upon the day'[12]). Sometimes the idea of anticipatory stillness ('sated upon the stillness of the bride') mocks itself, with an equally disquieting gentleness:

> The wooden wings of justice borne aloof,
> we close our eyes to Anselm and lie calm.
> All night the cisterns whisper in the roof.

The repose of nuns is as involuntarily incongruous as the fact that 'Theology makes good bedside reading'. *Tenebrae* is a perspective of jokes, seen in slow motion, gradually revealing themselves. 'Joke', of course, would have as special a sense with Hill as a phrase like 'exquisite, immaculate music' does. In 'Genesis', too, the point of the joke in the line 'There is no bloodless myth will hold' is the necessary bloodlessness of words in poetry. In respect of this kind of self-consciousness, Hill is very much a modern poet, too concerned with possibilities to take the normal short-cut to effects. There can be nothing '"simple, sensuous, passionate"'[19] here; only the exploration of states of being, their conjuration in grave elaborate mime.

Hence Hill's obsession with ritualised violence: the cavalcade of 'Florentines' with their 'stricken faces damnable and serene';[20] the huddled dead at Towton, most murderous of all English battlefields, where 'carrion birds/ Strutted upon the armour of the dead'; the preoccupation with 'ascetic opulence' and 'Self-wounding martyrdom ... true-torn among this fictive consonance'; with 'the miry skull/of a half-eaten ram'; with

> the stale head
> sauced in original blood; the little feast
> foaming with cries of rapture and despair.

Hill's closest relation here is with a very minor poet with whom he clearly feels a deep affiliation – Sidney Keyes – some of whose lines are quoted at the beginning of *Tenebrae*. Keyes did not have Hill's remarkable metaphysical delicacy, and his fascination with the relation between words and the acts and states they describe. His bookishness was more 'natural'. He also describes battles: Dunbar ('Iceweed and bleeding men'); Künnersdorf ('"fought in the shallow sand"') – the greatest scene of carnage in the war between Frederick of Prussia and Maria Theresa of Austria; and '"At Dunkirk I/ Rolled in the shallows, and the living trod/Across me for a bridge ..."'.[21]

This resemblance affords the most significant clue to Hill's position *vis-à-vis* not only poets of his own time but poetry in general. Keyes, the poet of bookish violence, amateur of arcane references and apocalyptic imagery, was actually killed in North Africa, serving as an army officer in the Second World War. Wilfred Owen, and Keyes's contemporary Keith Douglas, wrote poems that are, as it were, a part of their deaths in action, at one with their fates in spirit and will. But Keyes's fate seems wholly divorced from his image of it in poetry, and it is the nature and instances of such divorce which make up the inwardness of Hill's poetic medium. In the same way he is preoccupied with the gap between Celan's experience and his poetry; with Bonhoeffer the conspirator hanged from a meat-hook, and the world of his thought and theology; with Southwell the martyred Jesuit writing 'Passions I allow, and loves I approve ...', used by Hill as an epigraph to 'Lachrimae'; with the terror and desire of things as poetry fashions them, and as living deals them out. We love poetry as ourself (to paraphrase the epigraph to 'The Pentecost Castle' which Hill adopts from Simone Weil), because it satisfies us: whereas what we should love is the thing not ourselves which poetry cannot comprehend. To Hill, Keyes's fate would be far more significant than Owen's or Douglas's, because it is an exemplar of the distance between the poetic and the real; if poetry (Hill's poetry) can in its own way *become* that distance, it justifies itself.

Poetry itself, one might say, has always known its position, though poets have always pretended, whether ingenuously or not, that their power to move us is the product of straightforward mimesis, the power of their art to present and embody the truth. Pushkin's 'The Prophet' embodies the fervency of art's truth at the same time as it describes the fervency of the prophetic impact. Macbeth's lines about the murdered Duncan – 'His silver skin lac'd with his golden blood'[22] – operate in a way that is in some sense very like Hill's own method. The poetry summons up the true facts by calling attention to its distance from them; and moreover it uses the solipsism of poetry dramatically. Macbeth resorts to poetry to remove his own deed from himself in his own mind, as his words also give it pathos and dignity for public reception. Hill's art is not dramatic, and his words do not have the personal impact inherent in the dramatic form, but they institutionalise, as it were, the same covert purpose and method as Macbeth's at this moment.

All his poetry is founded on this sense of a division between itself and the world, a sense that is quite alien to the Romantic tradition. Yeats, who claimed to be among 'the last romantics', insisted on the unity of his poetry with both the natural and spiritual worlds ('Natural and supernatural with the self-same ring are wed').[23] Like a political one, such a poetic stance is merely assertive: the reader is not expected to 'believe' it any more than the citizenry is, but to respond to the fervency of the claim and the personality making it. The process is displayed with great panache in such a poem as 'Her Vision in the Wood', where Yeats imagines an old woman recalling physical love in an image from art and painting ('A thoughtless image of Mantegna's thought') of Adonis wounded by the boar:

> That thing all blood and mire, that beast-torn wreck,
> Half turned and fixed a glazing eye on mine.

– thus forcing into coincidence real violence and sex and art's imagination of them. The vision 'from a picture or a coin' 'had brought no fabulous symbol there/But my heart's victim and its torturer'.[24]

However personal to Yeats, and important to him, this claim is only a more deliberate and self-conscious assertion of what art has always implied, and has to imply in order to vindicate its own particular styles of reality. Hill's poetry uses many Yeatsian 'images', but in a wholly different way. As poet he cannot avoid 'Self-seeking',[25] but in his best art we seem to look not at the poet and his images, but into another world which the poet has glimpsed but knows to be not attainable in the words that both reveal and remove it. Hill is no more convincing than Yeats when he talks about the process, borrowing Simone Weil's terms like 'decreation', and her statement that art's difficulty and justification lies in its composition simultaneously on many different planes.[26] In fact he is less convincing, for whereas Yeats's statements are at one with his poetry, its will and personality, Hill's poetry depends not only on the absence of the poet but on an absence of his displayed technique and purpose.

The most significant thing about Hill is his solitary position on the contemporary poetic scene, the unlikeness of his tone to that of any other poets writing today. This solitude is essential to what his poetry does. In 1940, Pasternak explicitly rejected the 'communal' attitude towards poetry that Mayakovsky had fostered, the idea that 'the more poets we have the better'. That attitude is again found on the poetry scene today, in its appearance of sharing a communal medium. Pasternak in his poetry had to shun it, and so too in his own way does Hill. Not least among Geoffrey Hill's curious virtues as a poet is that in reading him we have no sense of an art other than his own: also that in re-reading him our sight goes more and more through the glass into the kingdom beyond, taking in further movements and features, in ever greater detail.

14

Reading Geoffrey Hill

Peter Robinson

'Difficult friend'[1] - Geoffrey Hill's poem dedicated to Osip Mandelshtam begins. In 1921, T.S. Eliot wrote: 'it appears likely that poets in our civilisation, as it exists at present, must be *difficult*.'[2] Twelve years later, finding a variety of reasons why poets might have been thought, rightly or wrongly, difficult, Eliot offers advice to the reader of poetry in the hope that he will become the 'more seasoned reader, he who has reached, in these matters, a state of greater *purity*, does not bother about understanding; not, at least, at first.'[3] In encountering new poetry receptivity is essential and, by 'greater *purity*', Eliot means an attentive openness to the many ways in which a poem can make itself felt. Irritably reaching after the meaning can be a way of defending ourselves against it. This openness, alert but not defensive, is also required for making a person's acquaintance: a necessary stage in becoming, and finding out if we want to become, someone's friend.

I

'Everybody has friends. Why doesn't the poet turn to his friends, to those people who are naturally close to him?' In 'About an Interlocutor',[4] Osip Mandelshtam argues that addressing living interlocutors, people close to the poet, 'takes the wings off the verse, deprives it of air, of flight. The air of a poem is the unexpected. Addressing someone known, we can only say what is known.' Mandelshtam's sense of risk in the choice of interlocutors has not been shared by many poets in English over the centuries; nor, beyond a casual and cursory sense of what it means to say we 'know' someone, can it be said to restrict to the known what may be addressed to living interlocutors, for even those to whom we are closest remain distinctly unknowable. 'There is no lyric without dialogue', Mandelshtam continues; but it is dialogue with an unknown interlocutor. Mandelshtam accepts a reductive presumption about other people so as to resist a style of poetry bound to reiterate trite lessons for an identified audience. If it is agreed that even those closest to us remain distinctly unknowable, Mandelshtam's suggestion that 'Fear of a concrete interlocutor, a listener from the same "epoch," that very "friend in my generation," has persistently pursued poets at all times' – is apt indeed. The attraction of hearing our own words in another's light and fear of what that light may be, such feelings between poets and readers as between potential friends, are among the engaged impulses that encourage attachment.

Geoffrey Hill rarely addresses his poems to identified living interlocutors.[5] The familiar style, one of whose virtues is to foster attachment and equality, was defined by Donald Davie when writing on Shelley as 'a quality of tone, of unflurried ease between poet and reader', and Davie notes that Shelley's poems in the familiar style were 'inspired by "the companions around us"'.[6] Davie implies that the tonal relations he admires between poet and reader may be substantiated and exemplified by such relations between poet and interlocutor. He argues that this style of poetry flourishes in societies with settled conventions of behaviour, and a homogeneous literary culture. Such poetry has survived into our day when such conditions – if they were ever other than ideal – do not obtain. There are poets now, and Davie is among them, who seek to compose a transition between public and private. The poet adopts an intimate tone where integrity of voice can be sustained, while remaining aware that the poem is intended to be overheard by people other than those to whom it is addressed. Geoffrey Hill has admired Swift's poetry for making such a transition, though in conditions more approaching the ideal. He singles out:

> ... in particular its power to move with fluent rapidity from private to public utterance and from the formal to the intimate in the space of a few lines. At times, in the letters to Bolingbroke and Oxford, what is private is simultaneously public in its implications. It is of course true that when one has a few good friends and those friends happen to be the most important men in England, E.M. Forster's injunction 'only connect' has a particularly happy significance.[7]

To write of relations between Hill's poetry and a readership in terms of difficult behaviour, of attraction and fear, might be to point towards an implied social context unlike that of Shelley's Pisan circle, or, differently again, of Swift's '... few good friends'.

Hill has often touched on the artist's past subservience to men of power. In 'Annunciations, 1' from *King Log*, troubadours appear at such men's banquets representing 'all who attend to fiddle or to harp/For betterment'. Geoffrey Hill's own gloss notes: 'they listen to violin and harp, because the function of art is to instruct by delight ("for betterment" = "for moral improvement"). At the same time they fiddle and harp, in the vulgar sense of the term, they pull strings to get on (they try to "better themselves").'[8] The

apparently remote setting of his poem should not blind us to one of Hill's
objects, which is to render a dilemma of poetry in its commerce with contem-
porary social usage and abuse. Its concluding line contains the word 'gobbets'
which the *OED* gives as 'Piece, lump, esp. of raw flesh or food; extract from
a text set for translation or comment.' If society is regarded as a conspiracy
for mutual self-advancement, poetry's higher calling may justifiably want
nothing to do with it; but resistance to the banquet values might then inspire
the creation of particularly succulent morsels for 'comment'. Difficult poetry
is sometimes defended on the disputable grounds that in a society which
survives by conspicuous consumption the harder a poem is to swallow the
better: it is good insofar as it sticks in the craw. Yet a poem too may be *in*
the world, and not *of* it. The 'unflurried ease' that Davie found in the familiar
style is secured upon implicit agreement between reader and writer, such as
that which usually exists between friends, to take what is said on trust; it
assumes the good intentions of both sides in the literary exchange. Geoffrey
Hill, in writing sceptically of the 'poetry-banquet', has identified for literature
a context of mutual exploitation and suspicion – a society of people in
linguistic difficulties.

The commentary on 'Annunciations' by Geoffrey Hill was occasioned by
Kenneth Allott's dilemma when attempting to anthologise him for a revised
edition of *The Penguin Book of Contemporary Verse*. Allott recounts how
his own choice from *For the Unfallen* dissatisfied the poet and how Hill's
preferences were unintelligible to the anthologist:

> The alternatives then are to omit Mr Hill altogether from the anthology or to
> represent him by the most recent work with which he is content. I have chosen
> the latter course because I think Mr Hill is a poet. I understand 'Annunciations'
> only in the sense that cats and dogs may be said to understand human conver-
> sation (i.e. they grasp something by the tone of the speaking voice), but without
> help I cannot construe it. Mr Hill has kindly supplied the following comment on
> his poem . . ..

Geoffrey Hill's self-defence and self-exegesis is elaborate and interesting in its
dubiety about poetry consumers, such as ourselves; it also converts Allott's
politely mocking confessions of faith and perplexity into an image of social
relations between English speakers:

> I suppose the impulse behind the work is an attempt to realize the jarring
> double-takes in words of common usage: as 'sacrifice' (I) or 'Love' (II) – words
> which, like the word 'State', are assumed to have an autonomous meaning or
> value irrespective of context, and to which we are expected to nod assent. If we
> do assent, we are 'received'; if we question the justice of the blanket-term, we
> have made the equivalent of a rude noise in polite company.

By recognising a desire to assume the meanings of words 'irrespective of
context' this passage asks us to consider what a context is. T.S. Eliot said
that the music of a word 'arises from its relation first to the words imme-
diately preceding and following it, and indefinitely to the rest of its context;

and from another relation, that of its immediate meaning in that context to all the other meanings which it has had in other contexts'.[9] In doing so, he applied the word first in an intrinsic sense (the parts of speech or vocabulary that precede or follow a word and restrict its meaning), then extrinsically to suggest both other places in texts where the word is used, and other milieux or occasions in which the word has appeared. Where 'context' means milieu or occasion, speech may be said to be usually more context-specific than writing. We mainly speak to more or less identified auditors in more or less recognised contexts, and the meanings of our words are defined accordingly. A writer who specifies the occasion of his text by invoking a named or indicated interlocutor, and describing or implying an occasion, seeks to carry over into the intrinsic context of his work some of the external constraints that will help to secure the meanings of his words. For Osip Mandelshtam this is to take 'the wings off the verse', to ground it. By attention to syntactic ambiguity, to intrinsic context, 'double-takes in words of common usage' may be realised; but, as Geoffrey Hill's passage suggests, to follow that impulse is to grow distant and difficult with regard to extrinsic context – particular occasions, circumstances, interlocutors, and, by extension, readers. Placing together 'Difficult' and 'friend' in the opening line of his poem addressed to Mandelshtam, Hill effortfully relates disparate senses of what a literary context may be.

Mandelshtam, to whom the poem is in fact 'A Valediction ...', was at times a difficult man as well as a 'difficult' poet. The memoir by his widow Nadezhda, *Hope Against Hope* (her name means 'hope' in Russian), begins memorably, 'After slapping Alexei Tolstoy in the face, M. immediately returned to Moscow.'[10] In homage to his subject, Geoffrey Hill's poem is difficult, though far from impossible – a word Donald Davie applies to Mandelshtam and his contemporary Marina Tsvetayeva: 'Impossible persons, both of them.'[11] Hill's poem employs senses of 'difficult' applied to poetry and behaviour, but also draws to the word implications from its relation to, and distance from, 'hard':

> Tragedy has all under regard,
> It will not touch us but it is there –
> Flawless, insatiate – hard summer sky
> Feasting on this, reaching its own end.
> ('Tristia ...')

That summer sky can be unfeeling, painful to bear, difficult to understand, strenuous, severe, and strict in its enacting of tragedy's selective gluttony. Mandelshtam was also a hard poet (his poems are not easy, and they can be fiercely resolute); his '[Stalin Epigram]'[12] contributed first to his exile, and later his death when in transit to a labour camp. The relation of 'Difficult friend' to 'hard summer sky' implicates Mandelshtam in his predicament, without lessening an implicit condemnation of his treatment: if Mandelshtam had a tragic flaw in his difficulty as a social being and a hard poet, nevertheless the tragedy that did for him is 'Flawless'. Stalin's state, however evil it was, could not conceive itself capable of culpability. Mandelshtam's poetic difficulty was self-protective; he could imply criticism of the state by indirection. Yet such obliquity, such aesthetic difficulty, was itself regarded by the state as anti-social. Hill's poem is called 'Tristia ...' because Mandelshtam too wrote a poem of that name, and, naming his poem, he associated himself with Ovid, who, when in exile, sent a work of that title back to Rome. Both poets were banished from the capital by their respective rulers.

Closer to home, the subtitle to 'Tristia ...', 'A Valediction to Osip Mandelshtam', invites a reader to remember John Donne's use of the word in his title 'A Valediction Forbidding Mourning',[13] for Hill's poem is a refusal to mourn:

> The dead keep their sealed lives
> And again I am too late. Too late
> The salutes, dust-clouds and brazen cries.

He is too late not only because Mandelshtam is dead, but also because others have leapt on his hearse as if it were a bandwagon. The 'brazen cries' might be trumpet blasts, hard because they are made of the alloy brass. Both its obduracy and impurity might account for 'brazen' in its idiomatic sense; the cries are shameless in feeding off his fate. Those 'brazen cries' also almost rhyme with the 'hard summer sky'. Geoffrey Hill is aware that Mandelshtam's social and poetic context is neither his, nor a peril. Tragedy may have 'all under regard' but 'It will not touch us'. Hill implies a relation between that regard and his own with the title he gave to the group from which 'Tristia ...' comes: 'Four Poems Regarding the Endurance of Poets'. The difficulty of Hill's poem inheres in the adjustment of its regard: it must be hard, for, though distant from the events it alerts us to, it is yet conscious of their violent reality. However, it must not too readily visualise violence, taking its hardness from the forces it implicitly rejects. Nor can it be too close to its subject, thus assuming an unfounded intimacy with such suffering. Geoffrey Hill's general title is concerned with '... the Endurance of Poets', both the pains that some poets have had to bear, and how they have outlived their lives in poetry which survives them. 'Difficult friend, I would have preferred/ You to them' Hill begins, as if the speaker were himself a remote Augustus 'preferring' candidates for literary posts; thus, *they* may be Stalin's politically acceptable poets and critics. Yet 'prefer' has its less specialised meaning here too, and *they* may also be late mourners and followers. As Osip Mandelshtam died when Geoffrey Hill was six, and as the first person singular may also be the poet speaking, we can take it that Mandelshtam is a friend of his only in, and because of, the poetry which did survive him, thanks largely to the agencies and memory of his widow. If we are not too difficult, too brazen, or too hard, the poet in his poetry may be able to fulfil 'the great end/Of Poesy, that it should be a friend ...'[14]

*   *   *

Ben Jonson's 'Inviting a friend to supper' promises a fine social occasion through the skill with which it adopts and vivifies a literary context. It consolidates social trust by exercising trustworthiness in, for instance, the consistent freedom and restraint, the liberty of its couplets:

> No simple word,
> That shall be vtter'd at our mirthfull boord,
> Shall make vs sad next morning: or affright
> The libertie, that wee'll enjoy to night.[15]

To refuse such an invitation would be a social and a literary solecism, for it would suggest that the receiver could understand neither the poem's worth nor the good faith in which it had been issued to a friend. 'Solecism' is a word which combines a writer's behaviour in his words with points of social behaviour. The *OED* gives definitions and exempla under three main headings: '1. An impropriety or irregularity in speech or diction; a violation of the rules of grammar or syntax; properly, a faulty concord. 2. A breach or violation of good manners or etiquette; a blunder or impropriety *in* manners, etc. 3. An error, incongruity, inconsistency, or impropriety of any kind.' It is a word Geoffrey Hill has had recourse to more than once, for it holds together, in its social and grammatical meanings, related values which the distancing or separation of extrinsic context, of occasion, from intrinsic, textual context attenuates or threatens to break. The word keeps literary behaviour in touch with behaviour in other contexts, even when the literary context does not concern itself directly with non-literary behaviour. In his radio script for 'The Living Poet', Hill refers to the problem of banishing these literary rude noises from one's work:

> The most painstaking attention to detail does not necessarily preclude the perpetration of 'howlers'; grammatical or referential solecisms. It is arguable that, in the notorious 'middle years', the impulse to persist in writing poetry (and indeed certain kinds of meditative prose) is an impulse to restitution. There is an obligation to get the facts right; and when one has failed, one must seek to amend.[16]

There is an instance of the impulse to make amends in the postscript to *King Log*; Geoffrey Hill printed a revised version of 'In Memory of Jane Fraser' subtitled 'An Attempted Reparation', and with a note saying: 'I dislike the poem very much and the publication of this amended version may be regarded as a necessary penitential exercise.' Hill's versions are identical apart from three commas in the first stanza, the change of a comma to a full stop at the end of the penultimate line, and the final line – which originally read 'And a few sprinkled leaves unshook' and became 'Dead leaves upon the alder shook.' The phrasing is more resolute, the rhythm more conclusive, and the nonce verb 'to unshake' has been removed.[17]

'"They say that genius is an infinite capacity for taking pains," he [Sherlock Holmes] remarked with a smile. "It's a very bad definition, but it does apply to detective work."'[18] In 'Poetry as "Menace" and "Atonement"' Geoffrey

Hill considers Simone Weil's proposal for 'a system whereby "anybody, no matter who, discovering an avoidable error in a printed text or radio broadcast, would be entitled to bring an action before [special] courts" empowered to condemn a convicted offender to prison or hard labour.'[19] He opposes to her suggestion the reasonable doubt that the kinds of remorse a writer might feel about the failure of due care and attention resulting in a misprint or solecism, or that anyone might feel about committing a social gaffe or *faux pas*, are not of the same order as those human errors or irresponsible oversights that cause pain and death. Yet careless talk can cost lives. As Hill has said of the sinking of the *Titanic*, about which he has written a terse ode, it was the hubristic claim of its designers that falsely lulled the passengers and crew; they were, as Hill observes, 'swamped by a slogan'.[20] Charles Péguy has been an inspiration to Hill not least because he was 'a meticulous reader of proof',[21] and *The Mystery of the Charity of Charles Péguy* includes this *pièce de résistance*:

> To dispense, with justice; or, to dispense
> with justice. Thus the catholic god of France,
> with honours all even, honours all, even
> the damned in the brazen Invalides of Heaven.
>   (p. 19)

The stanza exemplifies how an inattention to commas in proof-reading can mean the difference between a legal process founded on ethical discrimination, and a judiciary that can do what it wants, such as 'to dispense/with justice' – where the quandary of the line-end gives pause for thought or just hurries on down injudiciously. The poet, bearing in mind a judging reader such as Simone Weil with her power of citizen's arrest, manifests by attention to the state of the text a resistance to a sloppy world, yet it is a world with which his mock-solecisms signify complicity. The aloofness of resistance and embrace of complicity are both contained in the conclusion of 'Annunciations, 2':

> 'O Love,
> You know what pains succeed; be vigilant; strive
> To recognize the damned among your friends.'

These lines combine two conflicting desires: to identify those who are 'damned', and happen to include our friends, so as to shun them; and to acknowledge 'the damned' as also friends, to pray for or tend them. By combining these, Hill dramatises the rivalry between self-interested and self-sacrificial impulses; he also settles the struggle in the irreducible and singular presence of the words themselves. The extended ambiguities present a conflict of motives and balance of opposed pressures; which is the combination of a further conflict. Played upon by diverse forces and driven to seek amends by writing more poems, further occasions for culpability, the poet continues to be impelled by what Hill has called 'yet another impure motive, remorse'.[22]

John Purkis, in a footnote on the imaginary Spanish poet Hill 'translated' for 'The Songbook of Sebastian Arrurruz', considered that 'Although this poet is a "spoof" – his name sounds like "arrowroot" and he is said to have been banished for committing a grammatical solecism so that his work was removed from all the anthologies – Hill takes him very seriously as a poetic *alter ego*.'[23] Taken seriously indeed, Sebastian Arrurruz is a fictional variant on the thematic similarities and differences in much of Geoffrey Hill's work between suffering for the sake of your art and martyrdom for others' sakes; see, for example, *For the Unfallen*'s 'Homage to Henry James', entitled 'The Martyrdom of Saint Sebastian', where we are asked to 'Consider such pains "crystalline": then fine art/Persists where most crystals accumulate.' The solemn joke about Arrurruz's banishment and removal from the anthologies hints at agreement with Simone Weil's sense of crime and punishment as well as an awareness of Mandelshtam's fate. At the risk of bathos and banality, Hill keeps such exemplary sufferings in contact with the more mundane errors to which we are all prone:

> 'A knitting editor once said "if I make a mistake there are jerseys all over England with one arm longer than the other".' Set that beside Nadezhda Mandelstam's account of the life and death of her husband ... and one can scarcely hope to be taken seriously. Men are imprisoned and tortured and executed for the strength of their beliefs and their ideas, not for upsetting the soup. And yet one must, however barely, hope to be taken seriously.[24]

In a broadcast talk, he says: 'I write very much by intuition and work hard, by means of scholarship and self-criticism, to satisfy myself of the validity of that intuition', but he removes from the word 'scholarship' any suspicion of privilege or self-praise.[25] The sonnet sequence 'An Apology for the Revival of Christian Architecture in England' in *Tenebrae*, employs the scholarly temptation to wax nostalgic so that the poem can chart a history of falsification and neglect. '6. A Short History of British India (III)' half-mourns a half-truth:

> the life of empire like the life of mind
> 'simple, sensuous, passionate', attuned
> to the clear theme of justice and order, gone.
>
> Gone the ascetic pastimes, the Persian
> scholarship. . . .

The most consistently presented scholarly passion is Sebastian Arrurruz's attenuated meditation on a lost *amour*. He has been called by his translator 'a shy sensualist with a humour that could be said to balance the sensuality except that the finer nuances have been lost in translation'[26] – and his work has the self-confessed manners of an academic poet:

> Already, like a disciplined scholar,
> I piece fragments together, past conjecture
> Establishing true sequences of pain;

> For so it is proper to find value
> In a bleak skill, as in the thing restored:
> The long-lost words of choice and valediction.

A 'disciplined scholar' is an academic trained in a certain discipline; he is also one who has been chastised, perhaps for scholarly error or 'past conjecture' that has proved untrue, and, mortifying himself by penance, he is taking pains to establish 'true sequences of pain' – a compact of both his disappointments and his recall of them. Attempting to restore what was 'long-lost' (as in a 'long-lost friend' often said of one re-encountered), he remains perpetually desirous while perpetuating his longings through his work. In the fifth fragment of Arrurruz's sequence of pain, his scholarly taste for exactitude conspires with the desolate emptiness of his yearning; this familiar conflation of reading and eating (another instance of the suspicious 'poetry-banquet') makes Arrurruz sound gluttonous, choosy, and more than half-starved:

> I find myself
> Devouring verses of stranger passion
> And exile. The exact words
>
> Are fed into my blank hunger for you.

The phrase 'I find myself' discovers Arrurruz surprised at who he finds himself to be; he has uncovered himself by study, given substance and sustenance to his feelings by reading poetry. That exact word 'blank' he might have chanced upon in a number of not unsuitable English poems, or his translator might have done. Coleridge, suffering from unrequitable extra-marital passion, gazes on the heavens 'with how blank an eye!';[27] Tennyson, recalling a dead friend, sees how 'On the bald street breaks the blank day';[28] while William Empson – though strictly speaking Arrurruz could not have known this – begins a poem about no longer writing poetry 'It is this deep blankness is the real thing strange.'[29] With his 'blank hunger' Arrurruz, a poet with an empty piece of paper before him, is also suffering from a writing-block; he reads to feed his inspiration. He is a skeleton at the feast.

II

Writing of the 'Lachrimae' sequence in *Tenebrae*, Jeffrey Wainwright notes that the sonnets 'are also a profound discussion and demonstration of artifice in expression. Truly it is a dangerous game. Our language has woven several connotations around the words "artifice" and "artificial" for good reasons.'[30] To say so much of our language is to credit the cumulatively collaborative efforts of the English-speaking peoples with beneficial results; his statement trusts the common tongue, whereas Geoffrey Hill – despite and because of his ear for the colloquial – cannot put his trust in that. For, as he has said: 'In handling the English language the poet makes an act of recognition that etymology is history. The history of the creation and the debasement of words is a paradigm of the loss of the kingdom of innocence and original justice.'[31] Hill feels the shudder of fall in words, words that are *of* this world, and conceives of the acts of composition as a resistance to, and a seeking to amend for, sin and shame. Employing the same old words, he attempts to restore to the world of usage, and to the world that usage may order, distinguishable senses and values embedded in them. Victor Erlich asked:

> could not this unique command of the ambiguity of human experience, this adeptness at conveying the 'formidable density' of the world's body (John Crowe Ransom), be construed as a counterpart of that density of the medium, which, according to the Formalists, is typical of poetry?[32]

Hill has accommodated such a view to a religious sense of the medium's density, 'a sense of language itself as a manifestation of empirical guilt'.[33] Amidst the slipperiness, confusion, sloppiness, and active deceit in language-users (and Hill would add in words themselves), it is always advisable to read the small print.

'Money is a kind of poetry', Wallace Stevens wrote.[34] His aphorism reiterates the terms of a time-honoured analogy. When Geoffrey Hill speaks of the 'debasement of words' he too is calling upon it, for 'to debase' means to 'lower in quality, value, or character', and to 'adulterate' coins. There is a poetic frame of mind which unequivocally admires rich imagery and likes its poets to have the Midas touch. The weakness of the pure gold of poetic speech, however, is that it is brittle and particularly vulnerable to debasement. Osip Mandelshtam (whose conflicting uses of monetary imagery led Clarence Brown to note 'a profound indecision of spirit'[36]), argued in his 'Notes about Poetry' (1923) for the place of alloy in verse:

> Colloquial language loves accommodation. Out of hostile chunks it creates an alloy. Colloquial speech always finds the middle, convenient way. In its relationship to the whole history of language it is inclined to be conciliatory and is defined by its diffuse benevolence, that is to say, by its opportunism. Poetic speech on the other hand is never sufficiently 'pacified,' and in it, after many centuries, old discords are revealed.[36]

The sceptical weighing of colloquial language's attributes in this passage does not extend to a preference for poetic speech over it; Mandelshtam is in favour of colloquial language which, he argues, 'brings good to the language, that is longevity, and helps it, as it might help a righteous man, to perform its ordeal of independent existence in the family of dialects.' Such speech, originating in exchanges between people, might manifest the values Mandelshtam attributes to it, because its various and hidden senses allow the expression of one idea or feeling while implying another, seeking in the explicit and implicit meanings of speech a tacit goodwill in the hearer, and offering room for his or her reply in possible confirmation or possible disagreement. It is the medium in which differences of opinion, value, idea, and belief can confront each other and themselves, while maintaining amicable relations by mutual accommodation.

For Hill, colloquial language – with its clichés and dead metaphors, idioms, slang – is a matter for vigilant adjustment, involving both attachment and resistance: '... because the nature of true poetic speech is the attempt to transfigure some of the negative liabilities of speech into more positive form.'[37] When Jesus went up into an high mountain with three of his disciples 'he was transfigured before them. And his raiment became shining, exceeding white as snow'. Peter suffered from one of the negative liabilities of speech when he blurted out 'let us make three tabernacles', for 'he wist not what to say' (Mark, 9.2–3 and 6). Hill adopts the word 'transfigure' in order to give poetic transformation a spiritual dimension; an explicit parallel is made in such discussion of poetic speech and colloquial speech between the falling and rising of Donne's 'Therfore that he may raise the Lord throws down',[38] and the debasement and redemption of words. However, while an event like the Wall Street 'Crash' has been related to the Fall of Man,[39] bankers' and governments' efforts to maintain or elevate or lower the value of a currency cannot be equated with entering the kingdom of heaven. The New Testament neither offers a simple nor single attitude to money and coin. When certain Pharisees and Herodians tried to 'catch him in his words', Jesus asked, 'Whose is this image and superscription?' His reply to their answer may perhaps be interpreted as reaffirming, in the context of an attempt to corner him into a treasonable utterance, the similarity and difference between the power men have in controlling a currency, and God's power: 'Render to Caesar the things that are Caesar's, and to God the things that are God's' (Mark, 12.13 and 16–7).

Of *Mercian Hymns* XI–XIII, Jon Glover remarks: 'Offa's coins appear as objects of wonder, symbols of power, relics, objects of curiosity and contempt.'[40] The first of these prose-poems, devoted to rendering to Offa the things that are Offa's, also advances an analogy between minting a coin and making a work of art:

> Coins handsome as Nero's; of good substance and
> weight. *Offa Rex* resonant in silver, and the
> names of his moneyers. They struck with account-
> able tact. They could alter the king's face.

The allusion to Nero hints at such an analogy: Nero, who burned Christians, 'fiddled while Rome burned', thinking himself an artist. The poem may explore the various forms of exchange value for which an artist can be responsible in his work. There is a regicidal aggression in 'They struck', somewhat pacified and weighed by 'tact' – where social delicacy is in touch with physical contact. The pressures behind and against the two senses are nicely judged in that rich ambiguity of 'accountable': the treasury's books balanced, the king's vanity about his profile understood.

> Exactness of design was to deter imitation; mutil-
> ation if that failed. Exemplary metal, ripe for
> commerce. Value from a sparse people, scrapers of
> salt-pans and byres.

The other side of the coin to that risky artistic freedom of being able to alter the king's face is found in the punishment for counterfeiters: the criminal disfigured, altered by mutilation. A poet too may design his work in the hope of preserving its 'originality', its difficulty of imitation. 'Exemplary' is one of Hill's much-loved and needed words. He has applied it to the art of poetry: 'Poetry is responsible. It's a form of responsible behaviour, not a directive. It is an exemplary exercise.'[41] 'Exemplary metal, ripe for commerce' is also what the poem's words are. Initially, it is tempting to think that Hill's words are an alloy of hostile chunks, made in the spirit of Mandelshtam – a coinage more durable than pure metal. Instances in this prose-poem, despite the allusion to colloquial language, suggest that a pure poetic speech has been designed with particular care as regards the retention of value. The phrase 'scrapers of salt-pans and byres' gains resonance by having the colloquial 'scraping by', and the familiar 'buyers', implied in the design; but these words are not in the piece. It preserves its own originality of diction against the debasement of such phrases – phrases which have the world too much with them.

Describing Robert Lowell's version, in *Imitations*, of some lines from Baudelaire's 'Le Cygne', Hill noted: 'It is as though we are intended to recognize, in Lowell's poem, that the lyric maintains a perilous autonomy against mundane attrition. It shows itself scarred at the edge, somewhat distorted, as though from a partial melting-down.'[42] Elsewhere, he glosses the word 'attrition' by quoting Jeremy Taylor: 'Attrition begins with fear, Contrition hath hope and love in it; the first is a good beginning, but it is no more'.[43] It is as perilous to be independent of attrition, since it is a good beginning, as to be worn out or consumed by its fear. Hill keeps colloquial language within hearing distance of his poems because he is aware of the danger; it does not appear in his poems as colloquial speech because such language is too compromised by the compromises embedded in it through centuries:

> Swathed bodies in the long ditch; one eye upstaring.
> It is safe to presume, here, the king's anger. He
> reigned forty years. Seasons touched and retouch-
> ed the soil.

> Heathland, new-made watermeadow.

The expression 'safe to presume' – which, like 'I dare say', has lost touch with the physical vulnerability in 'safe' and 'dare' – is contextualised with a violence and authority such as to set safety mortally in question, and make presumption a dangerous arrogance. You too could end up in the ditch. The comma'd-off 'here' points at the historical context of Offa's coins, at the point in the prose-poem we have reached, and so at our own moment in history, from which it is safe to presume, I dare say – a safety for which we may be grateful. Here, to recall Mandelshtam's distinction, Geoffrey Hill has transfigured the pacified colloquialism into a fearfully poetic phrase – a reminder of our past in the language. Yet how the seasons in their alterations seem to imitate the valuing and revaluing of coins and words: 'touched' is cognate with 'tact'; 'to retouch' is what painters do to improve the finish of their work. Like 'pose' and 'repose' in T.S. Eliot's 'La Figlia che Piange',[44] the collocation of touches gives a delicacy and persistence to the seasonal cycle, the circulation of currency, the exchanges of words. The epithet 'new-made' applied to a 'watermeadow' recalls Ezra Pound's renovative poetic slogan and title of a 1934 collection of essays: *Make it New*. It suggests, too, that, as the seasons retouch the earth, so to rinse and refresh the language is to refurbish the sensible world.

*   *   *

Ezra Pound believed that the poetic vitality of a language lay in the identity of word and thing. When T.S. Eliot wrote 'Language in a healthy state presents the object, is so close to the object that the two are identified',[45] we can hear Pound's influence on both the idea and its phrasing. There is also a literary nostalgia for rudimentary conditions:

> In tables showing primitive Chinese characters in one column and the present 'conventionalized' signs in another, anyone can see how the ideogram for man or tree or sunrise developed, or 'was simplified from', or was reduced to the essentials of the first picture of man, tree or sunrise.[46]

Pound's very way of putting this, with its three divergent possibilities for the relation of the primitive to the conventional, indicates the unlikeness of his English, and anyone's English, to the Chinese characters as he conceives them. It is as though the strain involved for him in writing poetry in English made him long for a state where the poetry came ready-made: 'Fenollosa was telling how and why a language written in this way simply HAD TO STAY POETIC; simply couldn't help being and staying poetic in a way that a column of English type might very well not stay poetic.' Donald Davie, discussing a distinction between fundamental identity and conventional relation of words and things, quotes the French poet St.-John Perse reporting a conversation with André Gide:

> He told me of the attraction that an exhaustive study of the English language was beginning to exert over him. I, for my part, deplored the denseness of such a concrete language, the excessive richness of its vocabulary and its pleasure in trying to reincarnate the thing itself, as in ideographic writing; whereas French, a more abstract language, which tries to signify rather than represent the meaning, uses words only as fiduciary symbols like coins as values of monetary exchange. English for me was still at the swapping stage.[47]

Reading Geoffrey Hill gives reason to suspect that Pound's primitivism is an impossible wish for English, and that neither St.-John Perse's view of English nor his discrimination between it and French is entirely convincing. The very richness of English – not only its seams of near-synonyms, but also the compounded ambiguity, the alloy of its plainest words – makes it a language which manifests in itself the ambiguous density of the experienced world, and which its users must consequently exchange as fiduciary symbols. The absence of absolutely and eternally fixed relations between words and things, or between the speaker and the spoken to, obliges English speakers to take or give words in trust. Moreover, it is context, both within writing and in the implied occasion of utterance, that can limit the meanings and values in exchange, help settle the conditions of trust.

Quoting Péguy's words, Geoffrey Hill incidentally tests St.-John Perse's distinction between the French language and the English:

> 'Encore plus douloureux et doux.' Note how
> sweetness devours sorrow, renders it again,
> turns to affliction each more carnal pain.
>   (p. 28)

The word 'renders' in Hill's stanza recalls St.-John Perse's fiduciary symbols, but finds in the French for sweet and sorrowful a texture of incarnate being and an opportunity for transfiguration which the paper currency metaphor might seem to disallow. Shakespeare's Juliet can express a continuity of pleasure in approaching separation because her English 'Parting is such sweet sorrow' has an initial alliteration which the vowels and terminal consonant of 'sorrow' depart from;[48] in 'douloureux et doux' the long drawn out suffering of the three vowels in 'douloureux' are compacted into the brief pout of 'doux', with its more closely related vowel sounds and consonants. Such differences are one of the reasons why the *OED* gives as an example of 'render', meaning 'translate': 'poetry can never be adequately rendered in another language'. An extract from Charles Péguy's writings entitled 'Politics and Mysticism' (in *Basic Verities*), dwells on the term 'mystique' in its conclusion: 'Everything begins in mysticism and ends in politics. – The interest, the question, the essential is that in each order, in each system, mysticism be not devoured by the politics to which it gave birth. – '.[49] In Péguy's life and work Geoffrey Hill found occasion to enact, in his own poetic diction, the attrition of 'la mystique' by 'la politique' while, at the same moment, seeking to transfigure that too worldly process into the absolutes of an irreducible piece of art, a resistance to such devouring. It is as though the French for 'sweet' had eaten the heart out of 'sorrow', leaving the husk of two consonants and a vowel. Those words, like 'la mystique' and 'la politique' are set in an aggressive feeding embrace; but the word 'renders', as well as calling upon artistic portrayal or translation, asks us to remember that discrimination: 'Render to Caesar the things that are Caesar's, and to God the things that are God's.'

*   *   *

Early in *The Mystery of the Charity of Charles Péguy*, questions are asked about the responsibility that a writer can be held to take for his words:

> Must men stand by what they write
> as by their camp-beds or their weaponry
> or shell-shocked comrades while they sag and cry?
>
> (p. 9)

The question has been framed to catch up diverse circumstances in which it is difficult and conceivably inadvisable to 'stand by'; nor can we avoid being sometimes merely 'by-standers'. If men do not or cannot ever be thought to 'stand by' their words (in those senses relating to vigilance, loyalty, and accountability), can poetry be considered, in Hill's words, 'a form of responsible behaviour'? One reason why it is difficult to stand by the words in a poem is because they move; that is, they have a rhythmical momentum which, with their density of meanings and associations, creates an emotion:

> But still mourn,
> being so moved: éloge and elegy
> so moving on the scene as if to cry
> 'in memory of those things these words were born.'
>
> (p. 28)

The bracketing, outer, full-rhymes of the stanza conjoin poetry's sweetness to the subject's sorrows, while the sardonic play on 'moved' and 'moving' hold that up for inspection, with their hints of piling on the agony so as to grab the stage. William Wordsworth thought that

> ... from the tendency of metre to divest language in a certain degree of its reality, and thus to throw a sort of half consciousness of unsubstantial existence over the whole composition, there can be little doubt but that more pathetic situations and sentiments, that is, those which have a greater proportion of pain connected with them, may be endured in metrical composition, especially in rhyme, than in prose.[50]

A poet of Geoffrey Hill's scrupulous scepticism would recognise the value of what Wordsworth observes, but suspect the ways that rhyme and rhythm may render sorrow sweet, make pain enjoyable beyond endurance. Such musical powers may also be seen in the light of Péguy's sense that 'la politique' would devour 'la mystique', that suffering is exploitable by poet and politician; and 'to divest language ... of its reality' might involve approximation both to redemptive suffering and transfiguration, but may also invite the use of suffering for the encouragement of a spurious national unity by 'church and civic dignitaries'.[51]

In some of his early work, Geoffrey Hill devised a compacted syntax and complex diction which almost brought his poetry to a stand-still. Edward Lucie-Smith found it 'difficult to avoid the word "costive"',[52] while Christopher Ricks felt that 'the poems, though they still have force, no longer have so much momentum.'[53] Scanning over 'The Lowlands of Holland', we may

Witness many devices; the few natural

Corruptions, graftings; witness classic falls. . . .
                    ('Of Commerce and Society, II')

The very short clauses, even single items of diction are parted and sutured by
punctuation and lineation; they ask readers to dwell on each word, while to
read on is to follow the staggering moves. Being moved from 'Corruptions'
to 'graftings' involves bearing in mind that the former are 'decompositions',
'moral deteriorations', 'corrupt practices', 'perversions of language'; and the
latter are 'transplanted tissue', 'hydrid plant growth', 'illicit spoils'. The halt-
ing rhythm was purposefully conceived. Hill wrote, at the time, about Allen
Tate's 'Ode to the Confederate Dead': 'The Union cavalry . . . are like
Milton's angels, who cannot be injured. Parting before the blow, they flew
together again. The self-healing properties of Capitalism are, of course, re-
nowned.'[54] Hill is still exploring the collusions of military, commercial,
governmental, and religious visions and actions; but rather than rhythmically
baulking their careering progress even while miming their processes as he had
done earlier, in *The Mystery* . . . his music answers to the sorrows, doing
what it can:

                    The line

    falters, reforms, vanishes into the smoke
    of its own unknowing; mother, dad,
    gone in that shell-burst, with the other dead,
    'pour la patrie', according to the book.
                    (p. 23)

That line-break 'the smoke/of its own unknowing' does not pass without
recalling the anonymous medieval mystical text *The Cloud of Unknowing*, as
if to go through the smoke of battle were to penetrate the Divine mystery.
The distance between that title and Hill's rephrasing of it, the faintly clumsy
'its own unknowing', echoes the settled, colloquial and even more sceptical
'its own undoing' – where the men merely meet their death. They die 'accord-
ing to the book', and we are asked to reflect whether this is a military training
manual, or a bible, and if and when it can be both. The relation of 'dad' to
'patrie', by way of 'other dead', which in turn remembers 'mother' – finds
connection and conflict between loyalties to the home and the homeland; and
the movement of the lines, in their laconic and mundane routine, bear one of
those 'more pathetic situations' which Wordsworth recognised as needing the
consolation of a 'still, sad music'.

    Yet Geoffrey Hill's paradigm of language as fallen, and always to be re-
deemed, seems to give little stated consolation. The Fall may be fortunate,
but only poetry gives consolations – and dubious ones at that. Hill's high
agnosticism infuses his poetry with the need for, and the suspicion of, some-
thing further. '7. Loss and Gain' from 'An Apology . . .' takes its title from

Cardinal Newman's novel of Catholic conversion – one context for losses and gains. Condensed into the phrase, and resounding in the sonnet, is a glimpsed balance-sheet of English nineteenth-century history: losses and gains for 'the ruined and the ruinously strong'. Conceiving of the two together conjures up labyrinthine bafflements. Is there a touch of self-delusion in the one who gains a vision of salvation, and, caught in Keats's quandary ('Was it a vision, or a waking dream? ... Do I wake or sleep?'[55]), imagines that history may be atoned for?

> Vulnerable to each other the twin forms

> of sleep and waking touch the man who wakes
> to sudden light, who thinks that this becalms
> even the phantoms of untold mistakes.

These 'untold mistakes', which are both unconfessed and so vast in number as to be uncountable, include a world of different blunders: self-deception, solecism, fatal error of judgement. Hill's scruple and discipline might suggest a further paradigmatic substitution: the state of the text for the state of the world. It is tempting to read the poems as emblems of an uncorrupted body politic,[56] his careful rhythmic adjustments regulating trustful, though not credulous, exchanges of meaning within the lines' contexts, their responsibly-moving words emblematic of the circulation of an ideal currency. But this would be to believe that Hill's poems, or anyone's, are capable of becalming 'even the phantoms of untold mistakes.' The scepticisms are not to be out-stripped. Can a poem ever atone for history? Does its currency bear any relation to the one we have?

III

When Mandelshtam characterised colloquial language, he also came to the conclusion that 'Poetic speech on the other hand is never sufficiently "paci-fied," and in it, after many centuries, old discords are revealed.' Geoffrey Hill also senses the way poetry may preserve 'old discords' and may therefore be menacing; but he proposes that '... it may sometimes be necessary to mimic a dilemma' in a poem, to hear discords so as to contain them.[57] *Mercian Hymns* XVIII contains a piece of poetic speech which reveals old discords after many centuries, and it mimics a dilemma so as to examine the uses and abuses of an historical and cultural scholarship and imagination. It also al-ludes to a political furore relating to quotation out of context and reference to sources:

> At Pavia, a visitation of some sorrow. Boethius'
> dungeon. He shut his eyes, gave rise to a tower
> out of the earth. He willed the instruments of
> violence to break upon meditation. Iron buckles
> gagged; flesh leaked rennet over them; the men
> stooped, disentangled the body.

> He wiped his lips and hands. He strolled back to the
> car, with discreet souvenirs for consolation and
> philosophy. He set in motion the furtherance of
> his journey. To watch the Tiber foaming out
> much blood.

The prurient visualisation of violence for dubious ends[58] begins with an ele-
vation of Offa's tourism ('Offa's Journey to Rome' the hymn is called) by
employing the ostentatiously Latinate 'visitation', while 'some' implies a cer-
tain connoisseurship of emotion, a simultaneous indulgence and withdrawal.
The sentence which mimics a crucial moral slip is 'He willed the instruments
of violence to break upon meditation.' It is menacingly unclear whether Offa
wills the instruments to be broken by the power of meditation, identifying
with Boethius; or, he wills them to break Boethius' meditation; or, he exploits
meditation to will that a body be broken.

Seamus Heaney has observed that in *Mercian Hymns* 'the Latinate and
local also go hand in glove',[59] but, rather than conspiring together, here there
is an impacted conflict between etymologies in the movement from 'instru-
ments', 'violence', and 'meditation' to 'Iron buckles gagged; flesh leaked ren-
net' – a body tortured on the rack, to which the Latinate, though it may
command the proceedings, does not lower itself. One source for the style of
Hill's prose-poems is Ezra Pound's *Homage to Sextus Propertius*, which also
deploys close confrontations of words from one etymological origin with
those of another. About Pound's lines 'The moon still declined to descend out
of heaven,/But the black ominous owl hoot was audible', Donald Davie
wrote:

> The absurdly misplaced formality of 'declined to', and the ludicrously stilted
> passive, 'was audible', exemplify the English of the bored schoolboy lazily con-
> struing his Latin homework, but equally the proud pompous clerk (Pakistani,
> Cypriot or whatever) using the language of those who were lately his imperial
> masters ... Thus it appears that by wholly transposing 'imperialism' into
> language, into the texture of style, by forgetting his own existence 'for the sake
> of the lines', Pound has effected a far more wounding and penetrating critique of
> imperialism in general...[60]

Geoffrey Hill, whose essay 'Our Word Is Our Bond' painstakingly traces
Pound's culpabilities, has praise for *Homage to Sextus Propertius*: 'The status
fought for, and accomplished, within the comedy and melodrama of this
sequence, is, therefore, that of standing by one's words in a variety of tricky
situations ...'.[61] The difficulty for the poet is that to enter the 'tricky situa-
tions' he must 'mimic a dilemma'; it might involve transposing 'imperialism'
into language as raw translatorese. At the same moment, the poet must stand
by the same words; he is obliged to compose them so that the movement of
his lines resists his diction's susceptibility to being the inert phraseology of
the various shibboleths that constitute the dilemma. A piece of art which

mimics a dilemma will show signs of what it is implicitly offering for inspection. This is one reason for Pound's troubles with critics over the supposed schoolboy howlers in *Homage to Sextus Propertius*. Or, as Hill replied to those who found nostalgia in 'An Apology for the Revival of Christian Architecture in England': 'To be accused of exhibiting a symptom when, to the best of my ability, I'm offering a diagnosis appears to be one of the numerous injustices which one must suffer with as much equanimity as possible.'[62] But this critical misunderstanding, which blunts the strategic ironies that seek to mimic and yet remain responsible for the mimicking words, is also an outcome of the distance between inner context, where the words ambiguously work, and outer context of explicit or implied addressees.

The second verset of *Mercian Hymns* XVIII begins by associating Offa with Pontius Pilate and the Pharisees; he enjoys washing his hands of a moral problem. 'He set in motion the furtherance of/his journey' hints at a self-interested furthering and careering from place to place in his tourism – which takes him, in the final clause, to Rome, the underworld, and the prophecy of the Cumaean Sybil to Virgil's Aeneas. Geoffrey Hill's footnote properly directs us to this; and we find that final clause is a piece of bona fide poetic speech: ' "To watch the Tiber foaming out much blood": adapted from Vergil, *Aeneid*, VI, 87, "et Thybrim multo spumantem sanguine cerno".' Old discords are revealed after centuries in this line, referring to the prediction of war given to Aeneas, and fulfilled later in the poem. The same Latin phrase differently rendered appeared in Enoch Powell's speech of 20th April, 1968: the year also in which Geoffrey Hill began *Mercian Hymns*. The speech was given to the Annual General Meeting of the West Midlands Area Conservative Political Centre at the Midland Hotel, Birmingham; that is to say, in the modern-day regional capital of Offa's Mercia. Nearing the end of his speech, Enoch Powell said:

> As I look ahead, I am filled with foreboding. Like the Roman, I seem to see 'the River Tiber foaming with much blood'. That tragic and intractable phenomenon which we watch with horror on the other side of the Atlantic but which there is interwoven with the history and existence of the States itself, is coming upon us here by our own volition and our own neglect. Indeed, it has all but come.[63]

To allude to bloodshed is not necessarily to invoke it; but Enoch Powell moves from 'I seem to see', through 'it has all but come', to 'All I know is that to see, and not speak, would be the great betrayal' – from mock-hesitant prophecy to expectation, justified by adopting a phrase from Virgil without its context of a war that will found an imperial power: he gives substance to his enmities. The allusion to Virgil is the only particular instance of bloodshed given; 'after many centuries' he reveals the 'old discords' to invite an emotive concurrence. Thus, he would set in motion the furtherance of his journey: to change British immigration policy, and, more immediately, to affront the shadow cabinet leader Edward Heath.

Elsewhere, Enoch Powell said:

A classical scholar is equipped with the pre-digestion of a great range of human experience, political and also non-political, so that amongst non-classics he is rather like a man who knows the times-table, compared with people who don't ... The classical scholar already knows that eight times seven are seventy-two [sic] because that's in the *Antigone*, as it were.[64]

This seems to suppose, whether the mistaken multiplication is deliberate or not, that the application of past literary experience to contemporary lived experience is as unambiguous as doing your sums. It cannot be: because words, and words in different languages, do not perform with the transparent utility of numbers. Powell's classical scholarship visualises violence to gain emotional assent for what is desired by invoking its opposite; similarly, in the phrase 'we watch with horror', the alarm in 'with horror' fails to conceal the delight at having that example to enforce his own case – 'we watch'. Powell's words, many believed at the time, appeared to encourage social discord in the name of alleviating or preventing it. In the opening paragraph of his speech, Powell released himself from injunctions to caution when referring to possible conflicts – a caution which would seem to separate the responsible public speaker from the rabble-rouser:

Above all, people are disposed to mistake predicting troubles for causing troubles and even desiring troubles: 'If only', they love to think, 'if only people wouldn't talk about it, it probably wouldn't happen'. Perhaps this habit goes back to the primitive belief that the word and the thing, the name and the object, are identical.[65]

Geoffrey Hill, unlike the young T.S. Eliot in his essay on Swinburne, does not hold this 'primitive belief'. When he speaks of poetry as 'a form of responsible behaviour', his phrase summons belief in speaking and writing as acts to be judged in a light sometimes reserved for more obviously physical acts by those who call their utterances 'merely words'. His phrase implies, too, that it is when words and things are not assumed to be identical that their fine adjustment, which is a form of responsible behaviour, grows urgent. Powell's introductory remarks do not release him from the obligation to speak with tempered caution; they locate him in a linguistic context where such care and attention is essential, in order to prevent 'predicting troubles' from having the possible effect of 'causing troubles'. When Geoffrey Hill asks 'Did Péguy kill Jaurès? Did he incite/the assassin?' he is brooding on a similarly vexed relation between the use of certain words and the foreseeable consequences.

By enacting in *Mercian Hymns* XVIII a show of scruple which includes unscrupulousness, and by enacting it in a literary context where adjusted regard makes the engagement of scruple possible, Geoffrey Hill restores moral attention to an occasion for scholarly accuracy and responsible behaviour, through the language of the prose-poem and the example of his notes. A final detail about Powell's speech may illuminate Hill's pointed scholarly tact: '"for consolation and philosophy": the allusion is to the title of Boethius' great meditation, though it is doubtless an excess of scruple to point this out.' Enoch Powell lost his place in Edward Heath's shadow cabinet for a speech which was 'racialist in tone and liable to exacerbate racial tensions';[66] he had offended against the protocol for members of Parliament by quoting at length a letter from Northumberland about the behaviour of immigrants in his Wolverhampton constituency. Powell neither gave precise details of his source – though he stated that it was not an anonymous letter – nor did he offer evidence for the assertions made there. The protocol of not quoting private correspondence derives from two conflicting obligations: it is right to protect the privacy of those who write to their member of Parliament; it is also right, when material is quoted, to give details of the sources and evidence so that they can be independently examined.

*   *   *

It might be objected that if *Mercian Hymns* XVIII does concern itself with the linguistic behaviour of contemporary politicians, its presentation of symptoms in aid of diagnosis is particularly oblique. When Geoffrey Hill praised the 'fluent rapidity' of movement in Swift's poems 'from private to public utterance and from the formal to the intimate', he recognised the necessary context for such fluency in Swift's social relations. We are likewise obliged to recognise that such relations do not obtain today for most poets who would address their work to the condition of public life.[67] For Geoffrey Hill to speak the burden of his prose-poem to Enoch Powell would not only drastically narrow its meaning, but also involve assuming a relation between speaker and auditor either in the public or the private sphere – and, if the latter, of the private made public, an assumption which does not have substance in experience. Nevertheless, oblique strategies, the absence of named living interlocutors for instance, enable his work to render some of the ethical matter of political life without the tonal falsifications that an assumed familiarity or public address could entail. Eric Griffiths has noted that Hill 'knows better than to rely simply on the bare underpinning of imagined auditors';[68] and, in the absence of extrinsic contexts in which such acts of imagination might be substantiated, the intrinsic contexts of his poems exemplify language as a thing which, like 'The wooden wings of justice', is 'borne aloof'[69] into the considerable realm of the poem.

Strictly speaking, the colloquial speech which Mandelshtam valued as a constituent of poetry's language cannot appear in lyric poems as true colloquial speech. The word 'colloquial' indicates at least two speakers who are also auditors. Hill has written on more than one occasion that lyric poetry's composition is 'dramatic'.[70] When he describes how a writer may enact the 'drama of reason' by including the 'antiphonal voice of the heckler',[71] his word 'antiphonal' indicates a problem: the church-music term converts into a composed counterpointing of voices a nettled inruption of dissent in another's seamless mid-flow. It has been reported of leading politicians that as young men they sometimes asked 'supporters to heckle them to enliven dull meetings'.[72] The composition of heckling voices into lyric poems is vulnerable to such party management; the poet may be tempted to 'enliven' his work, and the divide between an antiphony that is just veiled accord and the true challenge of confronted differences resides, for poetry, in a certain stylistic rawness. This is a quality Hill praised in Wordsworth's 'Resolution and Independence', where his 'creative gift was to transform the helpless reiterations of raw encounter into the "obstinate questionings" of his meditated art without losing the sense of rawness.'[73] Wordsworth's gift is beyond Geoffrey Hill's scope; but Hill, who is very much more drawn, as Keats could be, towards 'the high claims of poetry itself',[74] has stretched for 'rawness' by partly resisting those higher reaches. Again of Swift as a poet, Hill wrote:

> ... there will be a temptation to claim that a timely encounter with popular verse 'redeemed' Swift as a poet. But there is no simple and obvious way in which this could be affirmed. Some of Swift's poems may have achieved immediate popular success, but one still has reservations about calling him a 'popular' poet; he did not so much use as demonstrate the colloquial; the very kind of accuracy he achieved was the result of a certain aloofness.[75]

Those last two clauses are also true of Geoffrey Hill; and that 'very kind of accuracy' is one of his greatnesses. What is distanced in the achievement of such accuracy is the sound of other specified people being spoken to, or speaking the grain of their lives. His poems recognise that distance and judge it by demonstrating, through the composing of voices which is his poetry, tones which have become far cries from people:

> Not as we are but as we must appear,
> Contractual ghosts of pity; not as we
> Desire life but as they would have us live,
> Set apart in timeless colloquy:
> So it is required; so we must bear witness,
> Despite ourselves, to what is beyond us,
> Each distant sphere of harmony forever
> Poised, unanswerable. If it is without
> Consequence when we vaunt and suffer, or
> If it is not, all echoes are the same
> In such eternity. Then tell me, love,
> How that should comfort us – or anyone
> Dragged half-unnerved out of this worldly place,
> Crying to the end 'I have not finished'.

> ('Funeral Music, 8')

Plangent and exacerbated, a voice calls upon a living, nameless addressee to answer. Only, in reply, no word comes.

Geoffrey Hill's 'florid grim music broken by grunts and shrieks'[76] dramatises the achievement of poetry's harmonies – colloquial, answerable speech transfigured into 'timeless colloquy'; it also contains the dramatic exchanges of a discordant world, nevertheless and necessarily attuning them. Though friends are not contracted to each other, as the married are, and though Hill has been principally concerned with words as 'bonds', he has also alluded to the bonds of friendship. Of his Oxford years he has said, 'I remained ill-at-ease socially, but made and kept several good friends.'[77] One of Offa's school friendships is sorely tried in *Mercian Hymns* VII: 'Coelred was his friend and remained so' even after being flayed for losing a toy aeroplane. Friendship's bonds can be heard to break in 'While friends defected, you stayed and were sure',[78] or 'your friendship so forsaken'[79]; and also in Charles Péguy's life, where Hill notices 'the harsh severing of old alliances and friendships in the years that followed.'[80] It is a benefit of the attuned language of great poetry that it stays faithful and remains true. In the long run it can be a friend. As well as for the liberty and fidelity of our friends, we may be grateful for Geoffrey Hill's work with all its broken music, its concords for ever on the mend.

Notes

Editor's introduction

1 Geoffrey Hill, *The Fantasy Poets, Pamphlet No. 11*, (Oxford, 1952).
2 Anonymous, 'Isis Idol: Geoffrey Hill', *The Isis*, 18 November 1953, p. 17.
3 *For the Unfallen: Poems 1952-1958*, (London, 1959).
4 *King Log*, (London, 1968).
5 *Preghiere*, Northern House Pamphlet Poets, (Leeds, 1964); *Penguin Modern Poets 8*, (Harmondsworth, 1966), pp. 53–82.
6 *Mercian Hymns*, (London, 1971).
7 *Tenebrae*, (London, 1978).
8 *The Mystery of the Charity of Charles Péguy*, (London, 1983).
9 *The Lords of Limit: Essays on Literature and Ideas*, (London, 1984).
10 *Brand* by Henrik Ibsen: A Version for the English Stage, (London, 1978).
11 *King Log*, p. 42.
12 For Hill's observations on the 'fallen' nature of language, see *Viewpoints: Poets in Conversation with John Haffenden*, (London, 1981), p. 88, and *The Lords of Limit*, pp. 6–7; Hill discusses 'transfiguration' and 'redeeming the time' on numerous occasions in *The Lords of Limit*, for example, pp. 30 and 67 for the former; 54, 103 and 156 for the latter. The biographical information given in my introduction is drawn from the Haffenden interview.

1 Early poems

1 'Letter from Oxford', *The London Magazine* Vol. 1 No. 4, May 1954, p. 73.
2 Ibid., p. 72.
3 *The Lords of Limit*, p. 2.
4 'Robert Lowell: Contrasts and Repetitions', *Essays in Criticism* Vol. 13 No. 2, April 1963, p. 191.
5 'Genesis; A ballad of Christopher Smart', *The Fantasy Poets, Pamphlet No. 11* (Oxford, 1952), collected in *For the Unfallen*, pp. 15-7.
6 'An Ark on the Flood', *The Isis*, 10 March 1954, p. 18.
7 'The Revelation', *The London Magazine* Vol. 1 No. 10, November 1954, p. 72. 'Prospero and Ariel', 'Gideon at the Well', *Oxford Poetry 1954*. 'To William Dunbar', *The Fantasy Poets, Pamphlet No. 11*. 'Saint Cuthbert on Farne Island', *Oxford Poetry 1952*.
8 'Water and Fire', *The Isis*, 4 March 1953, p. 22.
9 *The Lords of Limit*, pp. 96-7.
10. 'Good Friday', *Oxford Guardian* Vol. 13 No. 3, 24 February 1951, p. 11.
11 'Merlin', *Oxford Poetry 1953*, collected in *For the Unfallen*, p. 20.
12 'A Writer's Craft – 5', *The Isis*, 17 February 1954, p. 14.
13 Yeats, *Letters on Poetry from W.B. Yeats to Dorothy Wellesley*, (New York, Oxford, 1940), p. 94.
14 Richard Eberhart, in the poem 'If I could only live at the Pitch that is near Madness', *Selected Poems 1930–1965*, (New York, 1965), p. 18.
15 A phrase originally from P.T. Forsyth; applied to T.H. Green in *The Lords of Limit*, p. 120.
16 Another phrase from P.T. Forsyth, in *The Lords of Limit*, p. 17.

17 'Pentecost', *Oxford Poetry 1952*.

18 Hobbes, *Leviathan*, (London, 1973), p. 367.

19 Letter to George and Thomas Keats, 22 December 1817, in *Letters of John Keats*, ed. Sidney Colvin, (London, 1891), p. 48.

20 *The Lords of Limit*, p. 96.

21 'I See the Crocus Armies Spread', *Trio* No. 3, June 1953, p. 12.

22 *The Lords of Limit*, p. 4.

23 St John of the Cross, *The Dark Night*, *The Collected Works*, translated by Kavanaugh and Rodriguez, (Washington DC, 1973), p. 361.

24 'Summer Night', *The Isis*, 19 November 1952, p. 33.

25 T.S. Eliot, 'Tradition and the Individual Talent', *Selected Prose*, ed. Frank Kermode, (London, 1975), pp. 38-9.

26 'Letter from Oxford', op. cit. p. 74.

27 *The Lords of Limit*, p. 68.

28 Hill explains these terms in *The Lords of Limit*, p. 94.

29 'The Dream of Reason', *Essays in Criticism* Vol. 14 No. 1, January 1964, pp. 93-4.

30 Melville, *Moby Dick*, (London, 1961), p. 337.

31 Ibid., p. 338.

32 *The Lords of Limit*, p. 5.

33 Ibid.

34 'Letter from Oxford', op. cit. p. 73.

35 Eliot, 'Tradition and the Individual Talent', *Selected Prose*, p. 39.

36 *Viewpoints*, p.77.

37 Ibid., p. 78.

38 For example, Philip Larkin, Thom Gunn, Donald Davie, Anthony Thwaite, Donald Hall, Adrienne Rich, George Steiner.

39 *Viewpoints*, p. 80.

40 'Under Judgment', *New Statesman*, 8 February 1980, p. 214.

41 'For Isaac Rosenberg', *The Fantasy Poets*, *Pamphlet No. 11*.

42 'In Memory of Jane Fraser', *New Poems* Vol. 1 No. 3, Spring 1953, p.4; collected in *For the Unfallen*, p. 23. 'The Tower Window', *The Isis*, 28 January 1953, p. 19. 'Captain Richard Fraser', *Trio* No. 2, January 1953, p. 16.

43 'The Poetry of Allen Tate', *Geste* (Leeds) Vol. 3 No. 3, November 1958, p. 11.

44 *The Mystery of the Charity of Charles Péguy*, p. 31.

2 *For the Unfallen*

1 '"I in Another Place." Homage to Keith Douglas', *Stand* Vol. 6 No. 4,1964, p. 10.

2 For a fine portrayal of this, see J.P. Stern's *Hitler: The Fuhrer and the People*, (London, 1975), especially Chapters 6, 9 and 10.

3 In the comment on 'Annunciations' which he supplied Kenneth Allott, Geoffrey Hill cited 'Love' as one of the words which

> are assumed to have an autonomous meaning or value irrespective of context, and to which we are expected to nod assent. If we do assent, we are 'received'; if we question the justice of the blanket-term, we have made the equivalent of a rude noise in polite company.

The metaphor of the 'poetry-banquet' combines the meaning of art refined from the raw materials of experience and made acceptable for 'conspicuous consumption', with 'lip-service to heritage'. See *The Penguin Book of Contemporary Verse*, ed. Allott, (second edn, Harmondsworth, 1962), pp. 391-2. In terms similar to, but less subtle than those of 'Annunciations', the world of 'To the (Supposed) Patron' is ruled by appetite, and supplies and consumes 'loves and barbecues' without distinction.

4 Geoffrey Hill, '"The Conscious Mind's Intelligible Structure": A Debate', *Agenda* Vol. 9 No.

4 – Vol. 10 No. 1, Autumn/Winter 1971–72, p. 21.

5 Coleridge's letter of January 28th 1810 to Thomas Poole, *Collected Letters of Samuel Taylor Coleridge*, (6 Vols), ed. Earl Leslie Griggs, (Oxford, 1956–71), III, p. 282. Hill cites the source and quotes the relevant passage in *The Lords of Limit*, p. 90:

> Of Parentheses I may be too fond – and will be on my guard in this respect –. But I am certain that no work of impassioned & eloquent reasoning ever did or could subsist without them – They are the *drama* of Reason – & present the thought growing, instead of a mere *Hortus siccus*.

Hill later in the essay (p. 93) says that Coleridge 'surely foresaw the obligation to enact the drama of reason within the texture of one's own work, since nothing else would serve. His parentheses are antiphons of vital challenge.'

The relevance of Coleridge's phrase to Hill's practice as a poet was first drawn to my attention by David James Jones in his 'Myth and History in the Poetry of Geoffrey Hill, Seamus Heaney and George Mackay Brown' (Ph.D. thesis, University College of Wales, Aberystwyth, 1981). Here he discusses the part played by the 'drama of reason' in Hill's embodiment of 'an intelligence checking and rechecking its own rhetoric, often depreciatingly' (p. 61). I wish also to acknowledge a general debt to Dr Jones both for his consideration of *For the Unfallen* in his thesis and for our many discussions of Hill's work.

6 In 'Beyond Modernism: Christopher Middleton and Geoffrey Hill', *Contemporary Literature* Vol. 12 No. 4, Autumn 1971, pp. 420–36.

7 Thomas Mann's novel about the fictional composer Adrian Leverkuhn, during the period of the rise of Nazism, is – among other things – a complex and penetrating analysis of the relationship between artistic 'transcendence' of the limitations imposed by morality and the critical intelligence in a release of full-blooded feeling, and the release of destructive energy in the 'mass-ego' of a whole society. It also shows in detail the spurious justifications that intellectual sophistication can find for espousing barbarism and diabolism. Thomas Mann's own irony is the exact opposite of the Faustian arrogance with which Leverkuhn 'frees' himself from the checks of morality and reason. Hill's irony is similar to Mann's and arises from a perception of the same dangers; as Erich Heller in *Thomas Mann the Ironic German* (1958) says of Mann, he had 'an ineradicable moral distrust of the artist'. Heller's observation that 'moral intelligence was the very fibre of the aesthetic sensibility' in Mann is also equally applicable to Hill.

8 The passion for unity is evident, for example, in his admiring treatment of Hopkins in 'Redeeming the Time' (*The Lords of Limit*, pp. 84–103) and his quotation in '"Perplexed Persistence": The Exemplary Failure of T.H. Green' (*The Lord of Limit*, p. 113) of Elizabeth Schneider on Hopkins's intention 'to create the closest unity of all human values in Christ'.

9 The importance of this poem for Geoffrey Hill is evident from his discussion of it in '"The Conscious Mind's Intelligible Structure": A Debate', pp. 20–1. It is a complex argument, but one highly suggestive phrase, which is relevant to my point, and may, perhaps, be abstracted from the discussion without damaging its integrity, is Hill's description of Yeats's 'acute historical intelligence drawing its energy from the struggle with that obtuseness which is the dark side of its own selfhood'.

3 *King Log*

1 The rhetorical figure involved here partly resembles *asyndeton*, which omits the connectives between a sequence of parallel phrases or clauses. Puttenham calls it 'loose language' and sees it as a defect, 'a figure to be used when we will seem to make hast, or to be earnest': *The Arte of English Poesie*, (Cambridge, 1970), p. 175. Its effect in Hill's poetry is the very opposite of loose. Alternatively, it could be seen as *synthroesmus*, Englished by Puttenham as 'the Heaping figure', but again neither the description nor the examples are at all close

to the effect in Hill. Puttenham talks of 'an earnest and hastie heaping up of speeches ... made by way of recapitulation' (pp. 236-7). But Hill's practice plainly involves less a rhetorical embellishment than an enactment of thought in syntax. Rhetorical terms offer the false gratifications of a kind of literary technology, though there may be no harm in reminding ourselves that a *techne* is involved. Presumably, rhetorical schemes had some descriptive force when believed to be knowingly applied in composition and knowingly received.

2 *Viewpoints*, p. 95.
3 Henry Rago, quoted in *The Lords of Limit*, p. 6.
4 Ibid., p. 9.
5 Ibid.
6 W.B. Yeats, 'The Symbolism of Poetry', *Essays and Introductions*, (London, 1961), pp. 156-9.
7 *The Lords of Limit*, p. 9.
8 The phrases are from 'History as Poetry', *King Log*, p. 41.
9 Part of a phrase quoted from *The New Orpheus*, p. 147, in *The Lords of Limit*, p. 6.
10 *The Penguin Book of Contemporary Verse*, ed. Kenneth Allott, (second edn, Harmondsworth, 1962), pp. 391-2.
11 Sigmund Freud, 'The Antithetical Meaning of Primal Words', 1910, in *The Standard Edition of the Complete Psychological Works*, (twenty-four vols.) trans. James Strachey, (London, 1953-66), XI, pp. 155-61.
12 See particularly Christopher Ricks, 'Geoffrey Hill and "The Tongue's Atrocities"', (Swansea, 1978), pp. 13-21.
13 *The Lords of Limit*, p. 4.
14 Robert Lowell, 'Afterthought', *Notebook*, (London, 1970), p. 262.
15 Plato, *Timaeus and Critias*, trans. Lee, (Harmondsworth, 1965), p. 123.

4 Mercian Hymns

1 'Geoffrey Hill', *Agenda* Vol. 13 No. 3, Autumn 1975, p. 26.
2 *Poetry Book Society Bulletin*, No. 69, Summer, 1971.
3 F.M. Stenton, *Anglo-Saxon England*, third edition, (Oxford, 1971), p. 222.
4 F.M. Stenton, 'The Supremacy of the Mercian Kings', *English Historical Review*, XXXIII, 1918, p. 446.
5 Christopher Brooke, *The Saxon and Norman Kings*, (London, 1982), pp. 100-1.
6 George Peele, *The Old Wives Tale*, edited by Patricia Binnie, (Manchester, 1980), 11.664-68, reading 'beard' with Dyce, rather than 'bird' as Binnie and the 1595 Quarto. I owe my references to Joseph Jacobs to Mrs Binnie's edition.
7 The word may also have been prompted by the extraordinary coiffure of the medieval graffito from All Saints, Sutton, Bedfordshire. See figure 20 in V. Pritchard, *English Medieval Graffiti*, (Cambridge, 1967) used on the dust-jacket of the first edition. It interestingly combines the childish and the archaic.
8 *The Lords of Limit*, p. 2.
9 *Viewpoints*, p. 90; the italics are my own.
10 *King Log*, p. 67.
11 *The Lords of Limit*, pp. 2, 10.
12 Ibid., p. 10.
13 *Viewpoints*, pp. 94, 95.
14 *The Lords of Limit*, p. 11, citing Rush Rees, *Without Answers*, 1969, p. 150.
15 Roger Little, *Saint-John Perse*, (London, 1973), p. 95.
16 St.-John Perse, *Anabasis*, translated by T.S. Eliot, revised edition, (London, 1959), p. 9.
17 Ibid., p. 87.

18 *Œuvres complètes*, Bibliothèque de la Pléiade, (Paris, 1972), p. 1108; my translation.

19 *Anabasis*, trans. Eliot, p. 25.

20 Eric Homberger, *The Art of the Real: Poetry in England and America since 1939*, (London, 1977), p. 211.

21 There is a direct allusion to *Aeneid* VI. 86-7 at the close of Hymn XVIII: 'To watch the Tiber foaming out much blood.'

22 *Œuvres complètes*, p. 1147; my translation.

23 St-John Perse, *Exil*, ed. Roger Little, (London, 1973), p. 17.

24 *Exile and Other Poems*, trans. Denis Devlin, second edn, Bollingen Series XV, (New York, 1949), p. 16.

25 *Anabasis*, trans. Eliot, p. 57.

26 'Virgil and the Christian World', *On Poetry and Poets*, (London, 1957), p. 128. Eliot's view of Virgil is well discussed by Frank Kermode, *The Classic*, (London, 1975), pp. 15–45. His entire chapter is pertinent to an understanding of *Mercian Hymns*.

27 Ibid., p. 130.

28 I cannot agree with Merle Brown that Hill's sense of the past is 'in combative, critical relationship' with Eliot's: *Double Lyric: Divisiveness and Communal Creativity in Recent English Poetry*, (London, 1980), p. 60. He fails to catch both tone and intention.

29 *Anabasis*, trans. Eliot, 1959, pp. 65, 23.

30 *The Lords of Limit*, p. 6.

5 *Tenebrae*

1 Published *University of Leeds Review*, 21 (1978), but delivered 5 December 1977. Reprinted in *The Lords of Limit*, pp. 1–18.

2 *The Lords of Limit*, p. 2.

3 Ibid., p. 17.

4 Ibid., pp. 6–7.

5 Merle E. Brown, *Double Lyric*, (London, 1980), p. 71.

6 On the record *The Poetry and Voice of Geoffrey Hill*, Hill does not read 'gone' and 'one' as full rhymes.

7 *Viewpoints*, p. 89.

8 William Empson, 'Recent Poetry', in *Nation and Athenaeum*, 21 February 1931, p. 672.

9 *The Lords of Limit*, p. 10.

10 (1975); ibid., p. 114.

11 *The Notebooks of Samuel Taylor Coleridge*, (three vols) ed. Coburn, (London, 1957-73), II, Entry 3231.

12 James Smith, 'On Metaphysical Poetry', *Scrutiny* Vol. II No. 3, Dec. 1933, p. 228.

13 Eric Partridge, *You Have a Point There*, (London, 1953), p. 134.

14 (1968); *The Lords of Limit*, p. 67.

15 *The Poetry Book Society Bulletin*, No. 98, Autumn 1978.

16 Jeffrey Wainwright, 'Geoffrey Hill's "Lachrimae"', *Agenda* Vol. 13 No. 3, Autumn 1975, p. 33.

17 (1983); *The Lords of Limit*, p. 144.

18 S. T. Coleridge, *Biographia Literaria*, (two vols) ed. Shawcross, (Oxford, 1907; reprinted 1979), I, p. 2.

19 E.g., in 'Holy Thursday', 'wolf' and 'she-wolf'; in 'Requiem for the Plantagenet Kings', 'blood' and 'blood-marks'; in 'Two Formal Elegies', 'witnesses' and 'witness-proof'; in *Mercian Hymns*, II, 'pet-name' and 'name'; in XIII, 'self-possession' and 'possession'; in *Brand* (Act V), 'war-clouds' and 'clouds'.

20 When the poem was first published, 'new-burgeoned' was 'far-dreamed-of'.

21 Eric Partridge, *Usage and Abusage*, (new edn, London, 1957), p. 148.

22 H.W. Fowler, *The King's English*, (1906; third edn reprinted Oxford, 1973), p. 284.

23 *Brand*, (second edn, revised, Minneapolis, 1981), p. 130.

24 H.W. Fowler, *Modern English Usage*, second edn, rev. Sir Ernest Gowers, (Oxford, 1965), p. 256.

25 T.S. Eliot, 'Leçon de Valéry', *Paul Valéry Vivant*, (Marseilles, 1946), pp. 74–6.

26 *The Lords of Limit*, p. 111.

27 'Literature Comes to Life ...', *The Illustrated London News*, 20 August 1966.

28 S.T. Coleridge, *The Friend*, No. 18, 21 December 1809, in *Collected Works*, (sixteen vols) ed. Coburn, Four II, ed. Rooke, (London, 1969), p. 241.

29 (1969); *The Lords of Limit*, p. 66.

30 In 'The Turtle Dove', 'half-sleep'; in 'The White Ship', 'half-appear'; in 'Of Commerce and Society, IV', 'Half-erased' and 'half-dead'; in VI, 'half-under'; in 'Funeral Music', 'half-unnerved'; in 'The Stone Man', 'Half-recognized'; in 'The Songbook of Sebastian Arrurruz', 'Half-mocking' and 'half-truth'; in *Mercian Hymns* VII, 'half-bricks'.

31 Preceded by the pamphlet, *The Fantasy Poets, Pamphlet No. 11*, (Oxford 1952).

32 Valerie Adams, *An Introduction to Modern English Word-formation*, (London, 1973), p. 100.

33 *Brand*, p. 179.

34 W.S. Milne, '"The Pitch of Attention": Geoffrey Hill's *Tenebrae*', *Agenda* Vol. 17 No. 1, Spring 1979, pp. 27–9.

35 Hill confronts innocence in, for example, 'Holy Thursday', 'Ovid in the Third Reich', and 'Locust Songs'. As to unpunctuation in *Tenebrae*: when first published, 'Te Lucis Ante Terminum' ('Two Chorale-Preludes: 2') had no punctuation – except a hyphen.

36 *The Lords of Limit*, p. 147.

37 Ibid., p. 158.

38 T.S. Eliot, Correspondence in *The Times Literary Supplement*, No. 1391, 27 September 1928, p. 687.

39 Eliot's words on the sleeve of his record of *Four Quartets*.

40 W.S. Milne, op. cit., p. 29.

41 Gone from the French translation of 'The Pentecost Castle': 'runes d'amour pour nous imprononçable'. Likewise 'chapelet d'enfant' and 'inépuisable', (tr. René Gallet, *Obsidiane*, No. 18, mars 1982).

42 Tennyson, in the Eversley edition; cp. Hallam Tennyson, *Alfred Lord Tennyson: A Memoir*, (two vols), (London, 1897), I, p. 50. The 22 lines of an early poem by Tennyson have 11 such unhyphenated compound words and the poem's title is 'Dualisms'.

43 '"It is stated that the train service on the Hsin-min-tun-Kau-pan-tse-Yingkau section of the Imperial Chinese Railway will be restored within a few days. – *Times*." Hsinmintun, Kaupantse, and Yingkau. These places can surely do without their internal hyphens in an English newspaper; and one almost suspects, from the absence of a hyphen between Y*ing* and *kau*, that the *Times*'s stock must have run short', *The King's English*, p. 285.

44 *The Lords of Limit*, p. 2.

45 'The plum-tree' and 'horse-flies' of 'Te Lucis ... 'were first published without their hyphens. Of earlier poems, 'Two Formal Elegies: I' revised 'sand-graves' to 'sand graves'; 'Canticle for Good Friday' revised 'carrion sustenance' to 'carrion-sustenance'.

46 *Modern English Usage*, rev. Gowers, p. 256.

47 *You Have a Point There*, p. 145.

48 'Robert Lowell: Contrasts and Repetitions', *Essays in Criticism* Vol. 13 No. 2, April 1963, p. 190.

49 On 'Hearth-stones', see Martin Dodsworth, 'Geoffrey Hill's New Poetry', *Stand* Vol. 13 No. 1, 1971–2, p. 62.

50 *Brand*, p. 36.

51 *The Notebooks of Samuel Taylor Coleridge*, III, Entry 3970.

52 John Peck, 'Geoffrey Hill's *Tenebrae*', *Agenda* Vol. 17 No. 1, Spring 1979, p. 22.

53 *British Poetry since 1970*, ed. Peter Jones and Michael Schmidt, (Manchester, 1980), pp. 91, 94.

54 See *The Poetry Society Bulletin*, No. 98, Autumn 1978; 'What Devil Has Got Into John Ransom?', *The Lords of Limit*, pp. 121–37; and the sermon preached by Hill at Great St Mary's, Cambridge, 8 May 1983.
55 *Brand*, Act V, p. 175.
56 *The Mystery . . .*, p. 21.
57 Sermon preached by Hill, 8 May 1983.
58 *The Lords of Limit*, p. 17.
59 Ibid., p. 113.
60 Jeffrey Wainwright, '"The Speechless Dead": Geoffrey Hill's *King Log*', *Stand* Vol. 10 No. 1, 1968, p. 49.
61 *Brand*, p. 14.
62 The (Cambridge) New Shakespeare, ed. John Dover Wilson and J.C. Maxwell, (1960), p. 126.
63 *The Lords of Limit*, p. 56.
64 *Coleridge on the Seventeenth Century*, ed. R.F. Brinkley, (London, 1955), p. 643; Hill (1960), *The Lords of Limit*, p. 50.
65 (1972–3); *The Lords of Limit*, p. 88.
66 *You Have a Point There*, pp. 130–1.
67 T.S. Eliot, *Knowledge and Experience in the Philosophy of F.H. Bradley*, (London, 1964), p. 131.
68 F.H. Bradley, *Ethical Studies*, (second edn, Oxford, 1927), pp. 323–4.
69 'A Writer's Craft (5)', *The Isis*, 17 February 1954, p. 14.
70 *The Notebooks of Samuel Taylor Coleridge*, III, Entry 4124.
71 'Isis Idol: Geoffrey Hill', *The Isis*, 18 November 1953, p. 17.

6 *Brand*

1 Michael Meyer, *Ibsen: A Biography*, (London, 1974), p. 266.
2 Hill's 'version for the English stage' was commissioned by the National Theatre and first presented at the Olivier Theatre in London in April 1978. It was published in 1978 by Heinemann Educational Books Ltd in association with the National Theatre. A second, revised edition with introduction by Inga-Stina Ewbank was published in 1981 by the University of Minnesota Press. This edition is not, however, at the time of writing easily available in the UK, so that *all references in this essay are to the first edition by Heinemann, 1978*, unless otherwise indicated.
   The revised Minnesota edition incorporates a number of lines cut from the London production, and accompanying first edition; there are also, independently, some amendments of words and phrases. The most extensive differences between editions are to be found in Act V, and in particular in Brand's monologue on the mountain heights after the crowd has turned back. This contains two substantial passages, of 20 and 14 lines, not to be found in the first edition. Those interested in pursuing the matter will find significant variations between the two editions on the following pages – Heinemann ed. first, Minnesota in brackets: 12 (16), 18 (23), 22 (27), 24 (30), 25 (31), 28 (34), 47–8 (55), 48 (56), 69 (81), 70 (82), 106 (122), 123 (139), 140 (158–9), 153 (173–4).
3 Catherine Ray, introduction to her translation of *Emperor and Galilean* (1876), quoted in *Ibsen: The Critical Heritage*, ed. Michael Egan, (London, 1972), p. 52.
4 *Tenebrae*, (London, 1978), p. 41.
5 *The Oxford Ibsen*, Vol. I, ed. and trans. James Walter McFarlane and Graham Orton, (London, 1970), p. 39.
6 *Viewpoints*, p. 97.
7 *The Lords of Limit*, p. 87.
8 *The Isis*, (16 June 1954), p. 22.

9 *New Poems*, ed. Donald Hall, (Fantasy Press, Winter 1952, Vol. 1, No. 2).
10 *Viewpoints*, p. 97.
11 Inga-Stina Ewbank, '*Brand:* The Play and the Translation', introduction to Henrik Ibsen, *Brand: A Version for the Stage* by Geoffrey Hill, second edition, revised, (Minneapolis, 1981), pp. vii–xxxvi. For a further discussion of the problems of translating Ibsen into English, see Inga-Stina Ewbank's chapter 'Ibsen on the English Stage', in *Ibsen and the Theatre*, ed. Errol Durbach, (London, 1980).
12 *Viewpoints*, p. 84.
13 Ibid., p. 96.
14 Ibid., p. 96.
15 *The Lords of Limit*, p. 102.
16 For an authoritative account both of the formal issues at stake and of the circumstances surrounding Hill's decision, see Inga-Stina Ewbank's introduction to the Minnesota edition.
17 *For the Unfallen*, p. 24.
18 *The Lords of Limit*, p. 96.
19 Ibid., p. 90.
20 *Mercian Hymns*, I.
21 Ibid., X.
22 *For the Unfallen*, p. 21.
23 *Tenebrae*, p. 41.
24 *Viewpoints*, p. 84.
25 *The Times Literary Supplement*, 16 June 1978, p. 660.
26 He is drawing some inferences from Simone Weil's 'law of artistic creation':

> Within the circumference of her 'law', lyric poetry is necessarily dramatic: indeed, the 'different planes' actually available to a director on his theatre-stage could even be regarded as an indication of what takes place 'simultaneously' in the arena of the poem. ('"The Conscious Mind's Intelligible Structure": A Debate', *Agenda* Vol. 9 No. 4–Vol. 10 No. 1, Autumn/Winter 1971–2, p. 15.)

7 *The Mystery of the Charity of Charles Péguy*

1 The words of the epigraph to this essay are Péguy's, quoted by Julian Green in his introduction to the selection of Péguy's work, *Basic Verities: Prose and Poetry*, 'Rendered into English by Ann and Julian Green', (London, 1943), p. 36.
2 *The Mystery of the Charity of Charles Péguy*, p. 28.
3 J.L. Austin, *How To Do Things With Words*, ed. J.O. Urmson, (Oxford, 1965), hereafter *Words*.
4 *The Lords of Limit*, pp. 138–59.
5 Austin, *Words*, pp. 6–7.
6 Austin, *Words*, p. 10.
7 See 'Charles Péguy', in *The Mystery of the Charity of Charles Péguy*, p. 30: 'a young madman, who may or may not have been over-susceptible to metaphor, almost immediately shot Jaurès through the head.'
8 Quoted in Marjorie Villiers, *Charles Péguy: A Study in Integrity*, (London, 1965), p. 290.
9 '9. The Laurel Axe', *Tenebrae*, p. 30.
10 Henri Bergson, *Creative Evolution*, trans. Arthur Mitchell, 1911; (New York 1944; Westport, Ct., 1975), pp. 7, 23.
11 See John Terraine, *The Great War 1914–18*, (London, 1965): 'At all levels French soldiers were taught the virtues of headlong attack' (p. 20). Terraine remarks on the 'lavish spending' of French officers' lives in the early days of the war (p. 48). Also John Ellis, *Eye Deep In Hell: Trench Warfare in World War I*, (London and New York, 1976), writes of 'a kind of military "spiritualism", a continual stress upon human capabilities at the expense of the potential of material forces'. He quotes Joffre in 1912: 'The French Army, returning to its

traditions, no longer knows any other law than that of the offensive...' (pp. 82–4).

12 Charles Péguy, *Œuvres Poétiques Complètes*, (Paris, 1967); the passage is also in *The Penguin Book of French Verse, 4: The Twentieth Century*, intro. and ed. Anthony Hartley, (Harmondsworth, 1966), p. 90.
13 *Harrap's Shorter French and English Dictionary*, ed. J.E. Mansion.
14 See *The Lords of Limit*, p. 159; Hill quotes Pound: 'And when one has the mot juste, one is finished with the subject.'
15 *The Lords of Limit*, p. 139.
16 Ibid., p. 139.
17 Ibid., p. 142.
18 Ibid., p. 151.
19 Ibid., p. 143.
20 Roland Barthes, *Elements of Semiology*, 1964, trans. Annette Lavers and Colin Smith, (Boston, 1967), pp. 88, 86.
21 *Twelfth Night*, III. i. 18–25.
22 Austin, *Words*, p. 9.
23 Ibid., p. 22.
24 *The Lords of Limit*, p. 143.
25 Jonathan Culler, *Structuralist Poetics*, (London, 1975), p. 130.
26 *The Lords of Limit*, p. 151; Hill is quoting Ransom from *The New Criticism*.
27 Ibid., p. 151.
28 Paul Ricœur, *The Rule of Metaphor*, trans. Robert Czerny et al, (London 1978), p. 115.
29 *Tenebrae*, pp. 15–21.
30 Daniel Halévy, *Péguy et Les Cahiers de la Quinzaine*, p. 188 (my translation).
31 Henri Bergson, *Time and Free Will*, trans. F.L. Pogson, (London, 1910; New York, 1912), p. 209.
32 *The Lords of Limit*, p. 150; Hill is quoting Kenneth Burke from *A Grammar of Motives*.
33 Ibid., p. 143.

8 War and the pity

1 William Blake, *Complete Writings*, ed. Keynes, (London, 1969), p. 172.
2 Merle E. Brown, *Double Lyric*, (London, 1980), pp. 20–72.
3 Charles Tomlinson, 'Poetry Today', *The Modern Age: The Pelican Guide to English Literature*, vol. 7, ed. Ford, (third edn, Harmondsworth, 1973), pp. 33–51.
4 See Jon Silkin, *Out of Battle*, (London, 1972), pp. 208–9, 233–4 and 246–7.
5 C.H. Sisson, 'Geoffrey Hill', *Agenda* Vol. 13 No. 3, Autumn 1975, p. 26.
6 Isaac Rosenberg, *The Collected Works*, ed. Parsons, (London, 1979), p. 239.
7 *Viewpoints*, p. 94.
8 See *The Lords of Limit*, pp. 84–103, and in particular pp. 89–90.
9 Isaac Rosenberg, *The Collected Works*, p. 151.
10 'Under Judgement', interview with Blake Morrison, *The New Statesman* Vol. 99 No. 2551, 8 Feb 1980, p. 212.
11 Part of the following discussion of 'September Song' is excerpted from my essay 'The Poetry of Geoffrey Hill', in *British Poetry since 1960*, ed. Schmidt and Lindop, (Manchester, 1972), pp. 143–164. It is now out of print, and I am grateful for the kind permission to reprint.
12 Shelley, *Poetical Works*, edn. Hutchinson (new edn, corrected by Matthews), (London, 1970), p. 514.
13 Simone Weil, 'Hitler and the Internal Régime of the Roman Empire'; see Simone Pétrement, *Simone Weil*, (Oxford, 1977), p. 358.
14 In *Preghiere*, (Leeds, 1964), p. 10.
15 S.T. Coleridge, *Biographia Literaria*, ed. Watson, (second edn, London, 1965), p. 167.
16 Allen Tate, *Poems 1920-1945*, (London, 1947), p. 22.

17. Wilfred Owen, *The Collected Poems*, ed. Day Lewis, (London, 1963), p. 49.
18 See also Christopher Ricks, 'Geoffrey Hill and "The Tongue's Atrocities"', (Swansea, 1978), p. 18.
19 T.S. Eliot, *Collected Poems 1909-1962*, (London, 1963), p. 40.
20 *3 Henry VI*, II. v. 122.
21 *Everyman and Mediaeval Miracle Plays*, ed. Cowley, (London, 1958), p. 232.
22. William Blake, *Complete Writings*, p. 164.
23 Osip Mandel'shtam, *Selected Poems*, trans. David McDuff, (Cambridge, 1973), p. xvi.
24 A.E. Housman, *A Shropshire Lad*, (Harmondsworth, 1961), p. 78.
25 *The Mystery of the Charity of Charles Péguy* requires separate although not different consideration. My essay was composed before the publication of Geoffrey Hill's poem concerning Jaurès and Péguy.

9 'How fit a title ...'

1 *The Poems and Letters of Andrew Marvell*, (two vols) ed. H.M. Margoliouth, (third edn, Oxford, 1971), I, p. 102.
2 Charles Rosen, *The Classical Style*, (London, 1971), p. 460.
3 Wallace Stevens, *Opus Posthumous*, (London, 1959), p. 167.
4 *King Log*, p. 25.
5 *King Log*, p. 53.
6 *Tenebrae*, p. 29.
7 In his interview with John Haffenden, Hill speaks of 're-reading the *Henry VI* plays at exactly the right time; discovering the power of a certain kind of rhetoric which I'd been educated to think of as inferior to Shakespeare's later work'. In *Viewpoints*, p. 81.
8 *King Log*, p. 41.
9 *King Log*, p. 42.
10 My argument here is indebted to Christopher Ricks's fine lecture 'Geoffrey Hill and "The Tongue's Atrocities"' (Swansea, 1978) in which he speaks of 'the taxing achievement of a decent detachment, a freedom from unjust appropriation of suffering and horror and war' (p. 28).
11 *For the Unfallen*, p. 26.
12 Hill's essay on Ben Jonson speaks sceptically 'of "timeless moments" in any art', *The Lords of Limit*, p. 54.
13 For example in the 'essay' in *King Log*, p. 68.
14 *Somewhere Is Such A Kingdom: Poems 1952-1971*, with an Introduction by Harold Bloom, (Boston, 1975).
15 Thomas Hobbes, *Leviathan*, ed. C.B. Macpherson, (London, 1970), p. 96.
16 Ibid.
17 *Tenebrae*, p. 32.
18 *Viewpoints*, p. 88.
19 There are other, less clearly significant cases of shared title in *For the Unfallen*, some of which may be accidental. 'Wreaths' could refer to the 'Wreath' poems of Herbert and Vaughan; 'Merlin' to Edwin Muir's poem of that name; 'The Turtle-Dove' to the folk-song in W.H. Auden's *Oxford Book of Light Verse*, (Oxford, 1938 and 1973), p. 375; 'The White Ship' to the poem by Dante Gabriel Rossetti – while 'The Emperor's Clothes' must allude to Hans Christian Andersen's story.
20 Robert Desnos, *Domaine Public*, (1953); Osip Mandelstam, *Tristia*, (1922).
21 Clarence Brown, *Mandelstam*, (Cambridge, 1973), p. 219.
22 Charles Causley, 'The Stone Man', *The Listener*, 2 January 1964, pp. 15-6.
23 'Notes' to *King Log*, p. 70.
24 *Sweet's Anglo-Saxon Reader* (twelfth edn, Oxford, 1950), Section XXXII, pp. 170-80.
25 Hill discusses his diagnostic relationship to nostalgia in the sequence in *Viewpoints*, p. 93.

26 There are numerous histories of British India, though I have seen none with this precise title. There is a 'Hereford Carol' in *The Oxford Book of Carols*, ed. Dearmer, Vaughan Williams, Shaw, (1928; reset edn, London, 1964), p. 20.

27 *The Mystery of the Charity of Charles Péguy*, p. 28.

28 In *Viewpoints*, p. 91.

29 *Tenebrae*, p. 19.

30 Perhaps this is best shown by a scatter of quotations from each book. From *King Log*: 'For none but the ritual king?' (p. 26); 'a stranger well-received in your kingdom' (p. 30); 'Seigneur' (p. 37); 'Suffragans of the true seraphs' (p. 39). From *Mercian Hymns*: 'King of the perennial holly-groves' (I); 'a king in his new-risen hat' (III); 'The princes of Mercia were badger and raven' (VI); 'O my masters' (XXVIII). From *Tenebrae*: 'weep for your lord' (p. 7); 'Crucified Lord' and 'your lords of revenue' (p. 15); 'conquistador of fashion' (p. 16); 'king of our earth' (p. 18); 'lords of unquiet or of quiet sojourn' (p. 22); 'Reverend Mother' (p. 31); 'So to celebrate that kingdom' (p. 34); 'Look at us, Queen of Heaven' (p. 35); 'abstinence crowns all our care' (p. 39); 'Lord of Misrule./He is the Master of the Leaping Figures' (p. 44). From *The Mystery of the Charity of Charles Péguy*: 'In Brutus' name martyr and mountebank/ghost Caesar's ghost' (p. 9); 'footslogger of genius, skirmisher with grace/and ill-luck, sentinel of the sacrifice' (p. 10); 'the sun-tanned earth is your centurion' (p. 11); 'Dear lords of life, stump-toothed with ragged breath' (p. 23); 'Good governors and captains' (p. 25).

31 Christopher Ricks has written perceptively on this: '"overlord" is a word both abjectly modern (not a style, but a style of government) and proudly ancient', in 'Overlord of the M5', *The Listener*, 26 August 1971), p. 274.

32 Christopher Brooke, *The Saxon and Norman Kings*, (London, 1967), p. 100.

33 *Viewpoints*, p. 88.

34 Hill pays affectionate tribute to the essay from which this is quoted in *The Lords of Limit*, pp. 88-90. My quotation comes from George Eliot, *Theophrastus Such*, (second edn, Edinburgh, 1879), 'Looking Backward', pp. 48-9.

35. *Viewpoints*, p. 94.

36 *Somewhere Is Such A Kingdom*, 'Introduction: The Survival of Strong Poetry', p. xxii.

37 *Complete Works of William Hazlitt*, (twenty-one vols) ed. P.P. Howe, (London, 1930-4), IV, pp. 214-6.

38 Ibid.

39 *The Works of John Milton*, (eighteen vols and supplement) ed. Patterson, Abbott, Ayres, (New York, 1931-8), VII and VIII. In the *Second Defence of the People of England* Milton argues that Cromwell is above any title but 'father of the country':

> Other titles, though merited by you, your actions know not, endure not; and these proud ones, deemed great in vulgar opinion, they deservedly cast from them. For what is a title, but a certain definite mode of dignity?

(translated by George Burnett), VIII, p. 223.

40 Walter Jackson Bate, *The Burden of the Past and The English Poet*, (London, 1971).

41 *King Log* pp. 13, 21, 24.

42 Ibid. pp. 35-8.

43 See, for example, *The Sonnets of Michelangelo Buonarotti and Tommaso Campanella*. Now for the first time translated into rhymed English by John Addington Symonds, (London, 1878). In Sonnet XV Symonds give Campanella the Hill-like line: 'Martyrdom is the stamp of royalty'. Nadezhda Mandelstam, *Hope Against Hope*, trans. Max Hayward, (Harmondsworth, 1975).

44 See Hill's own comments on this poem in *The Penguin Book of Contemporary Verse*, ed. Kenneth Allott (second edn, Harmondsworth, 1962), p. 392: 'The "germ", I think, is the key phrase in line 11. "Our God scatters corruption" = "Our God puts corruption to flight" or "Our God disseminates corruption". I may have been thinking of Mr Dulles' idea of God as Head of Strategic Air Command'.

45 Quoted in Walter Kauffman, *Nietzsche*, (New York, 1956), p. 158.

46 Hill confers comparable paradoxical victory upon other writers elsewhere. He describes *The Mystery of the Charity of Charles Péguy* as his 'homage to the triumph of his "defeat"' (p. 31), and entitles his essay on T.H. Green '"Perplexed Persistence": The Exemplary Failure of T.H. Green', *The Lords of Limit*, pp. 104–20. Some of the epithets he uses of Péguy convey a similar status, like 'raw veteran' and 'footslogger of genius' (p. 10).

47 The title of his inaugural lecture, see *The Lords of Limit*, pp. 1–18. The first paragraph of the lecture is itself a classic instance of Hill's elaborate sense of, and play with, title in both the senses I have been considering. In it he gives a tortuously self-referential account of the title he has conferred upon his lecture in relation to the titles that he himself bears of 'poet' and 'professor' (the lecture itself being the occasion at which the conferral of the latter title is effectively established).

48 *The Mystery* . . . p. 16.

49 In *The Necessary Angel*, (London, 1961), Wallace Stevens argues that

> There is no element more conspicuously lacking from contemporary poetry than nobility. There is no element that poets have sought after, more curiously and more piously, certain of its obscure existence ... The nobility of rhetoric is, of course, a lifeless nobility. Pareto's epigram that history is a cemetery of aristocracies easily becomes another: that poetry is a cemetery of nobilities. For the sensitive poet, conscious of negations, nothing is more difficult than the affirmations of nobility and yet there is nothing that he requires of himself more persistently, since in them and in their kind, alone, are to be found those sanctions that are the reasons for his being and for that occasional ecstasy, or ecstatic freedom of the mind, which is his special privilege (p. 35).

50 T.S. Eliot, *Selected Essays*, (third edn, London, 1951), p. 293.

51 '"The Conscious Mind's Intelligible Structure": A Debate', *Agenda* Vol. 9 No. 4–Vol. 10 No. 1, Autumn/Winter 1971–2, p. 21.

10 Hill and the dictionary

1 *The Letters of Emily Dickinson*, ed. T.H. Johnson (Cambridge, Mass., 1958), III, p. 858; II, p. 404.

2 Ibid., II, p. 791.

3 Michael Hamburger in *The Truth of Poetry*, (London, 1982), discusses the consequences for poetry of 'the terrible disparity between civilian and military experience' in the First World War (Chapter 7), and the new 'anti-poetry' arising from the Second World War (Chapter 9). See particularly his comments on the Polish poet Tadeusz Różewicz, who in writing 'for the horror-stricken', the 'survivors', claimed: 'We learnt language from scratch, those people and I'. Also relevant is George Orwell's essay of 1946, 'Politics and the English Language'.

4 Samuel Johnson, *Lives of the English Poets*, ed. G.B. Hill, (Oxford, 1905), III, p. 435.

5 Alexander Pope, *An Essay on Man: Epistle I*, 1.200.

6 David Jones, *In Parenthesis*, (London, 1937), pp. x and xi.

7 Dorothy Whitelock, *The Beginnings of English Society*, (Harmondsworth, 1952), p. 198.

8 R.W. Southern, *Western Society and the Church in the Middle Ages*, (London, 1970), p. 28.

9 William Wordsworth, 'Preface to *Lyrical Ballads*' (1802), in *The Poems*, (2 vols) ed. J.O. Hayden, (Harmondsworth, 1977), I, pp. 869, 875.

11 Hill's imitations

1 Francisco de Quevedo y Villegas, 'Retrato de Lisi que traía en una sortija', in *Agenda* (Geoffrey Hill special issue) Vol. 17 No. 1, Spring 1979, p. 59.
2 Lope de Vega Carpio, '¿Qué tengo yo que mi amistad procuras?', in ibid., p. 60 and J.M. Cohen, *The Penguin Book of Spanish Verse*, (Harmondsworth, 1956), p. 247. Geoffrey Hill acknowledges Cohen as a source for his imitations from the Spanish in the notes to *Tenebrae*.
3 T.S. Eliot, *Collected Poems 1909-1962*, (London, 1963), p. 214.
4 Francisco de Quevedo y Villegas, 'Afectos varios de su corazón, fluctuando en las ondas de los cabellos de Lisi', in Cohen, p. 264.
5 'The Masque of Blacknesse', in *Ben Jonson*, ed. Hertford, P. and E. Simpson, Vol. VII, (Oxford, 1941), p. 177.
6 Lupercio Leonardo de Argensola, 'Llevó tras sí los pámpanos otubre . . .', in Cohen, p. 202.
7 *A Midsummer-Night's Dream*, II. i. 99-100.
8 *Viewpoints*, pp. 89, 93.
9 *The Lords of Limit*, p. 105.
10 *Viewpoints*, p. 88.
11 See 'Robert Lowell: Contrasts and Repetitions', *Essays in Criticism* Vol. 13 No. 2, April 1963, pp. 188-97.
12 *Viewpoints*, p. 93.
13 Christopher Ricks, 'Cliché as "Responsible Speech": Geoffrey Hill', *London Magazine* Vol. 4 No. 8, November 1964, p. 98.
14 William Cookson, 'A Few Notes on Geoffrey Hill', *Agenda* Vol. 9 Nos. 2-3, Spring-Summer 1971, p. 146.
15 *Viewpoints*, p. 95.
16 Osip Mandelstam, *Journey to Armenia*, revised translation by Clarence Brown, (London, 1980), p. 32.

12 Hill's criticism

1 'Literature Comes to Life . . .', *Illustrated London News*, 20 August 1966.
2 John Milton, *Paradise Lost*, VIII, 11.250-1. I quote from *The Poems of John Milton*, ed. J. Carey and A. Fowler, (London, 1968).
3 Sigmund Freud, *New Introductory Lectures on Psychoanalysis* (1933), trans. James Strachey, (London, 1964), Lecture 35.
4 'Funeral Music, 4', in *King Log*, p. 28.
5 Ludwig Wittgenstein, *On Certainty*, trans. Denis Paul and G.E.M. Anscombe, (Oxford, 1969), p. 62e.
6 T. S. Eliot, *The Use of Poetry and the Use of Criticism*, (London, 1933; new edn, 1964), pp. 15, 23, 29, 127.
7 Ibid., pp. 27, 127.
8 *The Lords of Limit*, p. 133.
9 Raymond Williams, 'Base and Superstructure in Marxist Cultural Theory', *New Left Review* 82, November 1975, p. 5.
10 Ibid., p. 6.
11 Similar difficulties arise, for example, in Althusser's writing on ideology in *Lenin and Philosophy*, trans. B. Brewster, (London, 1971).
12 Williams, op.cit., p. 4.
13 Ludwig Wittgenstein, *Philosophical Investigations*, trans. G.E.M. Anscombe, (Oxford, 1953; third edn, 1967) p. 277e.
14 *The Lords of Limit*, p. 86.
15 Ibid., p. 105.

16 Ibid., p. 23.

17 Ibid., p. 2.

18 Samuel Johnson, *Rasselas*, (1759), Chapter 10, in *Johnson: Poetry and Prose*, ed. Mona Wilson, (1950, second edition 1957) p. 411.

19 P.B. Shelley, 'A Defence of Poetry', (1821), reprinted in *English Critical Essays: Nineteeth Century*, ed. E.D. Jones, (1916, re-issued London, 1971), p. 138.

20 *The Lords of Limit*, p. 159.

21 Ibid., p. 85.

22 Ibid., p. 127.

23 Ibid., p. 136.

24 Ibid., p. 147.

25 Ibid., p. 26.

26 Robert Southwell, *Epistle of Comfort*, quoted ibid., p. 28.

27 R.C. Trench, *On the Study of Words*, (London, 1851; fifth edn, 1853), p. 1.

28 William Empson, 'This Last Pain', in *Collected Poems*, (London, 1955), p. 33.

29 D.W. Harding, 'The Hinterland of Thought', in *Experience into Words*, (London, 1963; reprinted Harmondsworth, 1974), p. 176.

30 Ibid., p. 178.

31 Ibid., p. 176.

32 Ibid., p. 186.

33 *The Lords of Limit*, p. 146.

34 Ibid., p. 107.

35 Harding, op. cit., p. 191.

36 *The Lords of Limit*, p. 109.

37 Ibid., p. 130.

38 Ibid., p. 58.

39 Ibid., p. 104.

40 Ibid., pp. 84-5.

41 Frank Kermode, *The Romantic Image*, (London, 1957; reprinted 1971), Chapter 8.

42 T.S. Eliot, 'Milton II', (1947), in *On Poetry and Poets*, (London, 1957), p. 153.

43 *The Lords of Limit*, p. 149.

44 *The Correspondence of Gerard Manley Hopkins and Richard Watson Dixon*, ed. C.C. Abbott (London, 1935), pp. 147-8. Owen Chadwick defends concepts such as 'secularisation' and 'the Renaissance' with a related argument: 'By the nature of historical science, vagueness, blurred edges, recognition of the unchartable mystery in human motives and attitudes and decisions, are no necessary obstacle to an authentic through broad judgment in history. At least they offer scope for that humility of heart and openness of mind which are proverbially said to be indispensable to historical understanding.' *The Secularization of the European Mind in the Nineteenth Century* (Cambridge, 1975), p. 3.

45 William Wordsworth, 'There was a Boy'; *The Excursion*, III, 1.716ff.; ibid., IV, 1.1156ff. All quotations are from *The Poems*, (two vols) ed. J.O. Hayden, (Harmondsworth, 1977).

46 Geoffrey Hill, interviewed by the present writer for a talk, 'The Composed Voice', broadcast BBC Radio 3, 14 July 1981.

47 William Wordsworth, *The Prelude* (1805 text), IV, 1.247ff.; I quote from the edition of J. Wordsworth. M.H. Abrams, and S. Gill, (London, 1979).

48 F.R. Leavis, 'Literary Criticism and Philosophy', in *The Common Pursuit*, (London, 1952; reprinted 1966), p. 213.

49 Ibid., p. 214.

50 Broadcast talk, 'The Living Poet', BBC Radio 3, 6 August 1979.

51 *The Lords of Limit*, p. 68.

52 '"The Conscious Mind's Intelligible Structure": A Debate', *Agenda* Vol. 9 No. 4-Vol. 10 No. 1, Autumn/Winter 1971-2, p. 16.

53 *The Lords of Limit*, p. 82.

54 In the last sentence of 'Redeeming the Time', ibid., p. 103.
55 Ibid., p. 16.
56 Friedrich Nietzsche, *The Use and Abuse of History* (1874), trans. Adrian Collins, (Indianapolis, 1949), p. 7.
57 John Milton, *Paradise Lost*, VII, 1.635ff.

13 Somewhere is such a kingdom

1 George Herbert, *The Works*, ed. Hutchinson, (Oxford, 1941), p. 184.
2 See John Bayley, *The Uses of Division*, (London, 1976), pp. 171-82.
3 Philip Larkin, *The Less Deceived*, (Hessle, 1955), p. 13.
4 F.E. Hardy, *The Life of Thomas Hardy*, (new edn in one vol., London, 1962), p. 128.
5 T.S. Eliot, *Selected Essays*, (third edn, London, 1951), p. 17.
6 Geoffrey Grigson is attributed with relating the anecdote in Jeffrey Meyers, *The Enemy*, (London and Henley, 1980), p. 237.
7 T.S. Eliot, *Collected Poems 1909-1962*, (London, 1963), p. 104.
8 Thomas Hardy, *The Complete Poems*, ed. Gibson, (London, 1976), p. 349.
9 Philip Larkin, *The Whitsun Weddings*, (London, 1964), p. 38.
10 W.B. Yeats, *The Collected Poems*, (London, 1950), p. 225.
11 William Wordsworth, *The Poems*, (two vols) ed. J.O. Hayden, (Harmondsworth, 1977), I, p. 552.
12 Samuel Johnson, *The Lives of the English Poets*, (two vols), (reset edn, London, 1952), II, p. 485.
13 W.H. Auden, *The English Auden*, ed. Mendelson, (London, 1977), p. 246.
14 David Holbrook, *Selected Poems 1961-1978*, (London, 1980), pp. 19-20.
15 W.H. Auden, op. cit., p. 237.
16 *Tenebrae*, p. 26.
17 For a discussion of this poem, see John Bayley, *Pushkin*, (Cambridge, 1971), pp. 144-50.
18 For this and the two citations which follow: *Tenebrae*, pp. 19, 25, and 31.
19 Ibid., p. 27.
20 For this and the six citations which follow: *Tenebrae*, p. 40; *King Log*, p. 31; *Tenebrae*, pp. 19 (twice), and 37 (twice).
21 Sidney Keyes, *The Collected Poems*, ed. Mayer, (London, 1945), pp. 86 and 72-3.
22 *Macbeth*, II. iii. 110.
23 W.B. Yeats, *The Collected Poems*, pp. 276 and 328.
24 W.B. Yeats, *The Collected Poems*, p. 313.
25 *Tenebrae*, p. 19.
26 See '"The Conscious Mind's Intelligible Structure": A Debate', *Agenda* Vol. 9 No. 4-Vol. 10 No. 1, Autumn/Winter 1971-2, pp. 14-32.

14 Reading Geoffrey Hill

1 'Tristia: 1891-1938, A Valediction to Osip Mandelshtam', *King Log*, p. 38.
2 T.S. Eliot, 'The Metaphysical Poets', *Selected Essays*, (third edn, London, 1951), p. 289. Hill alludes to Allen Tate on Eliot's difficulty in *The Lords of Limit*, p. 131.
3 T.S. Eliot, *The Use of Poetry and the Use of Criticism*, (London, 1933), p. 151.
4 Osip Mandelstam, *Selected Essays*, trans. Monas, (Austin and London, 1977), pp. 59, 61, 62-3, and 61.
5 The dedication of poems to living people, where the dedicatee is not addressed in the poem,

should not be confused with the poetry of living interlocutors. Geoffrey Hill often dedicates his poems to relatives, friends, and colleagues; occasionally dedications included in magazine publications are later dropped, and vice versa.

6 Donald Davie, *Purity of Diction in English Verse*, (London, 1952), pp. 138 and 159 where Davie is quoting a phrase of Mary Shelley's.

7 *The Lords of Limit*, p. 68.

8 Geoffrey Hill, in *The Penguin Book of Contemporary Poetry*, ed. K. Allott, (second edn, Harmondsworth, 1962), pp. 390-3 for this and the two citations which follow.

9 T.S. Eliot, 'The Music of Poetry', *On Poetry and Poets*, (London, 1957), pp. 32-3.

10 Nadezhda Mandelstam, *Hope against Hope*, trans. Max Hayward, (London, 1971), p. 3.

11 Donald Davie, *The Poet in the Imaginary Museum*, (Manchester, 1977), p. 268. See also Davie, *Collected Poems 1971-1983*, (Manchester, 1983), pp. 140-1: here Davie considers Mandelstam's 'hardness', taking a cue from Mandelstam's 'About the Nature of the Word' where he writes 'man should be the firmest thing on earth'. Henry Gifford has informed me that the Russian word translated as 'firm' has the sense of 'hard' and 'steadfast', 'resolute'.

12 Osip Mandelstam, *Selected Poems*, trans. Brown and Merwin, (London, 1973), pp. 69-70.

13. Hill's title associates the well-known English love-poem of parting with Mandelstam's own poem of departure, which begins in the Brown and Merwin translation 'I have studied the science of good-byes' (*Selected Poems*, pp. 23-4).

14 *The Poems of John Keats*, ed. M. Allott, (London, 1970), p. 80.

15 *Ben Jonson*, ed. Herford, P. and E. Simpson, Vol. VIII, (Oxford, 1941), p. 65.

16 Broadcast talk, 'The Living Poet', BBC Radio 3, 6 August 1979.

17 In the first two printings of the poem (1953, 1954), the punctuation at the end of the penultimate line is a full stop. This became a comma in the first edition of *For the Unfallen* (p. 23), and reverted to a full stop in *King Log* (p. 69). In the third impression of *For the Unfallen*, the revised version with the dates '[1953-1967]' is printed, but the three commas from the first stanza which had been removed in the *King Log* text have returned, or remained.

18 Sir Arthur Conan Doyle, *A Study in Scarlet*, in *The Complete Sherlock Holmes Long Stories*, (London, 1929), pp. 29-30.

19 *The Lords of Limit*, p. 8.

20 'The Poetry of Allen Tate', *Geste* (Leeds) Vol. 3 No. 3, November 1958, p. 9.

21 'Charles Péguy', in *The Mystery of the Charity of Charles Péguy*, p. 30.

22 *The Lords of Limit*, p. 7; Hill's phrasing and his qualm here may derive from T.S. Eliot's 'About Donne there hangs the shadow of the impure motive; and impure motives lend their aid to a facile success', in 'For Lancelot Andrewes', *Selected Essays*, p. 345; and perhaps, 'the purification of the motive/In the ground of our beseeching', 'Little Gidding', *Collected Poems 1909-1962*, (London, 1963), p. 220.

23 John Purkis, in *Donald Davie, Charles Tomlinson, Geoffrey Hill*, A306 Twentieth Century Poetry, The Open University (Milton Keynes, 1976); Unit 31, p. 55.

24 *The Lords of Limit*, pp. 7-8.

26 Broadcast talk, 'The Living Poet', BBC Radio 3, 6 August 1979.

26 *Viewpoints*, p. 95.

27 'Dejection: An Ode', *The Complete Poetical Works of Samuel Taylor Coleridge*, (two vols) ed. E.H. Coleridge, (Oxford, 1912), I, p. 364; see also 'Blank misgivings of a Creature/ Moving about in worlds not realized', William Wordsworth, 'Ode: Intimations of Immortality . . .', *The Poems*, (two vols) ed. J.O. Hayden, (Harmondsworth, 1977), I, p. 528.

28 *The Poems of Tennyson*, ed. C. Ricks, (London, 1969), p. 871.

29 William Empson, *Collected Poems*, (London, 1955), p. 81; see also, 'An Order of Service', *King Log*, p. 20, and Hill's discussion of this and related words in *The Lords of Limit*, p. 151.

30 Jeffrey Wainwright, 'Geoffrey Hill's "Lachrimae" ', *Agenda* Vol. 13 No. 3, Autumn 1975, pp. 37-8.

31 *Viewpoints*, p. 88.
32 Victor Erlich, *Russian Formalism*, (The Hague, 1955), p. 180.
33 *The Lords of Limit*, p. 7.
34 Wallace Stevens, 'Adagia', in *Opus Posthumous*, (London, 1959), p. 165.
35 Clarence Brown, *Mandelstam*, (Cambridge, 1973), p. 104.
36 Osip Mandelstam, *Selected Essays*, trans. Monas, (Austin and London, 1977), p. 80.
37 *Viewpoints*, p. 86.
38 John Donne, *Poetical Works*, ed. Sir H. Grierson, (London, 1933), p. 337.
39 James Joyce played with the notion: 'The fall ... of a once wallstrait oldparr is retaled early in bed and later on life down through all christian minstrelsy.' *Finnegans Wake*, (London, 1939), p. 3.
40 Jon Glover, 'The Poet in Plato's Cave: A Theme in the Work of Geoffrey Hill', *Poetry Review* Vol. 69 No. 3, March 1980, p. 63.
41 *Viewpoints*, p. 99.
42 'Robert Lowell: Contrasts and Repetitions', *Essays in Criticism* Vol. 13 No. 2, April 1963, p. 193.
43 Jeremy Taylor, cited in *The Lords of Limit*, p. 16.
44 T.S. Eliot, *Collected Poems 1909-1962*, (London, 1963), p. 36; what I have in mind here is the way that Eliot, by rhyming 'pose' and 'repose', gives to the latter a flickering sense of 'pose again' as well as its accepted meaning; the device is similarly employed in 'Prufrock': 'a hundred visions and revisions' (p. 14).
45 T.S. Eliot, *Selected Essays*, p. 327; I may be exaggerating Pound's influence, but this statement does not accord with the view of poetic language in 'The Music of Poetry' cited above, (note 9) written more than twenty years later. For Pound's pronouncements on poetic language at the time of Eliot's essay on Swinburne, see 'A Retrospect', *Literary Essays*, ed. T.S. Eliot, (London, 1954), pp. 4-5.
46 Ezra Pound, *ABC of Reading*, (London, 1951), p. 21 and 22.
47 St.-John Perse, cited in Donald Davie, *Articulate Energy*, (London, 1955), p. 97. Hill alludes to Davie's discussion, and in particular op. cit. p. 121, in *The Lords of Limit*, p. 140.
48 *Romeo and Juliet*, II, ii.184.
49 Charles Péguy, *Basic Verities*, 'Rendered into English by Anne and Julian Green', (London, 1943), p. 107.
50 William Wordsworth, 'Preface to *Lyrical Ballads*' in *The Poems*, (two vols) ed. J.O. Hayden, (Harmondsworth, 1977), I, p. 885.
51 'Charles Péguy', in *The Mystery ...*, p. 31.
52 *British Poetry since 1945*, ed. E. Lucie-Smith, (Harmondsworth, 1970), p. 240.
53 Christopher Ricks, 'Cliché as "Responsible Speech": Geoffrey Hill', *London Magazine* Vol. 4 No. 8, November 1964, p. 101.
54 'The Poetry of Allen Tate', op. cit. p. 10.
55 *The Poems of John Keats*, p. 532.
56 See Geoffrey Hill's discussion of this way of reading a poem in *The Lords of Limit*, pp. 143-4.
57 '"The Conscious Mind's Intelligible Structure": A Debate', *Agenda* Vol. 9 No. 4-Vol. 10 No. 1, Autumn/Winter 1971-2, p. 21.
58 I am indebted to the discussion of this hymn in Christopher Ricks, 'Geoffrey Hill and "The Tongue's Atrocities"', (Swansea, 1978), p. 4.
59 Seamus Heaney, *Preoccupations*, (London, 1980), p. 160.
60 Donald Davie, *Pound*, (London, 1975), pp. 59 and 61; the lines Davie comments on are in Ezra Pound, *Collected Shorter Poems*, (London, 1952), p. 240.
61 *The Lords of Limit*, p. 156.
62 *Viewpoints*, p. 93.
63 Speech by The Rt Hon. J. Enoch Powell, MP, printed in T.E. Utley, *Enoch Powell*, (London, 1968), p. 190.
64 'Politicians and Other Artists: An Interview with Enoch Powell', John Goodbody and Robert Silver, in *Trinity Review*, Summer 1977, p. 12.
65 *Enoch Powell*, p. 179.

66 Ibid., p. 18. See also, *Enoch Powell on Immigration*, Smithies and Fiddick, (London, 1969), pp. 59–60 and 133–4.
67 Hill reflects on this consideration in *The Lords of Limit*, p. 131.
68 Eric Griffiths, 'Standing in the Shadows', in *Perfect Bound* 6 (Cambridge), Autumn 1978, p. 79; I am indebted to Eric Griffiths for drawing my attention some years ago to possible relations between *Mercian Hymns* XVIII and Enoch Powell's so-called 'Rivers of Blood' speech.
69 '10. Fidelities', in 'An Apology for the Revival of Christian Architecture in England', *Tenebrae*, p. 31. Hill's 'borne aloof' recalls 'a wailful choir of small gnats' which is 'borne aloft/ Or sinking as the light wind lives or dies', in Keats's 'To Autumn', *The Poems of John Keats*, p. 654.
70 See ' "The Conscious Mind's Intelligible Structure": A Debate', p. 75; and *The Lords of Limit*, p. 90.
71 *The Lords of Limit*, p. 90
72 *The Sunday Times*, 16 October 1983, p. 16.
73 *The Lords of Limit*, p. 109.
74 Ibid., p. 5.
75 Ibid., p. 82.
76 'Postscript King Stork', in *King Log*, p. 67.
77 *Viewpoints*, p. 77. Hill discusses literary friendship in 'Letter from Oxford', *London Magazine* Vol. 1 No. 4, May 1954, pp. 72–3.
78 '8. Vocations', in 'An Apology ...', *Tenebrae*, p. 29. For some of the implications of the word 'friend' here, see Cardinal Newman's sermon 'The Parting of Friends', his last preached as an Anglican, in *Sermons and Discourses* (1837–57), ed. C.F. Harrold, (London, 1949), pp. 122–33.
79 This is how the line 'as seeker so forsaken' ('The Pentecost Castle, 8', *Tenebrae*, p. 11) appeared in the second of 'Three Mystical Songs', *Agenda* Vol. 11 No. 4–Vol. 12 No. 1, Autumn/Winter, 1973–4, p. 54.
80 'Charles Péguy', in *The Mystery...*, p. 30; see also Section 4 of the poem itself, pp. 14–5.

Bibliography of works by and about Geoffrey Hill

Philip Horne

This bibliography is divided into three sections. The primary list, of Geoffrey Hill's works, gives details for each individual work of every separate appearance known to me until its first collection in a book by Geoffrey Hill. It gives only the first broadcast of radio and television programmes. Geoffrey Hill has helped greatly by looking over the results and giving many suggestions, without which the listing would be considerably less accurate and less representative. It unfortunately remains the case, however, that a number of items have baffled pursuit and escaped inclusion: I have been unable to trace any of the poems printed before Geoffrey Hill's arrival in Oxford, or the interview he gave soon after the publication of *For the Unfallen*, to a Leeds university magazine. No doubt there are further lacunae. Poems by Geoffrey Hill were read on BBC Radio on 13 September 1950 and 25 March 1952 in the programme *Midland Poets*.

Within each heading I have tried to present the items in chronological order of publication. Very often exact dating has proved impossible; I have given precedence to the *more* exactly dated items in any doubtful case and relegated others to what seems the latest possible date. The poems are listed first, and prose, criticism and interviews subsequently, for each year. Translations and musical settings of Hill's work are given in the second section.

I have applied the same chronological principle in the list of critical writing about Geoffrey Hill. There may well be criticism in small and foreign magazines that I have not come across. I give the full titles of articles and essays; reviews I simply describe as reviews. (This categorical distinction has a somewhat nebulous edge.)

I am indebted for the kindness of many people: first to Geoffrey Hill; to Christopher Ricks, who has tirelessly encouraged me; and to Kenneth Curtis, Eric Griffiths, Henry Hart, Robin Holloway, Pico Iyer, Adrian Poole, David Ricks and Katy Koralek, Peter Robinson, Tom Sutcliffe, Peter Swaab, Mrs Patricia Taylor, Anthony Thwaite, and Willa Van Deenan of the *TLS*. Also to an anonymous editor at *Stand*, and to staff at the University Library in Cambridge, the Bodleian in Oxford, the British Library in London and the New York Public Library. The final responsibility is my own.

I have used some symbols and abbreviations:

* = uncollected in major editions
(E) = edited by Geoffrey Hill
SMALL CAPITALS = a book with Geoffrey Hill as a named author
rev. = review
FTU = *For the Unfallen*
KL = *King Log*
MH = *Mercian Hymns*
SISAK = *Somewhere Is Such A Kingdom*
Péguy = *The Mystery of the Charity of Charles Péguy*

I   The works of Geoffrey Hill

1951

'Late Autumn'*; 'Jordan'* and 'Good Friday'*, *Oxford Guardian* (magazine of the Oxford University Liberal Club), Vol. 13 No. 3, 24 February 1951, pp. 5, 13.

1952

'For Isaac Rosenberg'*, *The Isis* (Oxford), 20 February 1952, p. 20.
'To William Dunbar'*, 'God's Little Mountain', 'Genesis: a ballad of Christopher Smart', 'Holy Thursday/of William Blake', 'For Isaac Rosenberg'*, in GEOFFREY HILL (*The Fantasy Poets, Pamphlet No. 11*), (Oxford, Fantasy Press), Autumn 1952.
'Summer Night'*, *The Isis*, 19 November 1952, p. 33.
'Flower and No Flower'*, in Donald Hall (ed.), *New Poems* Vol. 1 No. 2, Winter 1952, (Oxford, Fantasy Press), p. 5.
'Pentecost'*, 'Saint Cuthbert on Farne Island'*, in Derwent May and James Price (eds.), *Oxford Poetry 1952*, (Basil Blackwell), pp. 18–19.

1953

'The Tower Window'*, *The Isis*, 28 January 1953, p. 19.
'Captain Richard Fraser, Aged 24 Years'*, *Trio* (Oxford) No. 2, January 1953.
'In Memory of Jane Fraser', 'Epithalamion'*, in Donald Hall (ed.), *New Poems* Vol. 1 No. 3, Spring 1953, pp. 4–5.
'I See The Crocus Armies Spread ...'*, 'Merlin', *Trio* No. 3, June 1953, pp. 12–13.
Broadcast: 'Gideon at the Well'* read by Geoffrey Hill on *First Reading*, BBC Radio, 1 July 1953.
'Genesis', *Paris Review* No. 2, Summer 1953, p. 31.
'In Memory of Jane Fraser', 'Gideon at the Well (for Janice)'*, *Paris Review* No. 4, Winter 1953, pp. 84–5.
'The Bidden Guest', *Departure* (Oxford) Vol. 1 No 3, n.d., p. 11.
(E) 'Genesis', 'Merlin', 'The Bidden Guest', 'Holy Thursday' in Donald Hall and Geoffrey Hill (eds.), *Oxford Poetry 1953*, (Oxford, Fantasy Press), pp. 22–8.

Prose, criticism

Review of William Blake's 'Jerusalem', *The Isis*, 4 March 1953, p. 22.
'*Symposium:* a discussion between Alan Brownjohn, Alistair Elliot, Geoffrey Hill, and Jonathan Price, with Anthony Thwaite in the chair', *Trio* No. 3, June 1953, pp. 4–7.
Review of Michael Shanks, 'Fantasy Poets: Number 13', *Trio* No. 3, June 1953, pp. 23–4.
Review of Richard Eberhart's 'Undercliff', *The Isis*, 25 November 1953, p. 31.
(E) Jonathan Price and Geoffrey Hill (eds.), *New Poems* Vol. 2 No. 2, Winter 1953.

1954

'An Ark on the Flood'*, *The Isis*, 10 March 1954, pp. 18–19.
'The Revelation'*, *London Magazine* Vol. 1 No. 10, November 1954, p. 72.
'In Memory of Jane Fraser', 'An Ark on the Flood'*, 'Prospero and Ariel'*, 'Gideon at the Well (for Janice)'*, in Jonathan Price and Anthony Thwaite (eds.), *Oxford Poetry 1954*, (Fantasy Press), pp. 13–19.

Prose, criticism

'Personal Choice (4)' (on Housman), *The Isis*, 10 February 1954, p. 72.
'A Writer's Craft (5)', *The Isis*, 17 February 1954, p. 14.
'Letter from Oxford', *London Magazine* Vol. 1 No. 4, May 1954, pp. 71-5.
'Contemporary Novelists (4): François Mauriac', *The Isis*, 16 June 1954, p. 22.

1955

'Enemy of the People'*, 'Pennies for Charon'*, *Paris Review* No. 8, Spring 1955, pp. 72-3.
'The Turtle Dove', *Nimbus* Vol. 3 No. 1, Spring 1955, p. 29.
Broadcast: 'Solomon's Mines', 'The Metamorphosis' (sic), read on 'New Verse', BBC Radio, 12 June 1955.
'Solomon's Mines (To Bonamy Dobrée)', 'Epithalamium 1 and 2' (later 'Asmodeus 1 and 2'), *Nimbus* Vol. 3 No. 2, Summer 1955, pp. 87-8.
Broadcast: 'Enemy of the People' read on 'New Poems from the North', BBC Radio, 2 November 1955.
'Solomon's Mines (To Bonamy Dobrée)', 'The Re-birth of Venus', 'The Fear', 'Knowing the Dead..../(To the Jews in Europe, 1939-45)', 'The Distant Fury of Battle', 'On this side of Jove's Cloud'*, 'Asmodeus 1 and 2', POETRY AND AUDIENCE (Leeds) Vol. 3 No. 5, 11 November 1955 (these poems comprising the whole number).

1956

'The Fear', *Audience* (New York) Nos. 6-7, 4 May 1956, p. 16.
'The Distant Fury of Battle', in Stephen Spender, Elizabeth Jennings and Dannie Abse (eds.), *New Poems 1956: A P.E.N. Anthology*, (London), p. 124.
'Genesis', in G.S. Fraser (ed.), *Poetry Now*, (London), pp. 91-93.

1957

'Wreaths', *Poetry* (Chicago) Vol. 90 No. 2, May 1957, p. 80.
'Scapegoat' ("Through scant pride to be so put out! ..."), 'Drake's Drum', *Listen (Yorkshire)* Vol. 2 No. 3, Summer-Autumn 1957, p. 6.
'Wreaths', 'The Turtle Dove', in Kathleen Nott, C. Day Lewis and Thomas Blackburn (eds.), *New Poems 1957: A P.E.N. Anthology*, (London), pp. 70-1.
'Asmodeus 1 and 2', 'The Turtle Dove', 'The Re-Birth of Venus', 'In Memory of Jane Fraser', 'Gideon at the Well (for Janice)'*, 'God's Little Mountain', 'Genesis', in Donald Hall, Robert Pack and Louis Simpson (eds.), *New Poets of England and America*, (New York), pp. 120-5.

1958

'After Cumae', *The New Statesman* Vol. 55 No. 1404, 8 February 1958, p. 172.
'A Metamorphosis' ("Doubtless he saw some path clear, having found ..."), 'The Fear', *Gemini* 5, Vol. 2 No. 1, Spring 1958, p. 41.
'Orpheus and Eurydice', *The National and English Review* Vol. 150 No. 902, April 1958 (p. 10 of 'Life and Language: An Anthology of New Work by Contemporary Poets,' bound between pp. 152-3).
'The White Ship', *The Hudson Review* Vol. 11 No. 2, Summer 1958, p. 257.
'In Piam Memoriam', 'Picture of a Nativity', 'The Bibliographers', *Poetry and Audience* Vol. 6 No. 5, 7 November 1958, pp. 1-2.
'Doctor Faustus', 'Canticle for Good Friday', *Poetry and Audience* Vol. 6 No. 9, 5 December 1958, pp. 2-3.

'The Martyrdom of Saint Sebastian', 'The Lowlands of Holland', 'A Pastoral', 'Elegiac Stanzas', *Listen* Vol. 3 No. 1, Winter 1958, pp. 4–6.
'The Lowlands of Holland', in Bonamy Dobrée, Louis MacNeice and Philip Larkin (eds.), *New Poems 1958: A P.E.N. Anthology*, (London), p. 48.

Prose, criticism

'The Poetry of Allen Tate', *Geste* (Leeds) Vol. 3 No. 3, November 1958, pp. 8–12.

1959

'To the (Supposed) Patron', *The New Statesman* Vol. 57 No. 1459, 28 February 1959, p. 304.
'Canticle for Good Friday', 'Two Formal Elegies (for the Jews in Europe)', 'The Guardians', 'Requiem for the Plantagenet Kings', *Paris Review* 21, Spring–Summer 1959, pp. 98–100.
FOR THE UNFALLEN: POEMS 1952–1958, (London, André Deutsch), 16 October 1959.

Prose, criticism

Review of 'Isaac Rosenberg Exhibition, at Leeds University', *The New Statesman* Vol. 57 No. 1473, 6 June 1959, p. 795 (as 'G.H.').

Interviews

Interview in Leeds University magazine, quoted by *TLS* reviewer, 31 October 1968.

1960

FOR THE UNFALLEN: POEMS 1952–1958, (Chester Springs Pennsylvania, Dufour Editions), 1960.

Prose, criticism

'The World's Proportion: Jonson's Dramatic Poetry in "Sejanus" and "Catiline" ', in John Russell Brown and Bernard Harris (eds.), *Jacobean Theatre*, (London), pp. 112–31.

1961

'Ovid in the Third Reich', *The New Statesman* Vol. 61 No. 1562, 17 February 1961, p. 264.
'Two Sonnets' (later 'Annunciations'), *X: A Quarterly Review* Vol. 2 No. 1, March 1961, p. 35.
'Locust Songs/to Allan Seager', *Stand* Vol. 5 No. 2, n.d., p. 2.

1962

'A Pre-Raphaelite Notebook', *Shenandoah* Vol. 13 No. 2, Winter 1962, p. 12 (not collected till *Tenebrae*).
(E) 'The Assisi Fragments/To G. Wilson Knight', *Poetry and Audience* Vol. 9 No. 21, 8 June 1962, p. 10. (Editorial has note: 'Our thanks to Geoffrey Hill for helping to edit this special issue').
'The Assisi Fragments (to G. Wilson Knight)' (with epigraph: ' "– this delight in giving a form to oneself as a piece of difficult, refractory and suffering material –" (Nietzsche)'), *Stand* Vol. 6 No. 1, n.d., p. 6.
'Annunciations' (with comments by G.H.) in Kenneth Allott (ed.), *The Penguin Book of Contemporary Verse* (revised edition, Harmondsworth 1962), pp. 391–3. (Reprinted in 1982 as *English*

Poetry 1918-60, with a 'Prefatory Note' by Miriam Allott).
'Annunciations', in Donald Hall and Robert Pack (eds.), *New Poets of England and America: Second Selection*, (Cleveland and New York), p. 72.

Prose, criticism

'The Poetry of Jon Silkin', *Poetry and Audience* Vol. 9 No. 12, January 1962, pp. 4-8.

1963

Three poems: 'The Humanist', and 'Two Fragmentary Variations: 1) "For Justice is exilèd from the earth" (Thomas Kyd)' (version of 'Florentines', later collected in *Tenebrae*), and '2) "When Violence was ceas't, and Warr on Earth" (John Milton)' (later 'I had hope when Violence was ceas't' in *King Log*), *Stand* Vol. 6 No. 3, n.d., pp. 10-11.

Prose, criticism

'Robert Lowell: Contrasts and Repetitions' (review of Lowell's *Imitations* and H.B. Staples's *Robert Lowell: The First 20 Years*), *Essays in Criticism* Vol. 13 No. 2, April 1963, pp. 188-197. (Reprinted in Jonathan Price (ed.), *Critics on Robert Lowell: Readings in Literary Criticism*, (London, 1974), pp. 80-91).
Entries on 'Isaac Rosenberg' and 'Allen Tate' in Stephen Spender and Donald Hall (eds.), *The Concise Encyclopaedia of English and American Poets and Poetry*, (London), p. 278 and pp. 326-7. (Reprinted 1970).

1964

'Three Baroque Meditations', *The Listener* Vol. 71, No. 1815, 9 January 1964, p. 67.
'Domaine Public', *Living Arts 3* (London, I.C.A.), April 1964, p. 89.
Broadcast: 'Poetry Today: R.S. Thomas/Geoffrey Hill', BBC Radio, 22 October 1964.
'The Imaginative Life', 'History as Poetry', 'A Prayer to the Sun', *Paris Review* No. 31, Winter-Spring 1964, pp. 109-10.
'Tristia: A Valediction to Osip Mandel'shtam', *Stand* Vol. 7 No. 2, n.d., p. 36.
'Men are A Mockery of Angels', in John Butt (ed.), *Of Books and Humankind: Essays and Poems Presented to Bonamy Dobrée*, (London), p. 181.
PREGHIERE, (Northern House Pamphlet Poets, Leeds), 1964; containing 'Men Are a Mockery of Angels', 'Domaine Public', 'A Prayer to the Sun', 'Three Baroque Meditations', 'The Assisi Fragments', 'Ovid in the Third Reich', 'History as Poetry', The Imaginative Life'.

Prose, criticism

'The Dream of Reason' (review of "The Review: Special Number - William Empson"), *Essays in Criticism* Vol. 14 No. 1, January 1964, pp. 91-101.
'"I in Another Place": Homage to Keith Douglas' (review article), *Stand* Vol. 6 No. 4, n.d., pp. 6-13.

1965

'Broadcast: 'The Leeds Poets', BBC Radio, 28 March 1965 (discussion, with readings of 'Men Are a Mockery of Angels' and 'The Imaginative Life').
'Soliloquies' ('1. The Stone Man, 1878/for Charles Causley', '2. Old Poet with Distant Admirers'), *Agenda* Vol. 4 No. 1, April-May 1965, p. 7.

'From the *Songbook* of Sebastian Arrurruz' (No. 5), *TLS* No. 3309, 29 July 1965, p. 648.
Broadcast: 'The Living Poet: Geoffrey Hill', BBC Radio, 5 September 1965.

1966

Broadcast: 'Funeral Music', read by Alan Wheatley and introduced by Geoffrey Hill, 'Poetry Now', BBC Radio 3, 20 September 1966.
'From the *Songbook* of Sebastian Arrurruz' (Nos 1–4), *Agenda* Vol. 4 Nos. 5 and 6, Autumn 1966, pp. 34–6.
PENGUIN MODERN POETS 8 (Edwin Brock, Geoffrey Hill, Stevie Smith), (Harmondsworth), pp. 53–82. (Reprinted 1968.) Contains 'The Turtle Dove', 'Solomon's Mines', 'The Distant Fury of Battle', 'Asmodeus', 'Picture of a Nativity', 'Canticle for Good Friday', 'The Guardians', 'After Cumae', 'The Bibliographers', 'The Death of Shelley', 'Ode on the Loss of the *Titanic*', 'Doctor Faustus', 'A Pastoral'. 'To the (Supposed) Patron', 'Annunciations', 'Little Apocalypse', 'Men are a Mockery of Angels', '*Domaine Public*', 'A Prayer to the Sun', 'Ovid in the Third Reich', 'Three Baroque Meditations', 'The Humanist', 'Soliloquies', 'The Imaginative Life'.

Interviews

Interview with Michael Dempsey, 'Literature Comes to Life ...', *The Illustrated London News*, 20 August 1966, pp. 24–5.

1967

'Funeral Music', *Stand* Vol. 8 No. 3, n.d., pp. 4–6.
'September Song', *Stand* Vol. 8 No. 4, n.d., p. 41.
Record: THE POET SPEAKS 8, edited by Peter Orr. (Readings of 'Canticle for Good Friday', 'To the (Supposed) Patron', 'In Piam Memoriam', 'Little Apocalypse', 'The Assisi Fragments'.) (London, Argo Records), Argo No. PLP 1088 (recorded Leeds, 26 June 1966).

1968

'From *The Songbook of Sebastian Arrurruz*': '9. A Song From Armenia', *Stand*, Vol. 9 No. 3, n.d., p. 50.
KING LOG, (London, André Deutsch), August, 1968. (Also issued by Dufour Editions, Chester Springs, Pennsylvania, 1968.)

Prose, criticism

'Geoffrey Hill writes:' (about *King Log*), *Poetry Book Society Bulletin* No. 58, Autumn 1968.
'Jonathan Swift: The Poetry of "Reaction"', in Brian Vickers (ed.), *The World of Jonathan Swift: Essays for the Tercentenary*, (Oxford), pp. 195–212.

1969

Prose, criticism

'"The True Conduct of Human Judgment": some observations on *Cymbeline*', in D.W. Jefferson (ed.), *The Morality of Art: Essays Presented to G. Wilson Knight by his Colleagues and Friends*, (London), pp. 18–32.

1971

MERCIAN HYMNS, (London, André Deutsch), July 1971.

Prose, criticism

'Geoffrey Hill writes:' (about *Mercian Hymns*), *Poetry Book Society Bulletin* No. 69, Summer 1971.
' "The Conscious Mind's Intelligible Structure" ': A Debate', *Agenda* Vol. 9 No. 4-Vol. 10 No. 1, Autumn/Winter 1971-72, pp. 14-23.

1972

'The Pentecost Castle' (with epigraph from R.O. Jones, *A Literary History of Spain*; versions of 1, 2, 4, 6, 3 and 9), *Agenda* Vol. 10 No. 4-Vol. 11 No. 1, Autumn /Winter 1972-73, pp. 68-70.
'Copla by Sebastian Arrurruz', *Stand* Vol. 14 No. 1, n.d., p. 4.

Prose, criticism

'Redeeming the Time', *Agenda* ('Rhythm Issue') Vol. 10 No. 4-Vol. 11 No. 1, Autumn/Winter 1972-73, pp. 87-111.

1973

Broadcast: 'Mercian Hymns' read by Alan Wheatley and introduced by Geoffrey Hill, BBC Radio 3, 31 January 1973.
'Three Mystical Songs' (versions of 'The Pentecost Castle' 7, 8 and 13, with epigraph from David Jones), *Agenda* ('David Jones Issue') Vol. 11 No. 4-Vol. 12 No. 1, Autumn/Winter 1973-4, pp. 54-5.
Versions of Nos. 8, 12 and 3 from 'An Apology for the Revival of Christian Architecture in England' (with epigraph: ' "Sanctified by such passages/Let us exchange our messages"-George Barker'), in John Heath-Stubbs and Martin Green (eds.), *Homage to George Barker on his Sixtieth Birthday*, (London), pp. 46-7.

1974

'We Close our Eyes to Anselm and Lie Calm' (later '10. Fidelities' of 'An Apology ...'), 'Ecce Tempus' (later 'Veni Coronaberis'), *Poetry Nation* III (Manchester), p. 6.
Untitled, the second of 'Two Chorale-Preludes' (with note: 'after Paul Celan's "Kermorvan" and quoting a phrase from W.J. Ong S.J.'), *Stand* Vol. 15 No. 2, n.d., p. 6.

1975

'Lachrimae', *Agenda* Vol. 12 No. 4-Vol. 13 No. 1, Winter/Spring 1975, pp. 29-35.
Text of James Brown's Cantata *Ad Incensum Lucernae* (including sections 4, 6 and 8 of 'Tenebrae' and 'Christmas Trees'), first performed at University of Leeds Department of Music Spring Concerts, 5 February 1975 (programme prints text).
'Eight Poems': 'Terribilis Est Locus Iste', 'The Pentecost Castle' Nos. 10, 11, 12, 14 and 15, 'The Devotions of his Sacred Majesty in his Solitude and Sufferings Rendered in Verse, and Set to Music for Voice and an Organ or Theorbo' (sections 1 and 2 are versions of 'Tenebrae' sections 5 and 2), *Agenda* Vol. 13 No. 3, Autumn 1975, pp. 18-22.
'Lachrimae', in Patricia Beer (ed.), *New Poems 1975: A P.E.N. Anthology*, (London), pp. 153-7.

SOMEWHERE IS SUCH A KINGDOM: POEMS 1952-1971 (Boston, Houghton Mifflin). Brings together *For the Unfallen*, *King Log* and *Mercian Hymns*, without the epigraphs and dedications of those volumes, and with a new covering epigraph: ' "Sometimes a man seeks what he hath lost; and from that place, and time, wherein he misses it, his mind runs back, from place to place, and time to time, to find where, and when he had it ..."/Thomas Hobbes, *Leviathan*, 1651'. With 'Introduction: The Survival of Strong Poetry' by Harold Bloom.

Prose, criticism

'Perplexed Persistence: the Exemplary Failure of T.H. Green', *Poetry Nation* IV, 1975, pp. 128–45.

1976

Prose, criticism

Television broadcast: 'T.S. Eliot: "Marina" ' (contribution to Open University programme), first transmission BBC 2, 24 April 1976.

1977

Seven Sonnets from 'An Apology ...' (Nos. 1, 4, 5, 7, 9, 11 and 13), *Agenda* Vol. 15 Nos. 2-3, Summer/Autumn 1977, pp. 3–9.
'Homo Homini Lupus – after Anne Hébert's "Les Offensés" '*, *Agenda* Vol. 15 No. 4, Winter 1977-8, p. 6.
'Damon's Lament for his Clorinda, Yorkshire 1654', in Geoffrey Elborn (ed.), *Hand and Eye: An Anthology for Sacheverell Sitwell*, (Edinburgh), (unpaginated).

1978

BRAND BY HENRIK IBSEN: A VERSION FOR THE ENGLISH STAGE, (London, Heinemann), (first performed at the National Theatre, April 1978).
'On the Death of Mr Shakespeare' (Nos. 1, 7 and 11 of 'An Apology ...', with epigraph from *A Midsumer Night's Dream* II.1.102-111), in Roger Pringle and Christopher Hampton (eds.), *A Selection from Poems for Shakespeare*, (London), pp. 82–84.
TENEBRAE, (London, André Deutsch), Autumn 1978.

Prose, criticism

'Geoffrey Hill writes:' (about *Tenebrae*), *Poetry Book Society Bulletin* No. 98, Autumn 1978.
'Poetry as "Menace" and "Atonement" ', *University of Leeds Review* 21, 1978, pp. 66–88.

1979

Broadcast: 'The Living Poet: Geoffrey Hill', BBC Radio 3, produced by Fraser Steel, 6 August 1979.
TENEBRAE, (Boston, Houghton Mifflin), 1979.
Record: THE POETRY AND VOICE OF GEOFFREY HILL, with notes by Grace Schulman, Caedmon TC 1597, New York, 1979.

Prose, criticism

Choice of the year's books, *The Sunday Times*, 9 December 1979.

1980

Prose, criticism

'Under Judgement', interview with Blake Morrison, *The New Statesman* Vol. 99 No. 2551, 8 February 1980, pp. 212–4.
'What Hymn is the Band Playing?' (on David Wright), *PN Review 14*, Vol. 6 No. 6, p. 35.

1981

HENRIK IBSEN, BRAND: A VERSION FOR THE STAGE by Geoffrey Hill, Second Edition, Revised, with an Introduction by Inga-Stina Ewbank, (Minneapolis, University of Minnesota Press).

Interviews

Interview with John Haffenden, *Quarto* No. 15, March 1981, pp. 19–22. (Reprinted in *Viewpoints: Poets in Conversation with John Haffenden*, London 1981, pp. 76–99).
Broadcast: interview with Eric Griffiths, in 'The Composed Voice', BBC Radio 3, produced by Thomas Sutcliffe, 14 July 1981.

1982

Prose, criticism

Review of Edward Mendelson's *Early Auden*, *The Cambridge Review* Vol. 103 No. 2267, 26 February 1982, p. 172.

1983

Broadcast: 'The Mystery of the Charity of Charles Péguy', read by Paul Webster and introduced by Geoffrey Hill, BBC Radio 3, 1 February 1983.
'The Mystery of the Charity of Charles Péguy,' *TLS* No. 4166, 4 February 1983, pp. 101–3.
THE MYSTERY OF THE CHARITY OF CHARLES PÉGUY, (London, Agenda/Ándré Deutsch), April 1983.
'The Mystery of the Charity of Charles Péguy', *Paris Review* Vol. 25 No. 88, Summer 1983, pp. 41–59.

Prose, criticism

'Our Word Is Our Bond', *Agenda* Vol. 21 No. 1, Spring 1983, pp. 13–49.
'"Thus my noblest capacity becomes my deepest perplexity"', text of a sermon preached at Great St Mary's University Church, Cambridge, 8 May 1983.
'What Devil Has Got Into John Ransom?', *Grand Street* (New York) Vol. 2 No. 4, Summer 1983, pp. 81–103.

1984

Prose, criticism

'C.H. Sisson', *PN Review* 39, Vol. 11 No. 1, March 1984, pp. 11-5.
THE LORDS OF LIMIT: ESSAYS ON LITERATURE AND IDEAS, (London, André Deutsch), 1984.
'Gurney's Hobby' (F.W. Bateson Memorial Lecture delivered 15 February 1984), *Essays in Criticism*, Vol. 34 No. 2, April 1984, pp. 97-128.
Review of John Haffenden's *Berryman* and Eileen Simpson's *Poets in Their Youth*, *Essays in Criticism*, Vol. 34 No. 3, July 1984.

II   Translations and musical settings of Hill's work

TRANSLATIONS

Geoffrey Hill, 'Le Château de Pentecôte' traduit par René Gallet, *Obsidiane* 18, mars 1982, pp. 59-75 (English with facing translation).
René Gallet, 'Etude sur "Le Château de Pentecôte" de Geoffrey Hill', *Obsidiane* 21, Hiver 1982, pp. 4-12.
Geoffrey Hill, *Poems*: 'Ovid in the Third Reich', 'Men Are a Mockery of Angels'; *Mercian Hymns* I, VI, VIII, X, XVIII, XXX; 'The Pentecost Castle, 1-7' translated into Greek by John Stathatos, *XAPTHΣ* (*Chartis*) 2 (Athens), September 1982, pp. 167-71.
John Stathatos, '*Tenebrae:* An Introduction to the Poetry of Geoffrey Hill', including translated excerpts from 'Domaine Public', 'Funeral Music', *Mercian Hymns* and *Tenebrae*, *XAPTHΣ* 2, pp. 172-5.
Geoffrey Hill, *Hymnen aus Mercia*, translated by Uwe Kolbe, in Angus Calder (ed.), *Englische Lyrik 1900-1980*, (Leipzig, 1983), pp. 313-24.

MUSICAL SETTINGS

Gordon Crosse, 'For the Unfallen Op. 9' (settings for tenor voice, solo French horn and string orchestra of four poems by Geoffrey Hill): 'Merlin', 'In Memory of Jane Frazer' (sic), 'Requiem for the Plantagenet Kings', 'In Piam Memoriam'. Oxford. (No date; first performance 17 September 1968).
James Brown, 'Cantata: Ad Incensum Lucernae' (to text by Geoffrey Hill), first performed at University of Leeds Department of Music Spring Concerts, 5 February 1975.
Robin Holloway, 'The Lovers' Well, Op. 49' (partial setting for baritone and piano of 'The Pentecost Castle' sections 1, 2, 3, 5, 6, 11, 13, 14, 15). Composed 1981, performed April 1984 in Emmanuel College 400th anniversary celebrations.

III   On Geoffrey Hill

Anthony Thwaite, rev. *The Fantasy Poets, Pamphlet No. 11*, Trio (Oxford) No. 2, January 1953.
Alan Brownjohn, rev. *The Fantasy Poets, Pamphlet No. 11*, *The Isis*, 18 February 1953, p. 27.
Adrienne Cecile Rich, rev. *Oxford Poetry 1952*, *The Isis*, 11 March 1953, p. 26.
George MacBeth, (remarks), *The Isis*, 17 June 1953, p. 20.
Anthony Thwaite, 'Oxford Magazines', *The Isis*, 18 November 1953, p. 11.
John Gross, rev. *Oxford Poetry 1953*, *The Isis*, 18 November 1953, p. 23.
Anonymous, 'Isis Idol: Geoffrey Hill', *The Isis*, 18 November 1953, p. 17.

Anthony Thwaite, *Essays on Contemporary English Poetry*, Tokyo 1957, pp. 170–1 and 216.

Anthony Thwaite, *Contemporary English Poetry: An Introduction*, London 1959, pp. 158–9.

A. Alvarez, rev. *FTU, The Observer*, 25 October 1959, p. 23.

G.S. Fraser, rev. *FTU, The New Statesman* Vol. 95 No. 1494, 31 October 1959, p. 590.

Martin Dodsworth, rev. *FTU, The Isis*, 25 November 1959, p. 25.

Roy Fuller, rev. *FTU, London Magazine* Vol. 7 No. 1, January 1960, pp. 73–6.

Joan Forman, rev. *FTU, The Poetry Review* Vol. 51 No. 1, January–March 1960, p. 44.

Elizabeth Jennings, *Poetry Today (1957–60)*, London 1961, pp. 43–5.

Kenneth Allott, *The Penguin Book of Contemporary Verse*, (revised edition, Harmondsworth 1962; reprinted in 1982 as *English Poetry 1918–60*, with a Prefatory Note by Miriam Allott), pp. 390–1.

P.N. Furbank, rev. *Preghiere, The Listener* Vol. 72 No. 1843, 23 July 1964, p. 37.

Christopher Ricks, rev. *Preghiere, The New Statesman* Vol. 68 No. 1741, 24 July 1964, pp. 123–4.

Peter Dale, rev. *Preghiere, Agenda* Vol. 3 No. 5, September 1964, p. 35.

Frederick Grubb, rev. *Preghiere, The Poetry Review* Vol. 55 No. 3, Autumn 1964, pp. 175–9.

Christopher Ricks, 'Cliché as "Responsible Speech": Geoffrey Hill', *London Magazine* Vol. 4 No. 8, November 1964, pp. 96–101. (Drawn on, and changed, in 'Clichés' in Leonard Michaels and Christopher Ricks (eds.), *The State of the Language*, Berkeley, Los Angeles and London 1980, pp. 59–61; and revised again in Christopher Ricks, *The Force of Poetry*, Oxford 1984, pp. 356–68.)

James Dickey, *The Suspect in Poetry*, Madison Minnesota 1964, p. 44.

Anonymous, rev. *Preghiere, TLS* No. 3365, 25 August 1966, p. 765.

Roger Hecht, rev. *Preghiere, Poetry* Vol. 110 No. 2, May 1967, pp. 118–9.

Ian Hamilton, rev. *KL, The Observer*, 25 August 1968, p. 22.

Martin Dodsworth, rev. *KL, The Listener* Vol. 80 No. 2058, 5 September 1968.

Richard Holmes, rev. *KL, The Times*, 14 September 1968, p. 20.

Christopher Ricks, rev. *KL, The Sunday Times*, 15 September 1968, p. 62.

Alan Brownjohn, rev. *KL, The New Statesman* Vol. 76 No. 1958, 20 September 1968, p. 363.

Martin Seymour-Smith, rev. *KL, The Spectator* Vol. 221 No. 7317, 20 September 1968, p. 397.

Peter Porter, broadcast rev. *KL*, 'Poetry Now', BBC Radio 3, 28 October 1968.

Anonymous (Alan Page), rev. *KL, TLS* No. 3479, 31 October 1968, p. 1220.

Peter Dale, rev. *KL, Agenda* Vol. 6 Nos 3–4, Autumn–Winter 1968, pp. 150–1.

Gavin Ewart, rev. *KL, London Magazine* New Series Vol. 8 No. 9, December 1968, pp. 92–3.

Jeffrey Wainwright, '"The Speechless Dead": Geoffrey Hill's *King Log*', *Stand* Vol.10 No. 1, n.d., pp. 44–9.

Derwent May, rev. *KL, the Review* No. 20, March 1969, pp. 53–6.

Robin Skelton, rev. *KL, Poetry* Vol. 114 No. 6, September 1969, pp. 397–401.

William Walsh, entry on Geoffrey Hill, in Rosalie Murphy (ed.), *Contemporary Poets of the English Language*, Chicago and London 1970, pp. 504–6.

Edward Lucie-Smith, *British Poetry Since 1945*, Harmondsworth 1970, p. 240.

Alan Brownjohn, rev. *MH, The New Statesman* Vol. 82 No. 2107, 6 August 1971, pp. 183–4.

Christopher Ricks, rev. *MH, The Listener* Vol. 86 No 2213, 26 August 1971, p. 274.

Anonymous, rev. *MH, TLS* No. 3626, 27 August 1971, p. 1024.

Ian Hamilton, rev. *MH, The Observer*, 29 August 1971, p. 23.

Peter Porter, rev. *MH, The Guardian*, 2 September 1971, p. 12.

Cyril Connolly, rev. *MH, The Sunday Times*, 5 September 1971, p. 30.

William Cookson, rev. *MH, Agenda* Vol. 9 Nos. 2–3, Spring–Summer 1971, pp. 146–7.

Barbara Hardy, rev. *MH, The Spectator* Vol. 227 No 7478, 23 October 1971, pp. 592–3.

Wallace D. Martin, 'Beyond Modernism: Christopher Middleton and Geoffrey Hill', *Contemporary Literature* (Madison, Wisconsin), Vol. 12 No. 4, Autumn 1971, pp. 420–36.

Ian Wedde, rev. *MH, London Magazine* New Series Vol. 11 No. 5, December 1971/January 1972, pp. 126–7.

Peter Levi, S.J., rev. *MH, Agenda* Vol. 9 No. 4 – Vol. 10 No. 1, Autumn–Winter 1971-2, pp. 99–100.

Martin Dodsworth, rev. *MH, Stand* Vol. 13 No. 1, n.d., pp. 61–3.

Michael Wilding, rev. *MH, New Poetry* (Sydney) Vol. 20 Nos. 1–2, February/April 1972, pp. 56–8.

Michael Launchbury, rev. *MH, Delta* (Sheffield) No. 50, Spring 1972, pp. 44–7.

Michael Schmidt, rev. *MH, Poetry* Vol. 120 No. 3, June 1972, pp. 170–81.

Jon Silkin, 'The Poetry of Geoffrey Hill', in Michael Schmidt and Grevel Lindop (eds.), *British Poetry Since 1960*, Manchester 1972, pp. 143–64. (Also in *The Iowa Review* (Iowa City) Vol. 3 No. 3, Summer 1972, pp. 108–28.)

Calvin Bedient, rev. *MH, Parnassus* Vol. 1 No. 2, Spring–Summer 1973, pp. 84–6.

Jon Silkin (ed.), *Poetry of the Committed Individual: A Stand Anthology*, London 1973, pp. 31–4.

Richard Ellmann and R. O'Clair (eds.), *Norton Anthology of Modern Poetry*, New York 1973, pp. 1289–90.

Frank Kermode and John Hollander (eds), 'Modern British Literature', *The Oxford Anthology of English Literature* Vol. II, New York 1973, pp. 2183–4.

Geoffrey Thurley, *The Ironic Harvest*, London 1974, pp. 154–7.

C.H. Sisson, 'Geoffrey Hill', *Agenda* Vol. 13 No. 3, Autumn 1975, pp. 23–8.

Michael Alexander, '*Mercian Hymns*', *Agenda* Vol. 13 No. 3, Autumn 1975, pp. 29–30.

Jeffrey Wainwright, 'Geoffrey Hill's "Lachrimae"', *Agenda* Vol. 13 No. 3, Autumn 1975, pp. 31–8.

Harold Bloom, 'Introduction – The Survival of Strong Poetry', to Geoffrey Hill, *Somewhere Is Such a Kingdom*, Boston 1975. (Reprinted in Harold Bloom, *Figures of Capable Imagination*, New York 1976).

Donald Hall, rev. *SISAK, The Nation* Vol. 221 No. 19, 6 December 1975, pp. 600–2.

Christopher Ricks, rev. *SISAK, New York Times Book Review*, 11 January 1976, p. 6.

Irvin Ehrenpreis, rev. *SISAK, The New York Review of Books*, Vol. 22 Nos. 21 and 22, 22 January 1976, pp. 3–6.

Richard Howard, rev. *SISAK, The Yale Review* Vol. 65 No. 3, March 1976, pp. 425–7.

Richmond Lattimore, rev. *SISAK, The Hudson Review* Vol. 29 No. 1, Spring 1976, pp. 126–7.

Robert Morgan, rev. *SISAK, Parnassus* Vol. 4 No. 2, Spring–Summer 1976, pp. 31–48.

John Matthias, rev. *SISAK, Poetry* Vol. 128 No. 4, July 1976, pp. 232–40.

Edward Hirsch, rev. *SISAK, The Sewanee Review* Vol. 84, 1976, pp. xcvi–xcviii.

Stephen Utz, rev. *SISAK, The Southern Review* Vol. 12 No. 2, 1976, pp. 426–33.

Calvin Bedient, 'Absentist Poetry: Kinsella, Hill, Graham, Hughes', *PN Review* number 1, 1976, pp. 18–24.

John Purkis, *Donald Davie, Charles Tomlinson, Geoffrey Hill, A306 Twentieth Century Poetry*, Unit 31, The Open University, Milton Keynes 1976, pp. 49–64.

Seamus Heaney, 'Artists on Art: Now and in England' (about *MH*), *Critical Inquiry* Vol. 3 No. 3, Spring 1977, pp. 471–88. (Reprinted, as 'Englands of the Mind', in *Preoccupations*, London 1980).

Igor Webb, 'Speaking of the Holocaust: The Poetry of Geoffrey Hill', *The Denver Quarterly* Vol. 12 No. 1, Spring 1977, pp. 114–25.

A.K. Weatherhead, 'Geoffrey Hill', *The Iowa Review* Vol. 8 No. 4, Fall 1977, pp. 104–16. (Reprinted in A. Kingsley Weatherhead, *The British Dissonance: Essays on Ten Contemporary Poets*, Columbia, Missouri and London 1983, pp. 71–94).

Harry Thomas, rev. *SISAK, Michigan Quarterly Review* Vol. 16 No. 1, Winter 1977, pp. 94–6.

Eric Homberger, *The Art of the Real: Poetry in England and America since 1939*, London 1977, pp. 210–12.

Christopher Ricks, 'Geoffrey Hill and "The Tongue's Atrocities"', University College of Swansea: The W.D. Thomas Memorial Lecture, 15 February 1978, Swansea 1978. (Also in *TLS* No. 3978, 30 June 1978, pp. 743–7; reprinted in Christopher Ricks, *The Force of Poetry*, Oxford 1984, pp. 285–318.)

Michael Billington, rev. *Brand* at NT, *The Guardian*, 27 April 1978, p. 12.

Irving Wardle, rev. *Brand* at NT, *The Times*, 27 April 1978, p. 16.

Robert Cushman, rev. *Brand* at NT, *The Observer*, 30 April 1978, p. 28.

Bernard Levin, rev. *Brand* at NT, *The Sunday Times*, 30 April 1978, p. 37.

John Elsom, rev. *Brand* at NT, *The Listener* Vol. 99 No. 2558, 4 May 1978, pp. 579-80.

Benedict Nightingale, rev. *Brand* at NT, *The New Statesman* Vol. 95 No. 2459, 5 May 1978, p. 616.

Germaine Greer, rev. *Brand* at NT, *The Spectator* Vol. 240 No. 7818, 6 May 1978, pp. 29-30.

Kenneth Muir, rev. *Brand*, TLS No. 3976, 16 June 1978, p. 660.

Eric Griffiths, rev. *Tenebrae*, *Perfect Bound* 6 (Cambridge), Autumn 1978, pp. 72-80.

Peter Porter, rev. *Tenebrae*, *The Observer*, 19 November 1978, p. 39.

William S. Milne, '"Creative tact": Geoffrey Hill's *King Log*', *Critical Quarterly* Vol. 20 No. 4, Winter 1978, pp. 39-45.

Anthony Thwaite, *Twentieth Century English Poetry: An Introduction*, London 1978, pp. 120-2.

Brian Oxley, 'The "Grammar" of *Tenebrae*', *Poetry and Audience* Vol. 25 No. 2, pp. 24-31.

Craig Raine, rev. *Tenebrae*, *The New Statesman* Vol. 97 No. 2494, 5 January 1979, pp. 19-20.

Martin Dodsworth, rev. *Tenebrae*, *The Guardian*, 1 February 1979, p. 10.

Agenda: Geoffrey Hill Special Issue Vol. 17 No. 1, Spring 1979, (Contributions by C.H. Sisson, Jeffrey Wainwright, John Peck, W.S. Milne, John Bayley, Cathrael Kazin, Merle Brown, William Cookson), pp. 3-89.

Edwin Morgan, rev. *Tenebrae*, *The Listener* Vol. 101 No. 2614, 7 June 1979, pp. 790-1.

Terry Eagleton, rev. *Tenebrae*, *Stand* Vol. 20 No. 3, n.d., pp. 75-7.

Brian Oxley, 'Hill's "Christian Year"', *Essays in Criticism* Vol. 29 No. 3, July 1979, pp. 289-

John Needham, 'The Idiom of Geoffrey Hill's "Mercian Hymns"', *English* Vol. 28 No. 131, Summer 1979, pp. 139-49.

Stephen Tunnicliffe, rev. *Tenebrae*, *Poetry Wales* Vol. 15 No. 1, Summer 1979, pp. 114-9.

Peter Lewis, rev. *Brand*, *Stand* Vol. 21 No. 1, n.d., p. 55.

John Haffenden, rev. *Brand*, *PN Review* number 9, Vol. 6 No. 1, pp. 24-5.

William Milne, 'Geoffrey Hill's *Mercian Hymns*', *Ariel* No. 1, 1979, pp. 43-63.

Garth Clucas, entry on Geoffrey Hill, in James Vinson (ed.), *Great Writers of the English Language Vol. I: Poets*, London 1979, pp. 488-90.

Michael Schmidt, 'Geoffrey Hill', *An Introduction to 50 Modern British Poets*, London 1979, pp. 398-407.

Grace Schulman, sleevenote to record, *The Poetry and Voice of Geoffrey Hill*, Caedmon TC 1597, New York 1979.

Vernon Young, rev. *Tenebrae*, *The Hudson Review* Vol. 32 No. 4, Winter 1979-80, pp. 621-2.

Jon Glover, 'The Poet in Plato's Cave: a theme in the work of Geoffrey Hill', *Poetry Review* Vol. 69 No. 3, March 1980, pp. 60-4.

Donald Hall, rev. *Tenebrae* and Caedmon record, *Poetry* Vol. 136 No. 2, May 1980, pp. 102-110.

Colin Falck, rev. *Tenebrae*, *Delta* No. 60, 1980, pp. 1-5.

Hayden Carruth, 'Poets on the Fringe', *Harpers* No. 1 (1980), p. 81.

Thomas Getz, 'Geoffrey Hill's *Mercian Hymns* and "Lachrimae": The Languages of History and Faith', *Modern Poetry Studies* Vol. 10, 1980, pp. 2-21.

Andrew Waterman, 'The Poetry of Geoffrey Hill', in Peter Jones and Michael Schmidt (eds.), *British Poetry Since 1970*, Manchester 1980, pp. 85-102.

Merle E. Brown, *Double Lyric: Divisiveness and Communal Creativity in Recent English Poetry*, London 1980, pp. 20-72.

Neil Corcoran, entry on Geoffrey Hill, in James Vinson (ed.), *Contemporary Poets: Third Edition*, London 1980, pp. 702-3.

Clive Wilmer, 'An Art of Recovery: Some Literary Sources for Geoffrey Hill's *Tenebrae*', *The Southern Review* (U.S.), Vol. 17 No. 1, January 1981, pp. 121-41.

John Haffenden, 'An Interview with Geoffrey Hill', *Quarto* No. 15, March 1981, pp. 19-22 (reprinted in *Viewpoints: Poets in Conversation with John Haffenden*, London 1981, pp. 76-99).

Calvin Bedient, 'On Geoffrey Hill', *Critical Quarterly* Vol. 23 No. 2, Summer 1981, pp. 17–26.

Michael Schmidt, 'The Time and the Place', *The Kenyon Review* New Series Vol. 3 No. 3, Summer 1981, pp. 20–2.

Calvin Bedient, 'The Thick and the Thin of it: Contemporary British and Irish Poetry', *The Kenyon Review* New Series Vol. 3 No. 3, Summer 1981, pp. 44–6.

Eric Homberger, 'Geoffrey Hill: la langue dans la mâchoire couveuse', *Figures d'Une Poésie Anglaise, Courrier du Centre International d'Etudes Poétiques* 143–4, Bruxelles, August–September 1981, pp. 17–22 (translated by F. De Haes).

Inga-Stina Ewbank, '*Brand*: The Play and the Translation' (Introduction), Henrik Ibsen, *Brand: A Version for the Stage* by Geoffrey Hill, Second Edition, Revised, Minneapolis 1981, pp. vii–xxxvi.

David James Jones, 'Myth and History in the Poetry of Geoffrey Hill, Seamus Heaney and George Mackay Brown', Ph.D. thesis, University College of Wales, Aberystwyth 1981.

René Gallet, 'Etude sur "Le Château de Pentecôte" de Geoffrey Hill, *Obsidiane* 21, Hiver 1982, pp. 4–12.

Derek Attridge, *The Rhythms of English Poetry*, London 1982, pp. 316–21.

Henry W. Hart, entry on Geoffrey Hill, in Walton Beacham (ed.), *Critical Survey of Poetry*, La Canada (California) 1982, pp. 1344–54.

Philip Pacey, *David Jones and Other Wonder Voyagers*, Bridgend 1982, pp. 119–23.

Robert Nye, rev. *Péguy*, *The Times*, 28 April 1983, p. 11.

Conor Cruise O'Brien, rev. *Péguy*, *The Observer*, 8 May 1983, p. 31.

Paul Brasington, rev. *Péguy*, *Broadsheet* (Cambridge), 11 May 1983, pp. 10–1.

Christopher Reid, rev. *Péguy*, *The Sunday Times*, 12 June 1983, p. 45.

Martin Dodsworth, rev. *Péguy*, *The Guardian*, 16 June 1983, p. 8.

Edna Longley, rev. *Péguy*, *The New Statesman* Vol. 105 No. 2726, 17 June 1983, p. 25.

Henry Hart, 'The Poetry of Geoffrey Hill' (Ph.D. thesis, 21 June 1983; copy in Bodleian Library, Oxford).

C.H. Sisson, rev. *Péguy*, *PN Review* 33, Vol. 10 No. 1, July 1983, pp. 12–3.

Eric Griffiths, rev. *Péguy*, *The Listener* Vol. 110 No. 2820, 4 August 1983, pp. 22–3.

Dick Davis, 'The Periodicals, 1: *Agenda*' (on 'Our Word Is Our Bond'), *TLS* No. 4193, 12 August 1983, p. 857.

Robert Crawford, rev. *Péguy*, *Gloucester Green* (Oxford), Summer 1983.

Donald Davie, 'Editorial' (on *Péguy*), *PN Review* 34, Vol. 10 No. 2, September 1983, pp. 1–2.

Marina Warner, rev. *Péguy*, *Poetry Review* Vol. 73 No. 3, September 1983, pp. 64–5.

Henry Hart, 'Geoffrey Hill's *The Mystery of the Charity of Charles Péguy*: A Commentary', *Essays in Criticism* Vol. 33 No. 4, October 1983, pp. 312–38.

W.S. Milne, rev. *Péguy*, *Agenda* Vol. 21 No. 3, Autumn 1983, pp. 12–23.

Peter Robinson, rev. *Péguy*, *English* Vol. 32 No. 144, Autumn 1983, pp. 262–9.

Henry Hart, 'The Poetry of Geoffrey Hill', *Oxford Poetry* Vol. 1 No. 2, Autumn 1983, pp. 69–74.

John Lucas, rev. *Péguy*, *London Review of Books* Vol. 5 No. 20, 3 November 1983, p. 16.

Jeffrey Wainwright and Alan Massey, letters on *Péguy* to *PN Review* 35, Vol. 10 No. 3, November 1983, pp. 6–7.

N.H. Reeve, rev. *Péguy*, *Poetry Wales* Vol. 19 No. 1, November 1983, pp. 109–12.

John Mole, rev. *Péguy*, *Encounter* Vol. 61 No. 4, December 1983, pp. 64–5.

Harry Blamires, entry on Geoffrey Hill, in Harry Blamires (ed.), *A Guide to Twentieth-Century Literature in English*, London 1983, pp. 120–1.

Martin Dodsworth, 'Ted Hughes and Geoffrey Hill: An Antithesis', in Boris Ford (ed.), *The New Pelican Guide to English Literature Vol. 8: The Present*, Harmondsworth 1983, pp. 281–93.

M.L. Rosenthal and Sally M. Gall, *The Modern Poetic Sequence: The Genius of Modern Poetry*, Oxford and New York 1983, pp. 299–307 (on *MH*).

David Wright, rev. *Péguy*, *Sunday Telegraph*, 22 January 1984.

David Gervais, rev. *Péguy*, *The Cambridge Quarterly* Vol. 12 Nos. 2 and 3, pp. 201–14.

Stephen Medcalf, rev. *Péguy*, *TLS* No. 4217, 27 January 1984, p. 76.

Robert Richman, ' "the battle it was born to lose": the poetry of Geoffrey Hill', *The New Criterion* Vol. 2 No. 8, April 1984, pp. 22-34.

David Trotter, *The Making of the Reader*, London 1984, pp. 209-18.

Anthony Burgess, rev. *The Lords of Limit*, TLS No. 4231, 4 May 1984, p. 487.

Anthony Thwaite, rev. *The Lords of Limit*, *The Observer*, 6 May 1984, p. 21.

Philip Hobsbaum, rev. *The Lords of Limit*, THES No. 601, 11 May 1984, p. 18.

George Steiner, rev. *The Lords of Limit*, *The Sunday Times*, 13 May 1984, p. 42.

Grevel Lindop, 'Myth and blood: the poetry of Geoffrey Hill', *Critical Quarterly* Vol. 26 Nos. 1 and 2, Spring and Summer 1984, pp. 147-54.

Donald Davie, rev. *The Lords of Limit*, *London Review of Books* Vol. 6 No. 11, 21 June 1984, p. 10.

Eric Griffiths, rev. *The Lords of Limit*, *Encounter* Vol. 63 No. 2, July-August 1984, pp. 59-63.

Peter Robinson, rev. *The Lords of Limit*, *English* Vol. 33 No. 146, Summer 1984, pp. 167-78.

Index

Davie, Donald 197, 198, 199, 208, 234
  re Pound 213
dead, the 4, 5, 11–19
  'best' 140
  commemoration of 134
  elegies 4, 11, 12–19
  in *For the Unfallen* 20–3, 25–8, 132, 134
  poets 11, 15, 72–3
dedications 233–4
defeat and victory 2, 19, 144, 230
Delacroix, Ferdinand 186
demonology 28–30
Descartes, René 28–9
Desnos, Robert 125, 126
determination, cultural 174–5
devices 42, 119
Devlin, Denis 58, 165
Dickinson, Emily 149–50, 152
difficulty, in poetry 196–200
directness of response 114–16
Donne, John 206, 234
  'The Calme' 3
  'A Valediction' 200
Donoghue, Denis 189
Douglas, Keith 21, 193
Dowland, John 135, 159–60, 161
Dreyfus, Alfred 104, 107, 109
duration, theory of 110
Dykes, Revd. John Bacchus 43, 134

Eberhart, Richard 6, 15
'The Groundhog' 16
elegies 4, 11, 12–19
Ellis, John 226–7
Eliot, George 138, 229
Eliot, T.S.
  and Bradley 84–5
  Hill dissents from 34–8
  re language 208
  re past 11, 15, 131, 151, 178–9
  re Perse 55–6, 57–8, 61
  personality in poetry 187, 188, 189
  re poetry 34–7, 62–3, 173, 196, 198–9
  sea in works of 26
  symbols from poems of 6
  terms, choice of 24, 158
  re Valéry 73
  and Virgil 60–1, 223
  re wit 147
  Four Quartets 34–6:
    'Burnt Norton' 34
    'The Dry Salvages' 26, 35, 68
    'East Coker' 35, 74–5
    'Little Gidding' 35, 64, 161
  'Marina' 65, 77
  'Poetry and Drama' 37
  The Sacred Wood 161
  The Use of Poetry . . . 173–4
  The Waste Land 26
Empson, William 65, 204

Erlich, Victor 205
errors, punishment for 202, 203
Europe, corruption of 20–2
Ewbank, Inga-Stina, edition and translation
  of *Brand* 87, 88, 89, 94, 225, 226

fables 38–9
Fabre, Lucien 57
Fantasy Press 15
fire, symbol 6
forefathers 54
forgiveness 117–18
form 18, 173
  ceremonial 42–3
Fowler, H.W., *Modern English Usage* 72
French Army, in World War I 102–4, 106,
  110–11, 226–7
French language 104, 208–9
Freud, Sigmund 172–3
friendship 196–7, 200–1, 217–18

Gesualdo, Don Carlo 135
Gide, André 208
Glover, Jon 206
gods 28–30
  creation 25–7, 162
  see also Christianity
Gray, Thomas 152, 158
Green, T.H. 66, 165, 175, 178, 180, 230
Griffiths, Eric 216

Haffenden, John 53, 54, 132, 165, 228
Halévy, Daniel 110
Hamburger, Michael 230
Harding, D.W. 177
Hardy, Thomas 187, 188, 189
Hartman, Geoffrey 189
Hazlitt, William 139–40
Heaney, Seamus 213
Heller, Erich 221
Hernandez, Miguel 125
Hill, Geoffrey
  career ix
  criticism by 175–8, 179–81, 183–4
  family ix, x
  POETRY:
  'Annunciations' 202, 229
    artists in 197–8
    language of 142, 168
    ritual in 42
    'The Word' in 44–5
  'An Apology for the Revival of Christian
    Architecture in England' 68–9, 72, 79,
    103, 115–16, 141, 150
    ambiguous language 142–3
    nostalgia 163–4, 203, 214
    titles 129, 136
    see also titles of poems
  'An Ark on the Flood' 2, 3–4, 5, 6, 7, 12–
    14